Lecture Notes in Computer Science 10217

More information about this series at http://www.springer.com/series/7409

Andreas Braun · Reiner Wichert
Antonio Maña (Eds.)

Ambient Intelligence

13th European Conference, AmI 2017
Malaga, Spain, April 26–28, 2017
Proceedings

Editors
Andreas Braun
Fraunhofer IGD
Darmstadt
Germany

Antonio Maña
University of Malaga
Malaga
Spain

Reiner Wichert
Center for Research in Security and Privacy CRISP
Darmstadt
Germany

ISSN 0302-9743 ISSN 1611-3349 (electronic)
Lecture Notes in Computer Science
ISBN 978-3-319-56996-3 ISBN 978-3-319-56997-0 (eBook)
DOI 10.1007/978-3-319-56997-0

Library of Congress Control Number: 2017936916

LNCS Sublibrary: SL3 – Information Systems and Applications, incl. Internet/Web, and HCI

Printed on acid-free paper

This Springer imprint is published by Springer Nature
The registered company is Springer International Publishing AG
The registered company address is: Gewerbestrasse 11, 6330 Cham, Switzerland

Preface

The 2017 European Conference on Ambient Intelligence is one of the prime venues for research in ambient intelligence, with experts participating not only from Europe but from around the globe. After skipping the 2016 edition, we are now providing a fresh start for the interdisciplinary research community interested in the field of ambient intelligence and related fields such as Internet of Things, smart cities, etc., and approaching them from points of view ranging from computer science and engineering, to psychology and social sciences to design and architecture. Technologies that were part of the vision of ambient intelligence are becoming more and more common in our daily lives, with smart devices recognizing our speech, or intelligent agents providing us with personalized services, leading to new ways for us to interact with our environment.

The formal proceedings of this 13th edition of the European Conference on Ambient Intelligence are collected in Vol. 10217 of Springer's LNCS. The AmI 2017 conference solicited contributions with the themes of:

- Enabling Technologies, Methods and Platforms
- Objectives and Approaches of Ambient Intelligence and Internet of Things
- From Information Design to Interaction and Experience Design
- Application Areas of AmI and IoT

AmI 2017 attracted the interest of researchers from academia and industry, who contributed to our varied program on research in ambient intelligence. This year's edition received 29 submissions for the full and short paper track. Each of these papers received at least three reviews by members of our Technical Program Committee that comprised experts from industry, academia, and research organizations. This process led to the acceptance of 16 full papers and four short papers, with an acceptance rate of 69%. These were accepted for a presentation and are included in this volume.

In addition we include one keynote with accompanying paper by the distinguished speaker Dr. Norbert Streitz, founder of the Smart Future Initiative. He presented an inspiring talk on "Reconciling Humans and Technology: The Role of Ambient Intelligence."

We observed a trend toward declining conference attendance and a smaller than expected number of submissions. Nonetheless, the European Conference on Ambient Intelligence remains highly engaging for the research community, with the respective editions of the proceedings receiving a large number of chapter downloads. This gives us hope that the research community and industry can benefit from the presented works and get inspiration for future research, designs, and products.

We would like to extend our thanks to the authors who submitted their research to AmI 2017, contributing to the high-quality program. Most importantly, this would not have been possible without the help of our Technical Program Committee and the Organizing Committee. Our Program Committee members and several subreviewers dedicated their time to provide high-quality reviews of the submissions, within a very tight schedule. Without their help we would not have been able to offer such an engaging program. We would also like to thank our honorary chair, Norbert Streitz, for his counsel during all phases of making this conference happen.

March 2017

Andreas Braun
Reiner Wichert
Antonio Maña

Organization

Program Committee

Jan Alexandersson	DFKI GmbH, Germany
Claudio Ardagna	Università degli Studi di Milano, Italy
Paolo Barsocchi	CNR-ISTI, Italy
Helmi Ben Hmida	Fraunhofer IGD, Germany
Andreas Braun	Fraunhofer IGD, Germany
Rem Collier	University College Dublin, Ireland
Babak A. Farshchian	SINTEF ICT, Norway
Nikolaos Georgantas	Inria, France
Hristijan Gjoreski	Jozef Stefan Institute, Slovenia
Tobias Grosse-Puppendahl	Microsoft Research
Otthein Herzog	Jacobs University Bremen, Germany, and Tongji University, China
Achilles Kameas	Hellenic Open University, Greece
Kristian Kloeckl	Northeastern University, USA
Shinichi Konomi	University of Tokyo, Japan
Hristo Koshutanski	Safe Society Labs, Spain
Arjan Kuijper	Fraunhofer IGD and TU Darmstadt, Germany
Antonio Mana	University of Malaga, Spain
Irene Mavrommati	Hellenic Open University, Greece
Preben Holst Mogensen	Aarhus University, Denmark
Antonio Munoz	University of Malaga, Spain
Filippo Palumbo	CNR-ISTI, Italy
Fabio Paterno	CNR-ISTIm, Italy
Carsten Röcker	Fraunhofer IOSB-INA, Germany
Norbert Streitz	Smart Future Initiative, Germany
Manfred Tscheligi	University of Salzburg, Austria
Kristof Van Laerhoven	University of Siegen, Germany
Reiner Wichert	AHS Assisted Home Solutions, Germany

Contents

Reconciling Humans and Technology: The Role of Ambient Intelligence 1
Norbert Streitz

Engineering a Cyber-Physical Intersection Management – An Experience Report 17
Florian Wessling, Stefan Gries, Julius Ollesch, Marc Hesenius, and Volker Gruhn

Exploring Design Opportunities for Intelligent Worker Assistance: A New Approach Using Projetion-Based AR and a Novel Hand-Tracking Algorithm 33
Sebastian Büttner, Oliver Sand, and Carsten Röcker

AuthentiCap - A Touchless Vehicle Authentication and Personalization System 46
Sebastian Frank and Arjan Kuijper

Indoor Localization Based on Passive Electric Field Sensing 64
Biying Fu, Florian Kirchbuchner, Julian von Wilmsdorff, Tobias Grosse-Puppendahl, Andreas Braun, and Arjan Kuijper

Safety Services in Smart Environments Using Depth Cameras 80
Matthias Ruben Mettel, Michael Alekseew, Carsten Stocklöw, and Andreas Braun

Contextual Requirements Prioritization and Its Application to Smart Homes . . . 94
Estefanía Serral, Paolo Sernani, Aldo Franco Dragoni, and Fabiano Dalpiaz

Voices and Views of Informal Caregivers: Investigating Ambient Assisted Living Technologies 110
Christina Jaschinski and Somaya Ben Allouch

Easy to Install Indoor Positioning System that Parasitizes Home Lighting . . . 124
Takuya Maekawa and Yuki Sakumichi

Exploring the Use of Ambient WiFi Signals to Find Vacant Houses 130
Shin'ichi Konomi, Tomoyo Sasao, Simo Hosio, and Kaoru Sezaki

A Framework for Distributed Interaction in Intelligent Environments 136
Dario Di Mauro, Juan C. Augusto, Antonio Origlia, and Francesco Cutugno

Which Mobile Health Toolkit Should a Service Provider Choose? A Comparative Evaluation of Apple HealthKit, Google Fit, and Samsung Digital Health Platform 152
Babak A. Farshchian and Thomas Vilarinho

Visual End-User Programming of Personalized AAL in the Internet of Things 159
Yannis Valsamakis and Anthony Savidis

Opportunities for Biometric Technologies in Smart Environments 175
Olaf Henniger, Naser Damer, and Andreas Braun

New Approach for Optimizing the Usage of Situation Recognition Algorithms Within IoT Domains 183
Chinara Mammadova, Helmi Ben Hmida, Andreas Braun, and Arjan Kuijper

HUDConCap - Automotive Head-Up Display Controlled with Capacitive Proximity Sensing 197
Sebastian Frank and Arjan Kuijper

E-Textile Couch: Towards Smart Garments Integrated Furniture 214
Silvia Rus, Andreas Braun, and Arjan Kuijper

Context-Aware Monitoring Agents for Ambient Assisted Living Applications 225
Sofiane Bouznad, Abdelghani Chibani, Yacine Amirat, Sabri Lyazid, Edson Prestes, Faouzi Sebbak, and Sandro Fiorini

Mobility Competencies of People with Down Syndrome Supported by Technical Assistance: Results of the Requirement Analysis in POSEIDON Project 241
Anne Engler, Anna Zirk, Monique Siebrandt, Eva Schulze, and Detlef Oesterreich

An Exploratory Study on Electric Field Sensing 247
Julian von Wilmsdorff, Florian Kirchbuchner, Biying Fu, Andreas Braun, and Arjan Kuijper

A Framework for Responsive Environments 263
Ben Salem, Jorge Alves Lino, and Jan Simons

Author Index 279

Reconciling Humans and Technology: The Role of Ambient Intelligence

Norbert Streitz(✉)

Smart Future Initiative, Frankfurt, Germany
norbert.streitz@smart-future.net

Abstract. This keynote presentation explores the role of Ambient Intelligence in current technical and social contexts related to smart cities. Having identified some undesirable tendencies, conclusions and design recommendations are provided on how to remedy the situation. This includes the need for redefining the 'smart everything' paradigm, in order to reconcile humans and technology.

It starts out with placing Ambient Intelligence in the context of Ubiquitous Computing, Disappearing Computer and Internet of Things (IoT). The application areas discussed are motivated by living in the Urban Age, i.e. the increasing importance and preeminent role of cities. Examples are 'transient spaces' and airports viewed as 'transient cities'. Different notions of the 'smart city of the future' are introduced and complemented by the concept of 'hybrid cities', i.e. integrating the virtual, digital world with the real, physical world.

The current hype about abundant business opportunities of smart cities requires a critical investigation. The Internet of Things (IoT) provides the infrastructure for collecting data about urban objects and citizens including their behavior. A wide range of information is combined and subjected to extensive 'big data' exploitation efforts – very often conducted without explicit consent of the people involved. In order to explore the challenges, but also the venues towards a more human-centered IoT, resp. an Ambient Intelligence approach, one has to explore the implications of matching people's profiles with service options available at specific locations. A major focus is on the risks resulting from smart city installations, especially the serious infringements of privacy rights, i.e., usage of personal data without consent of the people concerned.

Our thesis is that a critical reflection of different manifestations of the 'smart everything' paradigm is needed in order to meet the overall goal of reconciling humans and technology. A central aspect of this goal is to keep the 'human in the loop' and in control. Therefore, a citizen-centered design approach for future cities is needed, helping us to go 'beyond smart-only cities' and transform them into Humane, Sociable and Cooperative Smart Hybrid Cities.

1 Ambient Intelligence in Context

While the origins of the term 'artificial intelligence' (AI) date back more than 60 years (Dartmouth Conference in 1956), the term 'ambient intelligence' (AmI) is relatively more

A. Braun et al. (Eds.): AmI 2017, LNCS 10217, pp. 1–16, 2017.
DOI: 10.1007/978-3-319-56997-0_1

recent, created in the late 1990s at Philips[1] and then made popular especially via the activities of the IST Advisory Group (ISTAG) of the European Commission (ISTAG 2001). AmI is building on the ideas of Ubiquitous Computing proposed by Mark Weiser around 1990 at Xerox PARC and communicated to the scientific community at large in his seminal article in Scientific American (Weiser 1991). Although Weiser addressed with his proposal of a 'calm technology' also the relationship of ubiquitous technology and the perception and behavior of people, most of the follow-up research in ubiquitous computing took a more technical route. The AmI proposal - in contrast - promotes an approach with a more elaborated emphasis on user-oriented design, the human perspective in general as well as on the social context addressed by social interfaces.

Complementing the ISTAG activities, a line of research with a similar spirit was also funded by the European Commission: The *Disappearing Computer* (DC) proactive initiative (DC 2000–2005), where I had the honor to chair the DC steering group. The initiative consisted of a cluster of 37 institutions from academia as well as industry in 13 countries participating in 17 projects. The Disappearing Computer approach was inspired by and shared several aspects of Weiser's notion of calm technology as described in Streitz (2001, 2008), partly also, because I was a visiting scholar at Xerox PARC in 1990. More information about the DC approach and results can be found in a special issue of the Communications of the ACM edited by Streitz and Nixon (2005) and a LNCS 'State-of-the-Art Survey' edited by Streitz et al. (2007).

My understanding of Ambient Intelligence was very much influenced by our work in the DC initiative and then also reflected in our mission statement for the ERCIM Working Group SESAMI (Smart Environments and Systems for Ambient Intelligence) (SESAMI 2007):

> "*Ambient Intelligence represents a vision of the (not too far) future where "intelligent" or "smart" environments and systems react in an attentive, adaptive, and active (sometimes even proactive) way to the presence and activities of humans and objects in order to provide intelligent/smart services to the inhabitants of these environments. Ambient Intelligence technologies integrate sensing capabilities, processing power, reasoning mechanisms, networking facilities, applications and services, digital content, and actuating capabilities distributed in the surrounding environment. While a wide variety of different technologies is involved, the goal of Ambient Intelligence is to either hide their presence from users, by providing implicit, unobtrusive interaction paradigms. People and their social situations, ranging from individuals to groups, be them work groups, families or friends and their corresponding environments (office buildings, homes, public spaces, etc.) are at the center of the design considerations.*"

This description is still valid now in 2017 without much to add, except maybe the explicit mentioning of more comprehensive application scenarios like smart cities, smart airports, or 'smart everything' being investigated in this decade and in the future. This includes also a shift from embedded or attached sensors and actuators to 'smart ecosystems' to be described later on. The human-centered design approach will be revisited when being applied as citizen-centered design placed in larger social, especially urban contexts.

The more technology-driven approach of the ubiquitous computing community is undergoing a revival as the Internet of Things (IoT) and in specific application areas as

---

[1] For a description of the history of AmI see Aarts and Encarnaçao (2006).

Industrial Internet or Industry 4.0. The underlying idea evolved from research on RFID and is rather straight forward: every physical object is connected to/communicates with the Internet and thus – in principal – with every other object. This can be realized in different ways, e.g., by attaching sensors in order to monitor different properties of the object and communicating its state changes. This corresponds to the previously used notion of creating a 'digital shadow' of an object. Another option is that the object itself gets an IP address and communicates with the internet and other objects/devices as an IP-enabled device. Furthermore, these 'smart objects' have sensors to observe their surroundings and thus 'know' about their context.

An extension of IoT is called Internet of Everything (IoE), a term developed at Cisco, where people, processes, data and things are connected and become part of the overall network structure. This includes machine-to-machine communication (M2M) as well as machine-to-people (M2P) and technology-assisted people-to-people (P2P) interactions. One can, of course, extend the range of living organisms from people to animals and plants; work on smart farming/agriculture is just doing this. Although people are listed as part of the IoE equation, this does not necessarily mean that IoE is following a human-/people-/citizen-centered design approach. It seems that people are more or less considered being only nodes in the IoE network. In contrast, Ambient Intelligence - as defined above - puts people and their social situations at the center of its design considerations and thus in the driver seat.

Many of the now intensively discussed relationships between Ubiquitous Computing, Internet of Things or 'Web of Things' (as we called it then), Disappearing Computer, Artificial Intelligence and Ambient Intelligence were already described and investigated in an extensive book chapter by Streitz and Privat (2009). We will make references to some of these ideas as we go along.

2 Urban Age

In order to provide some context, we refer to numbers from the United Nations. World population will rise from 7.3 billion in 2015 to 8.5 billion in 2030 and 9.7 billion in 2050. Population in cities will rise to about 6.5 billion in 2050. Then, 2/3 of the world population will live in cities with the growth taking place especially in Asia and Africa, where we can observe how urban migration results in so called 'megacities'. Because more than 50% of the population is living already now in urban areas, cities have been and will increasingly become the central hubs of determining life in the 21th century, resulting in what has been called the 'Urban Age'. While this context is always to be kept in mind, the focus of this article is on the role of information and communication technology for designing future cities. Beyond this, a wide range of issues exist, including socio-economic, ecological, sustainability aspects. They are very important, but beyond the scope of this article here. Furthermore, it should be made clear that the smart city proposal could be only one way of addressing some of the problems in the urban age. And it will only be convincing, in case that cities are designed according to the goals elaborated later on (i.e. towards *Humane, Sociable, and Cooperative Smart*

Hybrid Cities). Nevertheless, it is only one perspective and not at all a solution for all the problems cities and society are facing.

2.1 Urban Environments as Hubs and Transient Spaces

Quality of life and economic prosperity will largely depend on the ability of cities to exploit their full potential. Therefore, it is important to explore the type and range of different activities in urban environments. Contemporary life styles become less focused and increasingly multidimensional. People's lives are taking place betwixt and between multiple offers and options. People's roles change within short time frames due to polyphasic activities in co-located and distributed situations.

Urban environments are characterized by a multitude of features and built instantiations. While the majority is determined by living quarters, a larger variety of challenges can be found in public administration and enterprise office buildings, industrial facilities, markets, shopping and entertainment facilities, restaurants, hotels, sport facilities, parks, places, streets, bridges, towers - just to name a selection. Buildings and spaces have their infrastructures and are populated by people, animals, plants, vehicles and other mobile as well as stationary objects. These lists are not intended to be complete. They only serve the purpose of providing context for the following reflections. In my presentation, I am limiting the discussion mainly to applications in public urban spaces. Nevertheless, these considerations and requirements can also be applied to smart homes or office buildings as in our previous EU-funded projects.

Public spaces stand out from the rest, because they are accessible to more or less all citizens, often serving in a '*hub function*' connecting many of the urban objects listed before. The public parts of most urban environments (e.g., streets, parking lots, places, markets, parks, bridges, foyers, shopping malls, passenger areas in train/bus stations and airports) can be characterized as '*transient spaces*'. Within the limitations of this paper it is not possible to explore the concept of transient spaces in full detail here. Transient spaces in the urban and public context can be characterized by a certain degree of mobility when passing-through (e.g., getting from the entrance of the airport to the check-in area or the boarding gate) or by staying in such a space, e.g., in a waiting area, for a limited period of time, although it can sometimes turn out to be unexpected long when the plane is delayed or the train/subway/bus is even canceled.

2.2 Airports Viewed as Transient Cities

Airports are good examples of transient spaces, because passengers, crew members and other temporary personnel stay only for a limited period of time. On the other hand, the range and type of activities are very similar to activities of people in public spaces of cities; just think of the types of services and opportunities offered (shopping, restaurants, bars, gaming and entertainment). Thus, one can consider airports as '*transient cities*' and model airports with respect to several dimensions as scaled down cities with a prominent existence and distribution of transient spaces, especially when taking the passenger perspective.

While there is currently a strong emphasis on designing future cities, the application domain of 'future airports' is discussed only in limited communities. This is surprising, because airports are already now very important hubs of transportation and logistics activities and their relevance will increase affecting millions of people. One can compare their role in this century with highways in the 20th century, railroads in the 19th century and seaports in the 18th century. Furthermore, it is a very interesting domain for research and studies due to its well defined location and usage scenarios.

3 Smart Hybrid Cities

The notion of '*smart cities*' has undergone transformations resulting in new connotations. In many cases, it is just a buzzword or even reduced to fashionable name dropping. Nevertheless, there is some common ground. Building smart cities is based on establishing an information and communication technology (ICT) infrastructure that allows instrumenting all kinds of physical objects (including humans, animals, plants). Beyond having different types of connectivity in place, the emphasis is on embedded sensors and actuators and, more advanced, on integrated smart materials. The relationship to the Internet of Everything (IoE) mentioned before is obvious. Pervasive computing and ambient intelligence infrastructures are transforming urban environments into interactive information and action spaces that are meant to be adaptive, responsive and smart. It results in what one would call a 'Smart City'. Building a smart city should not be a goal in itself. It should rather be considered as a vehicle for realizing the overarching goal of a humane, sociable and cooperative city (Sect. 4).

3.1 Smart Ecosystems

While the current approach is mainly determined by embedding individual sensors and actuators, I predict a shift towards a computing, communication, sensing and interaction '*substrate*' that can be handled at the application or domain level. Outdoor examples would be smart street-surfaces, building façades and windows; indoors we will find smart table-cloth, smart wall-paper and smart paint. It requires a seamless integration of components with a high degree of diffusion leading to an emergent smartness of the overall environment that might soon parallel other existing ecosystems. Its realization is dependent on results in the area of '*smart materials*', a difficult but promising area of research. Results exist for smart textiles and as steps towards smart wall-paper. Example: 'Wallpaper-TV' (2.57 mm thin and 77 inch large) was shown by LG at the CES this year. It is flexible and seamlessly mounted to the wall with small magnets. Note: this is not a research prototype, but a consumer product.

In general, but especially in the context of a smart city, the computer disappears as a 'visible' distinctive device, either physically due to being integrated in the environment or mentally from our perception, thus providing the basis for establishing a calm technology. This is the core of the '*Disappearing Computer*' approach (Russell et al. 2005; Streitz and Nixon 2005; Streitz et al. 2007) mentioned earlier. But the 'disappearance' feature has also serious implications for privacy issues to be discussed later (Sect. 6).

3.2 Self-aware Cities

There is a wide range of 'smart city' related concepts and terms (digital city, intelligent city, ubiquitous city, green city, resilient city, sustainable city, etc.), too many to be covered here. Beyond the general accepted notion based on ubiquitous deployment of ICT (see above), I like to introduce a different interpretation.

This conceptualization is based on the proposal that the '*smartness of a city*' can also be characterized by how much *the city knows about itself* and how this is communicated to its citizens. There are two perspectives. First, city officials who are in charge of administering and managing the city obtain additional knowledge about the different urban parameters and can therefore take more informed decisions. Second, citizens are enabled to have a more comprehensive, augmented view of their city. At the same time, it empowers them to engage and participate in addressing open city-related issues. In several cases, citizens will even play an active role in the data collection process.

Examples are feedback on air and sound pollution levels in the city, congested traffic, numbers of bicycles used today and in the past, delayed trains, broken roads, non-functioning devices, etc. Providing direct location-specific awareness, e.g., on pollution by using an ambient display in a transient public space, is one way to convey the status of the city to its citizens. Other ways of communication are also useful: posting real time data on websites, providing personalized/individualized awareness, using visual information via overlay displays (e.g., augmented reality type glasses), using local sound (in earphones) or tactile hints using vibrations conveyed by your clothes. One has to decide which of the human senses is appropriate for which situation.

Konomi et al. (2013) developed a very good example of enabling and communicating self-awareness by measuring urban congestion in trains of the Tokyo subway. It applies a clever approach of using indirect measures (the CO_2 level in the train compartments) for determining the congestion level (the more CO_2, the more passengers). This method is an example that collecting necessary data involves active and consenting participation of citizens. Konomi calls it the '*civic computing*' approach.

3.3 Hybrid Cities

Taking the notion of an Internet of Things seriously, we end up with large ensembles of augmented physical objects. Physical objects in the real world will have a digital representation (also called 'digital shadow') in the virtual world. The term '*Hybrid World*' denotes now the combination of real worlds and digital/virtual worlds. Depending on the purpose and level of detail of modeling the real world, there are different digital representations. Using Augmented Reality (AR) methods and devices, one can generate overlays and multiple representations, thus providing views into the combined hybrid world and enabling a certain degree of transparency.

Applying this distinction to urban contexts, the term '*Hybrid City*' (e.g., Streitz 2015) is a direct consequence. I favor this conceptualization and have used it already for a long time (since 2008). It reflects my understanding that we have to address the connection, balance and interaction of real worlds and virtual worlds, if we want to get the full picture of what is relevant for the design of our future cities.

3.4 Opportunities and Applications of the Smart City Platform

After establishing a ubiquitous and pervasive computing infrastructure, the next step is to exploit it by collecting, aggregating, evaluating, and processing data from sensors distributed in the urban environment. The resulting data will enable creating knowledge about people as well as states and changes of associated mobile and stationary objects (ranging from smartphones to vehicles, from street lights to buildings, etc.). We will observe a transformation into environments, where all activities can be monitored and smart services can be provided as offers to people based on personal profiles by matching them with options available at these places (=> personalized location-based services). There is no space here to describe the range of existing and future applications and devices, but I will show in my presentation several examples: smart streets and their components (street surfaces, street lights), smart parking, smart cars, including issues of autonomous driving.

4 Humane, Sociable and Cooperative Smart Hybrid City

Our overall goal when designing future or refurbishing existing cities should be: A *Humane, Sociable and Cooperative Smart, Hybrid City reconciling humans and technology* by

- Establishing a calm technology providing ambient intelligence that supports and respects individual and social life by keeping the 'human in the loop'.
- Respecting the rights of citizens, especially in terms of privacy. Therefore, personal data should – as much as possible – only be collected based on consent by providing choices and control of the process, including models of temporary provision and access and/or obligations to delete data later on.
- Viewing the city and its citizens as mutual cooperation partners, where the city is smart in the sense of being self-aware and cooperative towards its citizens by supporting them in their activities. This requires mutual trust and respect for the motives and vested interests of all parties involved.
- Acknowledging the capabilities of citizens to participate in the design of the urban environment (=> participatory design), especially with respect to their local expertise, and stimulating their active participation.
- Motivating citizens to get involved, to understand themselves as part of the urban community, to be actively engaged by contributing to the public good and welfare (=> collective intelligence, aspects similar to the Greek 'agora').
- Enabling citizens to exploit their individual, creative, social and economic potential and to live a self- determined life, and thus
- Meeting some of the challenges of the urban age by enabling people to experience and enjoy a satisfying life and work.

Figure 1 indicates the merging of real and virtual representations of the city into what we call a 'hybrid city'. The combined representations provide the basis for modeling the city in order to define how the different parts can be augmented with smart properties in order to create an urban environment with ambient intelligence. One has to determine how this augmentation can be used for the overall benefit of the city and added value for each individual citizen. This is the idea of a 'cooperative city'.

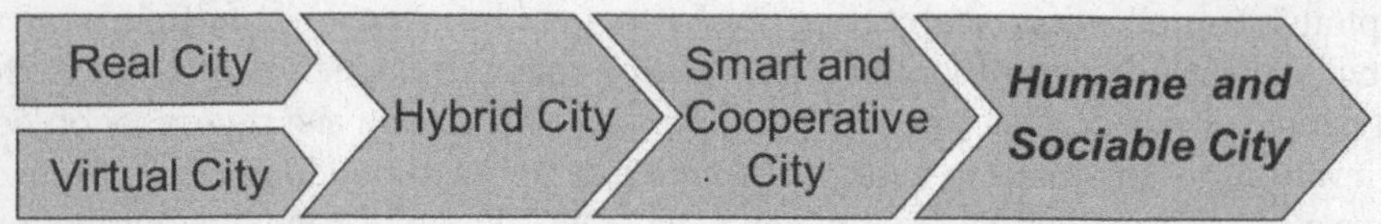

Fig. 1. Relationships of smart city characteristics

While the motivation for designing a humane and sociable city appears to be rather straight forward, the notion of a *Cooperative City* might need some explanation. It is based on our earlier work on Cooperative Buildings and Roomware (Streitz et al. 1998, 1999). In this tradition, I propose to apply human-centered design principles that have proven useful, e.g., in human-computer interaction and computer-supported cooperative work (CSCW), in this context as '*Citizen-Centered Design*'. We consider the 'cooperation' perspective as an overarching goal for the design process. It allows integrating functionalities and policies from the very beginning, viewing citizens as prospective 'users' or 'customers' of the city. This view could be called '*City as a Service*', where the urban environment is the interface between the city and the citizens. A transparent urban ambient intelligence environment enables city administration as well as citizens to make more and better informed decisions, because *both* (and this is essential) parties can access and exploit the wealth of data collected. Still, one always has to keep in mind, that 'smartness' is not a goal or value in itself, but has to be evaluated against the design guidelines stated before. Therefore, a discussion in a cooperative and respectful manner is needed in order to contribute to the objectives of the cooperative humane and sociable city.

Having painted this somehow ideal and optimistic picture, one has, of course, to be realistic and be aware that the smart city poses also new challenges. There are a number of potential pitfalls. One is the increasing privatization and commercialization of many aspects of urban life. It is no secret that the 'smart city' scenario is considered by many companies as the next big thing, where large profits are expected. If this trend continuous, it will result in fewer options for citizen participation in the decision making process and more privacy infringements, because the commercial objectives will – in many cases – be different to those outlined before.

Another issue is the danger of comprehensive and smart automation with its resulting dependencies and loss of control. Similar to the already existing dependency of our urban systems on a stable and continuous availability of electricity, we will be confronted with the dependency on smart systems, especially with the deployment of often non-transparent artificial intelligence components, e.g., in autonomous driving, voice-controlled smart homes. We will discuss this in more detail in the subsequent section on *the need of 'redefining the smart everything paradigm'*.

5 Redefining the '*Smart Everything*' Paradigm

5.1 Problems of the '*Smart Everything*' Approach

One can observe certain trends in the areas of IoT and AI when combined in different application fields as, e.g., smart home, smart cities, autonomous driving, etc. One major trend is a shift towards more or even complete automation of previously human operator controlled activities. Smart devices and underlying algorithms are controlling processes, services and devices as well as the interaction between devices and humans. Humans are increasingly removed from being the operator and thus from being in control. I label this the "*Smart Everything*" *Paradigm* which is gaining ever more ground. It results almost in an obsession to automate everything and AI is considered to be the Holy Grail. Only few people are aware or admit that AI is actually a pretty dated route towards the Promised Land. The current hype, amplified by abundant venture capital, forgets that progress was pretty limited when considering the history of AI since its origin in 1956. Take the status of speech understanding and translation systems as an example. How often were we promised in the last 60 years that the big breakthrough is just around the corner? Even when trying to anticipate a wide range of behavioral options, in the end the 'intelligent' system is following certain strategies in one way or the other. The often as human brain like described 'deep learning' approaches, currently very much in fashion, have their limitations, too, and are failing in many situations. They are certainly not the panacea to all problems. Some of the shortcomings might be overcome, but in any case it is still a long way to go.

Assuming these problems can be solved, there is – in my opinion – another more essential problem, i.e. 'AI behavior' is neither transparent nor comprehensible. Being untraceable implies in some way also that there is no reproducible outcome. We don't have to engage here in the discussion whether AI is deterministic or not. The important point is that we are already now confronted with the lack of transparency. Example: nobody (not even systems developers) can really understand, retrace and re-enact decisions of high frequency trading at the stock market carried out automatically and thus independently of human control and intervention. These new trading patterns have altered the financial landscape dramatically and certainly not for the better. Given this experience, what do we have to expect in domains like autonomous driving?

While these scenarios show high, but often incomprehensible flexibility, one can also observe the opposite, i.e. rigidity. Rigid behavior is another problem. It can be experienced especially by users and customers being confronted with fully automated call centers or on-line shops without any humans involved. It needs only some deviations from the standard routine and the system cannot handle the requests. People become desperate, because there is no human to turn to resolving the situation. One is not only questioning the pretended 'intelligence' of the system, but moreover the lack of it when thinking of the system developers. These systems are depriving people of their right to get appropriate services, individual attention and treatment. In many cases, one might even suspect the system is programmed on purpose not to understand, resp. not to react to certain inquiries, especially complaints about problems with products, so that the company can avoid dealing with them. The issue is that users and customers are and will be in the future even more completely at the mercy of companies and in loss of control.

In summary, feasibility problems and transparency deficits have to be considered as warning signs, especially when looking at the planned abundance of automating everything and seeking refuge and solutions in AI environments completely operated by algorithms. There has to be an alternative which is summarized in our proposal of '*keeping the human in the loop*' presented in the next section.

5.2 Smart Spaces Make People Smarter by Keeping the Human in the Loop

While the above remarks sound pretty negative and disillusioned, I like to propose an alternative or at least complementary approach for redefining the '*smart everything, everywhere and every time*' paradigm in order to reconcile the situation. It is based on earlier work we did more than 10 years ago (Streitz et al. 2005), but it is still valid and – as it seems – becoming increasingly important. It reflects the design approach of Ambient Intelligence we provided in the beginning and its role for reconciling humans and technology. For that purpose, we distinguish between '*System-Oriented, Importunate Smartness* and *People-Oriented, Empowering Smartness*'.

System-Oriented, Importunate Smartness
An environment is considered 'smart' if it enables certain self-directed (re)actions of individual artefacts or ensembles of artefacts based on continuously collected information. For example, a space can be 'smart' by having and exploiting knowledge about which people and artefacts are currently situated within its area, who and what was there before, when and how long, and what kind of activities took place. In this version of 'smartness', the space would be active (in many cases even proactive) and in control of the situation by making decisions on what to do next and actually take action and execute them without a human in the loop. It is more or less automated or even autonomous system behavior based on the interpretation of collected data.

Some of these actions could be importunate. Take the now almost classic example of a smart refrigerator in a smart home analyzing consumption patterns of inhabitants and autonomously ordering depleted food. While we might appreciate that the fridge makes suggestions on recipes that are based on the food currently available, we might get very upset in case it is autonomously ordering food that we will not consume for reasons beyond its knowledge, such as a sudden vacation, sickness, or a temporal change in taste or diet. Or the smart home locks me out, because my voice pattern does not match anymore the pattern stored in the data base due to a temporary illness.

People-Oriented, Empowering Smartness
The above view can be contrasted by another perspective where the empowering function is in the foreground and can be summarized as '*smart spaces make people smarter*'. This is achieved by keeping '*the human in the loop*' thus empowering people to make better informed decisions and take actions as mature and responsible people who are in control. In this case, the environment will also collect data about what is going on and aggregate these data but it communicates the resulting information for

guidance and subsequent actions still determined by the people. In this case, a smart space might also make suggestions and recommendations based on the information collected but the people are in the loop and in control. Here, the space supports smart, behavior of the people present (or in remote scenarios people being on the road but connected to the space). This approach is getting increasingly popular as work on soft actuation in pervasive computing shows. The people-oriented, empowering smartness is in line with the objectives of the Ambient Intelligence approach as defined in the beginning of this article. It is the approach favored by me for reconciling humans and technology.

Obviously, the two perspectives will rarely exist in their pure and distinct manifestations. They rather represent the end points of a dimension where we can position weighted combinations of both. What kind of combination will be finally realized depends very much on the application domain. There is also a relevant caveat: How much feedback do we want? How many data can we process? At which level of the data collection and aggregation process do we want or are we able to be involved? In some cases, it might be useful that a system is not asking for user's feedback and confirmation for every single step in an action chain because this would result in an information overload. The challenge for system design is to find the right balance. But despite the caveats, the important point is that human intervention and control is possible. The data belong to the people and the degree of automation is configurable by the human. The overall design rationale should be guided and informed by the objective to aim at having the '*human in the loop and in control*' as much as possible and feasible. This view is also reflected in what we conceptualized as the 'cooperative building' (Streitz et al. 1998) and now extended to the 'cooperative city'.

6 Privacy by Design

We agree that the smart city approach provides multiple opportunities which have been described by many authors and are therefore not repeated here. At the same time, there are threats that have been articulated. One is the increase of the already existing dependencies on reliable and working ICT-infrastructures. Another one is providing security by being prepared for and fighting criminal manipulations and cyber-attacks. In this presentation, we want to address especially the third major risk for citizens in a smart city, i.e. the loss of privacy in terms of losing the control over personal data. While the current discussions on privacy focus mainly on the virtual world (e.g., misuse in social networks), the more prevalent issues will surface in the smart city context concerning personal data of citizens in the real, resp. hybrid world. The discussion of privacy issues here is based on earlier work (Streitz 2016).

6.1 Trade-off Between Smartness and Privacy

There is a tricky trade-off between creating smartness and providing privacy. Obviously, a smart system will usually be smarter with respect to a service offered if it has more knowledge about the person compared to a system with no or insufficient data. Thus, there is an interaction and balance between collecting and processing data for tailoring functionality to make the system ‘smart’ and the right of citizens to be in control over which data are being collected, by whom, how they are used, i.e. the issue of privacy. As a side comment here, it is interesting to observe that many people are willing to provide their data for certain benefits (e.g., loyalty/payback cards, lotteries, sweepstakes). In some cases, they are even voluntary uploaded by the citizens, be it as unsolicited ‘selfies’ and videos, augmented glasses recordings of activities or sensitive health data being part of a fitness or ‘quantified self’ app.

6.2 Smart Cars and Street Lights as Urban Spies

Considering public and transient urban spaces, there are obvious design issues and implications for privacy. Beyond the almost ubiquitous and usually visible CCTV surveillance cameras, there are many sensors that are hidden in the environment.

Current and near future examples of privacy infringement are a result of providing urban objects with different types of sensors. Smart cars being enhanced for autonomous driving capabilities have a wide range of sensors (cameras, ultrasonic sensors, radar, laser-based LIDAR, GPS). Will they go off to sleep when the cars park on the curbside of the street? The fact that the engine is turned off, does not mean that the car is not active and sensing anymore. Nobody knows if and what the cameras and microphones are recording. Pedestrians walking by can be monitored. Peeking into the windows of the adjacent houses and apartments is no problem either. Who has control over the sensors and access to these data? The car company? Similar considerations apply to street lights being equipped with cameras and radar for the official and main purpose of monitoring the street looking for free parking spaces. But who knows what kinds of data are collected about the complete urban area within the view? Or take smart public displays used for advertisement (DooH = Digital out of Home). They are monitoring where passers-by are looking and analyze their emotional reaction to the content displayed. There are also options to identify the person and display individualized content. Does anybody ask for permission? Who owns the data?

The principal problem is: How can people know what is going on, when they are not aware of being tracked, when they cannot ‘see’ the different sensors, the manifold smart devices distributed in the urban environment due to the above mentioned Disappearing Computer approach?

6.3 Privacy as a Legal and Moral Right vs. Privacy as a Commodity

Although some people consider it old-fashioned, I like to recall that privacy used to be a legal and moral right, in many cases a socially negotiated feature. Now, privacy is turning into a commodity you pay for and you can trade – with the implication that privacy is becoming a privilege. In many cases, people are not really aware that the loss of their privacy is the price they pay for a seemingly free product or service, because they pay with their data. When discussing privacy, one should distinguish two aspects: Outgoing data (being collected via logging, tracking, and surveillance) vs. incoming data (resulting from intrusion, unsolicited communication). Both aspects have different but severe consequences.

While privacy is already an issue, it will become even more important in smart hybrid cities. While in the virtual world, you can – to a certain degree – still use fake identities and anonymization services, it will be more difficult to achieve this kind of disguise in the real world. The data that exist about you in the virtual world are now complemented by real world data and vice versa. Cameras are taking pictures of you entering a shop or a restaurant with known locations, while face recognition identifies your personal identity.

Real objects you are wearing, carrying, using, buying will be recognized by sensors in the environment because these objects are tagged. The car or bicycle you are using is a tagged object broadcasting its location and properties resulting in trajectories of your driving. But also your walking behavior is transparent when carrying a smart phone (based on radio signal multilateration or GPS). It will become more and more difficult to avoid object and person tracking, because soon all objects and their parts will be tagged, respectively have integrated IDs (=> smart artefacts). Location-based services in a smart hybrid city exploit not only your location and preferences but can also be used to build up a complete profile by monitoring your activities (e.g., buying goods, looking at public advertisements, contacting people), when and where, including also other people involved in the situation. Unsolicited offers and advertising on your mobile phones and soon on public displays you are looking at or passing by, may compromise your preferences in public to people around you. This future predicted for 2054 in the movie ‘Minority Report’ (created in 2002) seems to be very close now as it is the subject of the commercialization promises for the smart city.

Who can really predict what will happen to all the data generated in the real environment (either unobtrusively collected or voluntarily provided) and then stored up in the ‘clouds’ of numerous service providers and manufacturers, especially when these servers are based in a country that has no or very limited privacy and data security legislation? It should also be pointed out that Weiser - already at the time of his work on ubiquitous computing (Weiser 1991) - regarded privacy as a key issue for this kind of environments.

We argue therefore for so called Privacy Enhancing Technologies (PETs) (Streitz et al. 2007) and for Privacy by Design (Streitz 2016), i.e. to make privacy a first-order objective of system design. This requires addressing the conflict of unobtrusive data collection vs. human control over the data at an early stage of the overall system design.

Finally, I like to comment on often heard remarks by entrepreneurs and business people in Europe. They complain to have a disadvantage because of more restrictions on privacy, collection of data, and security compared to their competition in the US or in Asia. In contrast, I like to take an unequivocal stand on protecting and ensuring data security, personality rights and privacy. In Germany, we have legislation (since 1983) that personal data belong to the citizens and cannot be collected and used without consent (‘Recht auf informationelle Selbstbestimmung’). In Europe, we have the Data Protection Directive which was adopted in 1996. In the future, it will be superseded by the General Data Protection Regulation (adopted in April 2016) which is planned to be enforceable starting in May 2018.

The claim for privacy is more than a liberal rights movement as some might denigrate it. I am convinced that ‘privacy by design’ could even be a competitive advantage, a

USP (unique selling proposition) in the global market, where Europe could take a lead by reflecting on its basic democratic and ethical values.

7 Research Agenda for Ambient Intelligence and Conclusions

In order to foster the development of Humane, Sociable and Cooperative Smart Hybrid Cities, Ambient Intelligence plays a major role. Advancing progress in AmI can be facilitated by working on the following issues. These issues are based on earlier work in the EU-funded InterLink project, prepared as a road map for research in Ambient Computing and Communication Environments: "Towards the Humane City: White Paper on a Future Research Agenda" (Streitz and Wichert 2009). It is the result of joint efforts of a large group of collaborating researchers. Twelve research lines were identified and elaborated. For details see the final report available at the InterLink website or a summary in the InterLink booklet.

- Rationale for the Humane City
- Tangible Interaction and Implicit vs. Explicit Interaction
- Hybrid Symmetric Interaction
- Space-Time Dispersed Interfaces
- Crowd and Swarm Based Interaction
- Spatial and Embodied Smartness
- Awareness and Feedback Technologies
- Emotion Processing
- Social Networks and Collective Intelligence
- Self-organization in Socially Aware Ambient Systems
- Realization and User Experience of Privacy and Trust
- The Scaling Issue

While all themes are still valid, I like to emphasize a selection. Besides the always necessary continued reflection on a sound rationale and goal to be defined for the Humane, Sociable and Cooperative City, the following deserve special attention.

Hybrid Symmetric Interaction. Users' actions in real and virtual environments are often neither consistent nor can they be considered symmetric or reciprocal. This is especially important in hybrid environments where no particular world prevails. Usually, consistency is achieved when users explicitly update information in one or multiple virtual environments according to changes in the real world. More complicated, however, is the other direction: changing physical states due to virtual sensor measurements or virtual actions. The focus is on maintaining consistency of the representations, independent of the environment where the actions take place.

Space-Time Dispersed Interfaces. The future city requires the exploration of novel user interfaces that might be dispersed not only in space, but also in time. This research focuses on the ways in which humans can interact in time and space through and with computing devices.

Spatial and Embodied Smartness: Smart Spaces as Distributed Cognitive Systems. Smart spaces can be considered as a compound physical agent that acquires data from its environment through sensors and acts upon it via actuators. Contrary to a 'classical robot' that operates towards its outside, the cognitive capabilities of a smart space can be considered as an 'outside-in' robot, where the human user is an element of the internal environment of the smart space.

Realization and User Experience of Privacy and Trust. This theme has its origin in the basic conflict of data provision for enabling smart systems with human control and attention. Issues like privacy, trust and identity raise not only technical, but also social and ethical problems, particularly with regard to legal and moral rights as they have been discussed in detail here in the corresponding Sect. 6 before.

The Scaling Issue. The scaling factor can range from a body to a room, a building, public space, neighborhood, city, region or country. It can grow also according to the complexity due to the huge number of functionalities provided. The scaling of AmI spaces is not straightforward or trivial. Particularly interesting are: Fuzziness: one person's 'neighborhood' may be very different compared with its neighbors. Conflicts of interest among AmI spaces: moving between personal and public spaces having different characteristics. Moving from smaller to larger spaces, the number of people and AmI resources residing in them increases, and there are not always common goals or intentions. It is also very likely that different AmI environments are defined by different tasks and goals. This means that conflicts will inevitably arise. Availability, ownership and use of resources: environments of different size and scope require a seamless integration among private and public resources.

In summary, we can conclude that the smart city proposal contains many opportunities. But one should also be aware that there are several risks requiring the discussion of pros and cons. It is my opinion, that the smart city promises will only survive and be successful if our future cities are designed as Humane Sociable and Cooperative Smart Hybrid Cities, reconciling humans and technology. Urban environments should be designed to enable people to exploit their creative, social and economic potential and lead a self-determined life. Ambient Intelligence can play a major role in achieving this goal by reconciling humans and technology.

References

Aarts, E., Encarnaçao, J. (eds.): True Visions: The Emergence of Ambient Intelligence. Springer, Heidelberg (2006)

Disappearing Computer (2000–2005). http://www.smart-future.net/themes-and-issues/disappearing-computer/. Accessed 28 Feb 2017

ISTAG. Scenarios for Ambient Intelligence in 2010. Final report. February 2001. European Commission, Luxembourg (2001). http://cordis.europa.eu/pub/ist/docs/istagscenarios2010.pdf. Accessed 28 Feb 2017

Konomi, S., Shoji, K., Ohno, W.: Rapid development of civic computing services: opportunities and challenges. In: Streitz, N., Stephanidis, C. (eds.) DAPI 2013. LNCS, vol. 8028, pp. 309–315. Springer, Heidelberg (2013). doi:10.1007/978-3-642-39351-8_34

Russell, D., Streitz, N., Winograd, T.: Building disappearing computers. Commun. ACM **48**(3), 42–48 (2005)

SESAMI. Mission statement by A. Savidis and N. Streitz, the chairs of the ERCIM-Working Group SESAMI (2007). http://www.ics.forth.gr/sesami/index.html. Accessed 28 Feb 2017

Streitz, N.: Augmented reality and the disappearing computer. In: Smith, M., Salvendy, G., Harris, D., Koubek, R. (eds.) Cognitive Engineering, Intelligent Agents and Virtual Reality, pp. 738–742. Lawrence Erlbaum, Mahwah (2001)

Streitz, N.: The disappearing computer. In: Erickson, T., McDonald, D.W. (eds.) HCI Remixed: Reflections on Works That Have Influenced the HCI Community, pp. 55–60. MIT Press, Cambridge (2008)

Streitz, N.: Citizen-centered design for humane and sociable hybrid cities. In: Theona, I., Charitos, D. (eds.) Hybrid City 2015 - Data to the People, pp. 17–20. University of Athens, Greece (2015)

Streitz, N.: Smart cities need privacy by design for being humane. In: Pop, S., Toft, T., Calvillo, N., Wright, M. (eds.) What Urban Media Art Can Do - Why When Where and How, pp. 268–274. Verlag avedition, Stuttgart (2016)

Streitz, N.A., Geißler, J., Holmer, T.: Roomware for cooperative buildings: integrated design of architectural spaces and information spaces. In: Streitz, N.A., Konomi, S., Burkhardt, H.-J. (eds.) CoBuild 1998. LNCS, vol. 1370, pp. 4–21. Springer, Heidelberg (1998). doi: 10.1007/3-540-69706-3_3

Streitz, N., Geißler, J., Holmer, T., Konomi, S., Müller-Tomfelde, C., Reischl, W., Rexroth, P., Seitz, P., Steinmetz, R.: i-LAND: an interactive landscape for creativity and innovation. In: Proceedings of ACM CHI 1999 Conference, pp. 120–127 (1999)

Streitz, N., Kameas, A., Mavrommati, I. (eds.): The Disappearing Computer. LNCS, vol. 4500. Springer, Heidelberg (2007). doi:10.1007/978-3-540-72727-9

Streitz, N., Nixon, P.: The disappearing computer. Commun. ACM **48**(3), 33–35 (2005). Guest Editors' Introduction to Special Issue

Streitz, N., Privat, G.: Ambient intelligence. Final section "Looking to the Future". In: Stephanidis, C. (ed.) The Universal Access Handbook, pp. 60.1–60.17. CRC Press, Boca Raton (2009)

Streitz, N., Röcker, C., Prante, T., van Alphen, D., Stenzel, R., Magerkurth, C.: Designing smart artifacts for smart environments. IEEE Comput. **38**(3), 41–49 (2005)

Streitz, N., Wichert, R.: Towards the Humane City: White Paper on a Future Research Agenda. Final report (2009). InterLink website http://interlink.ics.forth.gr/central.aspx?sId=84I241I747I323I344337. Accessed 28 Feb 2017

Weiser, M.: The Computer for the 21st Century, pp. 66–75. Scientific American (1991)

Engineering a Cyber-Physical Intersection Management – An Experience Report

Florian Wessling, Stefan Gries(✉), Julius Ollesch, Marc Hesenius, and Volker Gruhn

paluno - The Ruhr Institute for Software Technology, University of Duisburg-Essen, Schützenbahn 70, 45127 Essen, Germany
{florian.wessling,stefan.gries,julius.ollesch,marc.hesenius, volker.gruhn}@paluno.uni-due.de
http://se.paluno.uni-due.de

Abstract. The engineering of cyber-physical systems (CPS) imposes a huge challenge for today's software engineering processes. Not only are CPS very closely related to real objects and processes, also their internal structures are more heterogeneous than classical information systems. In this experience report, we account on a prototypical implementation for an intersection management system on the basis of physical models in the form of robotic cars. The steps to implement the working physical prototype are described. Lessons learned during the implementation are presented and observations compared against known software processes. The insights gained are consolidated into the novel *Double Twin Peaks* model. The latter extends the current software engineering viewpoints, specifically taking CPS considerations into account.

Keywords: Software engineering · Cyber-physical system · CPS · Requirements engineering · Twin Peaks · Modeling · Experience report · Agile development · Software process model

1 Introduction

Cyber-physical systems (CPS) are an emerging topic for research and enable digital innovation in domains such as energy, health and transportation [13]. Equipped with computing power, networking and the ability to sense and actuate real world processes, CPS enable ambient intelligence to conduct process control. Furthermore, CPS may consist of heterogenous components unknown at development time, thus allowing dynamic extension at runtime allowing greater adaptability and the ability to cope with heterogeneous infrastructures. Being defined as systems at the crossroad between physical processes and information processing [12], CPS are vital for ambient intelligence.

CPS are key in the digital transformation – a development that brings the software engineering and traditional engineering domains closer together and creates new and interesting technical challenges and opportunities [14]. However,

A. Braun et al. (Eds.): AmI 2017, LNCS 10217, pp. 17–32, 2017.
DOI: 10.1007/978-3-319-56997-0_2

an often overlooked problem is the orchestration of experts to create CPS – i.e. the engineering process itself. To date, to the best of our knowledge there are no comprehensive accounts on the engineering methods for CPS. Thus, there is an urgent need to explore similarities and differences between information system engineering and engineering of CPS.

Road-going vehicles are currently undergoing a transformation to gradually become networked and autonomous [7]. The anticipated impacts are profound: greater individual productivity, less accidents and killings and new emerging business models to name only a few. Notably, a directly affected aspect of this transformation is traffic regulation.

Today, traffic signals and road signs are designed to be human-readable, but in the near future there is potential to optimize traffic flow by directly communicating with connected self-driving cars. While there are research groups focussing on analyzing and improving intersections and traffic flows in general, to the best of our knowledge, this is the first approach with a focus on the engineering of such an intelligent system.

The example of a intersection management system seems appropriate to study how CPS evolve as its engineering does not only concerns information systems but also mechanical components, sensors and actuators. To this point no general engineering process has emerged for CPS. Hence, we chose to investigate and observe the process of building a physical prototype using the example of an intersection with the aim to derive good practices that may be generalized in future work.

The paper is organized as follows: in Sect. 2 we will review related work on intersection simulation, physical prototyping and software engineering processes. Sect. 3 presents the project approach and describes the work done in the respective sprints. Section. 4 summarizes the results of the project in terms of intersection management and technical challenges while Sect. 5 describes the software engineering process which emerged from the development of the prototypical CPS. Eventually Sect. 6 provides an outlook in terms of future research directions.

2 Related Work

2.1 Software Engineering Process

Traditional software engineering processes are not directly applicable to cyber-physical systems due to the specific characteristics of CPS such as a close interdependency between hard- and software, uncertainty during operation, as well as the large scale, complexity and distribution of infrastructures [1,5]. As CPS lie at the intersection of multiple disciplines such as mechanical engineering, electrical engineering, control engineering, software engineering and physics, the CPS engineering process is multidisciplinary as well [1,6,10].

Al-Jaroodi et al. [1] give an broad overview of the software engineering challenges imposed by CPS. One of their findings is that the complexity strongly depends on the domain of the cyber-physical systems under development. While mobility and power limitation might be issues for CPS in the automotive domain this restriction is different for CPS developed in a smart home context. According to Al-Jaroodi et al. all software engineering phases such as analysis, design, implementation and testing need to be reconsidered and adapted when developing CPS [1]. Particularly during the analysis phase models and tools are required that enable a coherent specification while capturing CPS characteristics. For example Bures et al. consider the idea to use software architecture models that are extended with knowledge and insights "such as electro-mechanical elements, physical constraints and laws" from other areas [5].

The view from a software vendor is presented by Rüchardt and Bräuchle [18]. Their experiences support the initial assumption of this paper that the interdependency between hard- and software has a huge impact. The authors explain that the business model is influenced as well: "experiences with enterprise systems can be extrapolated and transformed into a new model of system operations, where product and service merge to form one common business model." [18].

Autonomous driving is currently gaining public interest and CPS are enabling this trend. Therefore we have chosen the domain of automotive traffic coordination and aim at creating a small-scale physical intersection in order to examine the software engineering process for CPS.

2.2 Simulating Intersections

There are several approaches working towards the future of intelligent transportation systems in which vehicles cross intersections autonomously.

A first step towards making intersections more efficient is analyzing the dilemma zone problem, which refers to the area in front of an intersection that is approached during the yellow light phase and the driver being indecisive about stopping or crossing the intersection. Petnga and Austin [17] describe this dilemma as a set of conditions that represent an unsafe state and present a simulation framework for implementing resolution algorithms. The authors conclude that for achieving a successful coordination it is necessary to consider cars and traffic lights simultaneously, i.e. both spatial and temporal data is required in order to prevent the system from reaching an unsafe state.

In a recent work from MIT the authors Tachet et al. examine slot-based systems known from aerial traffic coordination and present a framework to analyze the performance of different algorithms for a slot-based intersection for vehicles [20]. The common way of coordinating vehicles are traffic lights which grant access to an intersection area (i.e., the shared resource) exclusively to one of the traffic directions. In contrast to this approach, slot-based systems consider the trajectory of multiple vehicles and prevent collisions by coordinating the time slot in which the intersection can be crossed safely (simultaneously for multiple traffic directions). Their work shows that by using a slot-based intersection the capacity of an intersection can be doubled and delays significantly reduced.

Azimi et al. focus on Vehicle to Vehicle (V2V) communication in order to coordinate the crossing of an intersection [3]. Their algorithm segments the intersection into a grid of 4×4 cells. Each vehicle calculates possible collisions with other vehicles based on their desired trajectory and its respective occupied cells during the crossing. This communication process is triggered when approaching the intersection. The authors experiment with different algorithms ("intersection protocols") and compare the trip time and delay caused by crossing the intersection. Their results show that by avoiding single colliding cells on vehicle trajectories the delay caused by common traffic lights can be reduced from 48% up to 85% due to lower waiting time and a more fine-grained planning.

Wuthishuwong and Traechtler use a Vehicle to Infrastructure (V2I) approach in which a centralized system plans and coordinates the trajectories of vehicles crossing an intersection [21]. Based on discretization of the vehicle's two-dimensional trajectory and considering time as the third dimension the authors employ Dynamic Programming to calculate a collision-free route for each vehicle. Compared to the aforementioned approach Wuthishuwong and Traechtler achieve an even more fine-grained trajectory. Although the authors did not carry out exhaustive experiments they state that their approach reduced delay and supported an continuous flow of vehicles crossing an prototypical simulated intersection.

2.3 Simulations and Physical Prototypes

The examples mentioned in Sect. 2.2 are all software-based and simulate vehicle trajectories without any connection to physical devices.

The work by Paczesny et al. studies the link between simulation and prototyping of cyber-physical systems [16]. By providing a middleware combining aspects from both areas, it is possible during development to test and demonstrate a CPS composed of virtual nodes (i.e., simulated elements) and real nodes (e.g., objects and their sensors and actuators). This middleware also enables hybrid approaches as combinations of virtual and real nodes on both the cyber (i.e., software) and physical side.

Blech et al. call the combination of existing physical elements and software simulation "cyber-virtual systems" [4]. The authors highlight the importance of "visualization, simulation and validation of cyber-physical systems in industrial automation during development, operation and maintenance" supported by Hardware-in-the-Loop (HIL) approaches. HIL is known from the domain of embedded systems where hardware "parts of a system are simulated in software to test a distinct system component."

Kim et al. argue that conventional HIL simulations are not suitable for CPS as these simulations are usually built for specific systems in non-distributed environments [11]. Therefore the authors propose a human-interactive HIL simulation framework for CPS. It supports a fully distributed and scalable environment that connects human-interactive (i.e., physical) devices for input, distributed simulators and a physical system as the target to be tested.

3 Project Approach

The idea of this project is to interweave aspects from the above mentioned related work with an experimental setup while focussing on the primary goal to learn about the engineering process of CPS. Following this idea, we aim to develop problem solving techniques and guidance for work organization in CPS development projects. The actual results of the implementation are secondary. Therefore the following section is focussed on the work items and process and leaves out some technical details of the solution.

3.1 Project Setup

The project team consisted of software engineers, mainly the authors and one student who contributed to specific work items concerning simulation and intersection protocol algorithms. While high-level requirements were clearly set, detailed analysis of the real requirements was not possible and hence the team followed an agile approach [19, p. 57ff.] with weekly or bi-weekly meetings and an incremental development of features to explore technical boundaries (see Fig. 1). From the beginning, it was clear that due to resource constraints, the intersection needed to be modeled: no real cars, let alone a real intersection were available. Lego Mindstorms was chosen as framework for the physical model and accordingly the intersection needed to be built in a scaled-down indoor environment. Benefits and disadvantages of this approach will be discussed in the course of this chapter. The structure resembles the phases of the project and observations and lessons learned are outlined in the context of the sprint phase where they occurred.

3.2 First Sprint

The first sprint primarily served as a basis for subsequent work and guidance for the team members. In this regard, the sprint was primarily composed of two elementary tasks. First, the development hardware was examined and configured. Second, concepts and models to digitize the physical components were created.

In terms of hardware, we started with NXT and EV3 robots from the Lego Mindstorms series. The rationale behind this decision was that this is a proven framework for experiments in robotics. For better control over the hardware we used the LeJOS operating system [8], which allows execution of arbitrary Java software as opposed to the original Lego OS. After the construction of a prototypical vehicle, we started to implement the on-board software. In our concept, the vehicles should communicate their location to a central server in order to retrieve control information. The communication was to take place from the vehicle to a computer via Bluetooth. On the computer, a bridge software needed to be set up, which forwards the bluetooth communication via REST calls to a server. The NXT controllers that were used do not have the capability to implement IP-based communication themselves.

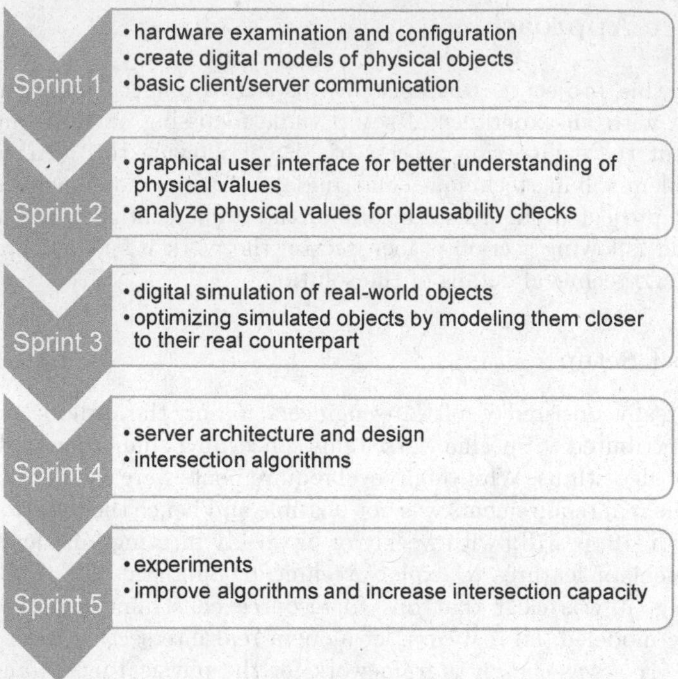

Fig. 1. Sprint overview

A special conceptual and technical challenge was the localization of the vehicles. As our experiment should be carried out indoor, GPS localization could not be used – the necessary precision of two to five centimeter for the scaled down car models cannot be achieved with normal GPS, especially not in an indoor environment. Also radio-frequency beacons are able to provide this spatial resolution. Instead, we decided to divide the lanes into fields (approximately five centimeter long), coded with different colors (see Fig. 2).

The unique color combination allowed localization of the vehicle across the lane. To read the color code, vehicles were equipped with two downward-facing color sensors whose values were sent to the server continuously. With that, the server can detect the position of the vehicle by matching its color combination and the color-coded model of the intersection.

The server component was implemented as Node.js server. In the first sprint, the server does not control any of the vehicles. Instead, only the transfer of the location from the vehicle to the server was implemented.

Lessons Learned: We learned that for the design decisions on how to abstract reality to a model, the available sensors play an important role. The characteristics and limitations of the sensors to be used need to be adequately studied to ensure that all functions can be implemented later. The sensors' specified capabilities are therefore a valid starting point for the model. However, the specification and documentation of the sensor must be read, tested and validated to ensure they can be used in the scenario – we found our designated color-sensors to massively underperform in the target environment. Also, we had to change the physical mounting and adjust the height of the color sensors to reach a better performance. Eventually the experimentation led to a reduced set of seven identifiable colors which was fed back to the modeling task in order to color code the intersection.

Fig. 2. Intersection prototype with robotic cars (Color figure online)

3.3 Second Sprint

In the second sprint, we focussed on creating a visualization to enable a more productive development and testing. While the messaging of the detected vehicle location to the server had already been implemented, it could only be written out to the console – a not well-readable form of information that makes the system difficult to debug. Thus, errors could not be detected directly, because they were not obvious to the human eye – especially, if the incoming values seemed plausible. To solve this problem, a graphical user interface (GUI) component was implemented. The GUI should enable developers to visualize the vehicle locations known by the server. Therefore, we constructed a digital twin of the intersection. Technologically, the implementation of the GUI was done in JavaScript to keep it close to the server codebase (especially for data structures and related code). HTML and the canvas element were chosen as native visualization means in this technology stack. As a result, movements on the physical intersection could be compared to the information of the server which were visualized on the screen. Each vehicle was represented by a simple rectangle in the digital model. The shape contains vehicle information such as location (including the color combination), speed, vehicle length, etc.

Lessons Learned: First, we depicted real-world objects in a machine readable format on the server. The problem here is that this model is not comprehensible enough for human developers in order to detect errors at first sight. Therefore we decided to visualize the created model as well. Even if this meant additional work, we invested the required time to accelerate the ongoing development process. HTML canvas proved to be a capable and well-performing, however not very comfortable option develop the GUI. Feedback from team members developing the intersection algorithms suggest that in fact identification of errors and troubleshooting got more productive and effective. Hence, we conclude that human readable models and visualizations help to structure the CPS development process and to increase its efficiency.

3.4 Third Sprint

It quickly became clear that the development was slowed down by the exclusive use of physical cars. The recurrent placement of vehicles increased the test effort further and slowed down debugging. The team therefore decided to simulate vehicles. Thus, this sprint focussed on developing a virtual car component. The idea was that the virtual instance of the vehicle would use the same interfaces as the physical robotic car. This way, the server does not know if a connected vehicle is a real or virtual (it is a blackbox). Other than the robotic vehicle, the virtual car component included the digital model of the intersection. To simulate driving behavior, it sent messages to the server with color codes from the model in the given order. Moreover, also the virtual vehicle could be controlled by commands from the server. Same as the robot, it would react to target speeds set by the server and behave accordingly. Effectively this meant that at higher speed, the color combinations were sent at shorter intervals to the server. At the same time, the experiments with robotic cars showed that the physical model needed extension. In some situations, the server assumed that cars had already cleared the intersection - but in reality they were still crossing. We speculated that the robotic cars varied their speed based on battery charge and available voltage. Thus we decided to add a color code to the lanes right after the intersection. By passing this color combination, the cars could declare themselves clear off the collision zone.

Lessons Learned: CPS focus on the interaction of physical objects, hardware and software. Real-world objects are sensed and measured and the system responds to their properties. Since the physical properties change constantly, scenarios are very difficult to reproduce. Furthermore, the continuous use of physical objects in the development process creates an enormous test and debug workload on software developers. The simulation of these objects can reduce the workload and accelerate the development process. The fact that simulated components are at work should be intransparent to other CPS components, otherwise the validity of the simulation is at risk.

3.5 Fourth Sprint

Once we were able to transmit the locations of real and virtual vehicles without errors to the server, the performance of any intersection algorithm could digitally be visualized on the screen. The next step was to deal with the control of the vehicles. In our setup, the server stored all locations of all vehicles at all times. This centralized server should now decide how fast each vehicle should move. The primary goal of any intersection control should be that there are no collisions, the secondary goal being optimal use of the road capacity. In this sprint, we implemented two competing routing algorithms that pursued different strategies in reaching the aforementioned goals.

The algorithms were designed as modules in the server, so that they could easily be switched and compared. Both routing algorithms got access to the location of all vehicles, their main task being the calculation of a target speed for each vehicle. The server then sent this information to the vehicles that adjust their speed accordingly. By using the virtual cars we were able to test the algorithms with unlimited vehicles and observe the behavior. As stated before, the main focus was to avoid collisions.

Lessons Learned: While implementing the routing algorithms, the virtual vehicles were used successfully to simulate the intersection. We learned that without simulations, no productive development is possible, as the iteration cycles between implementation and testing are very frequent and short. Often, changing a piece of code only took a few minutes to complete. Afterwards, a brief test needed to be performed in each case. Doing these tests during implementation with real vehicles is virtually impossible because this takes too much time and effort.

3.6 Fifth Sprint

In a final sprint we experimented with the different vehicles and tried to optimize the functions of the system. Focus here was to increase the capacity of the junction without causing collisions. To make the comparison more objective, a collision counter was implemented together with the option to freeze the GUI at the event of a collision. Prior to this, longterm testing was effectively useless as collisions needed to be observed by a human. The routing algorithms' code was cleaned and partially rewritten. In the experiments we also tried to combine real and virtual cars to observe if they behaved similarly and if the intersection could handle this situation.

Lessons Learned: After we had reviewed much of the implementation using virtual vehicles, we had to perform integration tests with real hardware. This showed how important it was that the virtual vehicles act as precisely as possible like their physical counterpart. The test on real hardware was completed quickly – only small changes to the code were necessary, e.g. to synchronize the speed of virtual cars to real cars. The routing algorithms and server components did not require further changes.

4 Project Results and Critical Acclaim

The project ended with a successful test of the intersection with both robotic and virtual cars, as well as a combination. At this stage the following artifacts have been developed:

- Physical model of the intersection and three physical model cars
- Bluetooth bridge for cars connected to the server module
- Two intersection protocol implementations
- Digital model of the intersection and graphical user interface
- Virtual car simulation module

With this setup, different use cases are supported. The virtual components together with the GUI proved very valuable to simulate behavior and visualize problems. In this use case, the virtual cars are controlled by the server according to the given protocol. Algorithms can be interchanged and collision numbers compared. The same applies when physical cars are used. These also are controlled through the server and the bluetooth bridge component. The latter being necessary for coupling of devices and tunneling of IP-based communication with the server component. Our experiments showed that the concept of indoor localization with color coded lanes worked rather precisely. The physical robotic cars worked well, although their physical properties in terms of speed and maneuvering capabilities are certainly in need of improvement. Although our analysis lacks detailed statistics, the results are promising as the throughput of the intersection seems ample and collisions could not be observed.

One main limitation of the scenario is that cars do not change their direction, i.e. they do not turn. While it is certainly possible to build Lego cars and software that enables precise turning maneuvers, we decided to not spend time on this feature. Secondly, we did not use ultrasonic distance control, despite the availability of the sensor in the Lego NXT framework. With this, it would have been relatively easy to ensure that a certain safety distance is kept by cars. We decided against this in order to focus on the algorithmic quality, however these sensors are widely used today for park distance control and are also part of the sensor package in autonomous vehicles. Another limitation is that we decided not to use vehicle to vehicle (V2V) communication. V2V is speculated to be a major feature of connected cars and enable better peer-to-peer coordination (amongst other benefits). This also would make the algorithmic control problem more interesting. While all these features would add realism and more complexity to examine the algorithms, it would have been just more iterations through physical and virtual models and software. Hence, we conclude these would not have added value for our focus area: the engineering process.

5 Results on Methodology and Engineering Process

Our observations are presented in two steps. First we elaborate on the differences between a CPS development process and an information system development process. Then we take those differences and generate a preliminary model for a CPS software engineering process and its phases.

5.1 Observations on CPS-Specific Tasks

CPS-specific tasks are naturally connected to the physical aspects otherwise missing in a software project.

The first step in our experiment was the construction of a viable physical model. This is due to the design decision to use building blocks instead of more integrated components. Certainly the idea to use Lego Mindstorms/NXT is a compromise between fabricating a physical model from scratch and choosing a fully integrated system like Anki Overdrive. As described, sensors and actuators need special attention. To information system developers it may come as a surprise that the sensor's capabilities, to a large extent, dictate the data model and even many functional aspects. In our case, the color sensor limitations influenced not only the physical architecture of the car but also the model of the intersection, such that localization was finally possible with the data generated. These constraints can be interpreted as technical requirements, well known to software engineers. However, their nature is different as they need to be developed and deducted from the physical processes in scope and are not given by stakeholders during the classical requirements elicitation phase methods such as interviews or scenarios [19, p. 99ff.]. This physical aspect is usually not present in the construction of information systems. It creates a greater uncertainty in the specification phase which leads to even more iterations between requirements and architecture. These iterations are similar to component tests, where a subsystem is tested individually in a prototypical and explorative manner.

Second, after the physical model has been developed and translated into an information and data model, the software implementation phase started to influence physical aspects again. When the first algorithm was tested with physical cars, we found that cars would collide because the algorithm assumed they had already cleared the intersection. So, in order to have a robust method to determine if the intersection was clear or not, it was decided to add a unique color code after the intersection to each lane. Cars would send this marker to the server and thereby declare that they leave the scope of control. Clearly, this measure could have been foreseen at an earlier stage. But to us it only became apparent when tested with physical model cars, that behaved physically correct. While it can be credited to a lack of experience in building CPS, it does seem realistic to assume that implementation aspects of CPS are likely to be overlooked until first tests of the integrated system are conducted. While it is certainly desirable to follow a holistic plan-driven approach in any safety-critical environment [19, p. 57] such as traffic control, the heterogeneity of CPS might render this ambition unfeasible. Thus, the CPS engineering process must not prohibit later adjustments to aspects of the system but rather enable change.

Third, the behavior of the physical cars was again modeled into a virtual simulation component. This component acted like the physical car and communicated with exactly the same protocol reading color codes and processing speed commands. As a result, it was not transparent for the server if a car was virtual or real. Being able to instantiate an almost arbitrary amount of (virtual) cars made testing and simulating the intersection algorithms a lot more convenient and productive. However, we found it difficult to recreate the exact physical behavior of the cars in terms of acceleration and speed. The physical cars would sometimes come off track or show faster or slower speeds (possibly due to higher or lower battery charge states). Nonetheless, the virtual cars made it possible to develop algorithms in a more reasonable time. Simulation is therefore both an accelerator, as well as a threat to development process. The danger is mainly rooted in the fact that a simulation can never fully account for the variability of real world applications and therefor cannot guarantee faultless operation.

5.2 Preliminary Model of CPS Software Engineering Phases

Throughout the different phases of our development, we saw strong parallels to the *Twin Peaks* model [15]. Twin Peaks emphasizes the interrelation of requirements and architecture, the notion being that there is a permanent exchange of information between the two. Moreover, Twin Peaks conveys the idea that one starts with a general understanding of requirements and architecture and iteratively generates a detailed view.

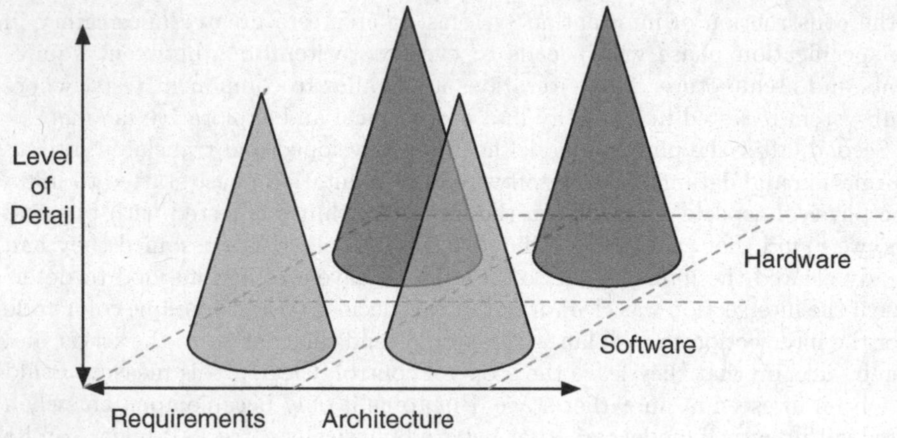

Fig. 3. *Double Twin Peaks* overview

Based on our observations, we propose to add the notion of physical (real-world) objects to this model. We found that often physical properties and constraints were only discovered when applying our architectural decisions. Therefore the iterations are not purely software-based but clearly there is a hardware-related loop to the CPS engineering process. As with Twin Peaks, this is a bidirectional information gain: software needs to be adapted when physical aspects change and the physical part of the CPS evolves when new software is implemented and tested. For example the requirement to localize vehicles indoors led to the development of a physical color-code schema. This in turn incurred that vehicles needed color sensors. Experiments with the latter showed that the positioning of the sensors

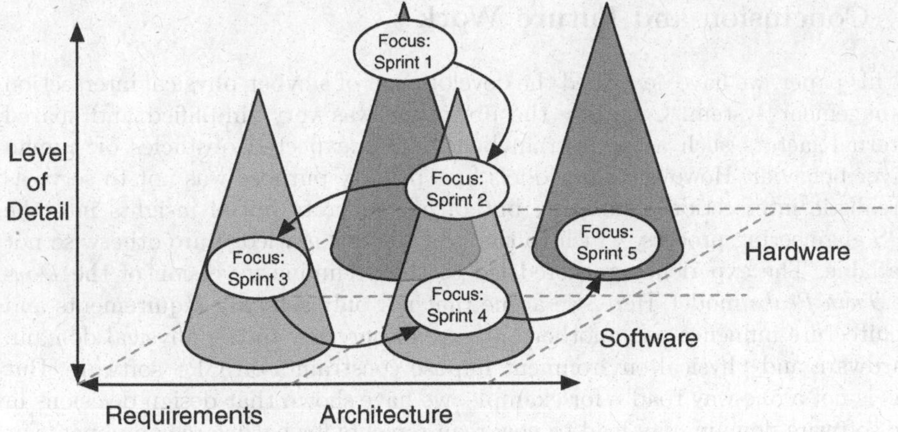

Fig. 4. Illustration of the observation that focus areas of sprints alternated over the course of engineering through different domains in *Double Twin Peaks*.

is crucial to obtain enough reliable data. The number of colors supported by the sensor influenced the software data model, and so on. We think it is crucial to understand that CPS components cannot be developed separately, but in fact the development of cyber and physical parts are closely aligned and interdependent. Therefore we present the *Double Twin Peaks* model, as shown in Fig. 3 below. In the foreground, it depicts the Twin Peaks of software requirements and architecture, adding a layer for the respective doubles in the physical domain – hardware requirements and hardware architecture.

Double Twin Peaks emphasizes the strong influence of physical properties on the design and development of CPS. As described in the original Twin Peaks publication, similar attention needs to be put on software requirements, architecture as well as hardware design and physical constraints. It can be hypothesized that as with software there exist CPS-patterns, i.e. solutions that can be applied in a range of similar problems. What can be said for sure is that a modular, well-defined and reusable system architecture is desirable for CPS in order to cope with complexity and shorten development cycles. However, this ambition is challenged as the physical part of CPS tend to be specifically tailored to the physical environment and relevant constraints. As physical components influence the software part, the entire CPS drifts towards a specific solution. Figure 4 depicts the described development journey in the *Double Twin Peaks* model. Despite the limited number of sprints, we experienced a constant interchange between domains which did not follow the textbook approach in software engineering.

While *Double Twin Peaks* is a preliminary result and needs validation, the generated insight might help developers aiming to build CPS to realize possible faux pas such as strict separation of teams or lack of communication.

6 Conclusion and Future Work

In this paper, we have described the development of a cyber-physical intersection management system. Certainly the prototype was very simplified and spared external factors such as pedestrian behavior, unexpected obstacles or human driver behavior. However, our models first priority purpose was not to serve as a realistic intersection simulation but rather generate initial insights into the CPS engineering process, which to the best of our knowledge are otherwise not available. The experience gathered led to the preliminary version of the *Double Twin Peaks* model. Here, we argue that not only software requirements and architecture influence one another but extend our view to the physical domain. Hardware and physical environment impose constraints on CPS software. But this is not a one-way road – for example, we have shown that design decisions in the software domain may lead to new requirements for hardware components or new ideas how to interact with the physical environment. We are currently developing a follow-up project. With this second generation prototype we would like to validate the *Double Twin Peaks* development model presented previously. The model should consistently be applicable throughout the phases of the CPS engineering life cycle. The focus is requirements engineering, architectural design, implementation and concurrent testing.

In this prototype setup we had used building blocks from the Lego NXT robotics framework. From a functional perspective, it is desirable to move away from this system as the NXT control units lack computing power and modern communication. In addition, to improve the cars speed and precision of movements, the mechanical design would need to be generally revised. Thus for the following project, we aim to use Anki Overdrive [9].

Higher speed and greater flexibility are not the only changes compared to NXTs – Anki vehicles are equipped with modern communication technology, optical sensors and artificial intelligence. The cars are fully-integrated devices whose software can not be customized [2]. Hence, a major benefit of using Anki is that we are able to observe if our findings still hold true for a more integrated platform, where most physical aspects are predetermined.

Thus, the focus of future research is no longer the software implementation of the vehicle itself. Instead, we will concentrate on the network of vehicles and the intelligent intersection control algorithm. With this slight change in focus, we are keen to see if the hardware layer in the *Double Twin Peaks* model is still relevant. Apart from that, Anki brings further possibilities to extent the project scope: up to four vehicles can travel side by side on the track. The track could therefore be divided into two tracks per direction, resulting in new possibilities for the control system and more realism compared to real world traffic. Moreover, we are planning turn maneuvers on the intersection to further increase the option space for the prototype.

Acknowledgments. This work has been supported by the European Community through project CPS.HUB NRW, EFRE Nr. 0-4000-17.

References

1. Al-Jaroodi, J., Mohamed, N., Jawhar, I., Lazarova-Molnar, S.: Software engineering issues for cyber-physical systems. In: 2016 IEEE International Conference on Smart Computing (SMARTCOMP), pp. 1–6, May 2016. doi:10.1109/SMARTCOMP.2016.7501717
2. Anki Inc.: Anki drive SDK (2016). https://github.com/anki/drive-sdk
3. Azimi, R., Bhatia, G., Rajkumar, R., Mudalige, P.: Intersection management using vehicular networks (2012). http://papers.sae.org/2012-01-0292/
4. Blech, J.O., Spichkova, M., Peake, I., Schmidt, H.: Visualization, simulation and validation for cyber-virtual systems. In: Maciaszek, L.A., Filipe, J. (eds.) ENASE 2014. CCIS, vol. 551, pp. 140–154. Springer, Cham (2015). doi:10.1007/978-3-319-27218-4_10
5. Bures, T., Weyns, D., Berger, C., Biffl, S., Daun, M., Gabor, T., Garlan, D., Gerostathopoulos, I., Julien, C., Krikava, F., Mordinyi, R., Pronios, N.: Software engineering for smart cyber-physical systems - towards a research agenda: report on the first international workshop on software engineering for smart CPS. ACM SIGSOFT Softw. Eng. Notes Arch. **40**(6), 28–32 (2015). doi:10.1145/2830719.2830736. ISSN 0163–5948
6. Derler, P., Lee, E.A., Vincentelli, A.S.: Modeling cyber-physical systems. Proc. IEEE **100**(1), 13–28 (2012). doi:10.1109/JPROC.2011.2160929. ISSN 0018-9219, 1558-2256. http://ieeexplore.ieee.org/lpdocs/epic03/wrapper.htm?arnumber=5995279
7. Gao, P., Kaas, H.-W., Mohr, D., Wee, D.: Automotive revolution - perspective towards 2030, January 2016. http://www.mckinsey.com/~/media/mckinsey/industries/high%20tech/our%20insights/disruptive%20trends%20that%20will%20transform%20the%20auto%20industry/auto%202030%20report%20jan%202016.ashx
8. Griffiths, L., Shaw, A., Bagnall, B.: LeJOS, Java for lego mindstorms (2009). http://www.lejos.org
9. Heidloff, N.: Node.js controller and MQTT API for Anki over-drive, May 2016. https://github.com/IBM-Bluemix/node-mqtt-for-anki-overdrive
10. Kim, K.D., Kumar, P.R.: Cyber-physical systems: a perspective at the centennial. Proc. IEEE **100**, 1287–1308 (2012). doi:10.1109/JPROC.2012.2189792. ISSN 0018-9219
11. Kim, M.J., Kang, S., Kim, W.T., Chun, I.G.: Human-interactive hardware-in-the-loop simulation framework for cyber-physical systems. In: Second International Conference on Informatics and Applications (ICIA), pp. 198–202 (2013). doi:10.1109/ICoIA.2013.6650255
12. Lee, E.A.: CPS foundations. In: DAC 2010 47th ACM/IEEE, pp. 737–742 (2010). doi:10.1145/1837274.1837462. ISSN 0738-100X
13. Lee, E.A.: The past, present and future of cyber-physical systems: a focus on models. Sensors **15**(3), 4837–4869 (2015). doi:10.3390/s150304837. ISSN 1424-8220. http://www.mdpi.com/1424-8220/15/3/4837/
14. Leitao, P., Colombo, A.W., Karnouskos, S.: Industrial automation based on cyber-physical systems technologies: prototype implementations and challenges. Comput. Ind. (2015). doi:10.1016/j.compind.2015.08.004. ISSN 01663615
15. Nuseibeh, B.: Weaving together requirements and architectures. Computer **34**(3), 115–117 (2001). doi:10.1109/2.910904. ISSN 0018-9162. http://dx.doi.org/10.1109/2.910904

16. Paczesny, T., Domaszewicz, J., Konstańczuk, P., Milewski, J., Pruszkowski, A.: Between simulator and prototype: crossover architecture for testing and demonstrating cyber physical systems. In: Pentikousis, K., Aguiar, R., Sargento, S., Agüero, R. (eds.) MONAMI 2011. LNICSSITE, vol. 97, pp. 375–385. Springer, Heidelberg (2012). doi:10.1007/978-3-642-30422-4_27. ISBN 978-3-642-30422-4
17. Petnga, L., Austin, M.A.: Safe traffic intersections: metrics, tubes, and prototype simulation for solving the dilemma zone problem. Int. J. Adv. Syst. Meas. **8**, 241–254 (2015)
18. Rüchardt, D., Bräuchle, C.: A large software vendor's view on cyber physical systems. In: 3rd International Workshop on Emerging Ideas and Trends in Engineering of Cyber-Physical Systems (EITEC), pp. 29–34 (2016). doi:10.1109/EITEC.2016.7503693
19. Sommerville, I.: Software Engineering, 9th International edn. Pearson, Boston (2011). ISBN 0137053460
20. Tachet, R., Santi, P., Sobolevsky, S., Reyes-Castro, L.I., Frazzoli, E., Helbing, D., Ratti, C.: Revisiting street intersections using slot-based systems. PLoS One **11**(3), e0149607 (2016). doi:10.1371/journal.pone.0149607. ISSN 1932-6203. http://journals.plos.org/plosone/article?id=10.1371/journal.pone.0149607
21. Wuthishuwong, C., Traechtler, A.: Vehicle to infrastructure based safe trajectory planning for autonomous intersection management. In: 13th International Conference on ITS Telecommunications (ITST), pp. 175–180 (2013). doi:10.1109/ITST.2013.6685541

Exploring Design Opportunities for Intelligent Worker Assistance: A New Approach Using Projetion-Based AR and a Novel Hand-Tracking Algorithm

Sebastian Büttner(✉), Oliver Sand, and Carsten Röcker

Ostwestfalen-Lippe University of Applied Sciences, Lemgo, Germany
{sebastian.buettner,carsten.roecker}@hs-owl.de,
oliver.sand@stud.hs-owl.de

Abstract. This paper presents a prototype of an intelligent assistive system for workers in stationary manual assembly using projection-based augmented reality (AR) and intelligent hand tracking. By using depth cameras, the system can track the hands of the user and makes the user aware of wrong picking actions or errors in the assembly process. The system automatically adapts the digital projection-based overlay according to the current work situation. The main research contribution of our work is the presentation of a novel hand-tracking algorithm. In addition, we present the results of an user study of the system that shows the challenges and opportunities of our system and the hand-tracking algorithm in particular. We assume that our results will inform the future design of assistive systems in manual assembly.

Keywords: Augmented reality · Mobile projection · Hand tracking · Manufacturing · Industry 4.0

1 Introduction

In recent past, there has been a huge trend in industrial manufacturing towards a higher flexibility. Products become more variable, development periods and product life cycles become shorter and consequently lot sizes decrease [12]. While there is in general a tendency towards automation, manual human work will still be required due to a high complexity in the assembly tasks or the uniqueness of the task itself. To support humans in assembly tasks, assistive systems have been presented that guide users through the process of manual assembly (e.g. [1,4,7,13]). While earlier work focused on the interaction with different output technologies, e.g. head-mounted displays or projection-based augmented reality, little work has been done with respect to the question, of how such assistive systems can become more intelligent in terms of supervising the work and giving automatic feedback according to the current work situation. With this paper, we present a projection-based assistive system that includes a novel hand-tracking

A. Braun et al. (Eds.): AmI 2017, LNCS 10217, pp. 33–45, 2017.
DOI: 10.1007/978-3-319-56997-0_3

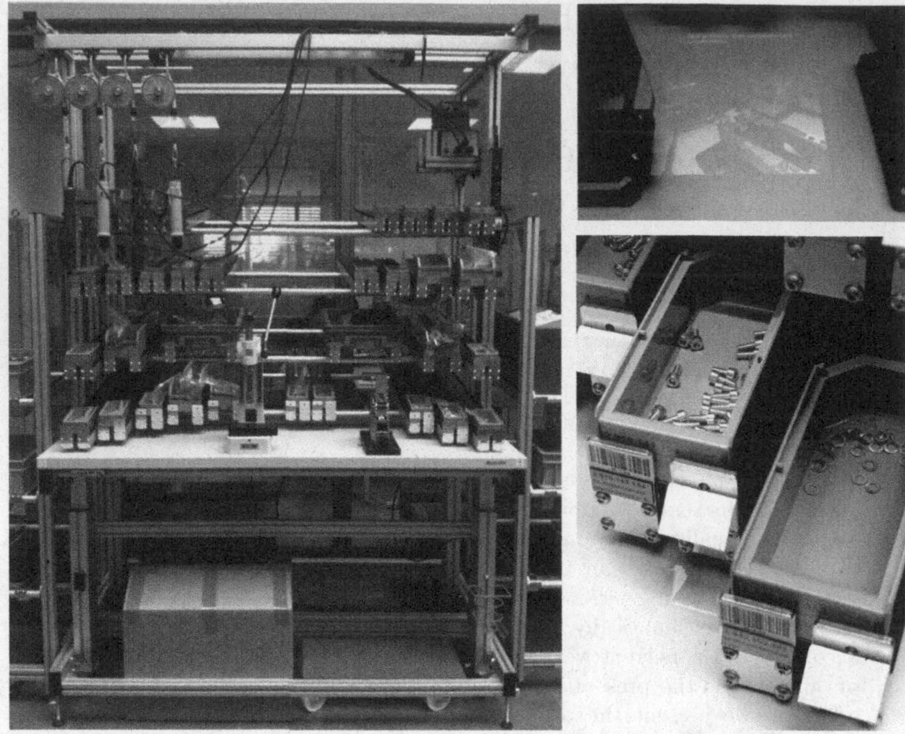

Fig. 1. Conventional manual assembly station (left) that was later equipped with assistive system with projection-based AR and intelligent hand tracking. Video-instructions are projected into the user's workplace (right, top). In-situ projections highlight the boxes for picking with green light (right, bottom). (Color figure online)

algorithm and guides users through the assembly process (Fig. 1). The paper presents the related work, describes our concept and its implementation with a focus on the new hand-tracking algorithm. Furthermore, we present a user study that shows the opportunities of the new hand-tracking system and the complete prototype as well, which will inform the future design of intelligent workplaces in manual assembly.

2 Related Work

In this section, we will consider the related work from the following two fields: First, we present related work on how to support humans with AR assistive systems in manual assembly. Second, we consider work related to the field of progress detection in assembly including hand- and tool-tracking in an assembly context.

2.1 AR Assistive Systems

A lot of publications have dealt with the topic of assisting industrial workers with new interaction technologies. Early work focused mainly on picking tasks e.g. by using head-mounted displays (HMDs, e.g. [15,16]). The empirical studies conducted indicated the potential of the systems, e.g. Guo et al. [9] showed that picking with AR support with HMDs is faster than the use of conventional paper instructions. In the last decade, the support of more complex assembly tasks has been evaluated. Billinghurst et al. [2] presented assembly support with a mobile device. Among others Paelke et al. [13] showed the feasibility of augmented reality assistive systems for picking and assembly tasks. Tang et al. [17] presented a system with spatially registered instructions and showed that they can improve the performance significantly. However, drawbacks of HMDs have been presented as well: Grubert et al. [8] conducted a study in which picking tasks had to be accomplished by users wearing HMDs for about four hours and showed that the users stress level increased. Lately, the research focus has shifted to projection-based assistive systems for manual assembly. In a comprehensive study, Funk et al. [6] compared different types of instructions in a workplace scenario in a projection-based assistive system for manual assembly. In their study, they compared projected contour, pictorial, video instructions and an uninstructed baseline. Their results showed that in-situ projected contour instructions lead to unified performance over three types of performance groups. Furthermore Funk et al. found that using in-situ projected instructions can significantly increase the productivity of cognitively impaired workers in assembly tasks [7]. Zheng et al. [18] compared the use of non-spatially instructions displayed on a centralized HMD, a peripheral HMD, a tablet computer, and paperbased instructions. They found that centralized instructions on an HMD lead to faster assembly times. In contrast, the study of Büttner et al. [3] found no significant difference between HMD instructions and a paper baseline. However, they found that the assembly time using projections is much faster and the error rate decreases in comparison with HMDs and a paper baseline. The related work shows some of the drawbacks of conventional instructions and indicates that (apart from HMDs) projection-based AR could improve manual assembly work.

2.2 Progress Detection

In early assistive systems, progress was detected by using proximity sensors to detect hands [9], but this approach is limited to the recognition of picking actions and requires an expensive installation of sensors. Kirch et al. [11] presented an alternative approach in which each part to assemble is equipped with a Radiofrequency Identification (RFID) tag. The user is wearing a wristband that is able to read the RFID tags automatically and confirm the picking actions. However, this approach is not suitable for small parts. Alternative approaches use hand tracking to capture the workers actions. Several data gloves or wristbands are available that can be used to capture the users arm, hand, and finger movements [5]. These physical approaches have the advantage that they work even when the hand is occluded, for example while picking a part from a box. However, the gloves are not very comfortable to wear and might not be suitable for an 8-hour shift. Bannat et al. [1] presented camera-based activity recognition. They developed a system with projection-based AR and body-worn grasp detection in combination with an RGB camera to detect whether the user picked a part from the correct box. While also considering the assembly process, Funk et al. [7] presented a system with a depth camera for checking both the picking and the correct assembly. In their user study, they used an assembly task of LEGO Duplo bricks that had to be picked from 1 out of 8 boxes. Our work is highly inspired by the related work above and especially by the presented work of Funk et al. [7]. While we constructed a very similar system from a hardware perspective, we focused on improving the hand-tracking algorithm in terms of accuracy for scenarios, where very small parts need to be picked from small boxes and assembled with other parts. Therefore we ran a human-centered design process that included a real assembly task from industry, where belt tensioners had to be assembled. Therefore, we contribute to the research on assistive system with the presentation of a new hand-tracking algorithm.

3 Basic Ideas and Concept

The assistive system presented in this work targets a commercial manual assembly station. It has a table with tools such as screwdrivers and a stationary press, a mount for the product during assembly, and a rack containing the boxes with the required parts. The commercial system has been extended with two depth-cameras that cover the whole picking and assembly area, two LED projectors for the instructions and feedback to the user and an ultrasound sensor for localization of tools. All the mentioned devices are mounted on the structure at the top of the assembly stations and are oriented downwards onto the table surface and boxes. The complete setup is shown in Fig. 1. With this setup, the system is able to track multiple hands with the depth-cameras in the three-dimensional space with an accuracy of a few centimeters and detect both picking and assembly actions. The projectors cover all boxes and the table and project the digital overlay into the workspace. Boxes are highlighted by color and a number that indicates how many parts should be picked. Videos, images and texts are used to provide instructions. The user interface can be adapted individually by using hand gestures to move or scale the content on the table, similarly to a touchscreen.

4 Implementation

In this section, we will present the implementation details relating to projection-based user interface and intelligent hand tracking. This section focuses the description of the hand-tracking algorithm.

Fig. 2. The figure shows a projected button. By using the projections in combination with the hand tracking, the table can be used as a touch screen.

4.1 Projection-Based User Interface

Our system projects the user interface into the physical workspace of the user. The projectors cover the complete assembly station including the table and all the boxes. The boxes are highlighted in a green color (see Fig. 1) if parts need to be taken from the specific box. Additionally a number is shown on the box that represents the number of parts to take. In case of errors, the boxes are colored red and alarm occurs that draws the users attention. Furthermore, the system shows media elements, such as images and videos on the component to be assembled or beside of it to assist with the assembly process. Another feature is the projection of virtual buttons into the workspace. The whole table can be considered as a touch-sensitive area. While the table does not recognize touch gestures itself, the depth-cameras are used for recognizing touches onto the virtual buttons (see Fig. 2). This enables the worker to interact with the system with minimal distraction.

4.2 Intelligent Hand Tracking

Our system uses two Asus Xtion Pro depth cameras. The cameras use a PrimeSense depth sensor, which is based on the structure light technique. It emits a pseudo random pattern using an infrared diode, which is reflected and captured by a camera sensor the depth is retrieved based on the deformation and warping of the pattern [14]. Due to the size of the assembly station, the use of two cameras is required to capture the whole space, as their field of view is not sufficient. We installed the cameras with a low amount of overlapping to avoid crosstalk (errors due to overlapping patterns of the infrared light). Figure 3 shows an image captured by the two cameras.

The raw depth images are retrieved using OpenNI and processed with OpenCV. In the first step, the foreground is extracted from the depth images.

Fig. 3. Image taken by the two depth-cameras.

Our system uses an approach based on mixture of gaussians to segment to foreground like arms, hands, and parts the user is holding from the background like the assembly stations structure, table surface, and boxes. Static, non-moving pixels are classified as background while moving parts are classified as foreground. The used background model is adapted over time to react to changes to the assembly station. After the background is removed, the Canny edge detection algorithm is used to extract contours from the depth image. Afterwards, the contours need to be classified to find the users hands. For this classification, we take into account the orientation and origin of the contours. First, contours that only enclose a very small area are discarded. Then, the knowledge of the users position which is always in front of the assembly station is used to classify hands. Only contours that are touching the images edge on the side that the user is standing on are classified as hands. The position of the hand itself is defined as its peak which is the point of the contours that has the largest distance to the images edge. Using the image coordinates of the point and its depth value, a spatial position can be reconstructed based on the cameras intrinsic parameters. As multiple cameras are used, the positions of the detected hands are transformed into a global coordinate system shared by all cameras. Possible duplicates due to hands that are visible in multiple cameras, are discarded. The detected hands are combined with the hands from the previous frames to perform temporal tracking. Each hand is assigned a unique identifier that stays constant between frames. A Kalman filter is optionally applied to smooth out the resulting hand positions. The resulting hand positions are compared to previously taught spatial regions defined as axis-aligned bounding boxes (AABB) that represent the boxes in the rack. In case a hand is detected inside such a region, we register a picking action of the user, respectively we register a certain user action in the workspace. Figure 4 shows the complete process described above.

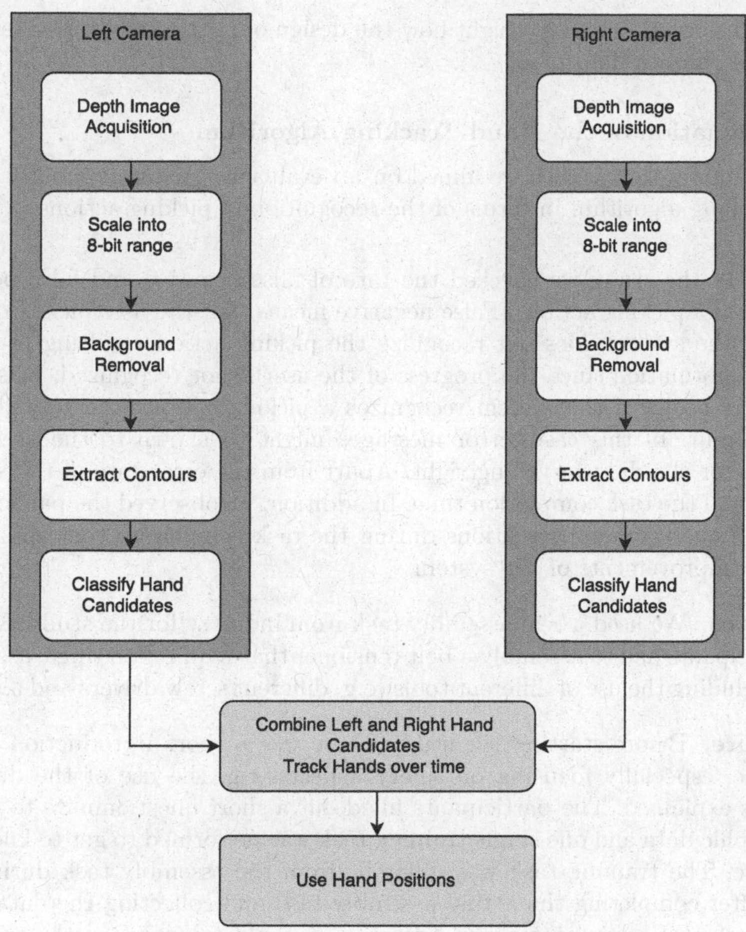

Fig. 4. The graphic shows the steps of the hand-tracking process. The process starts with capturing and processing the depth image. The processing is done for the left and right side individually. After the possible hand positions are retrieved, the data of the left and right camera are combined.

5 Evaluation

The development of the system followed a human-centered design process. There have been intermediate evaluations during the development process, e.g. the evaluation on how to present instructions that have been described in [3] and intermediate evaluation of the hand-tracking algorithm. In this paper we will present an evaluation of the system that is two-fold. First we ran a study focusing on the hand-tracking algorithm. The second part of the evaluation is a user study that compares the conventional work process with the work process by using the assistive system, when executing an industrial assembly task. With these studies we present an insight how the design of future assistive systems for manual assembly is informed.

5.1 Evaluation of the Hand-Tracking Algorithm

Before running user studies we aimed on an evaluation of the reliability of the hand-tracking algorithm in terms of the recognition of picking actions.

Design. In the study we checked the rate of false negative and false positive recognition of picking actions. False negative means that the user picks from the rack, but the system does not recognize the picking action resulting in wrong assistive information since the progress of the user is not recognized. False positive errors occur, if the system recognizes a picking action even though they did not occur. In this case, error messages might be shown to the user even though he or she did everything right. Apart from the error rate of the system we measured the task completion time. In addition, we observed the participants and noted qualitative observations during the task completion that could lead to future improvements of the system.

Apparatus. We used a real assembly task from industry for the study. Each of the participants had to assembly a belt tensioner that requires 28 single assembly steps, including the use of different tools (e.g. different screw drivers and a press).

Procedure. Before starting the study, there was a short introduction to the workplace, especially focusing on safety aspects, e.g. the use of the different tools was explained. The participants filled out a short questionnaire to collect demographic data and one single training task was performed to get to know the workplace. The training task was different from the assembly task during the study. After completing the actual assembly task and collecting the data there was a short post-session interview, where users could comment on the system.

Participants. We recruited 9 participants (1 female, 8 male) who where aged from 23 to 32 ($\mathrm{M} = 26.56, \mathrm{SD} = 3.27$). Three of the participants were engineers; the other six participants were students. There were three left-handed and six right-handed participants. The participants did not have any previous experience with the system or the assembly task.

Results. During the study 252 single picking and assembly steps have been executed. The average task completion time of the 28 steps was 540.78 s (SD = 152.02 s). Within the 252 picking steps, there was only one single false negative error. However, there were on average 0.89 (SD = 0.57) false positive errors, so almost every participant had a situation where the system recognized picking actions in the case there was none. Using the data of the observations we could conclude that all except one false positive error occurred when users hovered over another box before picking. As a result of the study, we adapted the system in the next iteration (and before the second study) by adding a very short delay before a box is actually triggered, to reduce the false positive rate.

5.2 User Study of Assistive System

The second study presented here focused on a user evaluation by comparing the assistive system with a paper baseline that is currently used in industrial practice.

Design. The study was designed following a repeated measures design with the instruction method (paper manual vs. assistive system) as independent variable. Each of the participants had to assemble two belt tensioners using the same assembly task that was presented in the first study. One belt tensioner had to be assembled with a paper manual and one with the presented assistive systems, while the order of the instruction methods was alternating assigned (within-subject design). We measured the following dependent variables: assembly time, picking errors, assembly errors. We used the NASA-TLX [10] to measure mental, physical and temporal demand as additional independent variables.

Procedure. In the same way as in the first study, there was a short introduction focusing on safety aspects as well as a questionnaire to collect demographic data. In this study, there was no training task. However the single tools of the workplace have been explained and could be tested by the participants before starting. After continuing each of the assembly tasks the participants filled out the NASA-TLX questionnaire. After completing both of the tasks there was a post-session interview to receive further qualitative data.

Participants. For this second study we recruited 10 new participants in the age of 21 to 27 ($M = 23.60, SD = 1,91$), all male, students, and all right-handed.

Results. The average task completion time with a paper manual was 572.40 (SD = 201.54) seconds and with our assistive system 611.30 (SD = 214.59) seconds (see Fig. 5a).

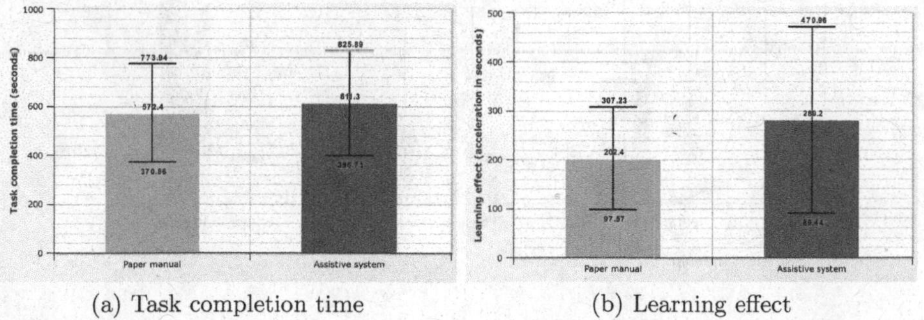

(a) Task completion time (b) Learning effect

Fig. 5. While the results of the study show no significant difference in the task completion time, when comparing the different instruction methods, there seem to be a learning effect, when using the assistive system first. The error bars depict the standard error

The collected data was analyzed regarding its variances (ANOVA), which revealed that the differences of the mean in the task completion time was not statistically significant ($F = 0.2, p = 0.661$). In this second study the mean of picking and assembly errors was 1.20 (SD = 2.57) when using the paper manual and 1.70 (SD = 2.50) when using the assistive system. Our ANOVA shows that the differences in the error rate are not statistically significant ($F = 0.19, p = 0.664$). Additionally to the analysis above, we analyzed the learning effect, which we consider as the time difference between the first and the second task completion time. In terms of the learning effect, we noted a difference between the systems: When using the paper manual first and the assistive system second, there was an average acceleration of 202.40 (SD = 104.83) seconds for the second task. Using the assistive system at first reduces the second task completion time by 280.20 (SD = 290.76) seconds (see Fig. 5b). This observation of a difference of 77.8 s in the mean acceleration of the task completion time could mean that there is a better learning effect when using the assistive system compared to the paper manual. We plan to address this question in our future research. The results of the NASA-TLX show the following ratings, based on scales ranging from 0 to 100: The mental demand had a mean rating of 34.50 (SD = 17.87) with paper instructions and a mean rating of 31.50 (SD = 24.27) when using our assistive system. The physical demand had a mean rating of 28.00 (SD = 20.71) with paper instructions and 23.50 (SD = 20.01) with the assistive system. The temporal demand had a mean rating of 37.00 (SD = 22.26) with paper instructions and a mean rating of 59.50 (SD = 18.33) with the assistive system. This results are shown in Fig. 6.

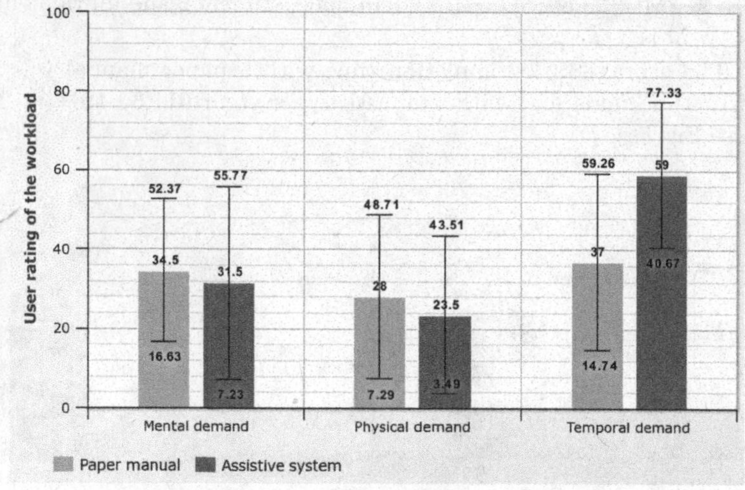

Fig. 6. The results of the NASA-TLX show a significant difference between the ratings of the temporal demand, when comparing the assistive system with the use of a paper manual. The differences in the rarings of the mental and physical demand are not significant.

Analyzing this results by running a Wilcoxon Signed-Rank test for each of the scales, shows that the results are significant on a level of $\alpha = 0.05$ for the temporal demand ($z = -2.50, p = 0.013$), but not for the mental demand ($z = -0.42, p = 0.677$) and physical demand ($z = -1.12, p = 0.262$). From this observation we conclude that the introduction of assistive technology that monitors the progress of assembly workers and adapts its user interface accordingly might put users under temporal pressure. Our system is self-paced by the actions of the users and users do not have to make any explicit input. This self-pacing could be a reason for the observation. However, this is a hypothesis and none of the participants mentioned something related to temporal demand in the post-session interviews, so we will analyze the reasons for the high ratings on the temporal demand more deeply in our future work. Regardless of the reasons for the high rating, reducing this temporal demand will be a concern for the future design of assistive systems for manufacturing.

6 Conclusion

In this paper we presented a prototype of an intelligent assistive system for workers in stationary manual assembly using projection-based augmented reality (AR). Particularly, we presented a new hand-tracking algorithm that is part of the system. The evaluation of the hand-tracking algorithm shows a high reliability in the recognition of picking-actions. We furthermore contribute to the research in assistive technology in the context of Industry 4.0 by presenting the results of a user study that compares our presented system to a paper manual as baseline. While our user study on the overall system did not show significant results in terms of task completion time or error rates, we could observe that the task completion time of following tasks could be reduced after using our assistive system. We therefore assume that the assistive system might have a better learning effect than paper manuals and could be beneficial for training purposes, which is a big concern in the future of manufacturing with shorter lifecycles and higher product variations. Collecting data about the workload of the users with the NASA-TLX questionnaire, we could show, that our self-paced assistive system puts a higher temporal demand on users than a paper manual. We conclude that reducing the felt temporal demand is one main concern for the future design of assistive systems in manual assembly. We plan to further investigate this observation in our future research.

References

1. Bannat, A., Wallhoff, F., Rigoll, G., Friesdorf, F., Bubb, H., Stork, S., Müller, H., Schubö, A., Wiesbeck, M., Zäh, M.F., et al.: Towards optimal worker assistance: a framework for adaptive selection and presentation of assembly instructions. In: Proceedings of the 1st international Workshop on Cognition for Technical Systems, CoTeSys (2008)

2. Billinghurst, M., Hakkarainen, M., Woodward, C.: Augmented assembly using a mobile phone. In: Proceedings of the 7th International Conference on Mobile and Ubiquitous Multimedia, pp. 84–87. ACM (2008)
3. Büttner, S., Funk, M., Sand, O., Röcker, C.: Using head-mounted displays and in-situ projection for assistive systems-a comparison. In: Proceedings of the 9th ACM International Conference on PErvasive Technologies Related to Assistive Environments, vol. 8. ACM (2016)
4. Büttner, S., Sand, O., Röcker, C.: Extending the design space in industrial manufacturing through mobile projection. In: Proceedings of the 17th International Conference on Human-Computer Interaction with Mobile Devices and Services Adjunct, pp. 1130–1133. ACM (2015)
5. Dipietro, L., Sabatini, A.M., Dario, P.: A survey of glove-based systems and their applications. IEEE Trans. Syst. Man Cybern. Part C (Appl. Rev.) **38**(4), 461–482 (2008)
6. Funk, M., Bächler, A., Bächler, L., Korn, O., Krieger, C., Heidenreich, T., Schmidt, A.: Comparing projected in-situ feedback at the manual assembly workplace with impaired workers. In: Proceedings of the 8th ACM International Conference on PErvasive Technologies Related to Assistive Environments, p. 1. ACM (2015)
7. Funk, M., Mayer, S., Schmidt, A.: Using in-situ projection to support cognitively impaired workers at the workplace. In: Proceedings of the 17th International ACM SIGACCESS Conference on Computers and Accessibility, pp. 185–192. ACM (2015)
8. Grubert, J., Hamacher, D., Mecke, R., Böckelmann, I., Schega, L., Huckauf, A., Urbina, M., Schenk, M., doil, F., Tümler, J.: Extended investigations of user-related issues in mobile industrial AR. In: 2010 9th IEEE International Symposium on Mixed and Augmented Reality (ISMAR), pp. 229–230. IEEE (2010)
9. Guo, A., Raghu, S., Xie, X., Ismail, S., Luo, X., Simoneau, J., Gilliland, S., Baumann, H., Southern, C., Starner, T.: A comparison of order picking assisted by head-up display (HUD), cart-mounted display (CMD), light, and paper pick list. In: Proceedings of the 2014 ACM International Symposium on Wearable Computers, pp. 71–78. ACM (2014)
10. Hart, S.G., Staveland, L.E.: Development of NASA-TLX (Task Load Index): results of empirical and theoretical research. Adv. Psychol. **52**, 139–183 (1988)
11. Kirch, M., Poenicke, O.: Using the RFID wristband for automatic identification in manual processes-the RFID wristband in the automotive industry. In: 2014 European Conference on Smart Objects, Systems and Technologies (Smart SysTech), pp. 1–7. IEEE (2014)
12. Lasi, H., Fettke, P., Kemper, H.G., Feld, T., Hoffmann, M.: Industry 4.0. business and information. Syst. Eng. **6**(4), 239 (2014)
13. Paelke, V., Röcker, C., Koch, N., Flatt, H., Büttner, S.: User interfaces for cyber-physical systems. at-Automatisierungstechnik **63**(10), 833–843 (2015)
14. Scharstein, D., Szeliski, R.: High-accuracy stereo depth maps using structured light. In: Proceedings of the 2003 IEEE Computer Society Conference on Computer Vision and Pattern Recognition, vol. 1, pp. I-195. IEEE (2003)
15. Schwerdtfeger, B., Klinker, G.: Supporting order picking with augmented reality. In: Proceedings of the 7th IEEE/ACM international Symposium on Mixed and Augmented Reality, pp. 91–94. IEEE Computer Society (2008)

16. Schwerdtfeger, B., Reif, R., Gunthner, W.A., Klinker, G., Hamacher, D., Schega, L., Bockelmann, I., doil, F., Tumler, J.: Pick-by-vision: a first stress test. In: 8th IEEE International Symposium on Mixed and Augmented Reality, ISMAR 2009, pp. 115–124. IEEE (2009)
17. Tang, A., Owen, C., Biocca, F., Mou, W.: Comparative effectiveness of augmented reality in object assembly. In: Proceedings of the SIGCHI conference on Human factors in computing systems, pp. 73–80. ACM (2003)
18. Zheng, X.S., Foucault, C., Matos da Silva, P., Dasari, S., Yang, T., Goose, S.: Eye-wearable technology for machine maintenance: effects of display position and hands-free operation. In: Proceedings of the 33rd Annual ACM Conference on Human Factors in Computing Systems, pp. 2125–2134. ACM (2015)

AuthentiCap - A Touchless Vehicle Authentication and Personalization System

Sebastian Frank[1(✉)] and Arjan Kuijper[1,2]

[1] TU Darmstadt, Darmstadt, Germany
sebastianfrank87@gmx.de
[2] Fraunhofer IGD, Darmstadt, Germany

Abstract. Current authentication systems in vehicles use portable keys or biometric and/or touch based inputs. They can be outwitted by stealing the keys or by copying the biometric information and analyzing the touch marks. This has to be inhibited, since vehicles are not only an expensive property, that would be lost in non-authenticated hands, but wrong permitted access also can unleash heavy machine power to inexperienced drivers or even people without a driver's license. We present a system that authenticates drivers and unlocks personalization features without any portable keys or touching. Moreover, it is invisibly integrated into a vehicle structure, the steering wheel. In contrast to biometric authentication, the password pattern is adjustable and changeable. With the presented system, vehicle manufactures are able to install driver authentication systems without any visible design changes. The manufacturer thus provides more freedom and responsibility to the driver by giving him the option to choose his own unlock pattern. Still, the security is increased by avoiding common vulnerabilities like smudge attacks, the stealing of keys, or copying of biometric data. Our experiments show excellent recognition rates for multiple string patterns. A small user study shows that our system achieves 86% accuracy for inexperienced users, up to 96% for experienced ones. The users appreciated the easy of use.

1 Introduction

Vehicular driver authentication systems provide a plenty of different physical methods to validate the motorists identity. Some rely on carrying keys with included radio for authentication security (e.g. key-less go). This setup narrows the personalization and authentication validation to the driver's key. Furthermore, key-less go systems can be outwitted, because of the key-only authentication. Any person that carries an authenticated key is automatically authenticated, too [10]. Besides key-bond systems, other systems rely on the integration of finger print sensors for at least two step identification system (finger print and key). In this case, the driver personalization would be possible due to the drivers' different finger prints. Nevertheless, biometric identification systems have the disadvantage, that the key cannot be changed at any time, because the person

A. Braun et al. (Eds.): AmI 2017, LNCS 10217, pp. 46–63, 2017.
DOI: 10.1007/978-3-319-56997-0_4

is tied to his or her biometric data [1]. The fingerprint sensor requires contact to the driver's finger. Moreover, it requires a visible position that can be inappropriate for vehicle interior design. Another, touch based, authentication system is mobile phone's screen unlock pattern system. The user draws a pattern on the touch screen to unlock the work space. Due to the mandatory touching and swiping, the system is vulnerable to the so called smudge attack. The smudge attack relies on the user's fingers' arrears on the screen. Directed light sources can reveal the unlock pattern [2]. Furthermore, several systems use cameras to recognize the driver's face. Cameras need a direct line of sight. Therefore, their integration into vehicle structures cannot be invisible. Moreover, camera systems can capture the driver's picture and therefore cause privacy issues [13]. AuthentiCap faces the issues of privacy protection, design intrusive application, biometric limited vehicle locking and smudge attack vulnerability. We provide a system that uses commonly apparent vehicle structures. Its vehicle integration does not need visible design changes. Its topology cannot record privacy immersive data. Its authentication system can be adjusted to the user's desire which provides personalization features. Due to the used sensors' measurement principle, the system does not need any touching of the user. Therefore, it is invulnerable to smudge attacks. Its usage is traceless. Besides AuthentiCap's concept (Sect. 3), we provide a proof of concept system prototype (Sect. 4). We use the prototype to gather training and testing data for the classification models. This prototype is used for system evaluation, in which possible users test several locking patterns. (Section 5) Moreover, the users rated the systems usability and their belief in the systems security. They added several ideas about further usage of the system, too.

2 Related Work

The National Highway Traffic Safety Administration (NHTSA) investigated the influence of driver distraction on driving security as presented in a report in 2016. The report shows that in the group of drivers with an age between 15 and 19 years, accidents are often caused by distraction. This group shows the greatest bias to distraction based accidents. Examples for distractions are the adjustment of audio, climate controls, or talking at the cell phone [16]. Besides distraction, drivers with an age between 15 and 24 show the biggest percentage of speeding caused accidents. In particular, the group of male drivers between 15 and 20 years shows 37% accidents caused by speeding, whereas the female driver's percentage is 24%. The female group between 21 and 24 shows 19% speeding caused accidents, the male group shows an unchanged 37% [15].

While driving experience is mandatory for save driving, especially parents do not want to submit their children to the risk of their self-induced risky driving behavior. Nevertheless, they want to let their children drive their car. One of the solutions for this issue is the driver identification technology. The NHTSA summarizes several identification systems in its 2010 report about monitoring of novice teen drivers. They name the fingerprint as identification system, voice recognition, facial recognition, eye scan and smart keys [14]. Ford provides its "MyKey" smart key system. While the first key acts as a key with full features activated, the secondary keys, which could be provided to teen drivers, can activate/deactivate several vehicle features. In particular, distraction and speeding relevant conditions get minimized. Ford provides to limit the vehicle's top-speed or the maximum audio volume level. Furthermore, active safety systems like speed warning or passive safety systems like restraint systems cannot be deactivated or the warnings cannot be disabled anymore [9].

2.1 Identification Systems

The NHTSA [14] already states the smart key's problem, that a possibly unauthorized driver can gain access to unlimited speed/distraction devices if he possesses the main key. While NHTSA's only limitation to biometric identification is the required high performance computing on facial and voice recognition, Alsaadi shows several limitations to biometric systems [1]. Due to the analysis of the users skin, the finger and the lens must be clean.

Another problem is the immutablity of biometric data. While passwords may change, it is hard to change the finger print of a thumb (or the iris, the ears, etc.). The imitation of fingerprints is a known spoofing technique. Printed fingerprints or mold copies can outwit identification systems. Xia et al. [22] published an approach to detect live fingers while using fingerprint recognition devices. The publication shows that the improvement of biometric identification is required. But not only finger prints can be imitated. Masks can trick face recognition identification devices or ear recognition devices. Other systems use cosmetic contact lenses to imitate iris features to trick iris recognition systems [3].

One solution to avoid immutable protection, like biometric identification, is the usage of changeable pass codes or patterns. For example the screen unlock pattern of mobile phones. Nevertheless this locking method is alterable, they are often touch based and therefore vulnerable, because touching leaves marks on the touch surface. The analysis of this marks is called smudge attack [2]. Schneegass et al. presented a smudge attack safe approach to keep the mobile screen locked. Instead of a static pattern unlock screen, he alters the position of the background screen image similar to the basic unlock pattern. The SmudgeSafe method reduces the tested guessing rate of unlocking patterns from 87.5% to, in dependence on image manipulation, a value between 0 and 30% [19].

2.2 Authentication Systems

The analysis of user authentication systems is a common field of study of today's security relevant devices. Garcia et al. present an investigation on automotive remote key-less entry systems. They analyzes the vulnerability of different key-less entry systems. The concerned automotive brands are VW Group, Alfa Romeo, Peugeot, Lancia, Renault and Ford. Their evaluation on exploitation systems like the Hitag2 show the vulnerability of millions of vehicles, yet a proof for the necessity of more reliable authentication mechanisms [10]. Alsaadi addresses this issue. Therefore, he tests biometric authentication systems since these systems shall provide further security since the systems are hard to outwit. He shows that the attributive accuracy is not applicable in all cases. For example, the ear recognition's accuracy is not that high [1].

Braun et al. provided an invention that facilitates driver authentication by use of invisible integrated capacitive proximity sensors. He uses an array of driver seat integrated capacitive proximity sensors. The user has to take seat on the driver seat. His biometric unique signature in the capacitive proximity sensors' measurement data in this specific position is used to identify and authenticate the driver [4,5,7]. Braun et al. not only use CPS for user authentication in vehicles. They already integrated capacitive proximity sensors as user input device [8]. User interaction is captured as finger movements on the vehicle's arm rest. The aim is to identify gestures. On the one hand as inputs with touch contact. On the other hand as movements in the air next to the armrest without touching. Their investigation shows that the touch based gesture recognition is preferred by users and works more stable than the contact-free gesture recognition [6].

Not only vehicle authentication systems shall be accurate. Other systems rely on non-biometric authentication mechanisms, too. For example the unlock screen pattern of mobile phones with android OS. Sun et al. [21] dissect this authentication mechanism. They analyze the characteristics of several unlock patterns. In their conclusion, they state that the limited pattern space leads to a limitation of touch based pattern unlock security. In the evaluation, they already state possible problems like the smudge attack or the shoulder surfing attack [21].

3 Our AuthentiCap Concept

Our approach is inspired by several disadvantages of the in Sect. 2 stated systems. These systems rely on biometric identification which is not changeable or touch based systems that can leave marks on the input device. Furthermore, camera based systems require a line of sight and therefore, are visible. Moreover the visible vehicle interior design must integrate those devices. The challenge here is to build a touchless authentication device that does not leave marks and the unlock password/pattern should be changeable. Furthermore, to avoid interior design changes, the system ought use given vehicle structures. Due to capacitive proximity sensors' (CPS) characteristics, they are the selected sensor system for AuthentiCap [11,12]. CPS react on changes of the electric field. In dependence on the sensing electrodes geometry, the range of the sensor is sufficient to detect object intrusion in an area about approximately 30 cm. Moreover, CPS can measure through non conductive materials. And therefore, can be placed under the cover of existing vehicle structures. The identification of the required vehicle structure for AuthentiCap is presented in Sect. 3.1. The user's first contact is the usage of the authentication mechanism. The designed process is described in Sect. 3.2. He needs to enter his selected password/pattern. The system needs to measure the conformity of the entered pattern. This process is described in

Sect. 3.3. The acquisition of the user input, the pattern, leads us towards the feature generation. Since the input of the CPS is not the direct content of the feature vector, we present the signature pattern acquisition in Sect. 3.4. But, the features of the recognition are related to the capacitive proximity measurement. Thus, Sect. 3.5 shows the conversion of the capacitive proximity sensing data to preprocessed data for feature generation.

3.1 Vehicle Structure Selection

Similar to the vehicle's ignition switch or the push button ignition switch, the driver should be able to use AuthentiCap from his driver seat. Furthermore, some systems of the vehicle already use capacitive sensors. One of these systems is the Hands-On/Hands-Off detection, provided by a patent of Peter Rieth (Continental Teves Ag & Co. oHG, 2008). Rieth equips a steering wheel with an array of capacitive proximity sensor electrodes. Figure 1 shows the patent drawing of the electrodes topology [17]. The metal core of the steering wheel (No 2) and the in line with the outer ring aligned electrodes (8,9) form a differential capacitor that represents, in combination with the driver, a device which output is related to the contact between hand and steering wheel [17]. Because of the, from the driver's perspective, directly reachable position of the steering wheel and already existing steering wheel setups with CPS, the vehicle's steering wheel is selected as AuthentiCap's used vehicle structure.

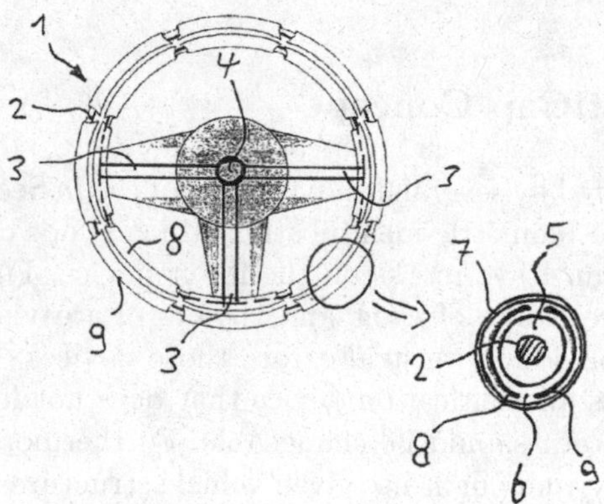

Fig. 1. Steering handle for motor vehicles and method for recording a physical parameter on a steering handle ([17], Fig. 1)

Figure 2 shows a sketch of a steering wheel. Because of the constraint not to use any touch based systems, we choose the inner steering wheel area as input area. The area is tagged in Fig. 2 (left: Input Area). The area is big enough to capture short strings or input patterns. This requirement refers to our authentication approach that relies on patterns/passwords. Since the area of focus is the

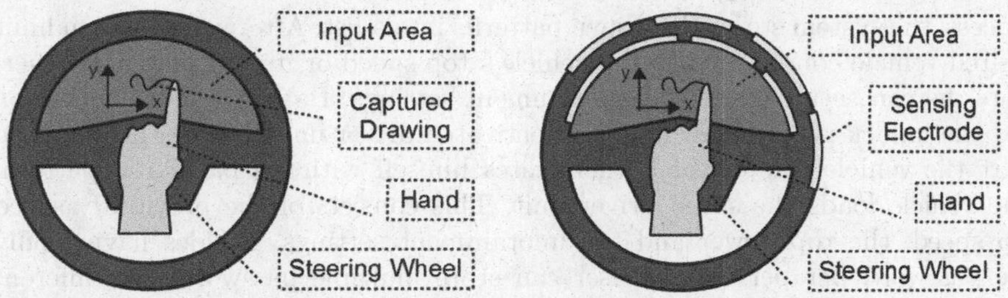

Fig. 2. Selected vehicle structure: steering wheel and sensing electrode position

upper steering wheel clearance, we surround the area with sensing electrodes. Eight electrodes are split into two groups of four entities. Figure 2 shows that each of this groups of four is equally spaced on a semi circle. One group on the inner diameter of the steering wheel, the other group on the outer diameter. The steering wheel's spokes and hub are not occupied by any devices, because we do not want to affect the airbag deployment area or cover.

3.2 Authentication Mechanism

We provide a generic input pattern creation to the user. He is free to write short texts, invented patterns, letters and any combination of these entities of any length. This approach is limited by the users ability to redraw his specified unlock pattern.

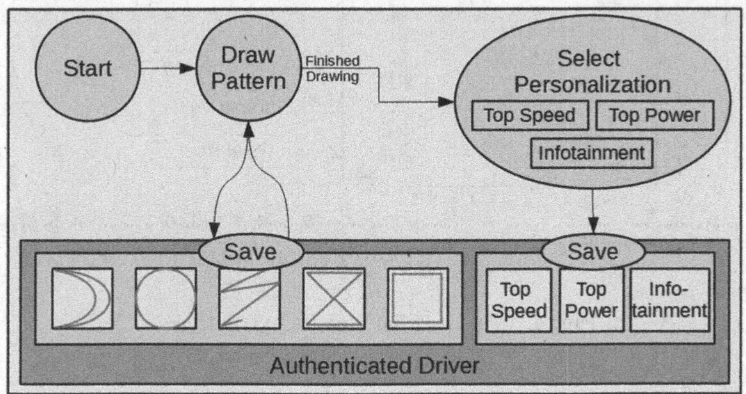

Fig. 3. Driver setup initialization process

Figure 3 shows the system training process. The user initiates a new pattern training process. Afterwards, he draws an arbitrary pattern. He can add further patterns until he thinks his password is safe enough. After he finishes his training process, the system stores the drawn patterns into a list. Afterwards, he can limit desired vehicle conditions like the vehicle's top speed or its top power. Furthermore, he can setup the initial infotainment settings. Both, the personalization and the unlock patterns form an authenticated driver unit. In later attempts to start the vehicle, the driver authenticates himself with his particular pattern. The vehicle loads the saved driver unit. This consists of the previously saved top speed, the top power and the infotainment settings. Besides having only one password per person, the user can store multiple passwords for different situations. For example further settings like the lighting position (for different vehicle loads) or airbag functions (driving with child's seat) can be individually personalized.

3.3 Signature Pattern Recognition

Each drawing of the driver is stretched into a quadratic, binary bitmap (black background, white "Pen" drawing). Each axis is stretched individually. The bitmap is converted into a feature vector. Its length is four time the bitmap edge length in pixel. Each index of the feature vector represents the considered measure of the corresponding bitmap edge-pixel position. The feature extraction is based on the common OCR feature "distance profile" (cf. [20]).

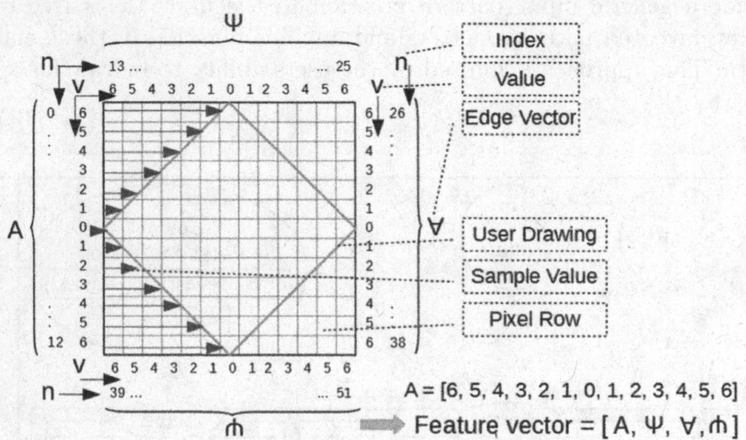

Fig. 4. User drawing feature extraction

Figure 4 shows the feature vector compilation of one sample drawing. It is comprised of four edge vectors. Each edge vector's length refers to the edge's number of pixels. The horizontal vector's length is the number of the bitmap's pixel columns. The vertical vector's length is the number of the bitmap's pixel rows. An edge vector's element value is the, perpendicular to the edge, distance to the first drawing pixel. For example the value of index $n = 4$, the first user drawing pixel is in column three. For index $n = 51$ the first user drawing pixel's distance is six pixel – therefore, the value of $n = 51$ is six. If the user wants to start the vehicle, he starts drawing his pattern. Each element of his drawing results in the presented feature vector. Our system verifies the user's identity by comparing the newly drawn pattern with the ordered, previously trained patterns. To compare the feature vectors, we compute the absolute deviation of each feature vector element. Afterward, the sum of deviations is divided by the feature vector length. This leads to the mean distance of new feature vector (x) and reference feature vector (y). If the mean distance is below a specified threshold (t), the pattern is recognized as pass and the user has to enter the next pattern. If the pattern is the last trained of the pattern list, the user is authenticated.

3.4 Signature Pattern Acquisition

The pattern acquisition starts if the user enters the input area. The first user-area intersection is set as the reference point for further movement. As long as the user intersects with the input area, the hands position, relative to the reference point is stored into an array. The hand position consists of an x and y coordinate where the x points towards the right of the user, rather the line between steering wheel and the right vehicle door. Further, the y part of the tracking points goes from the middle of the steering wheel to the upper edge of the outer steering wheel ring. The user drawing is not limited. If the user leaves the input area intersection, the system waits for a specific latency to gather further inputs. This ensures that the user is able to draw discontinuous patterns. If the user leaves the area, the current drawing is stored as a line. After the latency elapses, the current pattern acquisition is finished. The collected lines get stretched in the x and y directions. Each x position is mapped to a dedicated length which relies on the desired bitmap, shown in Fig. 5, in dependence on the minimum and maximum measured x position. We process similarly with the y positions. Afterward, the real number position data gets quantized by setting it to its integer values (floor). With respect to the signature pattern recognition, the lines of each drawing shall be continuous. Therefore, any missing values get computed by interpolation. Figure 5 shows the pattern acquisition process. The first part shows a two line input of the user. In the next part of Fig. 5, the lines

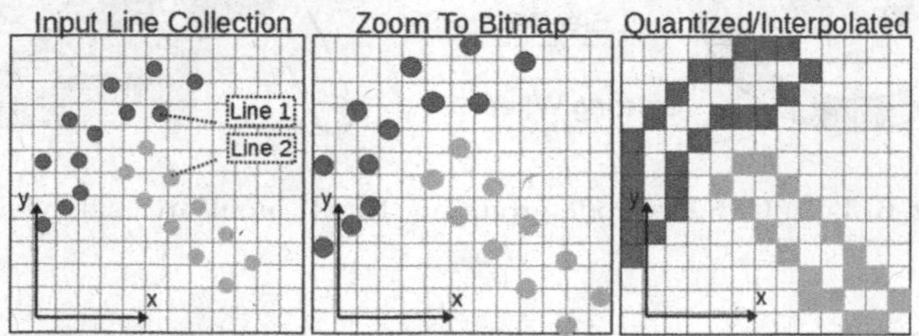

Fig. 5. Pattern acquisition

are zoomed until they match the bitmap boundary. Lastly, the last part of Fig. 5 shows the quantization and interpolation. This is the final pattern.

3.5 Hand Tracking

Aim of the hand tracking is to find a relation between the capacitive proximity sensor's (CPS) output and the actual hand position inside the steering wheel's input area. Furthermore, we need to distinguish between a driver's hand or finger that is inside or outside the drawing area. Rus et al. analyzed the relation between different material's distances to CPS electrodes. The dependence between distance and normalized sensor data is non-linear. Furthermore, they showed measurements with parallel aligned CPS electrodes [18]. The driver's hand or finger can be in any rotation or position inside and outside the input area. Due to these conditions, we skipped the attempt to find a correlation between position and CPS measurement data. We rely on a design based on support vector regression.

Before we can generate training data for our Support Vector Machine (SVM) approach, we need to define the pre-processing of the measured CPS data. Besides non-linearities induced by the physical setup of CPS and the hand position, environment conditions take influence on the measurement data. Two main conditions are the temperature and the moisture. Both manipulate the sensors bias and the CPS measurement curve. All AuthentiCap's CPS electrodes share the same environment. Therefore, we make the assumption that all sensors share the same influence on bias and curve. We group the CPS electrodes into two groups, as shown in Fig. 6. Each group represents an encapsulated measurement setup. Afterward, each electrode's measurement value is put into relation to its group's CPS measurement values. The measurement range is from zero to one. The grouping and putting into relation makes the measured data robust against bias and curve changes.

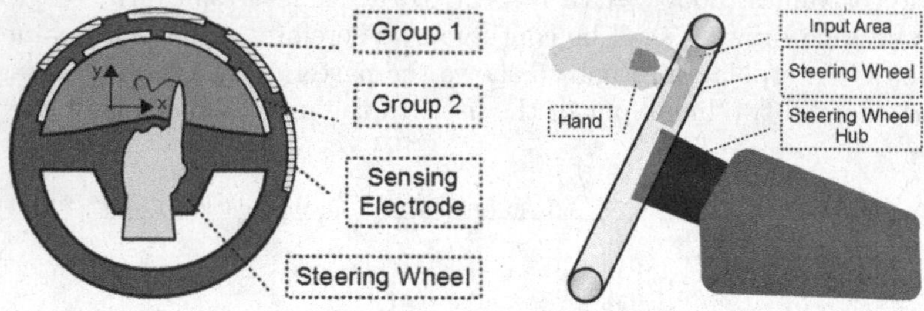

Fig. 6. Left: CPS electrode grouping. Right: input area side view

The generated measurement data, that is now set into each electrodes group's percentage data, is our support vector regression model's input data. In particular, each output dimension (x, y) relies on a regression of eight input dimensions.

One dimension per CPS electrode measurement. The support vector regression curve is computed separately for each output dimension, which leads to two regression models. To detect in area position, we use a support vector machine classifier. The classifier's input feature vector consists of the normalized CPS measurement data of all eight electrodes. The normalization is a mapping from zero to one correlated to the sensors' measurement range. Figure 6 also shows the input area from a side projection of the steering wheel while the user is inside the drawing area.

4 Prototype

The prototype setup consists of a steering wheel and attached electrodes. We first describe the setup of the electrodes. Then we show the practical electrode - steering wheel assembly.

4.1 Electrode Setup

The selected sensor toolkit provides eight capacitive proximity sensing channels. Each channel's measurement rate is 25 Hz. The connection and power supply of the toolkit relies on an USB connection. Each electrode has a width of 25 mm. Furthermore all electrodes have the same length of 100 mm. The electrodes material has to be flexible. Therefore, we select copper foil. The copper foil is coated with glue. Figure 7 (left) shows the electrode-shield assembly. The non-conductive buffer has a thickness of 0.5 mm. Setups with thinner buffer had a too small measurement range. To minimize the influence of the sensor-electrode connection, the electrode and the sensor are connected with shielded wires. The wire's shield is connected to the electrodes shielding.

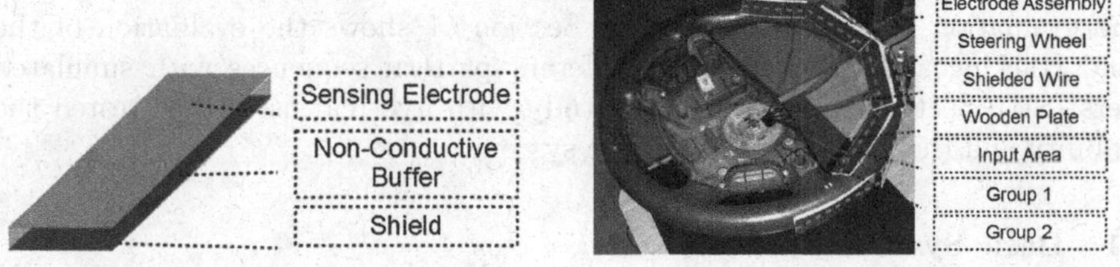

Fig. 7. Left: electrode setup Right: prototype assembly

4.2 Hardware Assembly

The basis of the prototype is a common steering wheel of a mass production vehicle. The steering wheel is mounted on a stand that is connected to a wooden plate. Figure 7 Shows an AuthentiCap prototype. The electrode topology relies on our proposed concept. Both sensing groups, presented at concept, are applied to the steering wheel.

Non-conductive adhesive tape fixes the electrode assembly at the steering wheel. The measurement principle's ability to sense through non-conductive materials allows us to cover the assembly with a slip cover. We select a silicone protective cover to proof the systems ability for non design intrusive application. In practical, the electrodes would be integrated under the steering wheel's envelope. Figure 8 shows the final prototype with protective cover.

Fig. 8. Prototype with protective cover

5 Evaluation

The evaluation consists of two parts. Section 5.1 shows the evaluation of the hand tracking and the analysis of different pattern sequences with simulated users (SU). Section 5.2 shows a user study with five real users that tested the usability and the reproducibility of the system.

5.1 Basic System Function

The basic driver input feature transduction mechanism is the support vector regression which correlates the CPS measurement input to planar positions in the input area of AuthentiCap. We collected 10,234 samples of training data for the x axis and 8,882 samples of training data for the y axis. Figure 9 shows the course of the trained regression model (Model output) and the measured data (Data output) for the x and y axes. They have a coefficient of determination (R^2) of 0.89 and 0.84, respectively.

AuthentiCap provides different pattern shapes. They can be of any length, a combination of any symbols, and even short strings like a signature. Figure 10

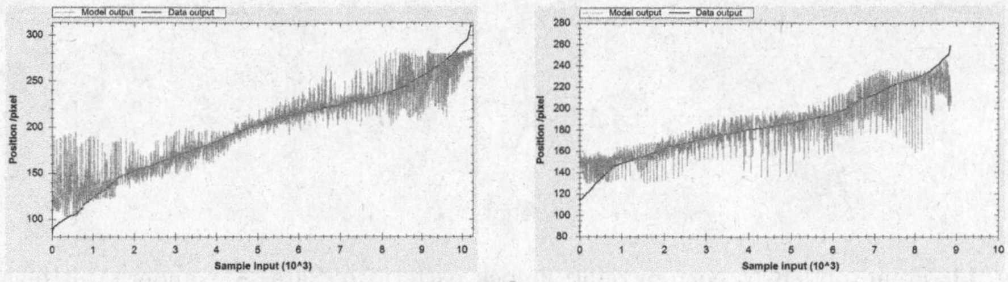

Fig. 9. Support vector regression results for the x (left) and y axes.

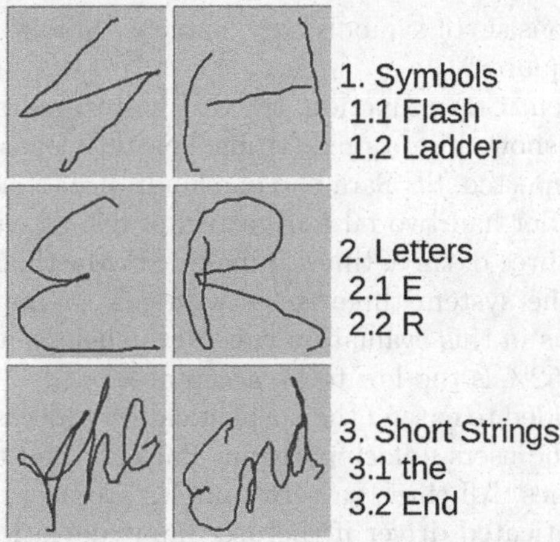

Fig. 10. Different user inputs

shows different possible user inputs. The first row in Fig. 10 shows two symbols. Symbol 1.1 is a stylized flash. Symbol 1.2 is a stylized ladder with one rung. It is an input with hand relocation outside the input area of AuthentiCap. Therefore it consists of three lines. The next two symbols are letters, we have the characters "E" (2.1) and "R" (2.2). The last row of Fig. 10 shows short input strings: "the" (3.1) and "End" (3.3). The characters, symbols, and strings in Fig. 10 show enough correlation to the intended characters, symbols, and strings so we can accept the coefficient of determination of 0.89 (x-axis) and 0.84 (y-axis). Thus we can simulate different users of AuthentiCap and evaluate AuthentiCap's user verification behavior.

We have four SU with different unlock patterns shown in Fig. 11. The first SU, Sara chooses a four digits pattern, a mix between symbols and letters. It consists of the letters "S" and "R". Furthermore, it contains two times the "Arc" symbol. The next SU, Alexander, extends the four digits pattern to a five digits pattern that only consists of alphabetic characters. His pattern consists of the letters "L", "E", "N", "N", "Y". SU Matthias' unlock pattern only consists of a short string, an abbreviation of his name: "Mat" in cursive. Finally, SU Sebastian

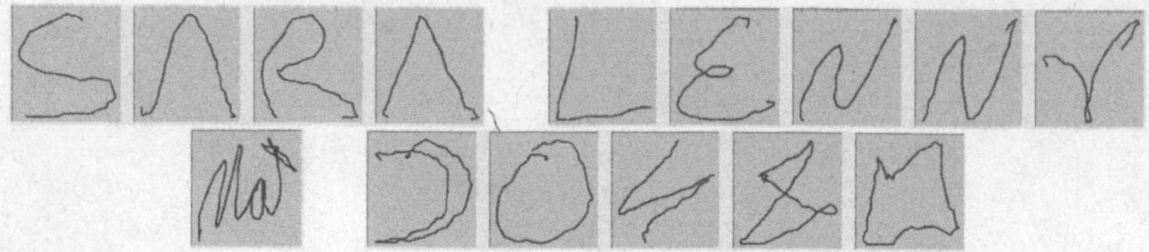

Fig. 11. From top left to bottom right: unlock patterns of Sara, Alexander, Matthias, and Sebastian.

uses a pattern that consists of symbols only, namely "Moon", "Circle", "Flash", "Sand glass" and "Square".

To evaluate AuthentiCap's function, the SUs had to redraw their pattern. A first naive evaluation shows that a single trained pattern leads to a system that is hard to unlock – as expected. SU Sara had one hindrance (false negative) in three attempts. SU Alexander had two false negatives of five attempts. SU Sebastian accessed the system three of three times. Finally, SU Matthias' performance was worst. He accessed the system three times with ten attempts. There were no false positive decisions in this evaluation run. Nevertheless, a total true positive rate of 12 out of 23, 52% is too low to be acceptable.

Therefore, we decided to extend the authentication process and added further training samples to the users unlock patterns. Each SU had to enter his specific pattern two more times. All three pattern samples are now treated equally and all lead to an authenticated driver if the user input deviation of all symbols is below the threshold (an average of 10 pixel distance). To test this small learning sample, each SU drew his pattern five times. Afterward, we entered 25 wrong patterns to check for false positives. Figure 12 shows the confusion matrix. The rate for true positive raised to 90%. At the same time, the false positive rate raised to 16%.

		Actual Class				
		Sara	Matthias	Alexander	Sebastian	Not Authenticated
Predicted	Sara	5				
	Matthias		5			4
	Alexander			3		
	Sebastian				5	
	Not Authenticated			2		21

Fig. 12. Confusion matrix

All false positive occurrences authenticated SU Matthias, the single string pattern. SU Matthias pattern was hard to redraw before the system gained further training patterns and leads to false positive authentication after the add of further training pattern. Figure 13 shows four false positive samples that predicted SU Matthias. This shows that for single input more training samples are needed and combinations of relatively simple letters or characters leads to a more secure identification. This trend was already visible in the training set with sample size one.

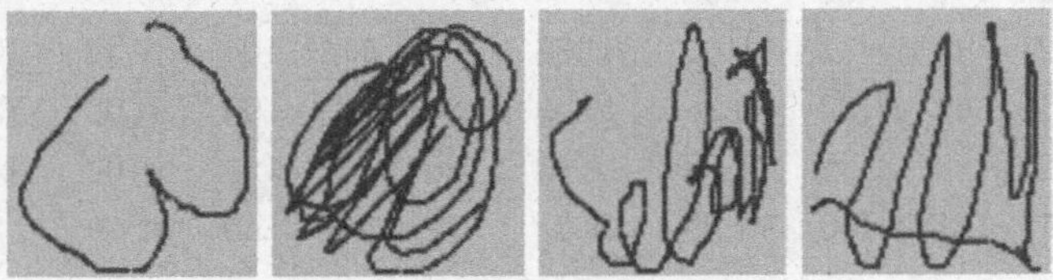

Fig. 13. False positive authentication "Matthias"

The system's authentication mechanism, that relies on a distance dependent input analysis, seems to be proper for pattern with more than four symbols. Nevertheless, the single string pattern can be distinct from the tested not-authenticated patterns. If we compare Fig. 13 with Fig. 11, the difference is obvious. Even if the authentication mechanism showed several issues, the user is able to redraw his pattern. Since authentication mechanisms from signatures are widely used, the core of our work (the touchless input device for authentication patterns) can be used with another authentication mechanism. The system proved that it can be invisibly integrated into existing vehicle structures, in this case the steering wheel. Furthermore, the usage did not leave any marks, because it works without contact. The variety of tested patterns shows that it can be adjusted to different patterns. The current evaluation leads to the recommendation to use more than a one-symbol pattern.

5.2 User Study

Given these findings, we started a small user-study including five real persons. All users were aged between 28 and 31. They all own a driver's license. Four users own a car as well. Their car's initial date of registration ranges from 2005 to 2014. The users were able to rate their experience with capacitive proximity sensing from 1 (no experience) to 10 (high experience). Except one user, who stated that his experience is 10, all users ranked their experience below or equal to 3.

For the recognition evaluation, we selected the pattern sequence of Sara. Each user had to draw the pattern sequence maximal 32 times. Because the pattern sequence consists of four single patterns, each user thus had the chance to draw maximal 128 patterns. If he did not succeed, he had to start at the beginning of the next pattern sequence, reducing the maximal number of possible patterns drawn. Besides the drawing of the pattern sequence, we asked the users several qualitative questions. The first task was to rate the usability of the system.

Table 1. Table user study

User	Pattern sequence					Single pattern				
	Pass	Fail	Sum	Pass %	Fail %	Pass	Fail	Sum	Pass %	Fail %
A	23	9	32	71.88	28.13	104	9	113	92.04	7.96
B	24	8	32	75.00	25.00	117	8	125	93.60	6.40
C	21	11	32	65.63	34.38	93	11	104	89.42	10.58
D	19	13	32	59.38	40.63	80	13	93	86.02	13.98
E	27	5	32	84.38	15.63	120	5	125	96.00	4.00
Sum	114	46	160	71.25	28.75	514	46	560	91.79	8.21

Second, they were asked if AuthentiCap can increase authentication safety and if they would use it in daily use.

Table 1 shows the results of the first part of the user study, the pattern sequence drawing. The user's pass rate for the whole pattern sequence ranges from 65.63% to 84.38% and the users' pass rate for the single patterns of these sequences ranges from 86.02% to 96%. As already stated, all users show different experience with capacitive proximity sensing. User E, who had the highest pass rate of 96% for single patterns and 84.38% for the pattern sequence, mentioned an experience level of 10. User D had a pass value of 86.02% for single pattern and 59.38% for the pattern sequence, the lowest pass rates. He also has the lowest experience, 1 (none), with capacitive proximity sensing. None of the users had false positive hits.

Figure 14 shows a chart of the users' experience with capacitive proximity sensing over the pattern pass rate. We included an exponential trend line. Its coefficient of determination (R^2) is 0.9. All users say that they think AuthentiCap can

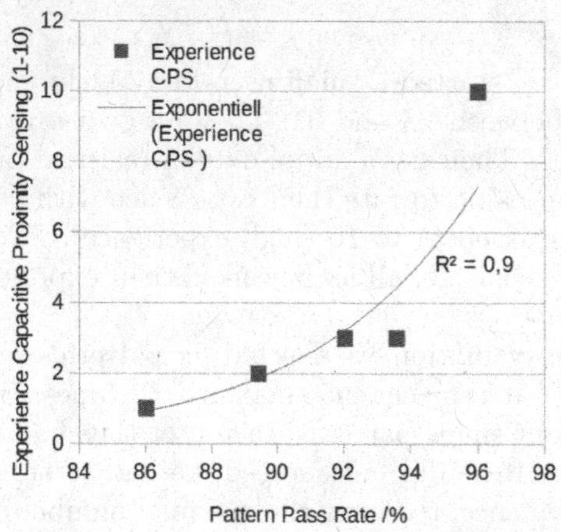

Fig. 14. Experience over pass rate

increase authentication safety. Moreover, except one user, all would use AuthentiCap in daily use. With a usability scale ranging from 1 (tough) to 10 (easy). The users rated the system's usability 5, 6, 7, 9, and 9. That is, a medium to easy usability.

At the end of the survey, the users were asked to think about further devices or systems that could use AuthentiCap. Most ideas focused on authentication systems. They say AuthentiCap could be the unlock mechanism of future desktops, safes, or smartphones. These samples show that AuthentiCaps usage is not limited to steering wheel containing automotive devices. One of the most often named purpose could be the unlocking of a door. A further interesting use could be the connection of AuthentiCap with signature cashless payment systems.

6 Conclusion and Outlook

We integrated two vectors of capacitive proximity sensing electrodes semi circle aligned in the upper outer ring of the vehicle's steering wheel. We identified the steering wheel as the best structure for our authentication system since it is already in use of capacitive proximity sensing for hands-on hands-off detection. Furthermore, we were able to integrate the sensors invisible. To face the limitations of touch based systems, we select the free area between steering wheel hub and upper steering wheel ring, the spyhole to the vehicle's speedometer, as input area. The provided system's unlock pattern is selected by the driver. Therefore, he can adjust it to his desired security level. We tested several unlock patterns. Patterns with more than one pattern element seem to be recommended since the current authentication process, that relies on the distance profile of the user's drawing seems to be vulnerable if the user selects a single string pattern as unlock pattern.

Moreover, the exact authentication mechanism of this system is only a placeholder for more reliable authentication mechanisms of future work. The aim of this paper is to check if AuthentiCap is able to provide reproducible and interpretable user input. The evaluation of this system proved that the user is able to provide distinct pattern's and even letters or symbols like hourglasses. The user study proved the usability of the system and the reproducibility of authentication patterns by different users. Due to the distinct user inputs, the chosen hand tracking algorithm seems to be proper even if the coefficient of determination is below 0.9 in all dimensions of the hand position. Furthermore, the accuracy of user inputs leads to further investigation of the usability of capacitive proximity sensing equipped vehicle structure like the steering wheel for HMI tasks like common gesture detection of Head-Up-Display cursor control.

References

1. Alsaadi, I.M.: Physiological biometric authentication systems, advantages disadvantages and future development: A review. Int. J. Sci. Technol. Res. 4(12), 285–289 (2015)

2. Aviv, A.J., Gibson, K.L., Mossop, E., Blaze, M., Smith, J.M.: Smudge attacks on smartphone touch screens. In: 4th USENIX Workshop on Offensive Technologies, WOOT 2010 (2010)
3. Bowyer Jr., K.W., Doyle, J.S.: Cosmetic contact lenses and iris recognition spoofing. IEEE Comput. **47**(5), 96–98 (2014)
4. Braun, A., Frank, S., Majewski, M., Wang, X.: CapSeat: capacitive proximity sensing for automotive activity recognition. In: Proceedings of the 7th AutomotiveUI 2015, pp. 225–232 (2015)
5. Braun, A., Frank, S., Wichert, R.: The capacitive chair. In: Streitz, N., Markopoulos, P. (eds.) DAPI 2015. LNCS, vol. 9189, pp. 397–407. Springer, Cham (2015). doi:10.1007/978-3-319-20804-6_36
6. Braun, A., Neumann, S., Schmidt, S., Wichert, R., Kuijper, A.: Towards interactive car interiors: the active armrest. In: Proceedings of the 8th Nordic Conference on Human-Computer Interaction: Fun, Fast, Foundational, pp. 911–914 (2014)
7. Braun, A., Wichert, R., Frank, S.: Verfahren zur feststellung der identität einer person auf einem sitz eines fahrzeugs, Patent DE 102014214978 A1, 04 Feb 2016
8. Braun, A., Wichert, R., Kuijper, A., Fellner, D.W.: Capacitive proximity sensing in smart environments. J. Ambient Intell. Smart Environ. **7**(4), 483–510 (2015)
9. Ford: Ford MyKey, now on 6 million vehicles, helps parents keep teens safe this summer, June 2013
10. Garcia, F.D., Oswald, D., Kasper, T., Pavlidès, P.: Lock it and still lose it - on the (in)security of automotive remote keyless entry systems. In: 25th USENIX Security Symposium, USENIX Security 2016 (2016)
11. Grosse-Puppendahl, T., Braun, A., Kamieth, F., Kuijper, A.: Swiss-cheese extended: an object recognition method for ubiquitous interfaces based on capacitive proximity sensing. In: Proceedings of the SIGCHI Conference on Human Factors in Computing Systems, pp. 1401–1410. ACM (2013)
12. Grosse-Puppendahl, T., Herber, S., Wimmer, R., Englert, F., Beck, S., von Wilmsdorff, J., Wichert, R., Kuijper, A.: Capacitive near-field communication for ubiquitous interaction and perception. In: Proceedings of the 2014 ACM International Joint Conference on Pervasive and Ubiquitous Computing, pp. 231–242 (2014)
13. Min, R., Choi, J., Medioni, G.G., Dugelay, J.: Real-time 3d face identification from a depth camera. In: Proceedings of the 21st International Conference on Pattern Recognition, ICPR 2012, pp. 1739–1742 (2012)
14. NHTSA - National Center for Statistics, Analysis: An exploration of vehicle based monitoring of novice teen drivers: Final report (2010)
15. NHTSA - National Center for Statistics, Analysis: Traffic safety facts - speeding (2014)
16. NHTSA - National Center for Statistics, Analysis: Traffic safety facts - distracted driving 2014 (2016)
17. Rieth, P., Böhm, J., Linkenbach, S., Hoffmann, O., Nell, J., Schirling, A., Netz, A., Stauder, P., Kuhn, M.: Steering handle for motor vehicles and method for recording a physical parameter on a steering handle, US Patent 7,321,311, 22 Jan 2008
18. Rus, S., Sahbaz, M., Braun, A., Kuijper, A.: Design factors for flexible capacitive sensors in ambient intelligence. In: 12th European Conference on Ambient Intelligence AmI 2015, pp. 77–92 (2015)
19. Schneegass, S., Steimle, F., Bulling, A., Alt, F., Schmidt, A.: SmudgeSafe: geometric image transformations for smudge-resistant user authentication. In: The 2014 ACM Conference on Ubiquitous Computing, UbiComp 2014, pp. 775–786 (2014)

20. Singh, G., Kumar, C.J., Rani, R.: Performance analysis of different classifiers for recognition of handwritten Gurmukhi characters using hybrid features. In: International Conference on Computing, Communication Automation, pp. 1091–1095 (2015)
21. Sun, C., Wang, Y., Zheng, J.: Dissecting pattern unlock: the effect of pattern strength meter on pattern selection. J. Inf. Secur. Appl. **19**(4–5), 308–320 (2014)
22. Xia, Z., Lv, R., Zhu, Y., Ji, P., Sun, H., Shi, Y.Q.: Fingerprint liveness detection using gradient-based texture features. Signal Image Video Process. **11**, 381–388 (2016)

Indoor Localization Based on Passive Electric Field Sensing

Biying Fu[1(✉)], Florian Kirchbuchner[1], Julian von Wilmsdorff[1], Tobias Grosse-Puppendahl[2], Andreas Braun[1,3], and Arjan Kuijper[1,3]

[1] Fraunhofer IGD, Fraunhoferstr. 5, 64283 Darmstadt, Germany
{biying.fu,florian.kirchbuchner,julian.von.wilmsdorff, andreas.braun,arjan.kuijper}@igd.fraunhofer.de

[2] Microsoft Research, 21 Station Road, Cambridge CB1 2FB, UK
tgp@microsoft.com

[3] Technische Universität Darmstadt, Karolinenplatz 5, 64289 Darmstadt, Germany
arjan.kuijper@mavc.tu-darmstadt.de

Abstract. The ability to perform accurate indoor positioning opens a wide range of opportunities, including smart home applications and location-based services. Smart floors are a well-established technology to enable marker-free indoor localization within an instrumented environment. Typically, they are based on pressure sensors or varieties of capacitive sensing. These systems, however, are often hard to deploy as mechanical or electrical features are required below the surface. They might also have a limited range or not be compatible with different floor materials. In this paper, we present a novel indoor positioning system using an uncommon form of passive electric field sensing, which detects the change in body electric potential during movement. It is easy to install by deploying a grid of passive wires underneath any non-conductive floor surface. The proposed architecture achieves a high position accuracy and an excellent spatial resolution. In our evaluation, we measure a mean positioning error of only 12.7 cm. The proposed system also combines the advantages of very low power consumption, easy installation, easy maintenance, and the preservation of privacy.

Keywords: Indoor positioning system · Indoor localization · Electric field sensing · Electric potential sensing · Body charge distribution

1 Introduction

Accurate indoor positioning is of vital importance in many domains, such as building occupancy detection [6], energy conservation in smart living environments [14], and elderly care. Such systems can either be token-free or token-based approaches. The latter include systems like RFID [18], ultrasonic sensor arrays [9], or WiFi systems [15], which require the tracked object to carry a token actively. Token-free systems include camera systems [21] or capacitive smart floors, as proposed by Braun et al. [2]. These systems do not require the user to

A. Braun et al. (Eds.): AmI 2017, LNCS 10217, pp. 64–79, 2017.
DOI: 10.1007/978-3-319-56997-0_5

carry additional hardware. In this case, all the information about the location and state of the individual must be extracted from sensing devices embedded in the environment. Camera-based systems achieve a very high accuracy but raise privacy concerns and require considerable computational facilities. In a survey, Kirchbuchner et al. showed that especially older people are not comfortable having a camera installed in their private domain [11]. In this paper, we focus on a novel smart floor system. Our new approach uses passive electric field sensing, a technology that detects changes in the ambient electric field caused by human movement [8]. Unlike active capacitive proximity sensing methods, it is less susceptible to electromagnetic noise, has lower power consumption, and operates better in humid environments. In this work, we will introduce related work in the domain of indoor positioning systems and, then present our system's architecture to show its easy installation and maintenance, and report on the findings of a test installation in our living lab. To further investigate the accuracy of the system, we evaluated our proposed system using a pre-marked reference path and compared the results with a visual system using Microsoft Kinect V2. We conducted the evaluation with two different settings with participants wearing shoes and walking barefoot to investigate their influence on the recognition performance.

2 Related Work

Various technologies have been investigated for token-free indoor localization. Camera-based positioning systems, as presented by Dockstader et al. [3], can reach a high spatial accuracy. Williams et al. use a distributed smart camera network to recognize falls and localize people standing in the system's detection area [21]. The authors argue that, with a sparse distribution of only three cameras, they are able to localize falls with an error of 40 to 60 cm. Further affordable systems are also available, such as AmbiTrack, as introduced by the group Braun et al. [18]. This system is based on low-cost cameras, tracks multiple persons, and uses contextual information for improving recognition rates and simplifying the installation. A general disadvantage of camera-based systems is, however, visual occlusion. Although occlusion can be mitigated by using multiple cameras [3], privacy concerns are still prevalent with camera-based systems [11]. Instead of using camera-based systems, we propose a capacitive system that is deployed underneath the floor. While the installation effort is considerably higher compared to cameras, it is not affected by occlusion, operates in darkness, and works under any kind of non-conductive material.

Other approaches, for example, based on WiFi [16], can track activities even through walls in a building. The advantage of using a WiFi signal is its range, as it can be transferred even through walls and no direct line of sight is needed. Furthermore, the presented system enables the interaction between the user and the sensing device without the prerequisite of wearing any additional devices or tokens. Such techniques often exploit the Doppler effect to extract the relative motion of the body relative to the sensing device. A radar-based system proposed by Bahl et al. [1] also showed promising results with respect to indoor positioning systems. However, such a system needs the user to be tracked and equipped with a mobile host.

Passive infrared sensors usually provide analog signals that can be analyzed to detect movements. The advantag of such a system is its low power consumption and small privacy impact. Apart from the motion information, relatively little contextual information can be extracted from PIR sensors due to ambiguous readings and potential losses of line-of-sight. However, in Lee et al. [13], the authors use a triangulation technique with three IR emitters with known positions to achieve indoor positioning. The authors discuss that due to noise and signal conditioning problems, their experiment has been conducted in a controlled environment, which has achieved acceptable results.

In a floor-based system, we focus on perceiving human beings with passive capacitive sensors. Such a system has its main advantages in elderly care, as it supports simultaneous indoor localization and fall recognition. Our architecture is based on a grid of single conductive wires deployed underneath a floor surface. Capfloor, proposed by Braun et al. [2], has already shown promising results in terms of this architecture. This work, however, uses an active capacitive sensing approach, which is susceptible to electromagnetic interference, such as that caused by TVs or switch-mode power supplies. Steinhage et al. [19] and Valtonen et al. [20] presented similar smart floor concepts using active capacitive sensing methods. We use in our novel system a sensing technology that is based on unobtrusively tracking the body's electrical field changes caused by the natural process of walking and moving in general. During the walking motion, the body's electrical potential changes through two effects: static charging due to the triboelectric effect and capacitive coupling due to the changing distance of the uplifting foot towards the ground, as explained by Ficker et al. [5] and Grosse-Puppendahl et al. [7].

3 Passive Electrical Field Sensing

In the following, we describe how a passive sensing electrode is affected by a person walking in close range. Here, we make use of the ambient electric field distortions that had occurred due to the presence or motion of a human body. Although the concept of measuring electric field distribution is not new, the use-case and the measurement method proposed by our system is, to our best knowledge, novel. Our proposed system benefits from the fact that each object, carrying a charge, emits an electric field. During walking motions or movements in general, every human being is subject to charge accumulation as described by the triboelectric effect [5], and changing capacitive coupling to the environment, e.g., caused by lifting a foot. Changes in accumulated charge and capacitive coupling result in the fact that a person emits an electric field caused by the varying body electric potential in the person's body. We can immediately experience this electric potential when rubbing our hair with a balloon. During everyday activities, this effect is less obvious but still present. To perceive such fields, we measure the induced charge on a sensing electrode in proximity to the field source, i.e., the human person. Every time a person lifts up or sets down a foot near the measuring electrode while walking, it will cause a charge redistribution on the surface of the sole, which will induce an opposite current on the remote measuring electrode. Also, with varying distance, the capacitive coupling between foot and ground changes while walking, which affects the body voltage. The relationship between the charge Q, the capacitive coupling between the person and the floor C_c, and the body electric potential difference is $V = \frac{Q}{C_c}$. We can approximate the capacitive coupling with the example of a plate capacitor equation, with $C_c = \epsilon_0 \epsilon_r \frac{A}{d}$ with A as the sole area and d as the foot-to-floor distance. The coupling capacitance increases with decreasing distance of the foot towards the sensing electrode.

Because of most events only last a short time and the charges are comparatively small, a challenge arises in how to measure the induced current in the electrode before it drains off. To address this problem, we use an impedance converter or current buffer as depicted in Fig. 1. Its input has a high impedance so that those very small displacement currents can be sensed reliably. The sensing electrodes are affected not only by changes in the electric field, which are induced by human activity, but also by the power line and other electrical equipment in the vicinity. We solve this issue by low-pass filtering the signal with a cut-off frequency of 15 Hz. This enables us to reliably detect walking activities while suppressing most environmental electric-field noise around 50/60 Hz. In Fig. 2, we depict an exemplary signal of a typical step caused by a person, who is periodically stepping over the measuring electrode as indicated by Label 1 and returning from the other side as indicated by Label 2. Notice that we lift our baseline to a positive voltage, so that in neutral or non-activated situations, the voltage stays a positive constant value and that change of body potentials while walking does not cause a sign flip. As observed in Fig. 2, as soon as the person

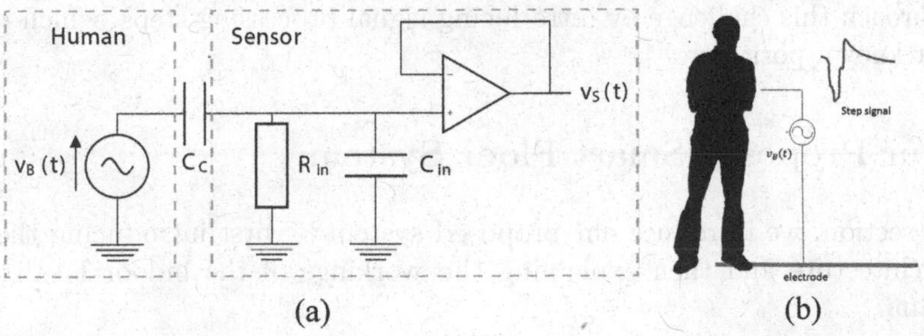

Fig. 1. (a) Impedance converter to ensure the current generated by human movements does not discharge immediately [7]. The first part represents a human body with a varying body voltage v_B due to movement, while the coupling capacitance is given by C_c and the resistance R_{in} and capacitance C_{in} affect the cutoff frequency of the hardware lowpass filter. The sensed voltage v_s is actually measured by our sensor. (b) A step signal of a person stepping on the electrode is illustrated.

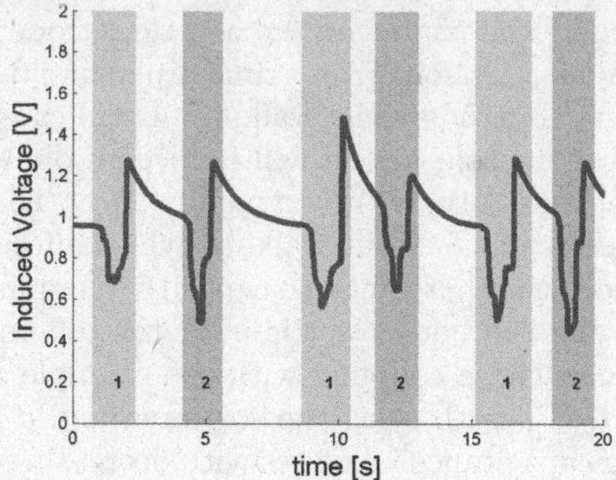

Fig. 2. Figure depicts a typical step signal measured by our sensing electrode. We measure the change of body voltage induced on the sensing electrode via walking. Label 1 indicates a step forward towards the sensing electrode and Label 2 indicates a step towards to the sensing electrode from the other side.

lifts his or her foot, the voltage decreases and increases again at the moment the foot contacts the floor. The same procedure can be observed when we step over the sensing electrode from the other side. If a person stands still without any movement, the electrode will discharge to a constant voltage and will stay there until new movement occurs. However, it is to notice that a typical step signal could also be reversed, depending on the current charge of the person. The advantage of passive electric field sensing over active capacitive measurement is that it is purely passive. The sensors do not emit any electromagnetic waves and only measures the induced changes of voltage caused by human beings who are walking nearby; thus, they consume a low amount of power. The only limitation of our proposed system compared to active capacitive sensing is that signals will only be generated if there is a movement in the vicinity of the sensing electrode. We approach this challenge by introducing signal processing steps, which retain the last known position.

4 Our Proposed Smart Floor System

In this section, we introduce our proposed system by first introducing the system architecture and then explaining the workings of the indoor localization algorithm.

4.1 System Architecture

The developed system is divided into three parts: a sensor array on the ground, a sub-controller for each ground segment and a central control unit for data analysis. On the square floor, electrodes starting from two adjacent sides build a grid structure. The electrodes are simple insulated copper wires and, thus, introduce very low cost. The wire spacing of 20 cm ensures that an average footprint is reliably detected. The wires are laid out manually, which still entails relatively high labor costs. For a potential market introduction, a laying with roll-out mats should be examined. The sensors are attached to two edges of the bottom surface. Therefore, a replacement of the sensors in case of failure or malfunction is possible without opening the bottom surface. This also results in low maintenance costs. Our measurement method ensures that it is possible to place any non-conductive floor covering above the electrodes. It is also feasible to enclose the electrodes in the screed. In our living lab, we place a simple carpet above the wire mesh of our test system.

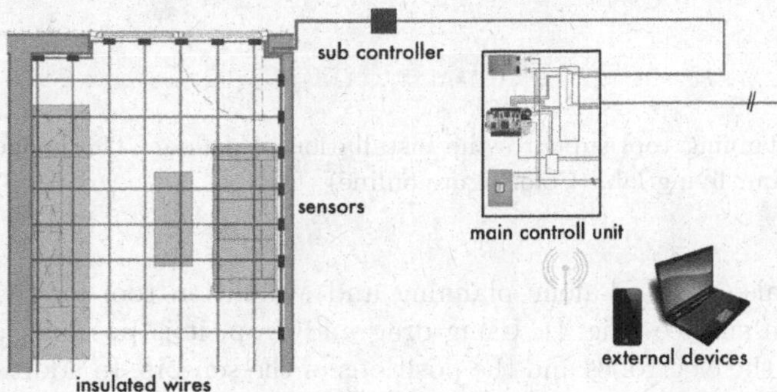

Fig. 3. The system overview shows the three parts of the system: sensors, a sub-controller, and a main controller.

For each floorspace or segment, the sensors are connected via an RS485 driven bus to a sub-controller. This unit manages the communication between the sensors and collects the sensor values with an update frequency of 10 Hz. Each sub-controller can manage up to 64 sensors. Subsystems can be used to cover rooms or single regions of interest in an apartment. Up to eight subsystems are connected via a CAT7 cabling to a central control unit. This main controller consists of a peripheral board connected to a BeagleBone[1] embedded computer, which performs the evaluation of the collected sensor signals. The BeagleBone Black is a low-cost, community-supported platform, based on an AM335x 1 GHz ARM Cortex-A8 equipped with 512 MB DDR3 RAM and 4 GB 8-bit eMMC onboard flash storage. On top of a customized Linux distribution, we are running Apache Karaf, a Java application container. This enables a modular software architecture which allows for successive updates of all components and remote management of the whole system. For each apartment, only one main controller is needed. This ensures that the data analysis is performed locally. If necessary, the system can communicate over the network with a home control or an emergency call system. The overall system layout is depicted in Fig. 3.

[1] www.beagleboard.org.

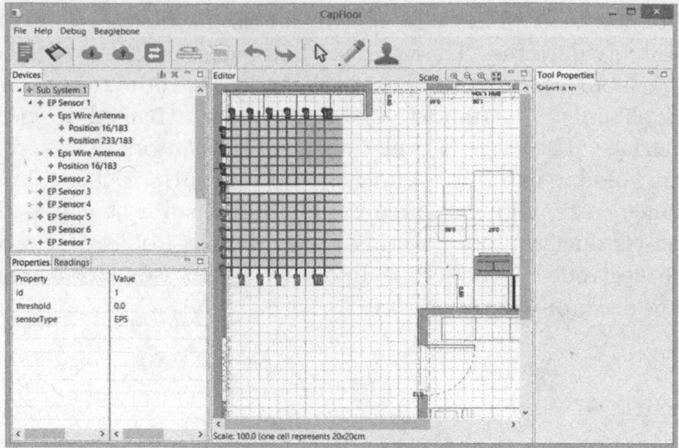

Fig. 4. The planning tool supports the installation of a floor. The image shows the setup used in our living lab. (Color figure online)

There is also a stand-alone planning and evaluation tool for the modeling of the bottom surface (Fig. 4). Using drag and drop, it is possible to draw the placement of the electrodes and the positions of the sensors. In addition, regions of interest, such as an entrance area, different floorspaces, and windows, can be marked. This information is stored in a hierarchical model on the main controller and offers the geometrical information to our indoor localization algorithm. In Fig. 4, the system installed in our living lab, consisting of two floorspaces, in gray and one entrance area in green, is depicted.

4.2 Indoor Localization Method

The algorithm used to perform the indoor localization benefits from the model-based structure of our proposed system. Using the designer introduced in the system architecture, our system is aware of the geometrical distribution of sensing electrodes within different floorspaces, e.g., the bedroom, kitchen, and entrance area. A floor space is a ground segment defined by the designer according to its geographical location and is, thus, important to smart home services.

The process of localization itself is divided into four steps, which will be introduced and detailed in the following section.

Positions of Activities Based on Floorspace. First, as soon as the foot breaks contact with the floor, a charge will be induced on the underlying sensing wire and, thus, will be measured. We set a threshold to determine the activity since environmental and electrical noise also has minor influences on the measurement. This environmental noise originates basically from the 50/60 Hz noise of the power lines. Even after applying the hardware-embedded low-pass filtering on the sensor itself, it still incorporates some noises due to the aliasing effect. To be certain, a proper threshold should be set to guarantee the proper performance of the indoor localization. We conducted the experiment of varying the threshold for the test runs without shoes. We discretized each floating point sensor value to a 12-bit integer value. Two thresholds of 50 and 100 were tested to illustrate the performance of localization accuracy. The mean positioning error increased from 16.34 cm for the threshold of 50 to 19.7 cm for the threshold of 100. Thus we chose a common threshold of 75. Based on the predefined floorspace, we determined for each floorspace activity based on the activated sensing electrode. We denote a sensor reading of a horizontally oriented electrode wire h_i as r_{h_i}. Likewise, we denoted the sensor reading of a vertically oriented electrode wire v_j as r_{v_j}. Per floorspace unit, we then have certain electrodes of interest forming floorspace activities $FA = (h_i, r_{h_i}), \ldots, (v_j, r_{v_j}), i = 1 \ldots N, j = 1 \ldots M$, where N and M are IDs of electrodes according their spatial placement.

Region of Interests per Floorspace. In the next step, for each 100 ms, a snapshot of events is taken. A region of interest (ROI) is a subset of floorspace activities, FA, which belong together. For each ROI certain activated horizontal and vertical sensing electrodes close by will be combined to form sub-regions of activities within one floorspace unit. We use $ROI = (h_i, r_{h_i}), \ldots, (v_j, r_{v_j}), i = a \ldots n, j = b \ldots m$, where n and m were the IDs of respective sensing electrodes, to illustrate one of such sub-region area.

Centers of Activity. In this step, we calculated the center of activity for an ROI_s containing n activated horizontal electrodes with (h_i, r_{h_i}) and m activated horizontal electrodes with (v_j, r_{v_j}) using a weighted average method by applying:

$$x_{ROI_s} = \frac{\sum_{j=b}^{m} r_{vj} x_j}{\sum_{i=b}^{m} r_{vj}}, y_{ROI_s} = \frac{\sum_{i=a}^{n} r_{hi} y_i}{\sum_{i=a}^{n} r_{hi}}, z_{ROI_s} = \frac{1}{m} \sum_{j=b}^{m} r_{vj} + \frac{1}{n} \sum_{i=a}^{n} r_{hi}$$

where the positions of x_{ROI_s} can be extracted using the activated vertical electrode and the positions of y_{ROI_s} can be extracted using the horizontal electrodes. The third component z_{ROI_s} provided the strength of this center of activity. With increasing z_{ROI_s} the probability increases that the person can be localized on this position (x_{ROI_s}, y_{ROI_s}). This way we calculated all the center positions of all possible K regions of interest $ROIs, s = 1 \ldots K$ within one floorspace.

Tracking of the Center Positions. Based on the possible options of the sub-regions of activities $ROI_s, s = 1 \ldots K$ and their center of activity $(x_{ROI_s}, y_{ROI_s}), ands = 1 \ldots K$, the most probable location needs to be chosen. For the first detected location, the position with the strongest z_{ROI_s} is chosen to indicate the most probable location and the successive positions are always chosen with respect to the last found position according to z_{ROI_s} from current step. Walking is a principal movement in humans. The biped motion is generally divided into a single support phase when only one foot is on the ground, and a double support phase, when both feet are on the ground [17]. Stride and step length are dependent on various factors, such as body size, the position of the feet, or hip mobility. These vary from person to person and even change with age. According to Elble et al. [4], compared to young adults, the elderly exhibit 17 to 20% reductions in the velocity of gait and length of stride. Therefore, in order to keep the computational effort for pure tracking low, a maximum stride length of 80 cm was assumed, according to Ibara et al. [10], which corresponds to a step width around 8 cm per sampling unit.

This proposed concept could be extended to multiple person tracking. However, in this paper, we only investigated the single user tracking. To adapt the current algorithm to perform multiple person tracking, we should pay further attentions to the found region of interests and not only select the one with the most probable center position and simply discard the other positions. A further optimized assignment algorithm should be included to assign the positions to different persons and keep track of them in the successive iterations. These concepts will be addressed in our next research scope.

5 Experiments and Evaluation

To test the spatial accuracy of our indoor localization algorithm we conducted a study. Further, we were interested in investigating various environmental influences on our proposed system, such as different footwear, especially the sole materials and the effects of walking barefoot. The charge accumulation is less prevalent when walking barefoot, and, thus, the voltage change induced on the measuring electrode is much weaker, which represents our worst-case scenario. For the test, we asked 12 participants to walk on a predefined path. The group of subjects included two women and ten men, between 23 and 37 years of age (average age 27), with a mean weight of 88.8 kg for the men and 53.5 kg for the women. Each test run followed a given path, which had been previously marked on the ground. The markers were 50 cm apart, which corresponds to a normal step length. An external system set the pace for the individual steps. For each participant, four test runs were performed, consisting of two test runs wearing shoes and two test runs with bare feet, in order to investigate the effect of sole material on our proposed system. The evaluation took place in our living lab, where we installed our indoor positioning system using two subsystems, as depicted in Fig. 5.

A walking speed of one step per second was chosen to simulate a slow human walking speed. Each second, a timer played a tone to help participants adjust their walking speed and to add the current position of the path to the recorder. The timing of the signal was used to get information about the time difference between the real world position and the position delivered by our system. The proposed system was further compared to a Microsoft Kinect V2. We mounted it horizontally on the side of our experimental setup to use the skeleton positions to track the person's movement. Since the entire area can be fully covered

Fig. 5. Test setup in the living lab with electrode grid and sensors.

without occlusion, this placement seems to be reasonable. Other possible setups like ceiling-mounted Kinect is also possible. However, since a skeleton tracking without further effort is not possible; thus an additional algorithm to track the position of the head is needed. For every marker, we measured the x- and y-coordinates to the origin point of our proposed system. In the next step, we transformed the Microsoft Kinect Skeleton positions to match the real-world coordinate system. The data acquisition of our proposed system communicates over an external MQTT server with our recording or evaluation system. With every new message, the position was determined and added to the recorder. The Kinect acquisition used the connected Microsoft Kinect V2 device and Microsoft Kinect API to retrieve the hip position to compare to our proposed system. We recorded each position with every incoming skeleton frame and marked it with a global timestamp. At the end of the recording, we stored all positions in different files for further processing and evaluation in Matlab R2013b.

We divided our test runs into two different sets. One set included all test runs conducted with participants wearing shoes and one set included all the remaining test runs conducted with participants walking barefoot on the sensing area. All conducted test runs with their resulted trajectories can be seen in Figs. 8 and 9. In Figs. 6 and 7, the average mean path for all test runs is depicted for each setting. This gives the reader an impression of how large the average positioning errors with respect to the reference positions were. The green dots show the prior marked reference positions on the ground, while the orange path connects the mean averaged positions over all test runs from one setting using our proposed system. In Fig. 6, the mean trajectory without shoes is depicted while in Fig. 7, the mean trajectory is shown when the participants wore shoes.

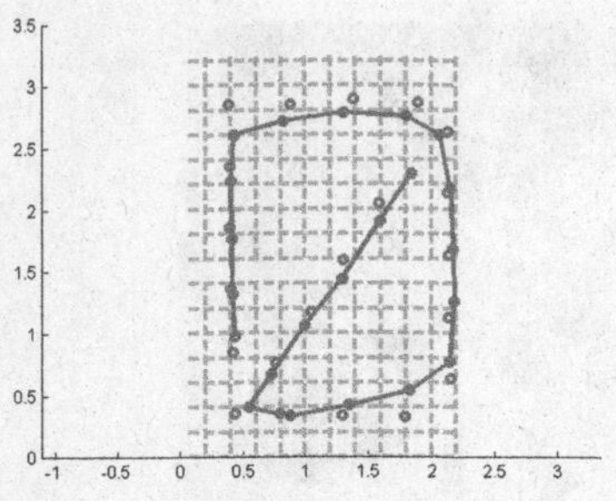

(a) Mean Trajectory Without Footwear From Proposed System

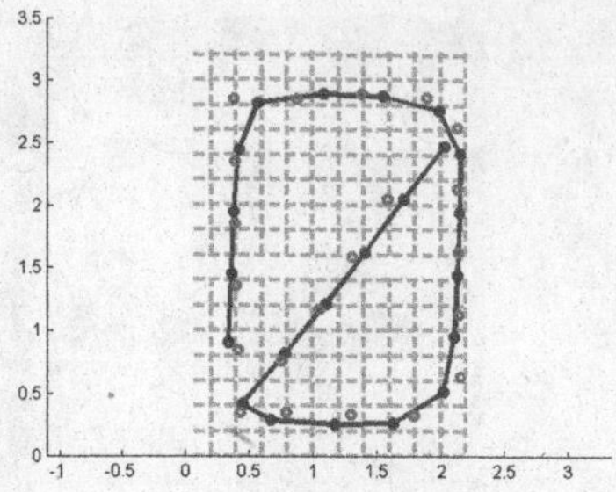

(b) Mean Trajectory Without Footwear From Kinect

Fig. 6. The orange curve shows the mean path on each position averaged over all the test runs with test persons walking barefoot. The purple curve shows the mean path from the comparing system using Kinect 2.0. (Color figure online)

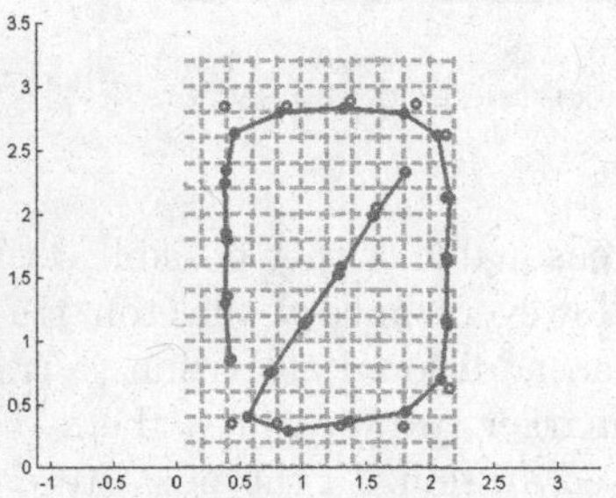

(a) Mean Trajectory With Footwear From Proposed System

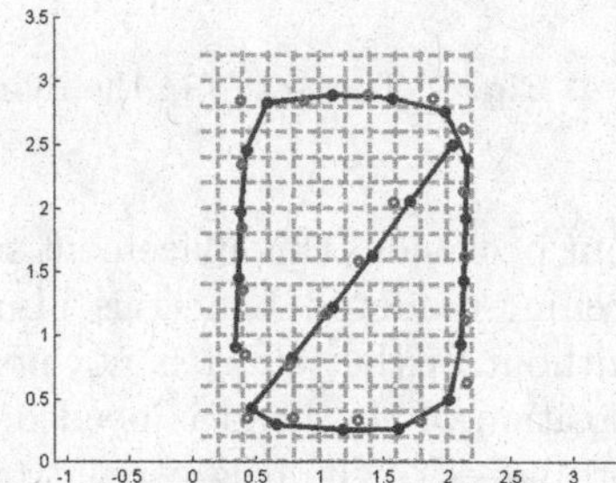

(b) Mean Trajectory With Footwear From Kinect

Fig. 7. The orange curve shows the mean path on each position averaged over all the test runs with test persons walking with shoes. The purple curve shows the mean path from the comparing system using Kinect 2.0. (Color figure online)

One obvious observation can easily be made from Figs. 7 and 6. As shown from using Microsoft Kinect as an input modality, the trajectories made no difference between walking barefoot and with shoes above the sensing area. In order to show the significance of footwear towards our proposed system, we further conducted the nonparametric Kruskal-Wallis H test [12] on our collected data points. To quantify the accuracy of our proposed system, we denoted the a priori known real-world positions of the reference path as p_{ref_i} in the form of $p_{ref_i} = (x_{ref_i}, y_{ref_i}), i = 1, \ldots, n$ and the test path as $p_{test_i} = (x_{test_i}, y_{test_i}), i = 1, \ldots, n$. The distance error was calculated using $d_{err} = ||p_{ref_i} - p_{test_i}||_2$ on each prior marked reference position. For each test run, we collected 22 distance errors between test position p_{ref_i} with respect to reference position p_{test_i}. Based on the data collected from 12 tested persons, each walking two times in each setting, we recorded $22 \times 2 \times 12 = 528$ distance errors for recordings with shoes and

528 distance errors without shoes. The results showed that walking barefoot had significantly different outcomes compared to walking in shoes ($p < 0.001$). The overall mean positioning error was 18 cm, with a standard deviation of 22.05 cm for recordings without shoes and a mean positioning error of 12.7 cm with a standard deviation of 13.6 cm for recordings with shoes, as shown in Table 1. The inferior performance of our proposed system from wearing shoes compared to being barefoot was partly due to the nature of our measuring principle itself. While the person walks barefoot on the sensing area, the charge separation induced by human walking is too small and, thus, drains off too quickly. On the contrary, for a person wearing shoes, the isolating sole material keeps the human body charge separated via constantly walking when it induces a change to the electrode.

Table 1. Positioning errors compared to pre-marked reference positions over all test runs with individual settings.

Setup	Mean	Median	Standard deviation
With shoes	12.7 cm	7.4 cm	13.6 cm
Without shoes	18.0 cm	8.8 cm	22.05 cm
Kinect hip	15.4 cm	14.7 cm	7.35 cm
Kinect right foot	22.0 cm	15.2 cm	15.8 cm
Kinect left foot	20.7 cm	13.9 cm	16.13 cm

To conclude our evaluation, we depict all of the walking trajectories for all participants in Figs. 8 and 9. We depict the positions from our proposed system as compared to the reference positions to illustrate the overall performance of our proposed system. Peculiar are the first two runs from participants 1 (c–d) and 2 (c–d) without wearing shoes. This could be explained by the reported changed habit or uncertainty from walking in shoes to without shoes. Giveno the instability of walking barefoot on the marked positions, these participants felt it was difficult to walk naturally on the given path.

Combining all the collected evaluation results, we can draw the conclusion that our proposed system possesses certain advantages compared to a vision-based system like Microsoft Kinect. The most common disadvantage of Microsoft Kinect is that sometimes, even the skeleton gets lost in the case of people wearing black clothes or moving out of the tracking area. Our proposed system tracks the person in the entire room without the problem of privacy concerns. The most important advantage is its low energy consumption because of its passive measuring nature that still offers precision in indoor localization.

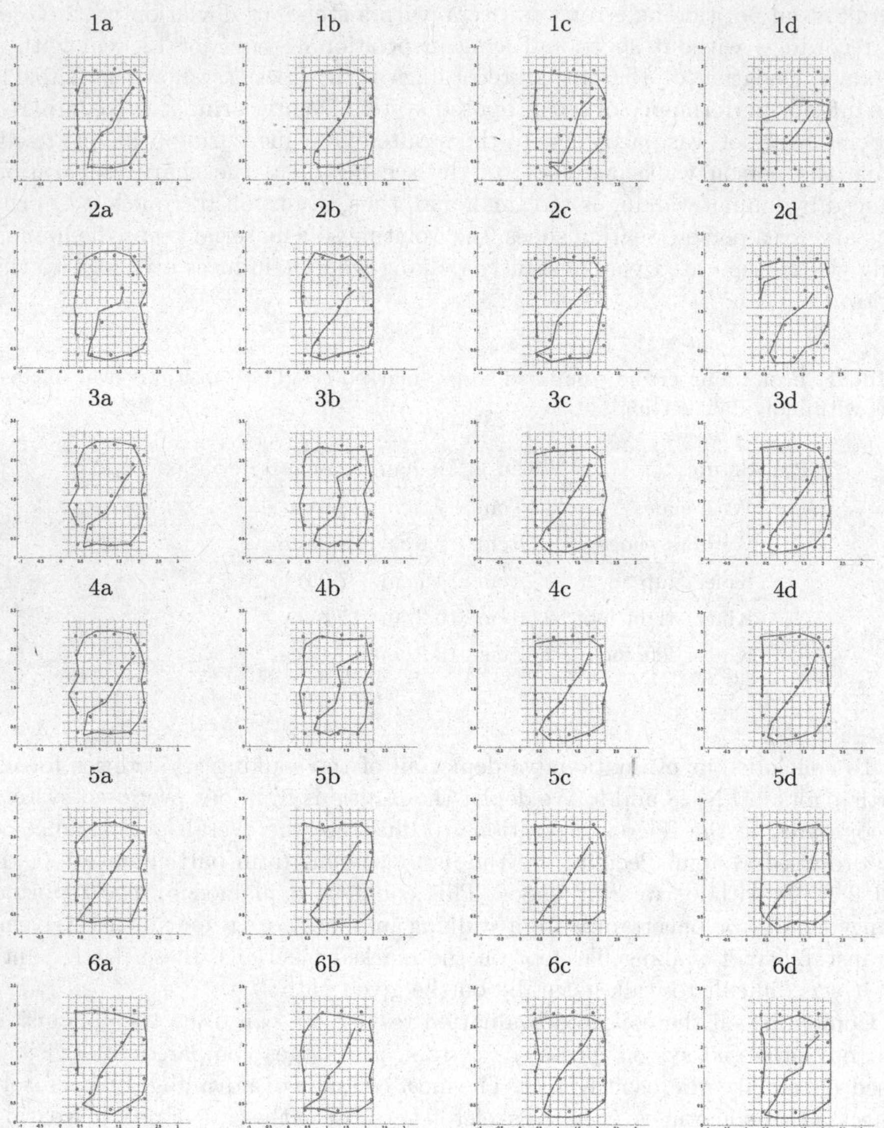

Fig. 8. Here we depict the participants 1 to 6 and draw the calculated trajectories from our proposed system using electrical potential sensing. The green dots are the pre-marked reference positions. The first two runs (a, b) are participants wearing shoes and the second two runs (c, d) are the same participant walking without shoes. (Color figure online)

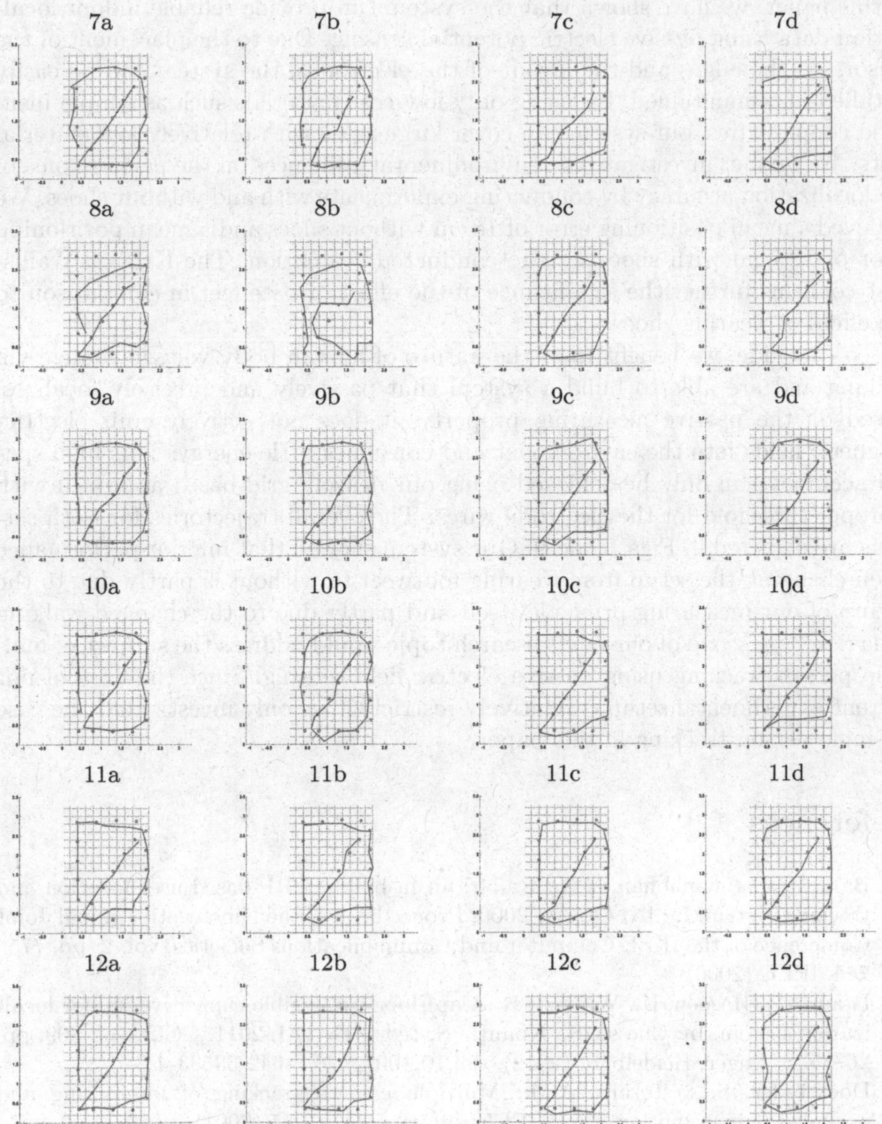

Fig. 9. Here we depict the participants 7 to 12 and draw the calculated trajectories from our proposed system using electrical potential sensing. The green dots are the pre-marked reference positions. The first two runs (a, b) are participants wearing shoes and the second two runs (c, d) are the same participant walking without shoes. (Color figure online)

6 Conclusion and Outlook

In this paper, we have shown that the system can provide reliable indoor localization data using passive electric potential sensing. Due to the placement of the sensors on the edges and the layout of the electrodes, the system can be easily installed and maintained. By using only low-cost materials such as simple insulated copper wires, our system can cover large areas with relatively low material costs. We further investigate the environmental influences on the performance of the localization accuracy by conducting experiments with and without shoes. We achieved a mean positioning error of 18 cm without shoes and a mean positioning error of 12.7 cm with shoes for the conducted evaluation. The Kruskal-Wallis-Test confirms further the significance of the effect of bare feet in comparison to the effect of wearing shoes.

To conclude, we benefit from the nature of human body voltage change via walking and are able to build a system that passively and precisely localizes. Based on the passive measuring property, it does not actively emit electric-magnetic fields into the environment and consumes little energy. This high spatial accuracy can only be achieved using our densely grid-based approach with a proper threshold for the electrode wires. The overall trajectories for both settings are depicted in Figs. 8 and 9. Our system showed that inferior performance when changing the setup from wearing footwear to without is partly due to the nature of our measuring principle itself and partly due to the changed walking behavior. The scope of our next research topic would address the subject of multiple person tracking using passive electric field sensing. Since the area of our current experimental setup is relatively restricted, we only investigated the case of single person tracking in this paper.

References

1. Bahl, P., Padmanabhan, V.N.: Radar: an in-building RF-based user location and tracking system. In: INFOCOM 2000, Proceedings of the Nineteenth Annual Joint Conference of the IEEE Computer and Communications Societies, vol. 2, pp. 775–784. IEEE (2000)
2. Braun, A., Heggen, H., Wichert, R.: CapFloor – a flexible capacitive indoor localization system. In: Chessa, S., Knauth, S. (eds.) EvAAL 2011. CCIS, vol. 309, pp. 26–35. Springer, Heidelberg (2012). doi:10.1007/978-3-642-33533-4_3
3. Dockstader, S.L., Tekalp, A.M.: Multiple camera tracking of interacting and occluded human motion. Proc. IEEE **89**(10), 1441–1455 (2001)
4. Elble, R.J., Thomas, S.S., Higgins, C., Colliver, J.: Stride-dependent changes in gait of older people. J. Neurol. **238**(1), 1–5 (1991)
5. Ficker, T.: Electrification of human body by walking. J. Electrostat. **64**(1), 10–16 (2006)
6. Filippoupolitis, A., Oliff, W., Loukas, G.: Occupancy detection for building emergency management using BLE beacons. In: Czachórski, T., Gelenbe, E., Grochla, K., Lent, R. (eds.) ISCIS 2016. CCIS, vol. 659, pp. 233–240. Springer, Cham (2016). doi:10.1007/978-3-319-47217-1_25

7. Grosse-Puppendahl, T., Dellangnol, X., Hatzfeld, C., Fu, B., Kupnik, M., Kuijper, A., Hastall, M., Scott, J., Gruteser, M.: Platypus - indoor localization and identification through sensing electric potential changes in human bodies. In: 14th ACM International Conference on Mobile Systems, Applications and Services (MobiSys). ACM (2016)
8. Harland, C., Clark, T., Prance, R.: Electric potential probes-new directions in the remote sensing of the human body. Meas. Sci. Technol. **13**(2), 163 (2001)
9. Holm, S., Nilsen, C.I.C.: Robust ultrasonic indoor positioning using transmitter arrays. In: 2010 International Conference on Indoor Positioning and Indoor Navigation (IPIN), pp. 1–5. IEEE (2010)
10. Ibara, K., Kanetsuna, K., Hirakawa, M.: Identifying individuals' footsteps walking on a floor sensor device. In: Yoshida, T., Kou, G., Skowron, A., Cao, J., Hacid, H., Zhong, N. (eds.) AMT 2013. LNCS, vol. 8210, pp. 56–63. Springer, Cham (2013). doi:10.1007/978-3-319-02750-0_6
11. Kirchbuchner, F., Grosse-Puppendahl, T., Hastall, M.R., Distler, M., Kuijper, A.: Ambient intelligence from senior citizens' perspectives: understanding privacy concerns, technology acceptance, and expectations. In: Ruyter, B., Kameas, A., Chatzimisios, P., Mavrommati, I. (eds.) AmI 2015. LNCS, vol. 9425, pp. 48–59. Springer, Cham (2015). doi:10.1007/978-3-319-26005-1_4
12. Kruskal, W., Wallis, W.: Use of ranks in one-criterion variance analysis. J. Am. Stat. Assoc. **47**, 583–621 (1952)
13. Lee, C., Chang, Y., Park, G., Ryu, J., Jeong, S.G., Park, S., Park, J.W., Lee, H.C., Hong, K.S., Lee, M.H.: Indoor positioning system based on incident angles of infrared emitters. In: 30th Annual Conference of IEEE Industrial Electronics Society, IECON 2004, vol. 3, pp. 2218–2222. IEEE (2004)
14. Li, N., Becerik-Gerber, B.: Performance-based evaluation of rfid-based indoor location sensing solutions for the built environment. Adv. Eng. Inform. **25**(3), 535–546 (2011)
15. Lim, C.H., Wan, Y., Ng, B.P., See, C.M.S.: A real-time indoor WiFi localization system utilizing smart antennas. IEEE Trans. Consum. Electron. **53**(2), 618–622 (2007)
16. Pu, Q., Gupta, S., Gollakota, S., Patel, S.: Whole-home gesture recognition using wireless signals. In: Proceedings of the 19th Annual International Conference on Mobile Computing and Networking, MobiCom 2013, pp. 27–38. ACM, New York (2013)
17. Rubio, J.P.B., Zhou, C., Hernández, F.S.: Vision-based walking parameter estimation for biped locomotion imitation. In: Cabestany, J., Prieto, A., Sandoval, F. (eds.) IWANN 2005. LNCS, vol. 3512, pp. 677–684. Springer, Heidelberg (2005). doi:10.1007/11494669_83
18. Saad, S.S., Nakad, Z.S.: A standalone RFID indoor positioning system using passive tags. IEEE Trans. Ind. Electron. **58**(5), 1961–1970 (2011)
19. Steinhage, A., Lauterbach, C.: Sensfloor (r): Ein aal sensorsystem für sicherheit, homecare und komfort. Ambient Assisted Living-AAL (2008)
20. Valtonen, M., Maentausta, J., Vanhala, J.: Tiletrack: capacitive human tracking using floor tiles. In: 2009 IEEE International Conference on Pervasive Computing and Communications, pp. 1–10 (2009)
21. Williams, A., Ganesan, D., Hanson, A.: Aging in place: fall detection and localization in a distributed smart camera network. In: Proceedings of the 15th International Conference on Multimedia, pp. 892–901. ACM (2007)

Safety Services in Smart Environments Using Depth Cameras

Matthias Ruben Mettel, Michael Alekseew,
Carsten Stocklöw, and Andreas Braun(✉)

Fraunhofer Institute for Computer Graphics Research IGD,
Fraunhoferstr. 5, 64283 Darmstadt, Germany
{matthias.mettel,andreas.braun}@igd.fraunhofer.de

Abstract. Falls of elderly persons are the most common cause of serious injuries in this age group. It is important to detect the fall in a timely manner. If medical help can't be provided immediately a deterioration of the patient's state may occur. In order to tackle this challenge, we want to propose two combined safety services that can utilize the same sensor to prevent and detect falls. The Dangerous Object Adviser detects small obstacles located on the floor and warns the user about the stumbling hazard when the user walks in their direction. The Fall Detection Service detects a fall and informs caregivers. This enables the caregivers to provide medical care in time. Both services are implemented by using the Microsoft Kinect, with the obstacles extracted from the depth image and the usage of skeleton tracking gives to provide the necessary information on the user position and pose.

Keywords: Safety services · Smart environments · Fall detection · Microsoft Kinect

1 Introduction

Smart environments can help their inhabitants to make their lives easier and more comfortable, as they support daily life activities and can control the different appliances that are installed. Their main objective is to establish services that support the users to avoid dangerous situations, such as stumbling over small obstacles placed on the floor. The support of a smart environment can help the user - especially when they are getting older - to live longer, independently in their own apartment.

Falls are the most likely event for injuries experienced by elderly people [1]. The fall detection is crucial for elder care, because the immediate assistance by caregivers can minimize the consequences of falls [1]. Technical solutions exist that catch the event of a fall and call for assistance. This combined functionality of detecting the fall and calling for help, is a Fall Detection Service. Often a fall is triggered by stumbling over an obstacle (e.g. a bag, an umbrella or a box) that is placed on the floor in the user's walking direction. If the system can

A. Braun et al. (Eds.): AmI 2017, LNCS 10217, pp. 80–93, 2017.
DOI: 10.1007/978-3-319-56997-0_6

detect such obstacles, it can warn the user and they can react by walking past or removing the obstacle.

Therefore, we propose a Dangerous Object Adviser (DOA) service, to prevent the user from stumbling over an obstacle and falling down, as well as a fall detection service to establish an automatic way to detect that the user has fallen and inform caregivers about the fall.

For the implementation of both services we require sensors, that can give us the following information about the user and his environment:

1. User location in the environment
2. User state
3. Obstacle locations in the environment

There are different approaches to provide the presented services. We chose to use a device that can provide both services - the Microsoft Kinect. "It is the world's first system that at reasonable price combines an RGB camera and a depth sensor. Unlike 2D cameras, the low-cost Kinect allows tracking the body movements in 3D. In the past years this device has been used in a variety of assistive applications for older adults [2]. It can serve as interaction device, or multi-sensor system installed in a user's home. Thus, if only depth images are used it can guarantee the person's privacy. The Kinect sensor is independent of external light conditions, since it is equipped with an active light source. As the Kinect uses infrared light it is able to extract depth images in a room that is dark to our eyes." [3]. In the scope of a larger research project this system was already installed as part of the overall architecture, primarily for emotion recognition from image and sound [4]. The primary idea is to use this existing infrastructure and evaluate the feasibility of creating a fall detection system using the sensors of the Kinect.

We use the second version of the device, the Kinect for Windows v2, whose SDK allows connecting a single device per system. In this work, we will present the considerations and design behind the Fall Detection and the DOA services, introduce the prototype system, and report on the results of a system evaluation that was performed to verify the general viability of the system. We conclude the paper with a discussion of the results and a short foray into potential future work.

2 Related Work

A variety of sensors have been utilized to detect falls. Chen et al. [5] use wearable acceleration sensors to detect falls. "These systems have the drawback that the user must remember to wear the sensors." [6]. This can be a particular challenge in the case of user's affected by dementia or Alzheimer's. Su et al. utilize a doppler radar [1]. "A human fall generates motion that creates frequency change between the sent and received signals of a Doppler radar. [..] A human fall typically reaches to about $v = 5\,\mathrm{m/s}$ before hitting the ground." [1] Floor mounted sensors are another common variety. Alwan et al. used vibration sensors that detect the mechanical waves created on the impact of a fall [7]. Braun et al. use capacitive sensors that can also detect the position of the user [8]. Capacitive sensors create weak electrical fields that are influenced by the presence of human bodies. Measuring and correlating their information they can be used for various forms of activity recognition [9]. "[These] systems eliminate the need for the user to wear a sensor; however, these systems are often expensive and are complex to install." [6].

These approaches are also more comfortable for the user, as there is no need to carry an additional device. They are installed in the environment without directly affecting the user. However, these systems typically need an initialization and learning phase and can only locate the user in the prepared environment. They can't analyze the environment itself. This is required for our DOA. Even though it is possible to attach further sensors to the environment, sometimes it may be better to reduce the sensor count in the environment, due to cost and performance considerations.

There are several works in the field of computer vision that use optical systems to detect falls. There are several advantages that cameras provide compared to other sensors, which includes a range of activity recognition methods. In addition, they can support the remote verification of fall events and are often unobtrusive. The main disadvantage are high requirements on installation and calibration. Most CCD-cameras require an external computing system for image processing, and there may be additional limitations due to difficult light conditions. A non-technical disadvantage is the perceived intrusion on the privacy of a user [10]. The addition of depth information can improve the quality of detection and prevent falls alarms. Rougier et al. describe in their paper "Demo: Fall Detection Using 3D Head Trajectory Extracted From a Single Camera Video Sequence" the utilization of a camera to track the head of a user, and a particle filter to get a 3D trajectory of the head [11]. After this the velocity of the head in floor direction can be calculated. If this velocity is higher than a threshold, a fall is detected.

Another computer vision approach employs the Microsoft Kinect depth image stream. Kepski et al. developed a system that utilizes a segmentation algorithm for the depth image and locates the user, the floor plane and the position of the user in relation to the floor plane [3]. Gasparrini et al. placed the Microsoft Kinect at the ceiling. "The system setup adopts a Kinect® sensor in top view configuration, at a distance of 3 m (MaxHeight) from the floor, thus providing a coverage area of 8.25 m^2. To extend the monitored area, the sensor can be elevated up to around 7 m; beyond this distance the depth data become unreliable." [12]. The approach applies background subtraction to find obstacles in the environment and the location of the user. If the user has fallen, the depth pixel values of the detected body are under a specific threshold. Additionally, this approach can track objects, even though the area is smaller than the area the sensor can monitor in a default setup. Another disadvantage is that the systems needs training to detect the user properly.

Kawatsu et al. apply the skeletal tracking feature of the Microsoft Kinect [6]. It calculates the distance between the floor plane and all skeleton joints as well as the velocity of the joints in floor direction. If the distance and the velocity fall below a specific threshold the system notifies a predefined user about a fall.

Most of these approaches for fall prevention focus on balancing issues of the user. The majority of systems provide supervised or unsupervised activity monitoring system to train the users [13]. Currently similar solutions to detect stumbling hazards do not exist. So we divided our project into sub-problems. The following approaches are different possibilities to solve the sub-problems, that have already been discussed or solved in other fields of work with a different context.

First there is the environment analysis. We need the positions of different obstacles located on the floor. In the field of robotics, laser or Kinect approaches are employed to navigate a robot through an environment. For trajectory estimation the map is recorded and can be utilized later to define trajectories. These maps have to be updated by the system as the robot is moving through the environment.

Lu et al. employs a laser scanner to create a map of the direct surrounding of the robot [14]. The laser measures the distance between the robot and the next obstacle. This distance is stored in a map.

Henry et al. describe an approach in their article "RGB-D Mapping: Using Kinect-style Depth Cameras for Dense 3D Modeling of Indoor Environments" that utilizes the depth image stream of the Microsoft Kinect to record a 3D map of the environment [15]. This approach is similar to the Kinect Fusion approach [16]. The 3D mesh can be converted to a 2D representation.

Another approach for map generation is the simultaneous localization and mapping (SLAM) described by Dissanayake et al. [17]. The idea behind this is, that by the continuous movement of a vehicle or robot the internal representation of the environment as map is updated and concurrently the position of the robot in the environment can be estimated.

3 Safety Services Using Depth Cameras

As previously mentioned, our implementation uses the Microsoft Kinect for Windows v2. It provides the necessary data for our services, as well as additional sensor information that can be used for more applications. The skeleton tracking delivers the user position [18]. This can be used to estimate the movement direction of the user and extract the dangerous obstacles in the environment from the depth image. Other services (e.g. speech recognition) can utilize other sensors (e.g. color image, audio).

The disadvantage of the Microsoft Kinect SDK is the limitation to one connected device per system. This requires one computer per area, where fall detection and dangerous object adviser have to be provided. Therefore, we need to find an optimal system setup to establish both services by using only one Microsoft Kinect device per room or area.

The final system setup adopts a Kinect sensor placed approximately two meters above the floor and has an angle of approximately 60° downwards to the floor plane as displayed in Fig. 1. For a proper floor plane segmentation, it is necessary that a large part of the floor plane is visible.

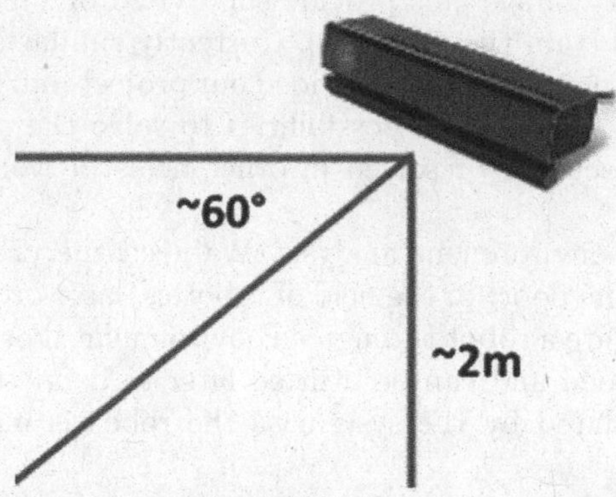

Fig. 1. The best Microsoft Kinect setup to combine both services with one device.

3.1 Fall Detection Service

The fall-detection combines a "static" and "dynamic" detection to detect a fall. The static detection checks whether a person is lying on the floor and the dynamic detection checks whether a person is currently falling to the ground. If the person is lying on the floor and has previously fallen to the ground, a fall is detected.

The joint position values tracked by the Microsoft Kinect are not completely stable as some joint position values can jump significantly in two successive frames, which is not reflected in the actual movement. First, our implementation fills a buffer for every joint with the distance to the floor, the current time, and whether the joint is tracked. The following equations are utilized to calculate the distances to the floor plane:

$$Plane : A \cdot x + B \cdot y + C \cdot z + D = d_{point} \quad (1)$$

$$JointDistance : d_{joint} = \frac{A \cdot x_{joint} + B \cdot y_{joint} + C \cdot z_{joint} + D}{\sqrt{A^2 + B^2 + C^2}} \quad (2)$$

To receive a correct detection, the buffer stores the joint data of at least 60 frames. The static and dynamic detection uses only the mean distance values for a certain number of frames (static = 30 frames, dynamic 25 frames). This mitigates an impact from outliers in joint positions and allows for smoothing of the joint distances to the floor overall.

Using the latest values in the joint distance buffer, the velocity for every joint is calculated by:

$$v_{joint} = \frac{d_{joint,i} - d_{joint,i-1}}{t_{joint,i} - t_{joint,i-1}} \tag{3}$$

With these joint velocities, the average velocity of every joint is calculated and used to calculate the average human velocity in floor direction in meters per second (m/s). If this value lies above a threshold of $-0.5\frac{\text{m}}{\text{s}}$ the dynamic fall detection is set to true for two seconds. We determined the threshold value from initial tests with different users. If the static fall detection is set to true within this two seconds, a fall is detected for a person.

For the static fall detection only head-, neck-, spine_shoulder-, spine_mid-, shoulder_left-, shoulder_right-, elbow_left-, elbow_right-, hip_left- and hip_right-joints are used. The other joints are either not needed to be detected near the floor, don't give a reliable prediction, or are too inconsistent in their values.

For all of joints used, the mean distance to the floor is calculated, followed by a check whether it is under the threshold of 0.65 m. This value is inspired by the work of Fryar et al. and adjusted on the basis of several test results [19]. Each successfully tracked joint has to be below this threshold, setting the static fall detection to true.

Our implementation is similar to the implementation by Kawatsu et al. [6]. The differences between them are that we utilize the floor plane coefficients provided by the Microsoft Kinect SDK, because we do not have the requirement to detect falls on stairs. Additionally, we combined the static and the dynamic detection, in order to avoid some of the false positives. A static detection triggers a fall only when the dynamic algorithm detects a fall before it.

The advantages of our solution are, that it is easy to implement, as the Microsoft Kinect captures all the required information. The skeleton tracking is independent from the lighting conditions of the environment and, as mentioned in Sect. 1, the user does not have to wear any sensors. The disadvantages are that a fall can only be detected, when a skeleton is tracked. The Microsoft Kinect was originally developed for gaming and controlling an XBox. The detection rate is the highest in the middle of the sensor viewing area [20]. This leads to the issue, that the skeleton is not tracked properly in the border sections of the depth image. The Kinect also needs some time to detect the skeleton when the user enters the viewing area. If the user is more than six meters away from the sensor, the skeleton can't be tracked properly. This approach can therefore not be applied to spacious rooms.

3.2 Dangerous Object Adviser Service

For the detection of dangerous objects we need the following information:

1. A set of objects which are located on the floor.
2. The position of the user in the room.
3. The movement direction of the user.

We convert the depth image of the Microsoft Kinect into a point cloud, before estimating the position of the floor plane with the random sample consensus (RANSAC) plane segmentation algorithm implemented in the Point Cloud Library [21].

After the segmentation of the floor plane, an image with the size of 800×800 pixel and a color value of two bytes per pixel is created. The x- and z-coordinates of the points are mapped to the x- and y-coordinate of the image and the pixel intensity represents the distance between the point and the floor plane. The size of the image is defined by the 8 m detection range of the Microsoft Kinect. The 3D values are noted in meters, with the image having a resolution of one centimeter [22].

As the RANSAC segmentation combines planes that have the same distance to the floor, we may run into the problem that some obstacles are detected with a large bounding box instead of two separate obstacles. Therefore we apply certain additional processing steps. To extract the locations and dimensions from the image, we apply opening (erode-dilate) and closing (dilate-erode) algorithms, in order to remove noise and use the canny algorithm to detect edges in the image. These can be utilized to receive the position and define an object-oriented bounding box of the obstacles.

The next step of the dangerous object adviser is the location and movement direction of the user in the room. This information can be extracted from the skeleton tracking data from the Microsoft Kinect. Contrary to the Microsoft XBox 360 Kinect, the Microsoft Kinect for Windows v2 does not provide a standalone value for the skeleton position. In this case it is practical to take the hip joint position instead. The skeleton position of the current frame can be considered as the user position, with the direction being calculated over the last five frames, by defining the sum of the vectors between the different positions of the user. Due to noise, the direction vector length has to be over a specific threshold of 0.065 m, otherwise the direction vector is a zero vector.

After extracting the information about the user and the obstacles, our algorithm performs intersection tests between the user ray and all obstacle bounding boxes. At the same time only obstacles that fulfill the following constraints are taken into account:

1. The obstacle height is smaller than the specific height threshold of 0.5 m.
2. The obstacle is not already marked as dangerous.
3. The obstacle is not set to the ignore list by the user.
4. The obstacle is not far away from the user.

To avoid the notification of obstacles, that are far away from the user, an intersection test with a circle with a radius of one meter is performed. The circle represents the purview of the user.

The static setup of this approach is a significant difference to the approaches that were mentioned in Sect. 2 that are all related to robotics. The sensor device is moving through the environment and has to find key points, in order to create detailed maps with environment information from different viewpoints of the sensor. In our approach the view can't change, as the Microsoft Kinect is mounted to a wall, or the view is changing just a little bit by accident, when it is placed on furniture or on a tripod. Accordingly, we can directly convert the depth image to a map. For finding dangerous objects, it is necessary to track the user position in the room and not the sensor position. Both algorithms can be performed separately, with the result of both being merged. This requires intersection tests between user direction, user range, and object bounding boxes.

The bottleneck of this algorithm is the floor plane detection, as the RANSAC algorithm to find planes in a point cloud is very slow. This value, however, is not a significant problem, because it is not necessary to analyze 30 frames per seconds, as changes in the environment typically occur at a lower frequency. In our case, we analyze one frame per second.

Another problem with the floor plane detection is that we do not have access to the inclination values of the sensor with the Microsoft Kinect for Windows v2. Previous versions provided access to an internal accelerometer, which would have allowed for easier determination of angles. Thus we have to manually determine the setup, as displayed in Fig. 1. If most of the floor is not visible, the coefficients are not calculated properly. This causes a misplaced floor plane, leading to some obstacles not being detected or a higher rate of false positives.

4 Evaluation

The crucial information we want to get from the evaluation is, how well the results of both services are with the in Sect. 3 described setup. We utilize the same setup for both evaluations, but evaluate them separately. The following subsections describe the performed evaluation and gives an explanation of the results.

4.1 Fall Detection Service

We evaluate both services in our living lab. For the fall detection, ten users (8m, 2f) were walking in the test area and were asked to fall down at four different locations:

1. Directly in the front of the camera. The user has a distance of around two meters, described by Microsoft as the ideal detection area of the Kinect [20,23].
2. The border area of the Microsoft Kinect field of view. The user walks from the background to the assigned spot.
3. In a distance of approximately four meters.
4. The same area as point 2, but the user enters the Microsoft Kinect view field of from the side.

In order to prevent injuries, a fall mat was used that dampened the shocks. It can be seen in Fig. 3. The events generated by the fall detection service were monitored. All described cases are highlighted in Fig. 2 and the results separated by the places are displayed in Table 2. The highlighted areas in magenta in Fig. 2

Fig. 2. Different test areas during the evaluation. The areas in magenta are not part of the depth image. (Color figure online)

Table 1. Short summary of the evaluation results.

Count	Skeletons	Detected falls	False positives
40	27	27	9

Table 2. Details of the results in the different tested areas.

Area	Count	Skeletons		Falls	
		Tracked	Not tracked	Detected	Not detected
1	10	7	3	7	3
2	10	5	5	5	5
3	10	9	1	9	1
4	10	6	4	6	4

display the parts of the color image that are not part of the depth image and can't be observed by the skeleton tracker.

In Table 1 we can see that the fall detection with another Microsoft Kinect setup can have a very good detection rate as well. Our implementation misses a fall only when the Microsoft Kinect does not track the skeleton. During the evaluation there were nine false positives triggered, from an overall count of 40 samples.

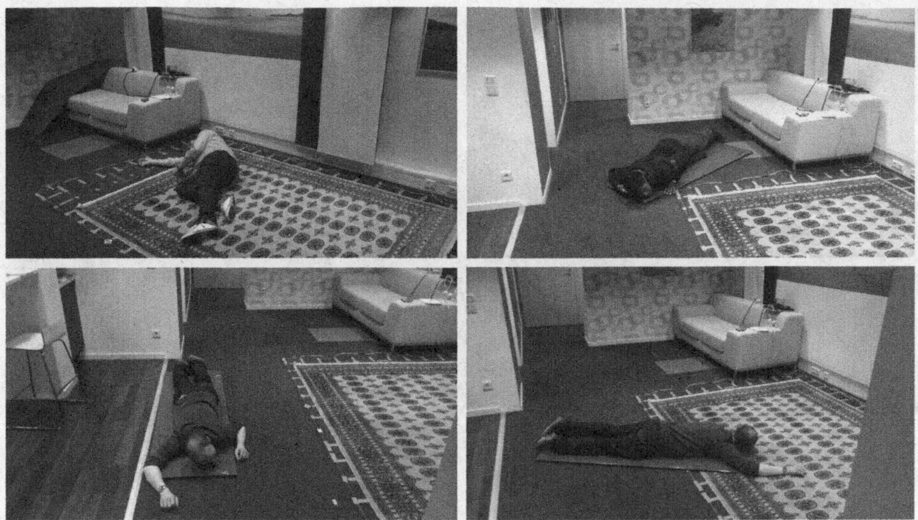

Fig. 3. The performed test cases from different test candidates

4.2 Dangerous Object Adviser Service

For the evaluation we place six different objects - specified in Table 3 - in the environment. Afterwards we check ten recorded frames of the Microsoft Kinect, if the objects are detected, and how many false positives occur in the recordings. We repeat these steps four times with different object locations. At the end we want to get the following information:

1. How many possible dangerous objects are detected?
2. How many false positives are detected in the environment?
3. Which dimensions has the smallest detectable object?

Table 3. The objects used in the evaluation.

Object	Dangerous	Dimension		
		Width	Height	Depth
Bag	Yes	0.44 m	0.28 m	0.33 m
Box	Yes	0.40 m	0.13 m	0.28 m
Small table	Yes	0.40 m	0.45 m	0.30 m
Wooden beam	Yes	1.00 m	0.06 m	0.06 m
Stack of journals	Yes	0.27 m	0.06 m	0.21 m
Bar stool	No	0.36 m	0.65 m	0.40 m

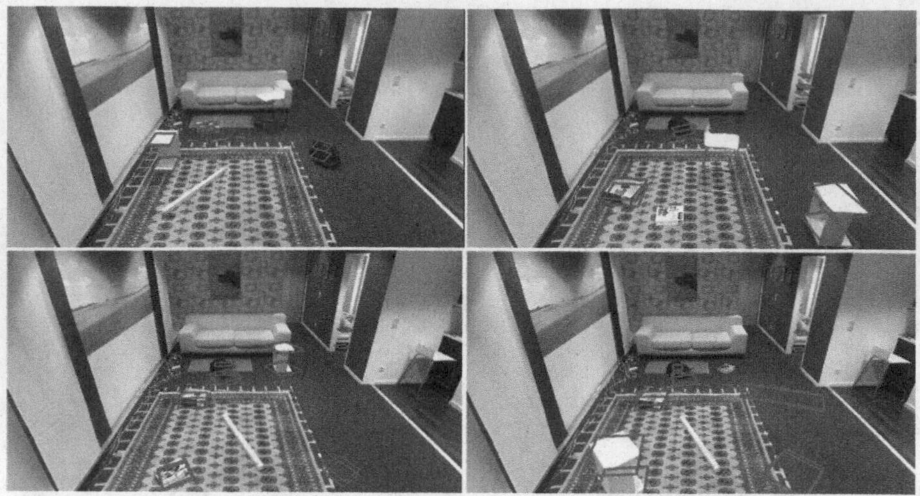

Fig. 4. Different scenes of a room with highlighted dangerous obstacles (Color figure online)

Table 4. Summary of the evaluation results

Object	Detected	Missed
Bag	35	5
Box	40	0
Small table	40	0
Wooden beam	0	40
Stack of journals	20	20
Bar stool	0	40
False positives	10	-
Other objects	40	-

The results listed in Table 4 shows that relatively large objects (e.g. the small table or the box) are detected robustly over all checked frames. The black bag is more challenging due to its color. The Microsoft Kinect has some problems measure the depth on black surfaces. In some frames the bag is divided into many small objects. Figure 4 shows the different recorded scenes with the detected dangerous obstacles. The biggest problem is that the system can't detect thin obstacles (e.g. umbrellas), represented in the scene by the wooden beam, because the Microsoft Kinect depth image is too noisy. We apply different filters to avoid too many false positives, but this removes thin objects from the map as well.

Depending on the filter parameters, the algorithm can detect fewer false positives (around 2 per frame), but in turn will not able to detect smaller obstacles anymore. In our evaluation setup the smallest detected object was the stack of journals with a dimension of 27 cm × 6 cm × 21 cm (width × height × depth), if it is near the camera. In a distance of four meters or more, the detection was not stable. The fine tuning depends on the composition of the environment. Sunlight, surfaces that absorb infrared light and a rough floor plane (e.g. carpet) can lead to noise in the depth image and, therefore, needs different parameter values.

The filter parameters are necessary to find relatively small obstacles. The algorithm can detect average dangerous obstacles like bags and small boxes over multiple frames. These obstacles can have a higher distance to the sensor as well. Objects like the bar stool are not detected, because they are not dangerous, due to their height. Our algorithm detected another dangerous object in the background. It was not part of the evaluation, but it is a bed in the neighbor room. Its height of 0.40 m it is a correctly detected dangerous object.

5 Discussion

The evaluation of both services shows the challenges that occur on trying to realize fall detection and obstacle detection in semi-realistic settings. While the system was able to track the majority of falls, the rate of 67.5% is not robust enough to install such a system in actual homes. The current algorithm based on the skeleton tracking largely relies on the availability of those skeletons, which was not often given in the evaluation scenario. The evaluation scenario is even a rather easy one for a Kinect, with a fairly open space and no large furniture, where detection is best. This will not be the case for many real-life applications, where common camera-positions, such as the TV will have lower viewing angles, or furniture in the best detection area. This could be observed in installations of the previously mentioned research project.

The performance of the DOA was reasonably well for the objects tested. Due to the sensor noise, somewhat flat objects at a larger distance are difficult to track and may be of particular interest, as they are more difficult to spot, yet may cause a fall. Currently, there is a strong technical limitation of the Kinect and the objects it may detect at further distances. Future systems may be able provide a better sensing resolution in the depth range to also detect those options.

Finally, we have to conclude that the real-life applicability for safety services in smart environments that are based on single-depth-camera installations per room are too limited at this point in time. Occlusion is a major factor, preventing a robust service in many situations. While this can be avoided by switching the location of the sensor (e.g. placed on the ceiling), or installing more sensors, there are currently technical limitations for those alternatives. The systems need high processing power, close to the sensor, which is difficult to accomplish for ceiling installations. In addition, multiple sensors per room are expensive and need additional processing power, more complex algorithms to correlate sensor data, and a more sophisticated installation.

6 Future Work

The biggest challenge of using computer vision, or skeleton tracking based approaches for the fall detection is occlusion in the environment. If the user falls behind an object (e.g. an armchair) the system can't detect this, because the cameras can't record enough information and the Kinect loses the tracked skeleton. A future approach should handle such problems in the environment.

The other problem, that we mentioned before, is the tracking distance of the Kinect. The skeleton can't be detected anymore in a distance more than four meters away from the device. The problem of the user tracking also affects the performance of the Dangerous Object adviser.

The proposed algorithm for finding obstacles in the environment is quite fast, but with a better plane segmentation algorithm the performance can be improved.

As mentioned in Sect. 3 the utilization of an accelerometer could be very useful to improve the algorithm. Due to the lack of access to the accelerometer of the Microsoft Kinect Device, it could be useful to attach an external accelerometer to the device.

In the future, we would also like to create a similar system with ceiling mounted sensors that have a larger field-of-view, which should significantly reduce any occlusion and provide room-scale services with a single sensor.

References

1. Su, B.Y., Ho, K.C., Rantz, M.J., Skubic, M.: Doppler radar fall activity detection using the wavelet transform. IEEE Trans. Biomed. Eng. **62**(3), 865–875 (2015)
2. Prediger, M., Braun, A., Marinc, A., Kuijper, A.: Robot-supported pointing interaction for intelligent environments. In: Streitz, N., Markopoulos, P. (eds.) DAPI 2014. LNCS, vol. 8530, pp. 172–183. Springer, Cham (2014). doi:10.1007/978-3-319-07788-8_17
3. Kepski, M., Kwolek, B.: Human fall detection using kinect sensor. In: Burduk, R., Jackowski, K., Kurzynski, M., Wozniak, M., Zolnierek, A. (eds.) CORES 2013. AISC, vol. 226, pp. 743–752. Springer, Heidelberg (2013). doi:10.1007/978-3-319-00969-8_73
4. Hanke, S., Sandner, E., Stainer-Hochgatterer, A., Tsiourti, C., Braun, A.: The technical specification and architecture of a virtual support partner. In: AmI (Workshops/Posters) (2015)
5. Chen, J., Kwong, K., Chang, D., Luk, J., Bajcsy, R.: Wearable sensors for reliable fall detection. In: 2005 IEEE Engineering in Medicine and Biology 27th Annual Conference, pp. 3551–3554, January 2005
6. Kawatsu, C., Li, J., Chung, C.J.: Development of a fall detection system with microsoft kinect. In: Kim, J.-H., Matson, E.T., Myung, H., Xu, P. (eds.) Robot Intelligence Technology and Applications 2012. AISC, vol. 208, pp. 623–630. Springer, Heidelberg (2013). doi:10.1007/978-3-642-37374-9_59
7. Alwan, M., Rajendran, P.J., Kell, S., Mack, D., Dalal, S., Wolfe, M., Felder, R.: A smart and passive floor-vibration based fall detector for elderly. In: 2006 2nd International Conference on Information Communication Technologies, vol. 1, pp. 1003–1007 (2006)

8. Braun, A., Heggen, H., Wichert, R.: CapFloor – a flexible capacitive indoor localization system. In: Chessa, S., Knauth, S. (eds.) EvAAL 2011. CCIS, vol. 309, pp. 26–35. Springer, Heidelberg (2012). doi:10.1007/978-3-642-33533-4_3
9. Braun, A., Wichert, R., Kuijper, A., Fellner, D.W.: Capacitive proximity sensing in smart environments. J. Ambient Intell. Smart Environ. **7**(4), 483–510 (2015)
10. Kirchbuchner, F., Grosse-Puppendahl, T., Hastall, M.R., Distler, M., Kuijper, A.: Ambient intelligence from senior citizens' perspectives: understanding privacy concerns, technology acceptance, and expectations. In: Ruyter, B., Kameas, A., Chatzimisios, P., Mavrommati, I. (eds.) AmI 2015. LNCS, vol. 9425, pp. 48–59. Springer, Cham (2015). doi:10.1007/978-3-319-26005-1_4
11. Rougier, C., Meunier, J.: Demo: fall detection using 3D head trajectory extracted from a single camera video sequence. J. Telemedicine Telecare **11**(4), 37–42 (2005)
12. Gasparrini, S., Cippitelli, E., Spinsante, S., Gambi, E.: A depth-based fall detection system using a kinect® sensor. Sensors **14**(2), 2756 (2014)
13. Hamm, J., Money, A.G., Atwal, A., Paraskevopoulos, I.: Fall prevention intervention technologies: a conceptual framework and survey of the state of the art. J. Biomed. Inform. **59**, 319–345 (2016)
14. Lu, F., Milios, E.: Globally consistent range scan alignment for environment mapping. Auton. Robot. **4**(4), 333–349 (1997)
15. Henry, P., Krainin, M., Herbst, E., Ren, X., Fox, D.: RGB-D mapping: using kinect-style depth cameras for dense 3D modeling of indoor environments. Int. J. Rob. Res. **31**(5), 647–663 (2012)
16. Microsoft Corporation: Kinect for windows SDK - kinect fusion, May 2016
17. Dissanayake, M.W.M.G., Newman, P., Clark, S., Durrant-Whyte, H.F., Csorba, M.: A solution to the simultaneous localization and map building (slam) problem. IEEE Trans. Robot. Autom. **17**(3), 229–241 (2001)
18. Shotton, J., Sharp, T., Kipman, A., Fitzgibbon, A., Finocchio, M., Blake, A., Cook, M., Moore, R.: Real-time human pose recognition in parts from single depth images. Commun. ACM **56**(1), 116–124 (2013)
19. Fryar, C.D., Qiuping, G., Ogden, C.L.: Anthropometric reference data for children and adults: United States, 2007–2010. Vital and Health Stat. Ser. 11, Data Natl. Health Surv. **252**, 1–48 (2012)
20. Microsoft Corporation: Kinect for windows SDK v1.8 - skeletal tracking, May 2016
21. Rusu, R.B., Cousins, S.: 3D is here: point cloud library (PCL). In: IEEE International Conference on Robotics and Automation (ICRA), Shanghai, China, 9–13 May 2011
22. Microsoft Corporation: Kinect for windows SDK - kinect API overview, May 2016
23. Microsoft Corporation: Kinect for windows SDK - features, May 2016

Contextual Requirements Prioritization and Its Application to Smart Homes

Estefanía Serral[1(✉)], Paolo Sernani[2], Aldo Franco Dragoni[2], and Fabiano Dalpiaz[3]

[1] KU Leuven, Leuven, Belgium
estefania.serralasensio@kuleuven.be
[2] Università Politecnica delle Marche, Ancona, Italy
{p.sernani,a.f.dragoni}@univpm.it
[3] Utrecht University, Utrecht, The Netherlands
f.dalpiaz@uu.nl

Abstract. When many requirements co-exist for a given system, prioritization is essential to determine which ones have higher priority. While the basic prioritization algorithms result in a total or partial order of the requirements, it is often the case that the priority of the requirements depends on the context at hand. This is especially true in ambient intelligence systems such as smart homes, which operate in an inherently dynamic environment that may affect the priority of the requirements at runtime. For example, depending on the health status of a smart home inhabitant, safety may become more important than comfort or cost-saving. In this paper, we make three contributions: (i) we introduce a novel method for the contextual prioritization of requirements, (ii) we propose an online platform for prioritizing the requirements for a smart home based on our method, and (iii) we report on results from an initial evaluation of the platform and the prioritization method.

1 Introduction

Requirements prioritization helps to identify which requirements in a given set are the most important for a system and its stakeholders [4]. Prioritization is typically conducted during the design or evolution of a system to distinguish between critical and optional requirements.

The basic prioritization algorithms return a total or partial order of the requirements in the set; this occurs, for instance, with popular techniques such as the MoSCoW method (which distinguishes between must have, should have, could have, won't have) [7] or the Analytic Hierarchy Process (AHP) [17].

For some systems, however, the priority of the requirements changes at runtime depending on the context at hand. This is true for context-aware [3] and self-adaptive systems [14], which adjust their behavior to the ever changing environment wherein they operate. A major trigger for such adaptation is that changes in the environment affect the relative importance of the non-functional requirements (NFRs) [5], or qualities, of the system.

A. Braun et al. (Eds.): AmI 2017, LNCS 10217, pp. 94–109, 2017.
DOI: 10.1007/978-3-319-56997-0_7

Ambient Intelligence systems and smart homes are a prominent example of systems that necessitate dynamic priority of NFRs and that can adapt their behavior based on the varying priorities. For example, if the health of a smart home inhabitant worsens, *safety* may become more important than *comfort* or *cost-saving*, and the home's behavior may switch to one where all monitoring devices are operational and the home becomes more intrusive by explicitly asking the inhabitant to provide information about her condition.

Existing work [8] proposes an approach for adaptive smart homes that relies on user- and context-specific priorities over NFRs. There, the smart home behavior is driven by an adaptive task model, which customizes the plans that the home carries out depending on the context and on user preferences. However, such approach provides no specific technique for eliciting those priorities.

In this paper, we address such limitations by proposing a novel elicitation technique for contextual priorities over NFR—that builds on and extends AHP—and by applying it to the smart homes domain. Specifically, we make three concrete contributions beyond the state-of-the-art:

- A method for the contextual prioritization of non-functional requirements that is intended for use by layman people with no expertise in prioritization.
- An online platform that supports the prioritization method for the context of smart homes. One key novelty of the platform is that it acts as a virtual proxy for the interaction between the analyst and the users.
- A preliminary evaluation of our platform with 25 users who employed the platform and judged how well the obtained adaptive smart home behavior complies with their preferences.

The rest of the paper is organized as follows. Section 2 discusses related work. The following sections describe our contributions: the contextual prioritization method (Sect. 3), the online platform (Sect. 4), and the evaluation results (Sect. 5). We conclude the paper and outline future work in Sect. 6.

2 Related Works

We review two strands of research that are relevant to the objectives of this paper: requirements prioritization and requirements elicitation in smart homes.

Requirements prioritization is defined the selection of the "right" requirements out of a given superset of candidate requirements so that all the different preferences of the end-users are fulfilled and the overall value of the system is maximized [16]. The purpose of any requirements prioritization technique is to assign values to distinct requirements that allow establishment of a relative order between them. To reduce costs, it is important to find the optimal set of requirements early, and then to develop the system according to this set.

There is a number of software requirements prioritization techniques [4], all of them with pros and cons. The 100-dollar test [13] requires to distribute 100 imaginary units (called dollars) among the individual requirements from the set: the more the dollars, the more important the requirement. Numerical assignment or grouping [11] requires to assign different labels to individual requirements that determine their priority groups (e.g., must have, should have, could have, won't have as in the MoSCoW method [7]). Ranking [4] requires the analyst to produce an ordinal scale of the requirements without ties in rank. The top-ten requirements approach [12] is useful when the wishes of multiple stakeholders are to be considered: each of them is required to list the ten requirements having the highest priority, and the results are then merged.

In our case, we have selected Analytic Hierarchy Process (AHP) [17], a systematic method that compares all possible pairs of hierarchically classified requirements in order to determine which has higher priority. The result is a weighted list on a ratio scale. AHP is one of the most complex methods but also provides fine granularity in the results and according to a recent survey [1], it is the most widely used technique. Moreover, it fits well our needs as our set of requirements is small (at most four requirements, as explained in Sect. 3).

As explained in Berander's survey [4], priorities should be determined by taking multiple aspects into account, including the importance of having the requirement (e.g., urgency or value), the penalty for not fulfilling the requirement [19], implementation cost, time, risk, and volatility. In this paper, we focus on the importance for the user, for we are interested in user-specific priorities.

Although many studies have been performed to study requirements prioritization in software engineering, the large majority of them only consider functional requirements since the prioritization process of NFR is harder [15]. Yet, NFRs are essential in AmI environments, for AmI systems are required to be sensitive to the needs of their inhabitants, anticipating their needs and behavior [18], and a viable way to do so is to use NFRs to guide adaptive behavior [8]. As far as our knowledge goes, no other work has proposed methods for prioritizing NFRs for smart homes or has considered contextual factors to adjust priorities.

In order to collect system requirements from end-users, many different techniques exist [21], such us interviews, task or domain analysis, focus groups, etc. Most of these methods require face-to-face communication, which has many benefits such as the ability to capture nuances in user requirements, but also several drawbacks. These techniques are time consuming, stakeholders are often incapable of expressing what they actually need (the say-do problem), and the interactions with software engineers may limit the exchange of information due to the influence of the engineer on the end user.

Other more advanced techniques can be used such as observation, monitoring or prototyping using living lab environments. An example is the Smart House Living Lab, which is fully equipped with the usual services of a conventional house where sensors and actuators are distributed in the living lab to offer a wide range of services [6]. However, living labs must be very flexible to offer all possible alternatives, and the development of environmental prototypes confronts many challenges such as cost-intensive and time-consuming experiments [2].

Finally, other alternatives have been proposed specifically to avoid these issues. For instance, Allameh et al. [2] propose the use of virtual environments to adjust the building design of a smart home according to users' preferences.

Their main outcomes are the possibility to use their approach for clustering target groups, the identification of living patterns, and the detection of spacial patterns. Unlike ours, their approach focuses mostly on functional aspects and does not explicitly consider the prioritization of NFRs.

3 A Method for Contextual Requirements Prioritization

We present our contextual prioritization technique, which can be used in the context of personalized systems that are able to customize their behavior to the preferences of the different users and contexts. A high-level illustration of the method is presented in Fig. 1 using the BPMN 2.0 notation.

The main goal of the technique is to obtain a contextual prioritization of non-functional requirements (NFRs); in other words, the priority of a NFR is not absolute but it depends on the context under consideration. Prior to system use, each user is expected to repeat the prioritization steps in order for the system to adapt to the individual preferences.

Three actors are involved: the *Designer* who prepares the environment for the prioritization activity, the *User* who expresses her preferences, and the *Platform* that algorithmically automates part of the process. The steps of our technique are described in the following and they are illustrated in Sect. 4.

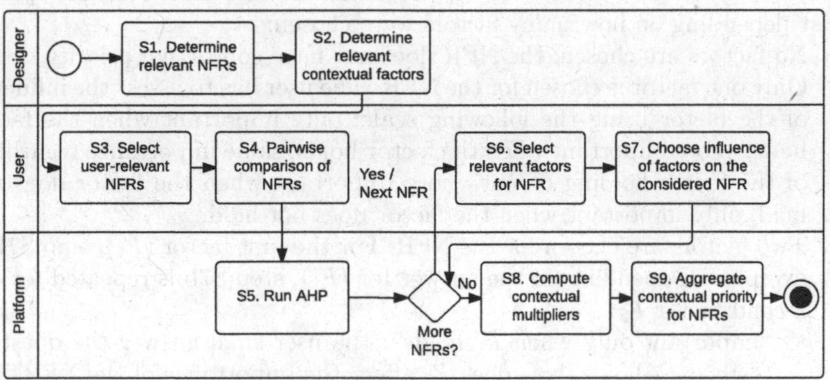

Fig. 1. Overview of the proposed contextual prioritization technique.

S1. Determine relevant NFRs. The designer of the system to-be determines the non-functional requirements (NFRs) to prioritize. We suggest to limit the number of NFRs to (at most) 4 to keep the process manageable, i.e., to minimize the required effort by the user.

S2. Determine relevant contextual factors. The designer identifies the contextual factors that may affect the NFRs' priority. For each factor, two descriptions are needed that denote when the factor holds and does not hold, respectively (e.g., "when it is hot weather" vs. "when it is cold weather").

S3. Select user-relevant NFRs. The user selects a sub-set of the NFRs to express which are the NFRs that she cares about. Not selecting a NFR corresponds to saying "I do not care at all about that NFR".

S4. Pairwise comparison of NFRs. The first prioritization activity employs classic AHP [17] and requires the user to perform a pairwise comparison of the NFRs to indicate their relative importance. To simplify the process, we use a simplified scale with 5 options to compare two NFRs: much less, little less, equally, little more, much more.

S5. Run AHP. Behind the scenes, the inputs of the pairwise comparison feed the AHP algorithms that returns the non-contextual relative importance of the NFRs. Together, the NFR importances sum up to 100%. We suggest to use the transitive calibration of the AHP verbal scale [9] to build the AHP matrix and compute a non-contextual relative importance of each NFR. A geometric progression is employed to calculate the priorities of the NFRs: the elements a_{ij} of the AHP matrix are equal to 1.0 when NFR_i and NFR_j have the same importance, 1.25 when the NFR_i is little more important than NFR_j and 2.441 when NFR_i is much more important than NFR_j.

S6. Select relevant factors for NFR. This step and the following one are repeated for each NFR that the user has not excluded. First, the user selects which factors affect the importance of the NFR. For simplicity, we limit the number of selectable factors to two.

S7. Choose influence of factors on the considered NFR. Multiple options exist depending on how many factors were chosen:

a. No factors are chosen: the NFR does not have contextual priority.
b. Only one factor is chosen for the NFR. The user has to assess the influence of the factor using the following scale: only important when the factor holds, more important when the factor holds, same importance regardless of the factor holding or not, more important when the factor does not hold, only important when the factor does not hold.
c. Two factors are chosen for the NFR. For the first factor (F_1), step S7b is executed. Depending on the answer for (F_1), step S7b is repeated for the second factor F_2:
   - "important only when F_1 holds": the user shall answer the question "when F_1 holds, how does F_2 affect the importance of the NFR?";
   - "important only when F_1 does not hold": the user shall answer the question "when F_1 does not hold, how does F_2 affect the importance of the NFR?";
   - "more/less important only when F_1 holds": the user shall answer two questions i. "when F_1 holds, how does F_2 affect the importance of the NFR?", and ii. "when F_1 does not hold, how does F_2 affect the importance of the NFR?";
   - "same importance regardless of the factor holding or not", step S7b is executed on F_2.

S8. Compute contextual multipliers. The platform automatically computes the effect of the contexts on the NFRs. For each NFR, the contextual multipliers are determined as follows:

- If "only if F" is selected, the multiplier holds corresponds to 1 when F holds and to 0 when F does not hold; formally, $M_F = 1.0$ and $M_{\neg F} = 0.0$;
- If "more if F" is chosen, $M_F = 0.\overline{6}$ and $M_{\neg F} = 0.\overline{3}$;
- For the "more if $\neg F$" option, $M_F = 0.\overline{3}$ and $M_{\neg F} = 0.\overline{6}$;
- For the "only if $\neg F$" option, $M_F = 0.0$ and $M_{\neg F} = 1.0$;
- If "equally" is chosen, the factor F is discarded: the user has actually stated that the factor has no contextual effect on the considered NFR.

When two factors are selected the contextual multipliers are the product of the multipliers of the individual factors for each combination of the factors holding or not. The syntax $M_{F_2|F_1}$ denotes the multiplier for F_2 which is selected in the context where F_1 holds (this is the answer to the questions of type "when F_1 holds..." in S7c); it corresponds to 0 when $M_{F_1} = 0$:

$$\begin{aligned} M_{F_1 \wedge F_2} &= M_{F_1} \cdot M_{F_2|F_1} \\ M_{F_1 \wedge \neg F_2} &= M_{F_1} \cdot M_{\neg F_2|F_1} \\ M_{\neg F_1 \wedge F_2} &= M_{\neg F_1} \cdot M_{F_2|\neg F_1} \\ M_{\neg F_1 \wedge \neg F_2} &= M_{\neg F_1} \cdot M_{\neg F_2|\neg F_1} \end{aligned}$$

S9. Aggregate contextual priority for NFRs. For each NFR, the contextual multipliers are applied to the non-contextual priority of the NFR x (P_x) from the AHP comparison as follows. First the platform finds the context y (boolean combinations of F_1 and F_2) having the highest multiplier M_{max}. Then, for each context y, the following equation results in the contextual priority value $CP_{x,y}$ for the NFR x in the context y:

$$P_x : M_{max} = CP_{x,y} : M_y \tag{1}$$

4 A Platform for Collecting Contextual User Preferences over Smart Home NFRs

Our aim is to apply the prioritization technique from Sect. 3 to regulate the behavior of a smart home according to its users' preferences. To do so, we developed a web platform that is used to conduct and to validate our method. Besides enacting the nine steps of our method (see Sect. 4.1), the platform collects metrics concerning how well the adaptive behavior of the smart home—guided by the contextual preferences—meets the users' expectations (see Sect. 4.2). Furthermore, the platform measures the users' perceived usability as well as information about users' demographics, education, and technical background.

4.1 Enacting the Contextual Prioritization Method

We created an online platform[1] that is structured as a questionnaire. The home page presents to the user the purpose of the questionnaire, i.e., "collecting users'

[1] https://goo.gl/ir65zM.

preferences concerning the behavior of their future smart home". The choice of using a website is made to maximize the ease of use and is enabled by the automated nature of the method described in Sect. 3. Should the target audience include people with little experience with computing, a human analyst can guide the users through the platform.

When the user begins the questionnaire, she is asked to select one to three aspects which she considers relevant. Such aspects are NFRs that are used to tune the smart home's behavior. We acted as designers (**S1** of our method), and chose three NFRs for the user to choose among, to avoid overwhelming her with too many questions:

- *Comfort*, representing the users' willingness to conduct tasks with minimal effort, and live in a comfortable environment (e.g., "I want my house to be always at the right temperature");
- *Efficiency*, representing the users' willingness to get things done quickly (e.g., "I want to skip breakfast if I have less time in the morning, and I want to take the fastest transport to go to work");
- *Utilities bill saving*, representing the users' willingness to pay lower utility bills (e.g., "I prefer to minimize the use of heating and air conditioning").

Table 1. The contextual factors supported by our platform.

Factor	Form 1 (factor holds)	Form 2 (factor does not hold)
Urgent tasks	I am in a rush	I do not have urgent tasks
Time period	I am not busy, e.g. I am on vacation	I am busy, e.g. I am working
Wealth	Money is an issue	Money is not an issue
Weather	It is good weather	It is bad weather

We also identified four contextual factors that are relevant for smart homes (see Table 1) as per **S2**: urgent tasks, time period, wealth, weather. For each of them, we defined two opposite forms that distinguish whether the factor holds (form 1) or not (form 2). It goes without saying that more factors could be considered, and our selection should be seen as illustrative.

If the user selects more than one NFR from the list (**S3**), she is asked to carry out a pairwise comparison of the selected NFRs, to perform the AHP [17]. For each couple of the selected NFRs (**S4**), the user has to state whether *(a)* the two NFRs are equally important, *(b)* one NFR is little more important than the other, *(c)* one NFR is much more important than the other (Fig. 2). The output is then processed by the platform that determines the AHP priorities (**S5**). In the example in Fig. 2, the non-contextual priorities are as follows: efficiency = 0.43, comfort = 0.35, utilities bill saving = 0.22.

Then, the user is asked to answer the question "Which of these aspects may affect how important <NFR-name> is for you?" to determine the influence of

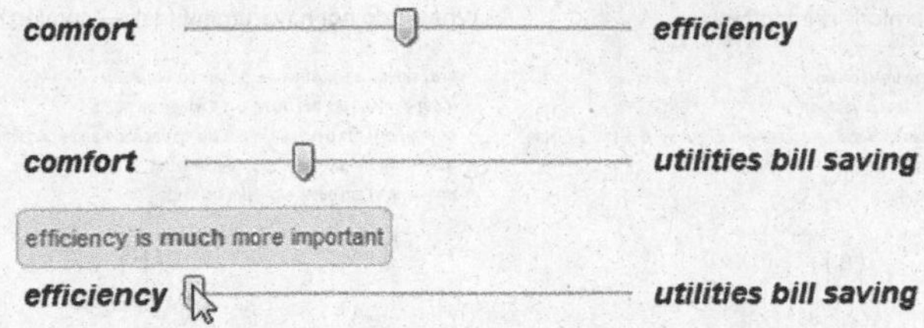

Fig. 2. The user pairwise compares the NFRs as part of the AHP process.

the context over the user's preferences. The user can select up to two factors (**S6**) for each NFR from the list shown in Table 1.

For each selected factor, the user is asked to state when it influences the NFR (see **S7** for the details): only when the factor holds (form 1 in Table 1), only when the factor does not hold (form 2), mostly when the factor holds/does not hold, or if the NFR has the same importance in both cases. Figure 3 shows an example related to the NFR "Comfort", when the user selected "Urgent tasks" as a contextual factor (**S7b**).

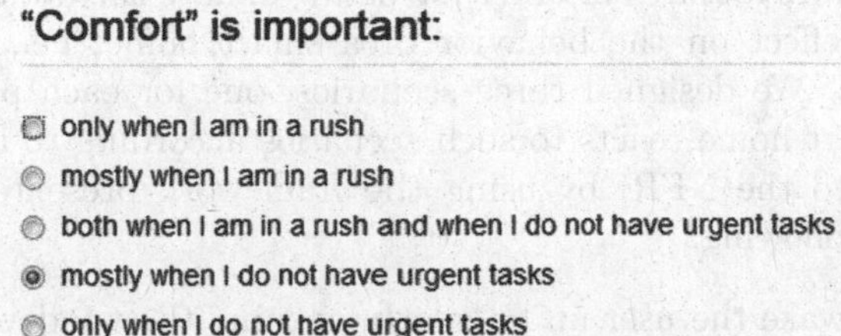

Fig. 3. Scoring how the factor "Urgent tasks" affects the NFR "Comfort".

Figure 4 shows an example assuming that a user selected both "Urgent tasks" and "Time period" as factors affecting "Comfort" (**S7c**). The user states that "Comfort" is important "mostly when I do not have urgent tasks". Consequently, the user is asked to rate how "Time period" affects "Comfort" when she is in a rush (Fig. 4a) as well as when she does not have urgent tasks (Fig. 4b). If the user had stated that "Comfort" is important "only when I do not have urgent task", the question of Fig. 4a would be omitted.

These choices determine the contextual multipliers (**S8**) for the various context. In Figs. 3 and 4, let F_1 be "urgent tasks" and F_2 be "time period". Figure 3 means "more if $\neg F_1$", while Fig. 4 indicates "more if $\neg F_2$" both when F_1 holds and when it does not hold. This leads to the following priorities:

- For context $F_1 \wedge F_2$, the multiplier is $0.\overline{3} \cdot 0.\overline{3} = 0.\overline{1}$
- For context $F_1 \wedge \neg F_2$, the multiplier is $0.\overline{3} \cdot 0.\overline{6} = 0.\overline{2}$
- For context $\neg F_1 \wedge F_2$, the multiplier is $0.\overline{6} \cdot 0.\overline{3} = 0.\overline{2}$
- For context $\neg F_1 \wedge \neg F_2$, the multiplier is $0.\overline{6} \cdot 0.\overline{6} = 0.\overline{4}$

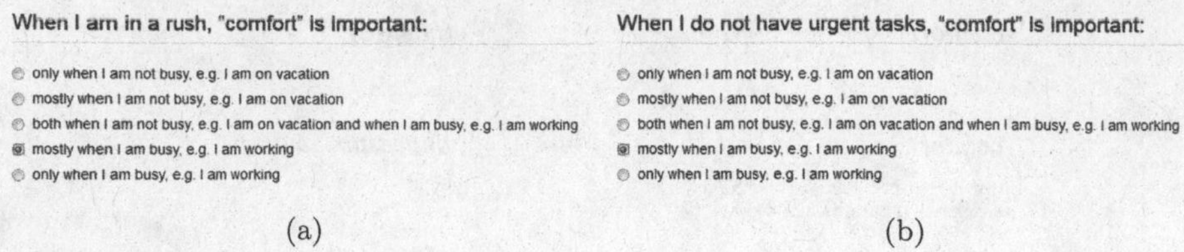

Fig. 4. Scoring how the factor "Time period" affects "Comfort", when the users selects that "Comfort" is important "mostly when I do not have urgent tasks".

The aggregated contextual priority is eventually defined by conducting step **S9**. In our example, the equation presented in Eq. 3 would lead to the following contextual priorities for the NFR "Comfort" (whose AHP priority is 0.35, as explained earlier in this section): 0.35 for context $\neg F_1 \wedge \neg F_2$, 0.17 for contexts $F_1 \wedge \neg F_2$ and $\neg F_1 \wedge F_2$, and 0.087 for context $F_1 \wedge F_2$.

4.2 Validating the Effect of the Priorities over Smart Home Behavior

The platform includes features in order for us to validate the obtained priorities by showing their effect on the behavior of a smart home, i.e., by activating different actuators. We designed three scenarios, one for each possible couple of NFRs. The smart home reacts to such scenarios according to the contextual priority assigned to the NFR, by using the framework presented in [8]. The scenarios are the following:

1. The home can wake the user up by gently opening the window blinds (comfort) or by activating the buzzer sound alarm (efficiency);
2. The home can refresh warm rooms by activating the air conditioning (comfort) or by opening the windows (utilities bill saving);
3. The home can activate the water heater (efficiency, as hot water is available more quickly) or employ the solar panel (utilities bill saving).

For example, in a context where comfort has higher priority than efficiency, the home will wake the user up by opening the window blinds instead of activating the buzzer sound alarm. For each scenario (thus, for each possible couple of NFRs), the platform shows two different contexts to the user: that where the first NFR has the maximum priority, and that where the second NFR has the maximum priority. The platform presents to the user the behaviors of the smart home in both cases, and the user is asked to express her agreement with such behavior on a Likert scale from 1 (strongly disagree) to 7 (strongly agree).

Besides the scenarios, the platform obtains further information on:

1. *perceived efficacy* of the platform for the user to express her preferences, via a 7-items Likert scale about agreement with the statement "The scenarios reflected the behavior I'd like for my smart home".

2. *usability* of the platform with the Usability Metric for User Experience (UMUX) [10] whose wording was customized for the platform as follows: *(a)* "The website enables me to express my preferences." *(b)* "Using this website is a frustrating experience." *(c)* "This website is easy to use." *(d)* "I have to spend too much time correcting things with this website."
3. *technical background* of the user. First, the user has to express her familiarity with Internet technologies (e.g., news websites and social networks), computer applications (e.g., word processors), and with programming languages via a Likert scale from 1 (not at all comfortable) to 5 (very comfortable). Then, the platform asks the user if she is working (or has worked) in the ICT sector. Finally, the platform asks the user if she is familiar with the "smart home" concept, by letting her select one of the following options: *(a)* "I never heard of smart homes" *(b)* "I heard the term, but I don't know what they are" *(c)* "I know what smart homes are" *(d)* "I am able to understand well how smart homes work (i.e. the technologies used)" *(e)* "I would be able to design/develop part of a smart home"
4. *demographics*, i.e., age, sex, country, and educational level.

5 Test Results

We report on a set of user tests concerning the perceived efficacy of our prioritization technique for the use case of a smart home, and the usability of the web platform that we developed. As described in Sect. 4, the web platform presents a questionnaire to the user; we discuss here the collected results concerning the obtained contextual priorities, the agreement with the proposed smart home scenarios, and the usability test.

Participants. The tests involved 25 users: 16 males and 9 females. The average age of the user is 31.96, with a standard deviation of 8.32 years. The users are from Belgium (11), Italy (6), and Spain (8). 11 users have a Ph.D. degree, 12 a master degree, 1 user has a bachelor degree and 1 user has a secondary school educational level. 20 users stated to have working experience in the ICT field: in particular, 9 of them stated to be able to develop components of smart homes.

Threats to Validity. The user tests that we performed to validate the prioritization should be considered preliminary due to the many threats to validity:

Conclusion. The small number of users does not allow to draw any statistically significant conclusion and has low statistical power. Also, due to the fact the participants are not native English speakers, the reliability of our measures (the questionnaires) may be limited. Although we tried our best to simplify the wording so to avoid misinterpretations, the threat is not nullified. Moreover, our choice to minimize the number of NFRs and factors to avoid overwhelming the users with too many questions (see internal validity) may affect the judgment of the users on the adequacy of the smart home behavior and on the ability of the platform to let them express their preferences.

Internal. The relevant internal threats categories for our tests are single group and social, according to Wohlin et al. [20]. Maturation threats are inevitable: while using the platform, some users may have kept motivated, while other may have been overwhelmed by the number of questions they were posed. To limit the effect of this threat, we limited the maximum number of selectable NFRs, contextual factors, and we employed simple questionnaires such as UMUX (that measures usability via four simple questions).

Construct. Design threats affect our tests: the link between NFRs and the adaptive behavior exhibited by the smart home was decided by the authors acting as designers. We did our best to choose scenarios that are clear illustrations of the prevalence of our NFR over another, but it is quite possible that the user's perception does not fully correspond to ours. Mono-operation bias also applies, given that we tested our contextual prioritization method only on specific behaviors of one smart home. To cope with hypothesis guessing, the home page of the website makes the context of our research clear.

External. The interaction of selection and treatment threat holds: we chose our subjects based on convenience sampling, and the obtained sample is certainly not representative for the whole population. While the sample group cannot be considered representative of current potential inhabitants of a smart home, the general increase in ICT skills of the human population makes the group more representative for the smart homes of the future. We need to repeat the tests with a larger and more representative audience to obtain more general results.

5.1 User Preferences and Validation of Scenarios

Concerning the distribution of the NFRs: 16 users selected comfort, 14 efficiency, and 17 utilities bill saving when asked to select the aspects relevant to them. In particular, 8 out of the 9 users who claim to able to develop smart home components selected comfort: according to smart home experts the comfort of the inhabitants is a key for a smart home to satisfy. On the contrary, most of the users who have just heard the term "smart home" (8 out of 11) selected Utilities bill saving: non-expert users seem to care more about the energy efficiency and the potential savings of living in an automated smart environment. This seems in line with having marginal knowledge on the fact that ambient assisted living goes beyond current trends in energy efficiency. Most users (14/25) have selected two NFRs, 7 have chosen only one NFR, and 4 have chosen all the three NFRs.

Table 2 highlights the selection of contextual factors per NFR. As expected, most of the users think that the factor wealth affects the importance of the NFR utilities bill saving: 14 out of the 17 users (82.4%) who selected such NFR. Urgent tasks is the most selected contextual factor for the NFR efficiency (78.6%): this is sensible, as a user would realistically prefer to do things quickly when she is in a rush. The most chosen factor for NFR comfort is time period: according to the users, the importance of comfort is mostly related to being in a working time period or on holiday (62.5%), although urgent tasks and wealth were also selected often (43.8%). Interestingly, weather was barely considered as an influencing

Table 2. Number (#) and percentage (%) of users selecting a factor per NFR.

	Comfort (n = 16)		Efficiency (n = 14)		Utilities bill saving (n = 17)	
	#	%	#	%	#	%
Urgent tasks	7	43.8	11	78.6	5	29.4
Time period	10	62.5	8	57.1	4	23.5
Wealth	7	43.8	4	28.6	14	82.4
Weather	2	12.5	0	0.0	2	12.5

factor, probably due to the fact that the users think of a smart home as a closed environment; we had included weather as a factor because the smart home described in [8] suggests a transportation means for reaching work.

Table 3 presents the average scores (on a Likert scale from 1 = strong disagreement to 7 = strong agreement) given by the users to the scenarios presented by the web platform. As explained in Sect. 4, the scenarios are computed by the platform to test whether the contextual priorities over NFRs lead to a behavior of the smart home that the users agree with. In each of the three scenarios, the home executes an action depending on the NFR with the highest priority. The results are weakly positive, with some scenarios being highly agreed upon and others obtaining neutral agreement ratings:

- The users give a score between weakly agreement and agreement (5.5) to opening the windows to refresh warm rooms (which happens when utilities bill saving is more important than comfort), while they are mostly neutral (4.22) on the converse scenario when comfort is more important and the smart home activates air conditioning;
- The users agree (6.11) with the scenario where the home employs solar panels to get hot water for the shower (this happens when the priority of utilities bill saving is higher than that of efficiency), while they are between neutral and weakly agreeing (4.57) on using the water heather when efficiency has higher priority;
- The users agree (6.22) that the home should wake them up by opening the blinds when comfort is preferred over efficiency; conversely, using the buzzer sound alarm in the same scenario is rated between weak disagreement and neutrality (3.9).

Note that most of the users selected utilities bill saving as an important factor, and we can notice higher agreement with scenarios where green and energy efficient actions are executed: opening the windows and using the solar panels.

Besides assessing the scenarios in isolation (as per Table 3), the users were asked to express their agreement with the following statement about the overall behavior of the smart home: *the scenarios reflected the behavior I'd like for my smart home*. The average score given by the users is 4.52 (standard deviation 1.45). This is inconsistent with the generally positive score assigned to the

Table 3. Average agreement of the users with the scenarios presented to them ($\overline{x}$), and standard deviation (σ).

Scenario		$\overline{x}$	σ
The home can refresh warm rooms by	Activating the air conditioning	4.22	1.62
	Opening the windows	5.50	1.71
To have hot water the home	Activates the water heater	4.57	1.59
	Employs the solar panel	6.11	1.45
The home wakes you up by	Activating the buzzer sound alarm	3.90	2.12
	Gently opening the window blinds	6.22	1.03

individual scenarios, and especially evident for the 5 users who state to know well smart home: they give an average score of 4 (neutrality, with a standard deviation of 0.89) to the statement, but they agreed with the three scenarios, with scores equal to 6 (std. dev. 0.82), 6.75 (std. dev. 0.43), and 5.6 (std. dev. 2.33). Our interpretation for such inconsistency is that, due to their expertise in developing smart homes, they may have expected the smart home to execute actions which are not covered by the current website.

5.2 Usability

Table 4 shows the average usability score for the platform using the Usability Metric for User Experience (UMUX) [10] framework. In a scale from 0 (lowest sense of usability) to 100 (highest sense of usability), our platform gets an average score of 66.50 (standard deviation 17.77). This indicates that usability is not particularly good, although we can notice quite some differences when analyzing sub-groups of the population based on their familiarity with smart homes. We discuss the results per group, although the findings should be taken with care due to the small sample size.

The 9 expert users (who state to be able to develop smart home components) are the most negative towards the web platform: the average UMUX score is 56.02 (standard deviation 17.58). 5 of such users agreed with the statement "Using this website is a frustrating experience", even if 3 of them agreed with the statement "This website is easy to use". A possible interpretation—that should

Table 4. The average UMUX score of the web platform ($\overline{x}$), with the standard deviation (σ).

Users	$\overline{x}$	σ
All (25)	66.50	17.77
Just heard the term "smart home" (11)	67.80	15.09
Know well smart homes (5)	82.50	8.08
Able to develop smart home components (9)	56.02	17.58

be confirmed with follow-up interviews—is that those experts are frustrated because the platform does not implement all the NFRs and smart home behaviors that they might expect. We chose to limit to three the number of NFRs and scenarios to avoid overwhelming users with too many choices, especially those who are not experienced with the field.

The 5 users who state to know well smart homes are the most positive towards the web platform: the average UMUX score is 82.5 and the standard deviation is 8.08 (the lowest). In fact, these are the users who agreed the most with the proposed scenarios and behaviors of the smart home.

The 11 users who have just heard the term "smart home" have an average UMUX score of 67.8 (standard deviation 15.09), quite similar to the total population.

6 Conclusions and Future Work

In this paper, we proposed an elicitation technique to compute contextual priorities over non-functional requirements (NFRs) according to end-users' preferences. The technique combines the need of personalized systems to respond to end-users' preferences with the goal of context-aware systems to adapt to the current context. In Ambient Intelligence, smart environments require both personalizations based on users' preferences and context-awareness. We applied our prioritization method to such domain, using three NFRs (*Comfort*, *Efficiency*, and *Utilities bill saving*) and four contextual factors (*Urgent tasks*, *Time period*, *Wealth*, and *Weather*) to regulate the behaviors of a smart home.

We developed a web platform, structured as a questionnaire, to carry out user tests with 25 participants. First, users were asked to indicate their preferences over the proposed NFRs and contextual factors. Afterwards, users were asked to validate the obtained prioritization: three scenarios (refreshing the home, heating water, and waking the user up) were shown presenting alternative behaviors of a smart home depending on the obtained priorities of the NFRs.

The results are encouraging for the use of our elicitation technique in the context of smart homes: in general, the users agreed with the proposed scenarios, based on the context they selected through the contextual factors, and on their preferences expressed by filtering the NFRs. Of course, the number of participants does not allow to draw any statistically significant conclusion, and large-scale replications are necessary to obtain more solid results as well as to assess the generality of the prioritization technique beyond smart homes.

The tests also show clear room for improvements: in fact, while the users agreed with the individual scenarios, they rated close to neutrally the statement "the scenarios reflected the behavior I'd like for my smart home". A possible explanation for this inconsistency is that the users—especially the more experienced ones with smart homes—would have expected some behaviors which are not included in the current implementation of the web platform.

An inherent trade-off exists for designers who aim to employ an automated platform for the collection of contextual requirements: that between ease-of-use and accuracy. Designers have to decide which and how many NFRs to let the user choose between, which contextual factors, and what scenarios. The challenge is to keep the prioritization simple enough that users do not feel overwhelmed, especially those with no experience in prioritization. Moreover, the platform could be improved by explicitly presenting the scenarios to the user before asking her to fill the questionnaire, so that she knows in advance the capabilities of the smart home and understands that the task at hand is to express preferences so that the smart home makes the "right" choice among existing alternatives.

At the end of the questionnaire, we also included an assessment of the users' perceived usability of the web platform. The average result (66.5) on the UMUX score (0 = lowest sense of usability, 100 = highest sense of usability) indicates a clear need for improvement. The average score is even lower (56.02) if we consider only the group of users who are smart home experts and able to use programming languages. Conversely, the users who stated they "know well smart homes" are rather positive about the user experience (82.5). While we chose a simple metric such as UMUX (four Likert-type questions) to avoid drop outs due to excessive complexity of the task, more in-depth qualitative studies are needed to assess what are the exact obstacles to usability.

We envisage that future work will engage two different research fields: Ambient Intelligence and Requirements Engineering. While the former community provides domain experience and can greatly benefit from contextual prioritization techniques that enable more dynamic and user-centric smart homes, further research in Requirements Engineering is necessary to build reliable algorithms. This paper paves the way for this interdisciplinary research collaboration.

References

1. Achimugu, P., Selamat, A., Ibrahim, R., Mahrin, M.N.: A systematic literature review of software requirements prioritization research. Inf. Soft. Technol. **56**(6), 568–585 (2014)
2. Allameh, E., Heidari Jozam, M., Vries, B., de Timmermans, H., Masoud, M.: Smart homes from vision to reality: eliciting users' preferences of smart homes by a virtual experimental method. In: The First International Conference on Civil and Building Engineering Informatics, pp. 297–305 (2013)
3. Baldauf, M., Dustdar, S., Rosenberg, F.: A survey on context-aware systems. Int. J. Ad Hoc Ubiquit. Comput. **2**(4), 263–277 (2007)
4. Berander, P., Andrews, A.: Requirements prioritization. In: Aurum, A., Wohlin, C. (eds.) Engineering and Managing Software Requirements, pp. 69–94. Springer, Heidelberg (2005). doi:10.1007/3-540-28244-0_4
5. Chung, L., Nixon, B.A., Yu, E., Mylopoulos, J.: Non-functional Requirements in Software Engineering, 1st edn. Springer, Heidelberg (1999)
6. Colomer, J.B.M., Salvi, D., Cabrera-Umpierrez, M.F., Arredondo, M.T., Abril, P., Jimenez-Mixco, V., García-Betances, R., Fioravanti, A., Pastorino, M., Cancela, J., Medrano, A.: Experience in evaluating AAL solutions in living labs. Sensors **14**(4), 7277–73111 (2014)
7. DSDM Consortium: DSDM public version 4.2 (2007). http://www.dsdm.org/version4/2/public

8. Dalpiaz, F., Serral, E., Valderas, P., Giorgini, P., Pelechano, V.: A NFR-based framework for user-centered adaptation. In: Atzeni, P., Cheung, D., Ram, S. (eds.) ER 2012. LNCS, vol. 7532, pp. 439–448. Springer, Heidelberg (2012). doi:10.1007/978-3-642-34002-4_34
9. Finan, J., Hurley, W.: Transitive calibration of the AHP verbal scale. Eur. J. Oper. Res. **112**(2), 367–372 (1999)
10. Finstad, K.: The usability metric for user experience. Interact. Comput. **22**(5), 323–327 (2010)
11. IEEE Computer Society: IEEE Recommended Practice for Software Requirements Specifications. IEEE Std 830–1993 (1994)
12. Lauesen, S.: Software Requirements: Styles and Techniques. Pearson Education, Upper Saddle River (2002)
13. Leffingwell, D., Widrig, D.: Managing Software Requirements: A Unified Approach. Addison-Wesley Professional, Boston (2000)
14. de Lemos, R., et al.: Software engineering for self-adaptive systems: a second research roadmap. In: de Lemos, R., Giese, H., Müller, H.A., Shaw, M. (eds.) Software Engineering for Self-Adaptive Systems II: International Seminar, Dagstuhl Castle, Germany, October 24–29, 2010 Revised Selected and Invited Papers. LNCS, vol. 7475, pp. 1–32. Springer, Heidelberg (2013). doi:10.1007/978-3-642-35813-5_1
15. Pergher, M., Rossi, B.: Requirements prioritization in software engineering: a systematic mapping study. In: 3rd International Workshop on Empirical Requirements Engineering (EmpiRE), pp. 40–44 (2013)
16. Ruhe, G., Eberlein, A., Pfahl, D.: Quantitative WinWin: a new method for decision support in requirements negotiation. In: Proceedings of the 14th International Conference on Software Engineering and Knowledge Engineering, SEKE 2002, pp. 159–166. ACM (2002)
17. Saaty, R.: The analytic hierarchy process–what it is and how it is used. Math. Model. **9**(3), 161–176 (1987)
18. Sadri, F.: Ambient intelligence: a survey. ACM Comput. Surv. **43**(4), 36:1–36:66 (2011)
19. Wiegers, K.E., Beatty, J.: Software Requirements, 3rd edn. Pearson Education, Upper Saddle River (2013)
20. Wohlin, C., Runeson, P., Höst, M., Ohlsson, M.C., Regnell, B., Wesslén, A.: Experimentation in Software Engineering. Springer, Heidelberg (2012)
21. Zowghi, D., Coulin, C.: Requirements elicitation: a survey of techniques, approaches, and tools. In: Aurum, A., Wohlin, C. (eds.) Engineering and Managing Software Requirements, pp. 19–46. Springer, Heidelberg (2005). doi:10.1007/3-540-28244-0_2

Voices and Views of Informal Caregivers: Investigating Ambient Assisted Living Technologies

Christina Jaschinski[1,2(✉)] and Somaya Ben Allouch[1]

[1] Saxion University of Applied Sciences, Enschede, Netherlands
{c.jaschinski,s.benallouch}@saxion.nl
[2] University of Twente, Enschede, Netherlands

Abstract. Ambient Assisted Living (AAL) technologies are on the rise in an attempt to ensure the sustainability of elderly care. Informal caregivers are an important stakeholder group for the successful adoption of AAL technologies. However, the number of studies that specifically address the attitudes, concerns and needs of this group is limited. With the aim to engage this underrepresented user group and to highlight their opinion and needs, we conducted in-depth interviews with 20 informal caregivers to evaluate different AAL solutions in the field of mobility and safety. While informal caregivers recognized the safety and mobility benefits and the increased peace of mind – privacy issues, the lack of human touch and an unfelt need for support formed major barriers towards adoption. Informal caregivers have an important influence on care decisions and should be closely involved when developing AAL tools.

Keywords: Ambient Assisted Living · Informal caregivers · Technology adoption · User needs

1 Introduction

Europe has one of the highest shares of older adults in the world. In 2013, already one out of five Europeans was 65 years or older and prognoses point to a further increase of this share for the next decades [1]. With population aging, it is expected that there will be more people with age-related chronic diseases and in need of long-term care. This together with the increasing old-age dependency ratio, forms a major risk for the sustainability of the current healthcare system.

1.1 Reliance on Informal Caregivers

Informal caregivers are crucial to the functioning of the care system as they are unpaid and usually the primary [2] and preferred [3] source of care. In the Netherlands, informal care is defined as "Long-term care that is provided beyond a caregiving profession to a person with care needs by one or more members from the close social environment, as such that care provision directly results from the social relationship" [4, p. 7]. According to a national study, 33% of the Dutch adult population has provided some form of

A. Braun et al. (Eds.): AmI 2017, LNCS 10217, pp. 110–123, 2017.
DOI: 10.1007/978-3-319-56997-0_8

informal care in 2014 [5]. Informal caregivers are typically female and spouses, children or children-in-law with a majority in the 45–65 age group [2, 6]. Tasks performed by informal caregivers include domestic support (e.g., groceries, prepare meals, cleaning); psychosocial support (e.g., administration, doctor visits, social activities, emotional support) and, usually to a lesser degree, personal care (e.g., bathing, dressing, feeding) and basic medical care (e.g., monitor medication intake, surgical dressing) [7].

In an attempt to cope with the increasing demand for health and social care and the accompanying financial pressure, the Netherlands recently implemented the new Social Support Act. One of the key aspects of the new Social Support Act is a stronger shift from intramural care to homecare and even more reliance on informal caregivers. However, changing family structures and a growing participation of women in the labor market put this reliance on informal caregivers at risks [1]. In addition, providing care to kin can be burdening and negatively affect the informal caregivers health and well-being [8, 9] - even more so when juggling care tasks next to a career and parenting responsibilities. Thus, while the demand for informal caregivers increases, it is expected that the number of informal caregivers declines over the next years [10].

1.2 Ambient Assisted Living (AAL)

According to the European Union, state-of-the-art information and communication technology (ICT) tools, introduced as Ambient Assisted Living (AAL) can be the answer to the economic and societal challenges of our aging population. AAL technologies are designed to facilitate healthy and active aging, thereby not only supporting the older adults but also their caregivers [11].

In AAL, advanced computational techniques (e.g., activity recognition, context modeling, location identification, planning and anomaly detection) and innovative technologies (e.g., smart homes, robotics, sensors) are used to create assistive tools that comply with the principles of Ambient Intelligence [12]. That is, assistive technologies that are unobtrusive; aware of the environment; tailored to the needs of the user; responsive to the user and the situational context; and anticipatory toward the user's needs [13]. Application domains of AAL technologies are broad as they aim to promote healthy and active aging in various contexts, i.e. at home, in the community and at work [11]. In this paper, we focus on AAL technologies for mobility and safety.

Mobility and safety are important aspects for shaping the older adult's level of independence and overall quality of life [14, 15]. With older age, problems in these areas increase. Common restrictions which affect the mobility include balance control, reduced perception of touch and vibration, reduced walking speed, gait disorders, strengths deficits and lower reaction time [16]. Those restrictions increase the likelihood of falls, which is one of the most prevalent safety risks for older adults. Safety and mobility are priority target areas of AAL technologies [11]. However, the success of these technologies is strongly dependent on the perceptions of the prospective users. Although the prospective users of AAL technologies are primarily older adults, most applications also directly affect the informal caregivers by relieving their tasks pressure or providing them with peace of mind. On the contrary, informal caregivers might also feel threatened by these technologies as they could take over some of their tasks and make them feel less needed. For the future success of AAL technologies, it is therefore crucial to consider the needs of the informal caregivers. This is also confirmed by Chen et al. [8], who call for more understanding of informal caregivers' physical, social and emotional needs when designing care technologies.

Adoption of AAL Technologies. Although research on AAL technologies is still a relatively new and emerging field, several researchers have explored user perceptions of AAL applications [e.g., 17–20]. For example, Demiris et al. [17] explored older adults' perceptions of various smart home applications. While added safety, health benefits and assistance with daily activities were perceived as predominant advantages of such technologies; concerns were expressed about privacy, the reduced human touch and the usability of the technology. Steel et al. [18] investigated older adults' attitude towards wireless sensor network technologies and suggested that independence was the strongest driver for acceptance, while cost was the most prevalent barrier. Interestingly, they also suggested that privacy might not be a major concern to older adults. Smarr et al. [20] found that older adults preferred robot assistance for domestic tasks such as chores, manipulating objects and information management while human assistance was preferred for personal care and leisure activities. However, most of these studies have a predominate focus on the attitudes and needs of older adults.

Informal caregivers play a vital role in the care of older adults and are therefore directly affected by the use of assistive technologies such as AAL systems. Moreover, research shows that they are closely involved in care-related decision making [21, 22]. Despite this close involvement, informal caregivers are either underrepresented or not included in most AAL studies. In the limited cases that informal caregivers are part of the user sample, data are often grouped together with the older adults' data, making it difficult to identify the perceptions belonging to the informal caregivers.

There are a few exceptions. In the Digital Family Portret Project [23] an ambient display was designed that provides awareness of older adults' daily activities with the aim to increase the peace of mind of distant family members. The design of the ambient display relied on the need analyses of both the older adults and their adult children and was evaluated with participants from both user groups in the subsequent field trials. The field trial showed that the Digital Family Portret indeed increased the peace of mind of the family member while increasing the older adult's feeling of safety. Moreover, the older adult reported to feel less lonely. A similar technology was introduced by Consolvo et al. [24]. The CareNet Display targets the different members of the care network with the aim to support and coordinate care activities. Through an ambient display information about the older adult's activities (e.g. meals, medication, visits) is displayed. The CareNet Display was tested among 4 older adults and 9 informal carers during a three week in-situ deployment. Results showed that the technology indeed supported the carers in the communication and coordination of care tasks, provided peace of mind and raised the general awareness of each carers' contribution. It also helped less involved carers to learn more about the older adults activities, which in turn lead to better conversations with the older adult. Ambience, usability and control were important design requirements resulting from the field trials. However, in both studies informal caregivers were also the primary users of the system.

Other AAL studies which actively involve informal caregivers are mainly centered around people with dementia [e.g., 25, 26]. In these studies, the informal caregiver is often considered as the main user or as the main decision maker and natural spokesperson for the care receivers' needs due to their cognitive impairment.

We argue that informal caregivers should be involved in acceptance studies, even when they are not the primary users and even when applications do not specifically target people with dementia. These informal caregivers will still be affected by the use of AAL technology and it is likely that they will be involved in the decision making process concerning the adoption decision. Looking at popular theories from behavioral sciences and the technology acceptance field, the need for including informal caregivers becomes even more apparent. Theory of Planned Behavior [27], Domestication Theory [28], as well as Diffusion of Innovation Theory [29] all stress the importance of the social environment in the process of adopting a new technology.

Therefore, this study highlights the perspective of the informal caregivers and investigates their attitudes, concerns and needs regarding AAL technologies for mobility and safety. As influential stakeholders and secondary users, their needs should be taken into account when developing AAL technologies.

2 Method

To get an in-depth insight into the informal caregivers' attitudes, concerns and needs, we conducted a qualitative study of semi-structured interviews with Dutch informal caregivers (n = 20). During the interviews the participants were asked to evaluate different AAL solutions targeting the older adults' mobility and safety.

2.1 Participants

The participants were conveniently sampled in the Eastern part of the Netherlands. Our sample was a good representation of the typical informal caregiver population with a large proportion of female participants (n = 18) and with almost all participants from the 45–65 age group (n = 19, M = 53.3, SD = 6.91). Most of the participants were working part-time (n = 14) or full-time (n = 3) next to their caregiving responsibilities. The large majority provided care to one or two family members, either parents (n = 17), in-laws (n = 1) or siblings (n = 1). Only two participants cared for a person outside their family circle (e.g., friend, neighbor). More than half of the participants (n = 11) had been an informal caregiver for at least 10 years. When asked about their time investment, nine participants indicated to spend less than 3 h a week on caregiving tasks, five participants spent 3–7 h a week, and only three participants spent 8 h or more a week on informal caregiving. All caregivers reported to provide some form of psychosocial support (e.g., administration, doctor visits, social activities, emotional support) and most of them (n = 19) also helped with domestic tasks (e.g., groceries, prepare meals, cleaning). Only three respondents were involved with personal care (e.g., bathing, dressing, feeding) and basic medical care (e.g., monitor medication intake). Concerning their overall ICT experience, all participants had experience with mainstream ICT' such as pc, laptop, smart phone or tablet and most of them (n = 14) used these tools on a daily basis.

2.2 Procedure and Data Analyses

The interviews were conducted in the participants' own home environment to create a comfortable interview situation. Each session started with some general information about the purpose of the study, the interview procedure and the consent for recording. After some questions about the context of informal care, several examples of AAL tools were presented to the participants. In the field of safety, visual sensors and ambient sensors for activity monitoring, detecting falls or unusual behavior and wearable (in-body) sensors for vital sign monitoring were used as an example. An intelligent wheelchair with an autonomous break system, wayfinding support and speech recognition; a smart wheeled walker with an autonomous break system and wayfinding support, an adaptive kitchen which moveable features and a domestic robot that assists with (instrumental) activities of daily living ((I)ADL) were used as an example from the mobility field. Each example was accompanied by a short textual description and visual representation of the AAL tool. To provide additional context on how these AAL tools could be used by the older adult in real life, two user scenarios, one focusing on safety and one focusing on mobility, were created.

Each session lasted about 60 to 90 min and was recorded and transcribed for subsequent analyses. All transcripts were carefully analyzed to identify common concepts and themes. When coding the data we applied a mixed-method approach, meaning that some of our themes were based on prior knowledge from literature (deductive approach) and some themes emerged directly from the participants' narratives (inductive approach) [30]. Following the constant comparative method we performed several rounds of coding to compare new codes to previous assigned codes to make sure the identified themes remained valid and to derive the final set of themes [31].

3 Results

3.1 Context Informal Care

The informal caregivers in this study were driven by various motives to provide care. Twelve informal caregivers reported giving care to be pleasant and rewarding, as stated by one participant: *"It's a wonderful job […]. I really enjoy it"*. Nine participants perceived care as 'a matter of course'. This was often connected to a feeling of reciprocity: *"I think it is normal, being a daughter. In the past, my mother cared for me; now I care for my mother"*. Some informal caregivers (n = 5) also felt a certain degree of obligation to provide support. Finally, less frequently mentioned drivers were the caregiver's own peace of mind (n = 2) and altruism (n = 1).

The most common problem the participants experienced as informal caregivers is workload. Eleven participants reported to sometimes feel overburdened especially in combination with their other responsibilities: *"If you work four days a week and you have one day off it is quite stressful"*. Others (n = 5) also felt emotionally challenged: *"At the moment it is really hard. It's not so much the time you invest but the psychological burden to see your father further deteriorate"*. Some participants (n = 3) mentioned that they encounter resistance on the part of the care receiver, in accepting their support. Other problems which were revealed by individual caregivers included lack of support, communication between caregivers, physical burden, financial burden, bureaucracy and confidence in one's own abilities. Five participants reported to experience no problems with regard to providing care.

3.2 General Evaluation of AAL Solutions

The main focus of the interviews was on the evaluation of different AAL solutions for mobility and safety, with the goal to identify different drivers and barriers towards AAL adoption from the perspective of the informal caregivers.

The majority of participants (n = 13) had a positive overall attitude towards AAL technologies. They appreciated the different possibilities for support and thought of AAL technologies as a positive development for the future of caregiving. In contrast, four of the interviewed participants were rather skeptical towards AAL technologies. Comments included among others: *"Rather weird"*; *"a bit science fiction"*; *"a scary idea"*; *"hard to imagine"* and *"going too far"*. In their view such technologies were a last resort and they would rather try to manage the necessary care by themselves. The remaining three caregivers had a mixed view of AAL technologies with some positive and some negative perceptions.

Comparing the different AAL solutions, that were used as an example in this study, the smart wheeled walker was positively perceived by most participants (n = 17), followed by the ambient sensors (n = 13) and the adaptive kitchen (n = 12). The participants especially liked that these tools could support the care receiver's mobility, prevent and signalize accidents and therefore, provide some peace of mind to them as caregivers. In contrast, most participants had a negative attitude towards the assistive robot (n = 16), followed by the wearable and visual sensors (n = 8). The participants complaint that these tools lack the human touch and invade the care receiver's privacy. The next section discusses the specific drivers and barriers of AAL adoption in more detail.

3.3 Drivers of AAL Technology Adoption

Safety. Safety is a strong driver of AAL technology adoption. Almost all participants (n = 19) recognized that AAL technologies could contribute to the safety of the care receiver. They appreciated that the various sensors could immediately trigger an alarm in case of emergency and therefore, falls or other accidents would not remain unnoticed by the caregiver: *"Essentially, you minimize the chance that somebody lies on the floor for one or two hours or maybe days"*. They liked that they could keep an eye on the care receiver's safety from distance and provide help when needed. With regard to the adaptive kitchen, participants pointed out that hazardous situations could be prevented, e.g. climb on a stool to reach the upper cupboard. The smart wheeled walker and the intelligent wheelchair were regarded as a tool to prevent dangerous situations and accidents outside the home, as becomes clear in this statement: *"Especially the wheelchair and I-walker could prevent a lot of accidents [...] Simply, because it is hard for older people to respond quickly"*.

Peace of Mind. Another strong driver that is closely related to safety is peace of mind. The majority of the participants (n = 15) mentioned that AAL technologies could increase their own peace of mind as well as the care receiver's peace of mind: *"Yes, I think they can provide peace of mind. For herself, [...] and surely for the family."* The caregivers pointed out that via the sensors they could check on the care receiver from distance whenever they felt worried and make sure that he or she is well. Interestingly, several participants (n = 7) were concerned that having all the sensor data could also have the opposite effect and burden them even more, as one participant stated: *"Sometimes, I think it is better that I don't know how she gets through the day. Because some stuff I don't want to see. Stuff that would scare me."* In line with this concern the majority of participants (n = 14) preferred to have the sensor data managed by a professional care center and then be alarmed in case of emergency.

Mobility and Support with Daily Activities. An additional 15 participants acknowledged that the presented AAL tools could increase the care receiver's mobility and support them with their daily activities. They pointed out that tools like the smart wheeled walker could encourage the care receiver to go more outdoors, walk small distances and increase the overall mobility radius. They also acknowledge that the adaptive kitchen and the assistive robot could compensate for the care receiver's physical limitations, e.g. getting dizzy when bending down to reach for objects, and help them with housework and personal care.

Independence. More than half of the participants (n = 11) mentioned the care receiver's independence as an important benefit of AAL tools, as becomes clear in this statement: *"I am advocate of staying independent for as long as possible; and if you use these technologies then you stay independent"*. According to the informal caregivers staying independent would preserve the care receiver's sense of freedom and self-worth. They also acknowledged that AAL technologies could enable the care receiver to stay in the familiar home environment for as long as possible. However, there were some critical voices towards keeping the care receivers home at all costs. Some informal caregivers (n = 3) indicated to prefer a care home over AAL technologies, when the health condition of the care receiver would change.

Support with Caregiving Tasks. Support with caregiving tasks was recognized as another driver of AAL technologies. Several participants (n = 8) pointed out that AAL technologies could support them in some of their usual caregiving task. For example, one participant stated with regard to the smart wheeled walker: *"I would not have to drive her to the hair dresser anymore, because she could do that herself"*. Participants recognized AAL tools would enable them to provide more care from distance, perform tasks more efficiently and ultimately relieve some of their workload.

Absence of Social Provision. A contextual driver of AAL technology adoption was the absence of social provision. Several participants (n = 6) stated AAL solutions were most suitable to older adults without a social support system or with family members living at some distance: *"If I would live at distance [...] then all the stuff that you have as an example here, yes, I think it could give some peace of mind."*

Finally, a few caregivers mentioned social involvement (n = 4) and health benefits (n = 3) as other drivers of AAL technologies.

3.4 Barriers Towards AAL Technology Adoption

Privacy and Intrusiveness. Privacy and intrusiveness form a strong barrier towards AAL technology adoption. Almost all participants (n = 18) were concerned that AAL technologies could invade the care receivers privacy. This was especially true for the visual sensors but also for the wearable and ambient sensors. Some informal caregivers stated that they would feel like a spy and that they would not want to have all kinds of information about the care receiver. Likewise, some participants also thought that the care receivers themselves would not appreciate it to be monitored by them as caregivers. They also feared that care receivers might not always be fully aware that they are monitored. Some caregivers stated that instead of feeling safe, the care receiver might feel uneasy about the sensors: *"Sensors under the skin measuring heartbeat and respiration – well that would get my heartrate up if everything is monitored"*. Other critical comments about the intrusiveness of the in-body wearable sensor included *"a bit like an alien"* and *"I would feel like a robot myself"* and *"animals are also tagged"*. While some participants regarded the care receiver's privacy as a priority, others believed the safety benefits to outweigh the privacy concerns (n = 6). Moreover, one caregiver indicated that privacy would not be a concern in the relationship with the care receiver: *"She has no secrets or privacy issues towards us"*.

Lack of Human Touch. Another strong barrier towards AAL technology adoption was the lack of human touch. The great majority of participant (n = 17) had some concerns that AAL technologies could reduce the human touch in care. The participant stated that contact, warmth and empathy is crucial to the care receivers and that technology could not offer these qualities. Participants were especially critical towards the assistive robot in that regard: *"You want someone with you to hold your hand and hug you from time to time. Well good luck with that robot"*. Another concern was that technologies might create more distance between care givers and care receivers and therefore, increase social isolation; *"Knowing they have those things at home, you might visit your mother or father less often to check on them"*. The majority of caregivers emphasized that technology could not and should not replace human care: *"You can have the greatest devices. But people will rather be bathed one time less and have a chat than being in a lonely home with all these technologies."* Or as another participant stated: *"I think [technology] can be a supporting tool but the humans should stay in control"*. Interestingly, one of the few male informal caregivers actually preferred an assistive robot over a human caregiver for his father as well as himself in the future. He argued, that often female professional caregivers carry out intimate tasks such as bathing. The same participant stated that the professional caregivers should not be responsible for the care receiver's social involvement: "*People always emphasize the human touch [...] but I think go visit clubs to get in touch with others. This should not depend on the caregivers*".

Unfelt Need for Support. The unfelt need for support was another significant barrier towards AAL technology adoption. Before even exposing participants to the AAL technology examples, they were asked if they would like any support in their caregiving tasks. The majority (n = 17) indicated that they would not need any support in their current situation. This can be explained by the fact that most of the participants shared their responsibilities with other family members and some already had support from professional care services. This unfelt need was also reflected by most participants (n = 17) when evaluating the AAL technology examples. Several participants (n = 9) stated that the care receiver was still independent and healthy enough and would not need a specific AAL tool (e.g., visual sensor) at the moment. Then again, other participants (n = 4) pointed out that the care receiver would be too restricted to benefit from a specific AAL tool, as becomes clear in this statement about the smart wheeled walker: "*This would not be suitable for my mother, because she rarely moves outside the house anymore*". Some informal caregivers (n = 5) felt there was no need for a specific AAL tool because they lived nearby and could provide the necessary care themselves or with the support from a professional caregiver. Others (n = 6) stated to be satisfied with their current assistive tool e.g., personal alarm system.

Technology Experience. Another barrier towards AAL technology adoption was technology experience. More than half of the caregivers (n = 11) were worried that the care receiver might lack the necessary experience and skills to be comfortable using AAL technologies. The participants emphasized that the care receivers have not grown up with technology and therefore, might not be open towards AAL technologies: "*She would not want that. Because she is from another generation and is not at all used to technology*". The care receivers might even be scared of tools like an assistive robot: "*A robot is scary to people*". Also, care receivers might have difficulties handling AAL tools: "*If my mother gets a kitchen like that, all the buttons would drive her crazy*". A few caregivers (n = 2) were also worried about their own technology skills. However, most participants were convinced that technology experience would not be a barrier for them as the next generation of care receivers. Nevertheless, it was emphasized that usability is an important requirement for AAL technologies (n = 4).

Reliability and Trust. Reliability and trust formed another barrier towards AAL technology adoption. Half of the informal caregivers (n = 10) had doubts about the reliability of AAL technologies. Several participants indicated that you could not completely trust AAL technologies because they might not work all the time: "*It's technology so it can break down, you can't completely trust those*". For example, one participant worried about potential accidents when the electronic breaks of the smart wheeled walker would malfunction. This lack of trust was often grounded in previous negative experience with care related ICT tools. Therefore, several caregivers (n = 5) emphasized that they would like to be able to test and experience an AAL tool before using it.

Resistance to Change. Resistance to change was another barrier mentioned by the informal caregivers. Several participants pointed out (n = 7) that the care receivers are not comfortable with new and unfamiliar situations and therefore, might be apprehensive towards AAL technologies: "*I doubt that people that age can handle such major changes*". Participants pointed out that AAL technologies that are based on familiar tools, e.g., adaptive kitchen, will be more acceptable than the more unfamiliar tools, e.g., assistive robot.

Contextual Limitations. An additional barrier towards AAL technology adoption were contextual limitations. Some informal caregivers (n = 7) stated that the care receiver's living environment could be problematic for some of the AAL tools. As one participants pointed out: "*It is all very narrow, so if a robot would need to get through, then I see a problem*". One caregiver also found the smart wheeled walker and the intelligent wheelchair less appealing for the care receiver because they lived outside the city center with everything far away.

Cost. Cost was also a barrier concerning AAL technologies. A few informal caregivers (n = 5) were concerned about the potential costs of AAL technologies: "*I think immediately, gosh this costs a lot of money. This is not affordable for the average older adult [...]*". Therefore, some participants demanded that AAL technologies must not be too expensive so that the less well-off older adults could afford them.

Pride. Finally, pride was another barrier towards AAL technology adoption mentioned by a few informal caregivers (n = 2). The participants stated that the care receiver had already trouble to accept support and therefore, would also be hesitant towards supporting tools such as AAL technologies.

3.5 Other Findings

Following our expectations, almost all informal caregivers (n = 18) played an important role in making care decisions. According to their statements, they regularly check on the care receiver's abilities to identify safety risks and care needs. Subsequently, they are often the ones who initiate the appropriate measurements to address these issues. However, the degree of social influence differed. Some informal caregivers pointed out to provide carefully phrased suggestions while others had a strong advisory role. A few informal caregivers even made decisions without consulting the care receiver first: "*As soon as needed, we bought a wheeled walker [...] although she did not want one in the beginning.*" Nevertheless, the majority of all informal caregivers (n = 15) emphasized that using an AAL technology would strongly depend on the wishes of the care receiver, and they would not use these tools without their consent: "*You have to honor their wishes. Do they want this or not*".

4 Discussion and Conclusion

The focus of this paper was to highlight the perspective of an often underrepresented target group: the informal caregivers. By conducting in-depth interviews with 20 informal caregivers we investigated their attitudes, concerns and needs regarding AAL technologies for mobility and safety. After coding and analyzing the data, eight drivers and nine barriers towards AAL technology adoption could be identified.

Our findings confirmed some of the results from existing literature on AAL adoption among older adults. This is not surprising, as the informal caregivers in this study did not just consider their own needs, but also spoke as advocates of the care receiver's needs. However, when looking at the results in more detail, new and interesting aspects of seemingly familiar topics could be identified. Moreover, we also observed some differences in the importance of the various drivers and barriers.

Similar to studies among older adults, the care receiver's safety [17, 19, 32] was a strong driver of AAL technology adoption among informal caregivers. The participants appreciated that AAL technologies could prevent accidents and immediately alert them in case of emergency. Clearly, the well-being and security of the care receiver is a number one priority to caregivers.

Peace of mind was another strong driver of AAL adoption. Informal caregivers reported that AAL technologies would help them to check-in with the care receivers and feel less worried about their well-being. Peace of mind was also an essential benefit for informal caregivers in the Digital Family Portrait studies and the CareNet Display project and [23, 24]. As Bossen et al. [33] suggest, family caregivers are emotionally invested in the care process and find it difficult to reach peace of mind. Therefore, they appreciate technologies which give them regular and detailed updates about the care receiver's well-being. Although, the caregiver's peace of mind is also mentioned in studies with older adults, it is usually a less prevalent driver.

Even though independence and aging in place typically is a priority among older adults [18, 19, 32], it seems a slightly less important driver to informal caregivers. A few participants even stated, that they would not want to keep the care receivers home at all costs and rather opt for a nursing home than using AAL technologies.

While results concerning privacy and intrusiveness are somewhat mixed in regard to older adults [18, 19, 32, 34], it was clearly a barrier for informal caregivers. The participants felt uncomfortable to 'spy' on the care receiver and have intimate information at their disposal. To counter this feeling, AAL tools could grant older adults control over what data points are shared and with whom as suggested by Consolvo et al. [24]. However, too much control can also lead to a loss of safety. Hence, it is important for developers of AAL tools to find a careful balance between privacy and security.

Surprisingly, like older adults [18, 35, 36] informal caregivers did not perceive the need for support, which was a strong barrier towards AAL adoption. Therefore, developers should closely involve caregivers (not just older adults) during the design process of AAL tools and allow them to experience prototypes in everyday life. This user-centered approach could aid the caregivers' understanding of the benefits of AAL technologies over traditional assistive tools. Moreover, it would be interesting to further investigate if caregivers indeed feel no need for support or are too ashamed or proud to ask for help, as suggested by de Klerk et al. [5].

Although the lack of human touch is a familiar topic [17, 37] it seems to be a more prevalent barrier among informal caregivers. Participants expressed the strong concern that AAL technologies could reduce the human touch in care and create a distance between them and the care receivers. To combat this barrier, AAL developers should emphasize that AAL technologies could also improve the relationship between caregiver and care receiver by providing mutual social awareness, providing input for meaningful conversations and relieving task pressure so there is more time for psychosocial support [24, 38, 39]. Interestingly one of the few participants who showed no concerns about this issue was a male informal caregiver. This could point to a gender bias and should be further investigated by future research.

The findings of this study should not be considered without taking into account several limitations. First, the results are based on a national sample that lived in a more rural part of the Netherlands. This could have affected the generalizability of our results. Second, visuals and use scenarios provide a somewhat limited view on the advantages and disadvantages of AAL technologies. However, the focus of this study was to access drivers and barriers in a pre-adoption phase, rather than investigating actual usage.

Despite its limitations, this study offers several interesting avenues for future research. First, given the fact that care tasks and the (subjective) task pressure can be highly diverse, future studies should compare different groups of informal caregivers (e.g. see caregiver roles by Consolvo et al. [24]) and other contextual factors and explore how these factors affect the perception of AAL technologies. Second, we believe that our in-depths findings can be leveraged for quantitative approaches to further investigate the influence of the identified drivers and barriers on AAL adoption. Third, considering that our results describe perceptions in a pre-adoption phase, it would be interesting to investigate if and how the meaning of the found drivers and barriers change in a later adoption stage when technologies are integrated in everyday life.

Awaiting future research to address these issues, the current study provides interesting insights into a user group that is often overlooked: the informal caregivers. Our findings show that informal caregivers are equally critical towards AAL technologies as older adults. Considering, that they are often the ones who initiate the discussion about assistive tools and subsequently could have a positively influence on the decision to adopt AAL technologies, their attitudes, concerns and needs deserve more attention and should be further investigated in the AAL community.

Acknowledgements. Our gratitude goes to the research assistants F. Mokkink and M. Heideman who supported us in the data collection process. Furthermore, we want to thank all participants for sharing their insights with us.

References

1. European Commission, Directorate-General for Economic and Financial Affairs: The 2015 Ageing Report - Economic and budgetary projections for the 28 EU Member States (2013–2060). Publications Office of the European Union, Luxembourg (2015)

2. Henz, U.: Informal caregiving at working age: effects of job characteristics and family configuration. J. Marriage Fam. **68**, 411–429 (2006)
3. Eckert, J.K., Morgan, L.A., Swamy, N.: Preferences for receipt of care among community-dwelling adults. J. Aging Soc. Policy **16**, 49–65 (2004)
4. House of Representatives of the Netherlands: Letter of the State Secretary for Health, Welfare and Sport, No. 65, 27401. The Hague, The Netherlands (2001)
5. de Klerk, M., de Boer, A., Kooiker, S., Schyns, P.: Unpaid help: who does what? The Netherlands Institute for Social Research, The Hague, The Netherlands (2015)
6. Huber, M., Rodrigues, R., Hoffmann, F., Gąsior, K., Marin, B.: Facts and Figures on Long-Term Care: Europe and North America. European Centre for Social Welfare Policy and Research, Vienna (2009)
7. Timmermans, J.M.: Informal care: about the help of and help for informal caregivers. The Netherlands Institute for Social Research, The Hague, The Netherlands (2003)
8. Chen, Y., Ngo, V., Park, S.Y.: Caring for caregivers: designing for integrality. In: CSCW 2013, pp. 91–102 (2013)
9. Pinquart, M., Sörensen, S.: Differences between caregivers and noncaregivers in psychological health and physical health: a meta-analysis. Psychol. Aging **18**(2), 250–267 (2003)
10. Hussein, S., Manthorpe, J.: An international review of the long-term care workforce: policies and shortages. J. Aging Soc. Policy **17**, 75–94 (2005)
11. van den Broek, G., Cavallo, F., Wehrmann, C.: AALIANCE - Ambient Assisted Living Roadmap. IOS Press, Amsterdam (2010)
12. Aarts, E.H.L., Encarnação, J.L.: True Visions: The Emergence of Ambient Intelligence. Springer, Berlin (2006)
13. Rashidi, P., Mihailidis, A.: A survey on ambient-assisted living tools for older adults. IEEE J. Biomed. Health Inform. **17**, 579–590 (2013)
14. Gabriel, Z., Bowling, A.: Quality of life from the perspectives of older people. Ageing Soc. **24**, 675–691 (2004)
15. Rubenstein, L.Z.: Falls in older people: epidemiology, risk factors and strategies for prevention. Age Ageing **35**, 37–41 (2006)
16. Rogers, M.E., Rogers, N.L., Takeshima, N., Islam, M.M.: Methods to assess and improve the physical parameters associated with fall risk in older adults. Prev. Med. (Balt.) **36**, 255–264 (2003)
17. Demiris, G., Rantz, M., Aud, M., Marek, K., Tyrer, H., Skubic, M., Hussam, A.: Older adults' attitudes towards and perceptions of 'smart home' technologies: a pilot study. Med. Inform. Internet Med. **29**, 87–94 (2004)
18. Steele, R., Lo, A., Secombe, C., Wong, Y.K.: Elderly persons' perception and acceptance of using wireless sensor networks to assist healthcare. Int. J. Med. Inform. **78**, 788–801 (2009)
19. Mahmood, A., Yamamoto, T., Lee, M., Steggell, C.: Perceptions and use of gerotechnology: implications for aging in place. J. Hous. Elder. **22**, 104–126 (2008)
20. Smarr, C.A., Mitzner, T.L., Beer, J.M., Prakash, A., Chen, T.L., Kemp, C.C., Rogers, W.A.: Domestic robots for older adults: attitudes, preferences, and potential. Int. J. Soc. Robot. **6**, 229–247 (2014)
21. Bass, D.M., Noelker, L.S.: The influence of family caregivers on elder's use of in-home services: an expanded conceptual framework. J. Health Soc. Behav. **28**, 184–196 (1987)
22. Byrne, D., Goeree, M.S., Hiedemann, B., Stern, S.: Formal home health care, informal care, and family decision making. Int. Econ. Rev. **50**, 1205–1242 (2009)

23. Rowan, J., Mynatt, E.D.: Digital family portrait field trial: support for aging in place. In: Proceedings of the SIGCHI Conference on Human Factors in Computing Systems, pp. 521–530 (2005)
24. Consolvo, S., Roessler, P., Shelton, B.E: The CareNet display: lessons learned from an in home evaluation of an ambient display design of the CareNet display. In: Ubiquitous Computing, pp. 1–17. ACM Press (2004)
25. Hwang, A.S., Truong, K.N., Mihailidis, A.: Using participatory design to determine the needs of informal caregivers for smart home user interfaces. In: Pervasive Computing Technologies for Healthcare, pp. 41–48. IEEE Press, New York (2012)
26. Rialle, V., Ollivet, C., Guigui, C., Hervé, C.: What do family caregivers of Alzheimer's disease patients desire in smart home technologies? Methods Inf. Med. **47**, 63–69 (2008)
27. Ajzen, I.: The theory of planned behavior. Organ. Behav. Hum. Decis. Process. **50**, 179–211 (1991)
28. Silverstone, R.L., Haddon, L.: Design and the domestication of ICTs: technical change and everyday life. In: Communication by Design: The Politics of Information and Communication Technologies, pp. 44–74 (1996)
29. Rogers, E.M.: Diffusion of Innovations, 4th edn. Free Press, New York (1995)
30. Ryan, G.W., Bernard, H.R.: Techniques to identify themes. Field Methods **15**, 85–109 (2003)
31. Strauss, A., Corbin, J.: The Basics of Qualitative Research: Techniques and Procedures for Developing Grounded Theory. Sage Publications, Thousand Oaks (1998)
32. van Hoof, J., Kort, H.S.M., Rutten, P.G.S., Duijnstee, M.S.H.: Ageing-in-place with the use of ambient intelligence technology: perspectives of older users. Int. J. Med. Inform. **80**, 310–331 (2011)
33. Bossen, C., Christensen, L.R., Groenvall, E., Vestergaard, L.S.: CareCoor: augmenting the coordination of cooperative home care work. Int. J. Med. Inform. **82**, e189–e199 (2013)
34. Beringer, R., Sixsmith, A., Campo, M., Brown, J., McCloskey, R.: The "acceptance" of ambient assisted living: developing an alternate methodology to this limited research lens. In: Abdulrazak, B., Giroux, S., Bouchard, B., Pigot, H., Mokhtari, M. (eds.) ICOST 2011. LNCS, vol. 6719, pp. 161–167. Springer, Heidelberg (2011). doi:10.1007/978-3-642-21535-3_21
35. Bright, A.K., Coventry, L.: Assistive technology for older adults. In: Proceedings of the 6th International Conference on Pervasive Technologies Related to Assistive Environments - PETRA 2013, pp. 1–4. ACM Press (2013)
36. Coughlin, J., D'Ambrosio, L.A., Reimer, B., Pratt, M.R: Older adult perceptions of smart home technologies: implications for research, policy & market innovations in healthcare. In: 29th Annual International Conference of the IEEE Engineering in Medicine and Biology Society, pp. 1810–1815 (2007)
37. Lorenzen-Huber, L., Boutain, M., Camp, L.J., Shankar, K., Connelly, K.H.: Privacy, technology, and aging: a proposed framework. Ageing Int. **36**, 232–252 (2011)
38. Cornejo, R., Tentori, M., Favela, J.: Ambient awareness to strengthen the family social network of older adults. Comput. Support. Coop. Work **22**, 309–344 (2013)
39. Lorenzen-Huber, L., Shankar, K., Caine, K., Connelly, K., Camp, L.J., Walker, B.A., Borrero, L.: How in-home technologies mediate caregiving relationships in later life. Int. J. Hum. Comput. Interact. **29**, 441–455 (2012)

Easy to Install Indoor Positioning System that Parasitizes Home Lighting

Takuya Maekawa(✉) and Yuki Sakumichi

Osaka University, Osaka, Japan
maekawa@ist.osaka-u.ac.jp

Abstract. This paper proposes a new indoor positioning system that utilizes home lighting. We design a beacon for use in the system that is inserted between a home light bulb and its socket, and is supplied with electricity from the socket. This means that the end user can easily install the system in his/her environment. In addition, we propose a fingerprinting-based indoor positioning method that employs signals received from the beacons. Because the ON/OFF states of our beacons change according to the ON/OFF states of the lighting, the signal strengths from the beacons also change greatly and this reduces positioning accuracy. So, we improve the positioning accuracy by estimating the ON/OFF states of the lighting based on the residents' life patterns.

1 Introduction

Fingerprinting-based WiFi positioning employs a training phase in which WiFi signals (i.e., the unique MAC addresses of APs and the signal strengths from APs) are observed at known coordinates. A set of APs and their signal strengths become a *fingerprint* that is unique to those coordinates. In the positioning phase, the observed WiFi signals at unknown coordinates are compared with the stored fingerprints to determine the closest match. The advantage of WiFi positioning is that the end user does not need to install any new equipment because the technique can employ WiFi APs at nearby houses, laboratories, shops, etc. However, because these APs are owned by other people, the user has very little control of them [2]. So, when the APs are moved or removed, the end user should recalibrate the system. In this paper, we attempt to deploy a few easy-to-install beacons in an environment of interest. Specifically, we set a beacon between a home light bulb (e.g., an electric bulb or fluorescent light) and its socket. The beacon is supplied with electricity from the socket and emits Bluetooth signals. The advantages of beacons that parasitize home lighting are as follows. (1) An end user can easily deploy a beacon because she simply inserts it between a bulb and its socket. (2) Every room has at least one lighting socket, so the beacons can cover all the areas related to the user's daily life. (3) Because the beacons are installed on the ceiling, they will not be moved or removed by residents unfamiliar with IT (e.g., the elderly).

To realize such an indoor positioning system, we design and develop beacons and an indoor positioning method with the following features. (1) Some rooms

A. Braun et al. (Eds.): AmI 2017, LNCS 10217, pp. 124–129, 2017.
DOI: 10.1007/978-3-319-56997-0_9

are not equipped with multiple sockets for light bulbs, e.g., many rooms have only one ceiling light, and we can install only one beacon in such rooms. Also, it is preferable for the end user to deploy only a few beacons. Thus, we design the beacons so that we can obtain good positioning accuracy with a small number. (2) Some people may spend the daytime in their living rooms without turning on any lighting. In such a case, the beacon cannot receive an electricity supply. To cope with the problem, we design beacons that have rechargeable batteries and that are power saving. (3) There are many lights in houses that we cannot expect to be used for long periods, e.g., a light in a bathroom. There is no point in including a rechargeable battery, which is expensive, in the beacon attached to such light bulbs because we cannot have sufficient time for charging. We plan to attach beacons without rechargeable batteries to such bulbs. However, the ON/OFF states of the beacon attached to such lights changes depending on the ON/OFF states of the corresponding lights. Thus, signal strength data measured at a certain position change greatly depending on the ON/OFF states of the beacons (lights). In such cases, we cannot simply adopt a fingerprint-based method that utilizes fingerprints collected *in advance*. In this paper, we propose a new indoor positioning method that takes account of the ON/OFF states of the beacons by employing the residents' life patterns.

2 Developed Beacon

Figure 1 shows our prototype beacon that is connected to an LED light bulb. Figure 2 shows our beacons attached to an electric bulb and ceiling light sockets. Because they are prototypes, they are not very small and the main body of the beacon (bottom right in Fig. 1) is separated from its socket adapter (top left in Fig. 1). Our beacons have the following features.

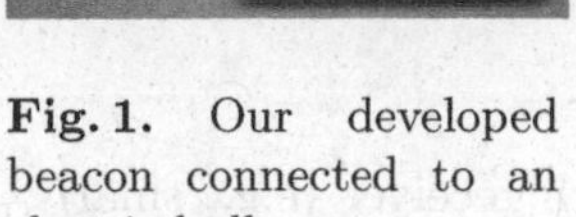

Fig. 1. Our developed beacon connected to an electric bulb.

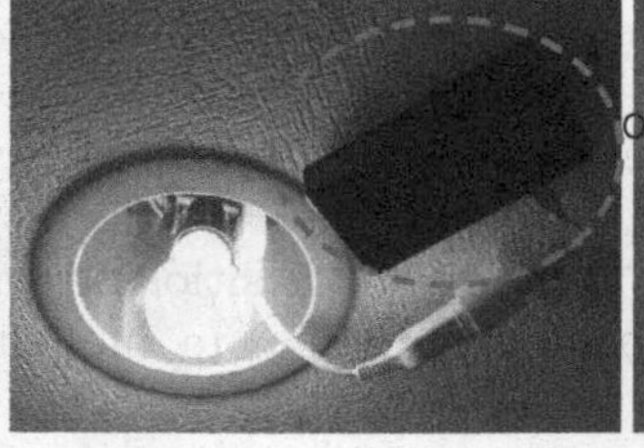

Fig. 2. Our beacons attached to a ceiling bulb and a fluorescent.

(1) When we want to perform indoor positioning, we cannot obtain accurate positions with signals from small numbers of Bluetooth modules. On the other hand, many rooms have only one light socket. To allow us to perform

accurate positioning in such environments, we incorporate multiple Bluetooth modules into our beacon. (We incorporated three modules based on the findings of previous studies [1].) We select a Bluetooth module whose signal propagation property is not uniform (i.e., has directionality), and incorporate the module into our beacon. In our preliminary evaluation, we were able to achieve accurate positioning (1.27 m mean distance error) with only one beacon. The accuracy was almost the same as that obtained when using three Bluetooth modules at the corners of a room (1.35 m mean distance error).

(2) Some people may spend the daytime in their living rooms without turning on any lighting. When a light is OFF, our beacon cannot receive an electricity supply. To cope with the problem, we equip our beacon with a rechargeable battery. The beacon can emit signals even when the light is OFF because its battery is charged when the light is ON. Here, to prolong the survival time of the beacon, it is designed to emit signals only during usual waking hours. In this work, we include a light sensor in the beacon, and this stops the beacon from emitting signals when it is very dark (i.e., late at night). There are also many lights in houses that are only turned on for short periods. We assume that beacons attached to such lights are not equipped with rechargeable batteries because of cost considerations.

3 Proposed Positioning Method

Here, we introduce our positioning method. Since the ON/OFF states of our beacons change depending on the ON/OFF states of the corresponding lighting (and ambient illuminance level), we cannot simply adopt existing fingerprinting techniques, which employ preset training data. Here we assume that training data are collected when all the beacons in an environment of interest are ON. So, if some beacons are OFF during the test (positioning) phase, the measured signal strength data are very different from those obtained during the training phase. Also, when the signal strength from a beacon is zero during the test phase, we cannot distinguish whether this phenomenon is caused by the OFF state of the beacon or the signal attenuation caused by the distance from the beacon. In this paper, we attempt to improve the positioning accuracy by estimating the ON/OFF states of beacons from the residents' life patterns.

3.1 Overview

We estimate the position of a user who has a Bluetooth receiver (e.g., smartphone) by employing received signal strength data $\boldsymbol{s}_t$ at time t. Our positioning method consists of two main procedures: (1) estimating beacons' ON/OFF states and (2) positioning with $\boldsymbol{s}_t$ and the estimated ON/OFF states.

3.2 ON/OFF State Estimation

We estimate the ON/OFF states of the beacons based on the following ideas. (1) The ON/OFF states change according to the residents' daily activity routines. For example, a beacon in the kitchen may be ON while meals are being prepared. (2) We consider that the lighting ON/OFF states are correlated. For example, beacons in the same room may be turned on at the same time. Also, in some houses, bedroom and living room lighting may not be ON at the same time.

Based on the above ideas, we estimate the ON/OFF states of beacons from $\boldsymbol{s}_t$ by using the Bayes' theorem as follows.

$$\hat{\boldsymbol{Y}}_t = \arg\max p(\boldsymbol{Y}_t|\boldsymbol{X}_t) = \arg\max \frac{p(\boldsymbol{X}_t|\boldsymbol{Y}_t)p(\boldsymbol{Y}_t)}{p(\boldsymbol{X}_t)}, \qquad (1)$$

where $\boldsymbol{X}_t$ is a vector that shows the ON/OFF states of Bluetooth modules created from observations $\boldsymbol{s}_t$ as follows.

$$X_{i,t} = \begin{cases} 1 \; s_{i,t} > 0 \\ 0 \; otherwise, \end{cases}$$

where $X_{i,t}$ shows the ith element of $\boldsymbol{X}_t$ and $s_{i,t}$ shows the observed signal strength of the ith Bluetooth module at time t. An example is $\boldsymbol{X}_t = [1\,0\,1\cdots 0]^T$. Each vector element shows whether or not a signal is observed from its corresponding Bluetooth module (1 or 0). Also, $\boldsymbol{Y}_t$ represents an estimation of the ON/OFF states. An example is $\boldsymbol{Y}_t = [1\,0\,1\cdots 1]^T$. Each vector element shows an estimation of the ON/OFF state of the corresponding Bluetooth module (ON:1, OFF:0). So, we find $\hat{\boldsymbol{Y}}_t$ that maximizes $p(\boldsymbol{Y}_t|\boldsymbol{X}_t)$ in the Eq. 1. We can expand the numerator of Eq. 1 based on our above ideas as follows.

$$\overbrace{\prod_{i=0}^{N} f_l(X_{i,t}, Y_{i,t})}^{p(\boldsymbol{X}_t|\boldsymbol{Y}_t)} \overbrace{\prod_{i=0}^{N} f_r(Y_{i,t}) \prod_{i,j,i\neq j} f_c(Y_{i,t}, Y_{j,t})}^{p(\boldsymbol{Y}_t)},$$

where N is the number of Bluetooth modules in the environment and $Y_{i,t}$ is the ith element of $\boldsymbol{Y}_t$. We describe each component in detail below.

$f_l(X_{i,t}, Y_{i,t})$ evaluates the consistency of estimation $Y_{i,t}$ compared with observation $X_{i,t}$ as follows.

$$f_l(X_{i,t}, Y_{i,t}) = \begin{cases} 0 \; X_{i,t} > Y_{i,t} \\ 1 \; otherwise. \end{cases}$$

That is, when the ith Bluetooth module is estimated to be OFF (i.e., $Y_{i,t}$ is 0) even if signals from the ith Bluetooth module are actually observed (i.e., $X_{i,t}$ is 1), we can say that the estimation is wrong and that $p(\boldsymbol{X}_t|\boldsymbol{Y}_t)$ is 0.

$f_r(Y_{i,t})$ relates to the residents' daily routine. This function evaluates the degree to which the estimation $Y_{i,t}$ at time t is consistent with the prior probability computed from ground truth data for the same time on previous days.

$f_c(Y_{i,t}, Y_{j,t})$ relates to the correlation of lighting ON/OFF states. This function evaluates the degree to which the pair of estimations $Y_{i,t}$ and $Y_{j,t}$ is consistent with the prior probability computed from ground truth data of previous days. So, we compute the probability $p_{i,j}$ with which both the ith and jth Bluetooth modules are ON (or OFF) at the same time in advance. For example, when both $Y_{i,t}$ and $Y_{j,t}$ are 1 (or 0), the $f_c(Y_{i,t}, Y_{j,t})$ value becomes $p_{i,j}$. When the $Y_{i,t}$ and $Y_{j,t}$ values are different, the $f_c(Y_{i,t}, Y_{j,t})$ value becomes $1 - p_{i,j}$.

3.3 Positioning

We estimate the position coordinates of the user from $\boldsymbol{s}_t$ and $\hat{\boldsymbol{Y}}_t$. When the ith Bluetooth module is estimated to be OFF, we do not use the $s_{i,t}$ value to estimate the coordinates. On the other hand, when the ith Bluetooth module is estimated to be ON, we use the $s_{i,t}$ value even if it is zero.

In the training phase, we obtain signal strengths from each Bluetooth module at known positions (training points). We model the observed signal strengths for each training point with a statistical model. By doing so, we can compute the probability with which $\boldsymbol{s}_t$ is observed at each training point. Then we obtain the training points with the top-k probabilities and compute the weighted average coordinates of the training points. (The weight corresponds to the probability.) Note that we should design the model by taking into account the above idea that we use $s_{i,t}$ *only* when the the ith Bluetooth module is estimated to be ON. In this work, we employ a Gaussian mixture model (GMM) to model each Bluetooth module's signal strengths at each training point, and obtain the final result (the probability related to the training point) by aggregating the probabilities related to *only* Bluetooth modules that are estimated to be ON as follows.

$$p(s_t, \hat{\boldsymbol{Y}}_t \| tp_n) = \sum_{i \in Y_{t,ON}} \sum_{m=1}^{M} \pi_m^i \frac{1}{\sqrt{2\pi\sigma_{m,i}^2}} \exp(-\frac{(s_{i,t} - \mu_m^i)^2}{2\sigma_{m,i}^2}),$$

where tp_n shows the nth training point, $Y_{t,ON}$ represents a set of indices of Bluetooth modules estimated to be ON in $\hat{\boldsymbol{Y}}_t$, M is the number of Gaussian mixtures, π_m^i is the mixture weight of the mth Gaussian related to the ith Bluetooth module.

4 Evaluation

4.1 Data Set

We collected *in-situ* sensor data at an apartment occupied by two people and shown in Fig. 3. Training data were obtained at the 26 points shown as filled circles in Fig. 3 for three minutes with all four beacons turned on. The test period lasted nine days, and the lighting was turned on/off naturally according to the residents' daily lives. Here our method requires the ground truth data of the ON/OFF states of the Bluetooth modules. In this study, we obtain pseudo ground truth data by aggregating Bluetooth scan data obtained from the smartphones that the two residents carried for ten days before the test periods.

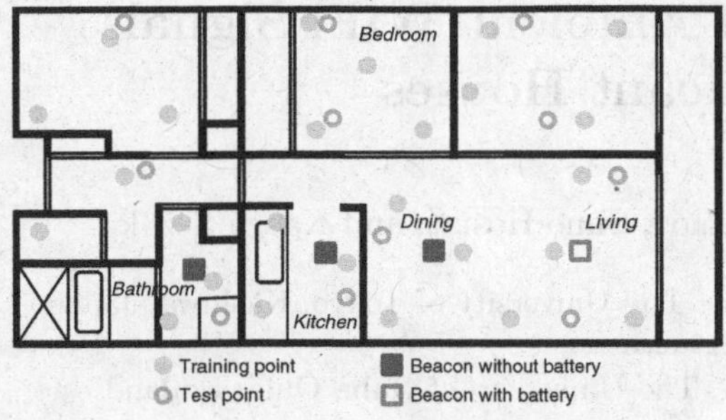

Fig. 3. Layout of experimental environment (12.6 m × 6.2 m).

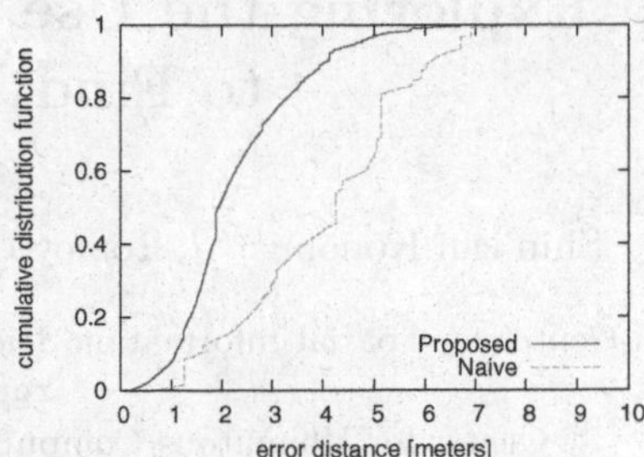

Fig. 4. CDFs of our method and naive method.

4.2 Results

Figure 4 shows the cumulative distribution functions (CDFs) of our method and a naive method that does not employ ON/OFF state estimation (i.e., as with the conventional methods, it estimates positions by using all Bluetooth modules in the environment even if they are turned off). Our method outperformed the naive method, and achieved about 50% precision within 2 m. The mean distance errors of our method and the naive method were 2.3 and 4.0 m, respectively. That is, with our method the positioning accuracy was improved by an average of about 1.7 m.

In particular, the positioning accuracies related to test points that were far from the beacon installed in the living room were greatly improved (about 2.0 m). Identifying the coordinates of the signal strength data obtained at the test point relied greatly on the signals from the other beacons, which were not equipped with a rechargeable battery, because we could not observe signals from the living room beacons at the test points. That is, when the beacons with no batteries were OFF, we could not observe signals from the beacons, which are useful for identifying the coordinates, at the test points. So when the signal strengths of such beacons were zero, the naive method mistakenly estimated that the signal strength data were observed at a place far from the beacon. On the other hand, our method can ignore beacons that are determined as being OFF when it estimates coordinates with the signal strength data.

Acknowledgement. This work was partially supported by JST CREST and JSPS KAKENHI Grant Number JP26730047 and 16H06539.

References

1. Kaemarungsi, K., Krishnamurthy, P.: Modeling of indoor positioning systems based on location fingerprinting. In: INFOCOM 2004, vol. 2, pp. 1012–1022 (2004)
2. Patel, S.N., Truong, K.N., Abowd, G.D.: PowerLine positioning: a practical sub-room-level indoor location system for domestic use. In: Dourish, P., Friday, A. (eds.) UbiComp 2006. LNCS, vol. 4206, pp. 441–458. Springer, Heidelberg (2006). doi:10.1007/11853565_26

Exploring the Use of Ambient WiFi Signals to Find Vacant Houses

Shin'ichi Konomi[1(✉)], Tomoyo Sasao[1], Simo Hosio[2], and Kaoru Sezaki[1]

[1] Center for Spatial Information Science, The University of Tokyo, Kashiwa, Japan
konomi@acm.org

[2] Center for Ubiquitous Computing, The University of Oulu, Oulu, Finland

Abstract. In many countries, the population is either declining or rapidly concentrating in big cities, which causes problems in the form of vacant houses in many local communities. It is often challenging to keep track of the locations and the conditions of vacant houses, and for example in Japan, costly manual field studies are employed to map the occupancy situation. In this paper, we propose a technique to infer the locations of occupied houses based on ambient WiFi signals. Our technique collects RSSI (Received Signal Strength Indicator) data based on opportunistic smartphone sensing, constructs hybrid networks of WiFi access points, and analyzes their geospatial patterns based on statistical shape modeling. We show that the technique can successfully infer occupied houses in a suburban residential community, and argue that it can substantially reduce the cost of field surveys to find vacant houses as the number of potential houses to be inspected decreases.

Keywords: Ambient WiFi signals · Vacant houses · Civic computing · Localization

1 Introduction

The population decline and movement to big population hubs is creating the urgent need to address the problems of vacant houses. A particularly challenging case can be found in Japan, where the number of vacant houses is increasing rapidly, and more than 30 percent of Japanese houses are projected to be vacant already in 2033 [6].

Vacant houses can be problematic, as they (1) decrease the quality of landscapes, (2) decrease safety and peace of mind related to crimes and disasters, (3) induce illegal dumping of garbage, (4) increase the risk of fire, (5) produce bad smell, (6) are more prone to damage by strong winds, heavy snow, or earthquakes, if improperly managed, (7) decrease vitality of community life, and so on. In certain places, local officials lack efficient means of keeping track of house vacancy situation, and thus there exists a clear need to find vacant houses before their condition deteriorates and to find new use for them. This should effectively

A. Braun et al. (Eds.): AmI 2017, LNCS 10217, pp. 130–135, 2017.
DOI: 10.1007/978-3-319-56997-0_10

happen via collaboration between local government, urban planners, and citizens. In Japan, typical means to do this is conducting costly field surveys to verify occupancy status.

In this paper, we propose a technique to infer the locations of occupied houses based on ambient WiFi signals. Our technique collects georeferenced RSSI (Received Signal Strength Indicator) data based on opportunistic smartphone sensing, constructs hybrid networks of virtual and real WiFi access points, and analyzes their geospatial patterns based on statistical shape modeling. We show that the technique can successfully infer occupied houses in a suburban residential community and thus reduce the cost of field surveys to map vacant houses.

2 Related Work

Chi et al. [2] use location records of Baidu users to analyze spatial distribution of vacant housing areas. Their analysis focuses on the issue of "ghost cities" in China and shows that location records of a large number of mobile users can reveal areas in which most houses are vacant. As our focus is wormhole-like sporadic vacant houses rather than entirely vacant city blocks, we must perform a much finer-grained analysis aiming to find the locations of individual vacant houses. Thus, we make inferences about individual houses based on the assumption that houses that contain active WiFi access points are likely occupied by people. Currently, more than half (53.6%) of the households in Japan use WiFi according to the government's survey in 2014, and the expanding market of household IoT devices can cause a rapid increase of WiFi and other radio signals in residential communities.

Our approach relies on a technique to determine precise locations of WiFi access points based on ambient WiFi signals. Existing research projects on indoor positioning show that locations of mobile users can be determined by using ambient WiFi signals. For example, Bahl and Padmanabhan [1] proposed a fingerprint-based algorithm that can determine users' indoor locations. Place Lab [5] uses estimated and known locations of WiFi access points and GSM cell phone towers in Seattle to compute users' locations at a city scale. Koo and Cha [4] proposed a multidimensional scaling-based approach based on relative distances between pairs of WiFi access points to estimate locations of WiFi access points in indoor spaces. Other researchers proposed to use probabilistic techniques for localizing indoor access points [3] and road-side access points [8]. Unlike existing approaches, we propose to use a hybrid network model along with multidimensional scaling to support mixed uses of various devices with or without the location sensing capability, thereby making it easier to deploy in local communities with sporadically distributed vacant houses.

3 Localizing WiFi Access Points in Local Communities

There are existing databases of WiFi signals, including the ones owned by private organizations and the others collected by the wardriving community (e.g., Wigle.net [7].) WiFi data can be collected easily by using off-the-shelf smartphones, tablets and notebook computers. Our method requires that WiFi mac addresses and RSSI (Received Signal Strength Indicator) data be recorded along with GPS-based location information if available. Volunteers can carry such devices in their pockets or bags while taking a walk, thereby collecting a sufficient amount of data relatively quickly (e.g., a few or several hours in total depending on the area of a local community.).

3.1 Constructing Hybrid Networks

We could infer the locations of WiFi access points (APs) by triangulation using the locations of mobile devices. However, this approach could not determine the locations of APs very accurately when individual access points are measured less than three times, or when mobile devices are not equipped with accurate GPS receivers. We thus employ a localization method based on statistical shape modeling. Unlike existing localization methods for indoor WiFi APs based on multidimensional scaling, which model collected measurements as a graph of WiFi APs [4], we model collected data as a hybrid network of real and virtual APs. A real AP (RAP) corresponds to an actual WiFi access point while a virtual AP (VAP) represents a measurement point by a mobile device. A mobile device creates n VAPs when it measures WiFi signals n times in a local community.

To construct a hybrid network with real and virtual APs, we first create vertices with all real and virtual APs based on mac addresses and timestamps. We next instantiate two types of edges, one connecting pairs of virtual APs, which we call V^2 edges, and the other connecting pairs of virtual APs and real APs, which we call VR edges. For all virtual APs that have location information, we simply compute their mutual distances on an Earth ellipsoid, and use them as weights for corresponding V^2 edges. The weights for VR edges are determined based on the RSSI values of WiFi APs (RAPs) as measured by mobile devices (VAPs). More precisely, we determine weights for VR edges according to Euclidean distance d, which is calculated as follows.

$$d(rssi) = \frac{MAX\_DIST}{L} * floor(10^{\frac{log10(L+1)*(MAX\_RSSI-rssi)}{(MAX\_RSSI-MIN\_RSSI)}}) \quad (1)$$

This is based on an oft-adopted model of the relationship between the distance and RSSI. The floor function quantizes the distances at L levels to mitigate the effect of unstable signals. MAX_RSSI and MIN_RSSI are the maximum and minimum RSSI values, respectively. MAX_DIST is the maximum distance. It is the distance at which the smallest level of RSSI would be observed.

3.2 Computing Relative and Absolute AP Locations

We first compute shortest-path distances between all vertices in the resulting hybrid network $\mathbf{G}$ to obtain a distance matrix $\mathbf{D}$. We next apply multidimensional scaling to distance matrix $\mathbf{D}$ to produce relative positions of all vertices in a two dimensional space. We then scale, rotate and translate the positions of real APs as follows to obtain their absolute geographical locations.

$$\mathbf{P_a} = s * \mathbf{P_r} \cdot \mathbf{R} + \mathbf{T} \tag{2}$$

$\mathbf{P_a}$ represents absolute geographical locations of real APs, which are obtained by scaling and rotating the relative positions of real APs, denoted as $\mathbf{P_r}$, with the scaling factor s and rotation matrix $\mathbf{R}$, and translating it by adding $\mathbf{T}$. Procrustes analysis is used to match the relative positions of virtual APs to the longitude and latitude values of the corresponding virtual APs, thereby deriving s, $\mathbf{R}$, and $\mathbf{T}$.

4 A Field Trial

This section presents our field trial in a suburban residential community. We collected ambient WiFi signals, inferred occupied houses based on the estimated locations of WiFi access points using the proposed method, and compared the results with the ground truth provided by the local community members. One researcher collected ambient WiFi signals in the community by walking along all the streets in the neighborhood (see map in Fig. 1), which took approximately an hour. The signals were recorded using WiGLE WiFi app [7] on two Android smartphones (Nexus 5 and Xperia Z Ultra) in the researcher's backpack pockets. Location data were captured via GPS, when available. Consequently, we captured data about 962 WiFi APs and 610 virtual APs. This implies that there are quite a few houses having multiple APs as there are only 286 houses in this community.

4.1 Constructing Hybrid Networks

As weak WiFi signals may be caused by multipath and obstructions, we ignored weak WiFi signals with their RSSI values less than −87 dB, which

Fig. 1. Comparative geovisualization. Yellow shows the houses inferred as occupied, and the purple shows actual vacant houses. (Color figure online)

approximately corresponds to the 80% cutoff point with the maximum RSSI of −57 dB and the minimum of −95 dB. We then computed the distances with $L = 3$, $MAX\_RSSI = -57\,\text{dB}$, $MIN\_RSSI = -87\,\text{dB}$, and $MAX\_DIST = 27\,\text{m}$ according to Eq. (1). The resulting distances have been used as the weights of VR edges to construct a hybrid network by using the *igraph* package of *R*.

4.2 Computing AP Locations

We computed shortest-path distances between all vertices and applied multidimensional scaling using *cmdscale* function of the *stats* package of *R*. We then derived scaling factor s, rotation matrix $\mathbf{R}$ and translation matrix $\mathbf{T}$ by using the procrustes function of the *vegan* package of *R*. Not surprisingly, and as depicted in Fig. 2, the matching was not perfect and the differences (i.e., arrows) are somewhat large for VAPs (i.e., circles) near the bottom left. Finally, we used s, $\mathbf{R}$, and $\mathbf{T}$ to compute the locations of the WiFi APs.

4.3 Detecting Occupied Houses

We establish that houses containing at least one WiFi access point are actively occupied. The yellow houses in Fig. 1 have been judged as occupied in this manner. Figure 1 also shows actual vacant houses in purple. The white houses were not inferred as occupied but they are actually occupied (i.e., false negatives). Of the 286 houses in the community, 278 are occupied and 8 are vacant. Our method detected 57 (20%) occupied houses without falsely detecting vacant houses as occupied houses (i.e., no false positives), suggesting to reduce the workload of field surveys accordingly. The number of detected houses is fairly lower than the number of detected APs, and improving the accuracy of AP localization could further reduce the workload for field surveys.

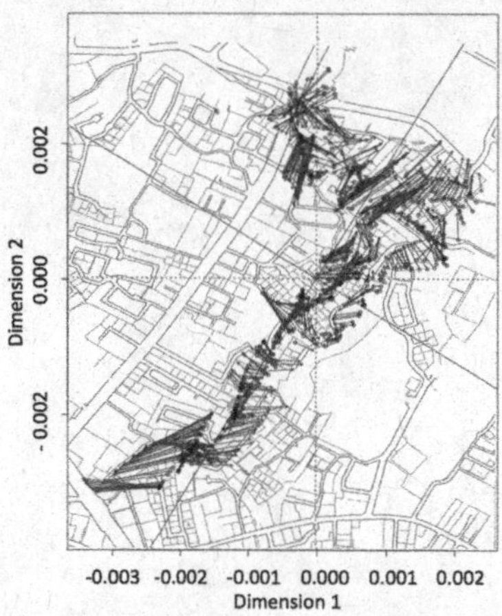

Fig. 2. Procrustes errors of our dataset

5 Conclusion and Future Work

We have proposed, implemented and verified a technique to infer the locations of occupied houses based on ambient WiFi signals. Our technique collects georeferenced RSSI (Received Signal Strength Indicator) data based on opportunistic smartphone sensing, constructs hybrid networks of WiFi access points, and analyzes their geospatial patterns based on statistical modeling. We have shown that the technique can successfully infer occupied houses in a suburban residential community.

While the detection accuracy is far from perfect (cf. false negatives in Fig. 1), the amount of correctly detected occupied houses is not small and the method did not produce false positives in our field trial. Potential explanations for not detecting a house occupied can be too weak signal strengths or no WiFi access point installed in those buildings (cable/mobile or no connection). Without exploiting the proposed method, field workers need to check all the houses. Using Fig. 1 as an example, the more yellow houses the method finds, the less workload is imposed on field workers to manually visit all houses multiple times.

In some cases, individuals may be wary of the SSIDs of their WiFi APs being used for finding their community's vacant houses. Encrypted hash IDs can be used to minimize such concerns, and they can also choose to disable the beaconing feature of their WiFi APs.

Naturally, more tests are warranted to further verify and optimize the method. The next step of our work seeks to find volunteers from local communities who are interested in urban development and public safety in their neighborhood to carry devices provided by us for logging purposes.

References

1. Bahl, P., Padmanabhan, V.N.: RADAR: an in-building RF-based user location and tracking system. In: Proceedings IEEE INFOCOM 2000, pp. 775–784 (2000)
2. Chi, G., Liu, Y., Wu, H.: "Ghost Cities" analysis based on positioning data in China (2014). arXiv:1510.08505
3. Ji, M., Kim, J., Cho, Y., Lee, Y., Park, S.: A novel Wi-Fi AP localization method using Monte Carlo path-loss model fitting simulation. In: Proceedings IEEE PIMRC, pp. 3487–3491 (2013)
4. Koo, J., Cha, H.: Unsupervised locating of WiFi access points using smartphones. IEEE Trans. Syst. Man Cybern. Part C Appl. Rev. **42**(6), 1341–1353 (2012)
5. LaMarca, A., et al.: Place lab: device positioning using radio beacons in the wild. In: Gellersen, H.-W., Want, R., Schmidt, A. (eds.) Pervasive 2005. LNCS, vol. 3468, pp. 116–133. Springer, Heidelberg (2005). doi:10.1007/11428572_8
6. Nomura Research Institute: News release, 7 June 2016. http://www.nri.com/Home/jp/news/2016/160607_1.aspx. (in Japanese)
7. Wigle.net (2017). https://wigle.net/. Accessed 3 Jan 2017
8. Wu, D., Liu, Q., Zhang, Y., McCann, J., Regan, A., Venkatasubramanian, N.: CrowdWiFi: efficient crowdsensing of roadside WiFi networks. In: Proceedings International Middleware Conference, pp. 229–240 (2014)

A Framework for Distributed Interaction in Intelligent Environments

Dario Di Mauro[1(✉)], Juan C. Augusto[2], Antonio Origlia[1,3], and Francesco Cutugno[1]

[1] University of Naples Federico II, Naples, Italy
{dario.dimauro,cutugno}@unina.it, antori@gmail.com
[2] Middlesex University, London, UK
j.augusto@mdx.ac.uk
[3] University of Padua, Padua, Italy

Abstract. Ubiquitous computing is extending its applications to an increasing number of domains. “Monolithic” approaches use centralised systems, controlling devices and users' requests. A different solution can be found in works proposing “distributed” intelligent devices that communicate, without a central reasoner, creating little communities to support the user. If the former approach uses all the available sensors being more easily context-aware, the latter is scalable and naturally supports multiple users.

In this work we introduce a model for a distributed network of entities in Intelligent Environments. Each node satisfies users' requests through Natural User Interfaces. If a node cannot produce the expected output, it communicates with others in the network, generating paths where the final target is undetermined and intermediate nodes do not understand the request; this is the focus of our work. The system learns parameters and connections in the initial topology. We tested the system in two scenarios. Our approach finds paths close to the optimum with reasonable connections.

1 Introduction

The human world is more and more interconnected. People have access to many computing devices and use them to communicate with each other. As a matter of fact technology is used to manage daily tasks more and more frequently and in a increasingly wider part of population: talk with friends, require information, enjoy art and manage appliances. Literature and market offer many solutions and, in order to maximise performances, they need to be contextualised in some domain, being more aware of how each system is changing the surrounding environment [2, p. 1]. The approaches proposed in literature are mainly divided in two groups; the former is based on a central reasoner that collects all the data coming from the available sensors and takes actions considering a monolithic core. The latter approach uses a distributed network of interacting devices; they have their own sensors and reasoners and are focused on smaller targets, usually

A. Braun et al. (Eds.): AmI 2017, LNCS 10217, pp. 136–151, 2017.
DOI: 10.1007/978-3-319-56997-0_11

related on the set of categories they belong to. If the first case is more easily aware of what is happening, the last is more flexible, and especially useful in dynamic contexts [25], where many users interact with the available technology together; moreover, the current market offers more and more devices focused on simple tasks, but that can be exploited to make the overall environment more intelligent. In all the adopted strategies, Human-Computer Interaction (hereafter HCI) plays a fundamental role. It is essential to make the users feel like *managers* of the environments they are in, moreover it influences the naturalness of the interaction with the system; it strictly depends on the domain, on the choices made concerning devices and design; however, considering interaction from a more abstract point of view, HCI, such as human-human and machine-machine communications, is performed by exchanging messages and data, also in a multi-modal way; domain and tasks infer more specific details. From this point of view, designing and developing different kinds of interaction requires to choose different sets of modalities, input devices, multi-modal fusion approaches and input managers, but the main need does not change: strive for a better communication. This concept is stronger in an Intelligent Environment (hereafter IE) [3], because different types of interaction are needed and, in a pervasive system, each entity in the world interacts with others in a specific way. In order to design a new IE, the needed steps are: modelling the environment and developing best interaction modalities for each chosen task. Modelling is always necessary to manage domain-related possibilities, constraints and involved actors; it is usually managed by experts of that domain and, for IEs, they should provide a set of sensors, devices and network protocols to reach some goals [8]. The latter part, indeed, is time-consuming and repetitive in many cases. Moreover, multiple users are supposed to independently use the network at the same time, so the system should be powerful enough to manage a large number of dialogues together. In a distributed system the resulting organisation can be seen as partitioned in communities that depend on the current interaction, and users are *leaders* of each set. The considered scenario is typical in smart museums, where works might talk to users: visitors follow their path and interact with a few entities per time; meanwhile their interaction is independent from other users and the rest of works of art. A centralised system cannot support all the visitors at the same time, while a distributed system can, but it should interact with others system nodes to process unknown requests.

In this work we will present a model for a distributed network of devices and a framework for HCI in IE, focusing on Natural User Interfaces (NUI) [21] and with a specific preference for natural language dialogues supported by gestures and augmented reality approaches; this work is in the direction of basic, natural interaction design thought to improve user experience quality. The framework provides a communication layer between machines, offering a pervasive/ubiquitous infrastructure and a comfortable environment to support Internet of Things (IoT) guidelines.

This paper is organised as follows: Sect. 2 reports works related to PHASER, that is the model presented in Sect. 3. In Sect. 4 we provide a solution for a problem related to distributed systems, named the "Navigation Problem". From

Sect. 5 we focus on a Smart House, showing some representative scenarios and reporting Experiments and Results in Sect. 6. Section 7 concludes the paper.

2 Motivation and Related Works

Our basic idea is to provide a distributed network of entities, where each node interacts with the user through multi-modal interaction following NUI guidelines. Knowledge is local to the node and limited to its own services. If the node is not able to produce the expected output for a request, it sends the received message to the others, without a prior determined target node. The Ambient Intelligence perceived by the users is built upon a collection of partial nodes' intelligence.

Other works facing the same problem have been found in literature. One of them is i*Chameleon [16], where the authors show an interaction among multiple devices, but the described system only supports a limited number of connected nodes. Moreover, the authors limit the work to exchanging signals, clearly defining starting (that sends requests and commands) and ending nodes (that receives and acts), but without considering a particular context, as differently proposed in this work. Peña-Ríos et al. [22] propose a framework to simply develop smart devices and test them by mixing real-life and simulated scenarios. That system presents interesting innovation points, but its use is limited to expert users only. An interesting system has been proposed by Dooley et al. [10]; it is a conceptual work, but it models ubiquitous computing in a smart environment aiming at supporting the user in IEs. The proposed model separates the world in spaces; each space is supposed to be an environment where people interact with distributed devices but their "reasoners" are still centralised. Considered spaces are homes, offices, local transports; different domains where technology can help people in their daily lives. Our model is complementary to Dooley's one, focusing on a distributed version of a single domain, supporting NUI.

A Multi-Agent System (MAS) point of view of an IE has been already explored in other studies [12,14]. Loseto et al. [17] propose a flexible multi-agent approach for smart-environments. Their work is based on the discovery of semantic resource and orchestration, including negotiation techniques between user and smart devices. Sun et al. [23] present a multi-agent design framework for a smart-home and home automation applications. Their work is a Belief-Desire-Intention model [5] for agent individual behaviour design and a regulation policy-based method for multi-agent group behaviour design. Valero et al. [26] propose a system based on Magentix2; differently from others, the authors introduced multiple users' roles and access policies based on that. MAS paradigms are very valid solutions for smart-environment support, but the listed works are usually directly connected to the right device or use a central system that collects the provided services. A distributed context provides flexibility and adaptability [25], while a central "service manager" presents some limitations, especially in very populated environments; however MAS solution of Valero et al. [26] inherits benefits by well known models such as JADE[1] and Jason[2].

[1] jade.tilab.com retrieved on December 2016.

[2] jason.sourceforge.net retrieved on December 2016.

3 PHASER

In this section we will present our model and its implementation in a framework, called PHASER (Pervasive Human-centred Architecture for Smart Environmental Responsiveness). In our concept, PHASER gives a role to each entity that interacts with others. Possible entities are *objects* and *people* that interact with those objects as well. For this reason, we define a node in an abstract way to include the needs of both entities. Each node interacts with others, offering services and responding to requests. We define a single node as a tuple:

$$N(\iota, Cnf_\iota, ClosePeers_\iota, DiscoveredPeers_\iota, oBC_\iota)$$

where ι is a unique identifier of the node in the environment; $ClosePeers$ and $DiscoveredPeers$ are sets of related nodes in the environment: ι interacts with those nodes. Details later in this Section. oBC collects partial information about the connected peers, acting as Business Cards; they include information gathered from a shared ontology (explained later in this Section) and the accepted inputs.

A configuration Cnf determines the behaviour of ι in the environment. It comprises inputs, outputs and the behaviour towards other nodes. In details:

$$Cnf_\iota = (name_\iota, type_\iota, class_\iota, env_\iota, I_\iota, O_\iota, P_\iota) \tag{1}$$

where *type*, *class* and *env* determine the role of ι in the environment according an ontology, *name* is chosen by an interaction designer; details are in Sect. 3.4. I and O represent input and outputs respectively; they divide data into channels as in Eq. 2 for multi-modal interaction, where c_x is a channel code and $RG_{c_x} = \{r_{i_1}, r_{i_2}, \ldots, r_{i_{c_x}}\}$ is a set of regular expressions. If N_{i_ι} and N_{o_ι} are the number of input and output channels, we define I_ι and O_ι in Eq. 3.

$$Ch_j = (c_j, RG_{c_j}) \tag{2}$$

$$I_\iota / O_\iota = \bigcup_{1 \leq x \leq N_{i_\iota/o_\iota}} \{Ch_x\} \tag{3}$$

Eventually P_ι, briefly described here, is a set of parameters for each node that determines how it reacts to connections and interaction requests.

Connections. Each node can interact with other peers and their reference is stored in $ClosePeers$; they compose the initial topology designed by a domain expert. However, sometimes new unforeseen connections can be discovered and included in $DiscoveredPeers$. New arcs may increase the power of the interaction for the user, because they create other bridges in the network, and if a node frequently connects to a discovered peer, this is automatically promoted to $ClosePeer$.

$$DiscoveredPeers = \bigcup (\kappa, c_\kappa, T_\kappa)$$

is a set of discovered nodes κ - we refer to them as "partial" connections -, where $c_\kappa \in [0..1]$ is the probability of making this connection fixed: κ will be included in $ClosePeers_\iota$ as $c_\kappa = 1$. T_κ is the last activity of this connection. As ι interacts with κ at time t, $c'_\kappa = UPC(c_\kappa, \Delta)$, where $\Delta = t - T_\kappa$. Details about the discovery of a node are in Sect. 4.2.

$$UPC(x, y) = x + \frac{x}{y\lambda(y)} \tag{4}$$

$$\lambda(x) = \phi_0 - (\phi_0 - \phi_1)\frac{1}{1 + e^{k_1 - x}} - (\phi_1 - \phi_2)\frac{1}{1 + e^{k_2 - x}} \tag{5}$$

$\phi_{0,1,2}$ and $k_{1,2}$ in Eq. 5 are constants that derive on the activity of the interaction. According to the activity of the interaction, $\lambda(x)$ assigns a factor ϕ. $\phi > 0$ means that the connection is strengthened, but for $\phi < 0$ it is discouraged. Typical relations are $1 \geq \phi_0 > \phi_1 > \phi_2$, with $\phi_2 \leq 0$ and $k_1 \ll k_2$.

Open Connection. As two nodes, ι and κ, open a connection, they share part of their local information composing a personal Business Card (BC):

$$BC_{\iota/\kappa} = (name_{\iota/\kappa}, type_{\iota/\kappa}, class_{\iota/\kappa}, env_{\iota/\kappa}, I_{\iota/\kappa}) \tag{6}$$

On open, $oBC_\iota = oBC_\iota \cup \{BC_\kappa\}$ and $oBC_\kappa = oBC_\kappa \cup \{BC_\iota\}$. On startup, ι asks a connection to each $p_i \in ClosePeers_\iota$. Partial connections will be opened following details shown in Sect. 4.2; in the latter case, collected BCs will be stored in the same way. Moreover, local information need to be updated:

$$DiscoveredPeers_\iota \cup \begin{cases} X_\kappa(t) & \text{if } (\kappa, c_\kappa, T_\kappa) \in DiscoveredPeers_\iota \\ \{(\kappa, 0, t)\} & otherwise \end{cases}$$

where $X_\kappa(t) = \{(\kappa, UPC(c_\kappa, t - T_\kappa), t)\} \setminus \{(\kappa, c_\kappa, T_\kappa)\}$ and t is the current instant. However, $X_\kappa(t')$ is added on every interaction between ι and κ, where t' are the considered next instants.

3.1 States

Each node in our model has a state. It determines which kind of work a node is doing and if it can accept other requests. A node starts in the *Idle* state; Table 1 summarise the states, while Fig. 1 reports all the allowed transitions; details about Forwarding in Sect. 4. The connection *Managing machine interaction (MMI)* → *Idle* is a "forced" transition and it happens if node ι is waiting for node κ for a *MMI*. If ι remains in *MMI* it would not be able to receive a response from κ, because it would be recognised as busy.

3.2 Network of PHASERs

In order to better support the communication, two nodes ι and κ share their Business Card as seen before. The result is a network where each node has partial information about its local connections. This is a real distributed context because

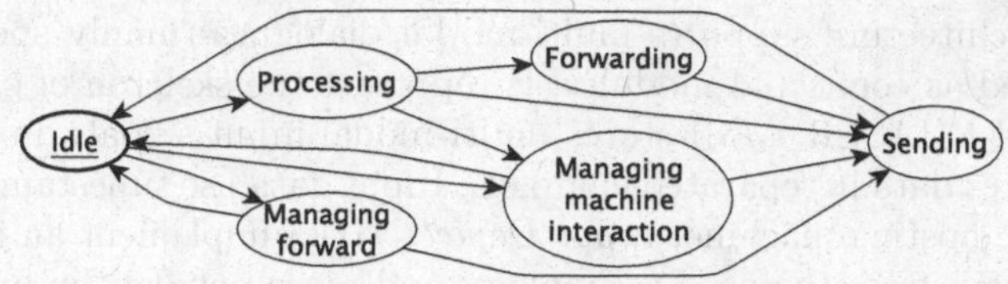

Fig. 1. Possible states and transitions for a node in PHASER

Table 1. Description of states of PHASER

State	Description
Idle	Initial state
Processing	The node is processing a request
Forwarding	The node is forwarding an unknown request
Managing forward	The node is processing a received forward
Sending	The node is replying or re-forwarding a request
Managing machine interaction	Two nodes are co-working for a request

there are no entities that collect all the information. Users interact with each node in the environment, but the actual topology is hidden for them. They, indeed, perceive the network as a compact system because each node involves other parts as in a centralised system, but PHASER is more flexible than a centralised system.

During a communication, ι may send a request to κ. A request R is a snapshot of the input for ι represented by $R = \{(c_j, r_{c_j}), 1 \leq j \leq N_{i_\iota}\}$, where N_{i_ι} is the number of input channels for ι, c_j is a channel and r_{c_j} is the value of the request on c_j. κ receives R, but it is able to accept it just if it represents a valid input for κ; for an element in the request $R_x = (c_x, r_{c_x})$ this is true if $\exists(c_x, R_c) \in \{Ch_{x_\kappa} \subseteq I_\kappa \mid r_{c_x}$ matches on $R_c\}$. "x matches on X" means that $\exists X_i \in X$ so that x complies on the format of X_i. This is wrapped in:

$$m\left(R_x, \kappa\right) = \begin{cases} 1 & \text{if } R_x \text{ is a valid input for } \kappa \\ 0 & otherwise \end{cases} \tag{7}$$

A request R is fully accepted by κ if $\sum_{1 \leq j \leq R} m\left(K_j, \kappa\right) = |R|$. We consider $|R|$ and not $|N_{i_\kappa}|$ because the request could not provide information for some channels. However, a fully accepted request is candidate to be manageable, but ι cannot take for granted that κ will process it successfully.

3.3 Architecture

The model presented above has been implemented and Fig. 2 presents the architecture of a node in the framework; it is an extended version of what already seen in [9]. The architecture supports multi-modal dialogues (manly speech+voice) and is designed as connected modules; it represent the skeleton of each node in the network of PHASER. MMI stores multi-modal input signals, in which a set of devices writes data in separated channels. Input data use timestamps gathered from the same hosting machine. *Input Devices* (IDs) implement an interface, in order to abstract from the used technology and represent data in an hardware-independent form. The diagram in Fig. 2 shows examples of IDs and ODs; their actual activation depends on configuration discussed above. Similar reasoning is replicated on *Output Devices* (OD): MMO collects multi-modal output data coming from ODs and presents their fission to users. An *Input Manager* (IM) manages the fusion of data taken by the MMI structure and passes their classification to the *Dialogue Manager* (DM); this is, here, just an interface towards a real dialogue manager; its behaviour, in fact, highly depends on the particular node and cannot be included in the overall description. The DM is mainly based on OpenDial [15], including it as an external tool, but other DMs may be integrated in PHASER. PHASER offers to the Dialogue Managers a support for network interaction, and for processing of requests as explained in Sect. 4.

The *Remote* module, instead, is used to communicate with non-human peers by standard protocols. They can be robots, smart-devices, technologically enriched works of art, etc. Relationships among these entities create a PHASER network in which each node has an internal logic. By including the *Remote* module as ID, we are able to equally manage human - through active IDs/ODs - and artificial entities - through *Remote* -. This aspect improves the user-centred point of view, because connections are hidden and users perceive the world as a single block, where parts of it process each request. With the proposed architecture, PHASER offers a ubiquitous infrastructure and a comfortable framework for an Internet of Things (IoT). The powerful aspect of this architecture is that its overall behaviour is not related to a single entity nor it is domain-specific but, with proper I/O devices and a DM, it allows to easily prepare an IE, concentrating efforts on each entity. Furthermore, if an environment is considered as "entities offering services" and by them in the Business Card, each system will be able to opportunely contact nodes to solve internal tasks. This is a typical concept in AI agent-based approaches, but we are proposing it in a multi-domain - interaction-oriented - abstract architecture.

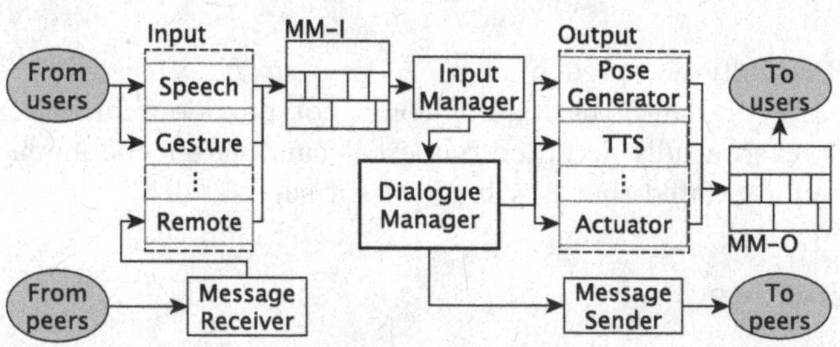

Fig. 2. The architecture of PHASER

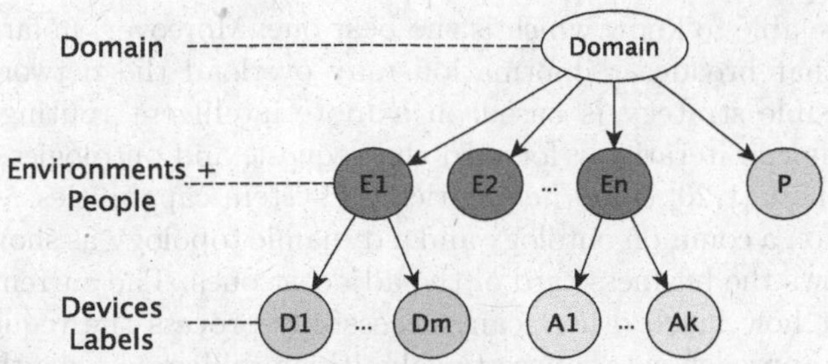

Fig. 3. The structure of a ontology accepted in PHASER

3.4 Ontology

PHASER uses an ontology that represents both the space and the devices. It currently relies on a new developed representation of an environment, but integration with well-known ontologies in this field is under investigation: we are considering soupa [7] and iot-lite[3]. An example of the ontology adopted in PHASER is in Fig. 3. Its structure is as follows:

- a node represents the domain;
- a number of environments are connected to *domain*: they represent physical rooms in the environment;
- each room contains devices. Multiple labels are supported (here with different grey levels);
- particular nodes are directly connected to the domain, because they have not a semantic relation with a single environment: devices that move through the rooms, or personal devices are considered in this class;
- devices working in multiple rooms (i.e. lights) are connected to multiple environments. The current room, that depends on where the device is, must be specified in the configuration, otherwise a random room will be selected at run-time.

Each instance of PHASER is an entity which belongs to a leaf of the tree. By specifying a class, PHASER derives at run-time information such as the environment and other devices in the same room. The selected class, is a parameter reported in the configuration each node requires, as seen before.

4 Navigation of a Request

As a node interacts with a user, it tries to locally process the requests. If the node is not able to do it, the system could deliver an error message or share the request within the network. It may broadcast the data, being sure to reach at least one valid node, if it exists, but if multiple available nodes arrive, the starting

[3] http://iot.ee.surrey.ac.uk/fiware/ontologies/iot-lite retrieved on December 2016.

node should be able to know which is the best one. Moreover, in large networks, many nodes that broadcast information may overload the network itself [11]. A second possible strategy is based on a more intelligent routing process [4], where the node can iteratively forward the request, and ontologies, history and context-awareness [1,20] could help enriching system capabilities.

By relying on a common ontology and a dynamic topology as shown in Sect. 3, each node knows the business card of the adjacent ones. The current node could easily find out how much others can successfully process the request and who they are. The approach we propose to solve this problem is a depth-first-search in a distributed graph where a greedy part chooses the local best nodes as first. Considered parameters are: current request, past interactions and context-awareness.

As a greedy method on a distributed system, the current node that is not able to locally process a request, sorts its adjacent entities in decreasing order, comparing them with Eq. 8.

$$Comp(s, c, n, R) = M(R, n) + Toll(s, c, n) + Friend(s, n) \tag{8}$$

where R the current request, in the form presented in Sect. 3.2, and s, c, n are respectively the starting, current and the next node in the path; the starting node is who received the user's request. The navigation ends if either a node provides a response or too many hops have been done. $M(R, n)$ is the match degree of the current request with the n's accepted inputs, where $M(R, n) = \sum_{0 \leq i < |R|} m(R_i, n)/|R|$. The higher $M(R, n)$ is, the more probably n can understand the request R. $M(R, n) = 1$ is a perfect match. R and m have both been presented in Sect. 3.2.

$Toll(s, c, n)$ represents a toll to pay in changing the environment. In our case:

$$Toll(s, c, n) = (-1)^{(E_c - E_n)(E_s - E_n)} \tau(E_c, E_n) \tag{9}$$

where E_A is an integer for the environment of node A, $E_A - E_B = 0$ *iff* nodes A and B are in the same environment and $\tau(x, y)$ is a function representing a toll going from x to y. Basically, the current node prefers to send the request in its environment, but if the request changes context, it is difficult to fall into the starting environment again.

If needed, $Friends$ assigns a bonus ϕ to requests coming from similar devices. Assuming that T_A is the type of device A in the ontology,

$$Friend(s, n) = \begin{cases} \phi & \text{if } T_s = T_n \\ 0 & otherwise \end{cases} \tag{10}$$

4.1 Sorting Nodes

If a node x needs to send a request, it uses $Comp(s, x, n, R)$ in the Eq. 8 to sort the connected nodes. Let s be the environment where the request started, x the current node, n one of the adjacent node and R the current request. Iteratively applying $Comp$ we obtain a sequence as in Eq. 11; oBC_x has been introduces in Sect. 3.

$$Sorted_x = (p_1, p_2, \dots, p_{|oBC_x|}) \tag{11}$$

where $Comp(s, x, p_i, R) \geq Comp(s, x, p_{i+1}, R)$, $\forall i \in [1..|oBC_x| - 1]$. x will forward R to the peers in the order of $Sorted_x$. At step i, peer p_i will be selected if p_{i-1} has failed at step $i - 1$; a final *"local fail"* is arisen by x if $p_{|oBC_x|}$ fails. In a centralised reasoner, the problem of forwarding is not relevant, because all the devices run in the same cluster. However, PHASER is flexible because the algorithm involves just active connections and it is recalled at each request.

4.2 Network Adaptability

On forwarding, a node x selectively chooses the nodes that could reply to the user on the submitted request. x has no knowledge about the identity of the "target" t - a node that is able to process the request - *a priori*. However, PHASER optimises the navigation of the request in two ways: *(i)* by using the tolls, PHASER learns that some directions could provide a response, fostering paths that worked in the past; *(ii)* if the forward successfully reaches a target t, the topology changes because t is a discovered peer and s opens a partial connection towards it.

The new connection is added to $DiscoveredPeers_s$ shown in Sect. 3. As well as permanent links, s and t share their BC, adding them in oBC_s and oBC_t respectively. A discovered connection is a temporary link, and it lasts just for the current session; they are not affected in the sort process because they are directly chosen with a highest priority by the forwarding algorithm. In reaching a target node t, nodes within followed path do not open new connections, but they update the related tolls of a constant μ, limited to a maximum level of τ_{max}. Possible tolls towards new environments will be included. For their value we assign a constant τ_i. τ_{max}, μ and τ_i are empirically defined.

5 Case Study in Smart House

Current technologies in the field of IE in Smart Houses rely on a single user interaction; this choice reduces the system complexity and optimises the ability of the system to understand users' needs according to their activities [24]. The most used communication device in this environment is the smart-phone. However, more than one person usually lives in a house and some studies have shown that people share the smart-phone [6,13,18]. On the contrary, recent solutions, such as Amazon Alexa[4], support multiple users and foster the interaction through a completely shared device connected to everything and everyone. Although it is possible to use more than one smart device in the house, Alexa, the virtual "assistant", centrally controls all processes.

[4] https://en.wikipedia.org/wiki/Amazon_Alexa retrieved on February 2017.

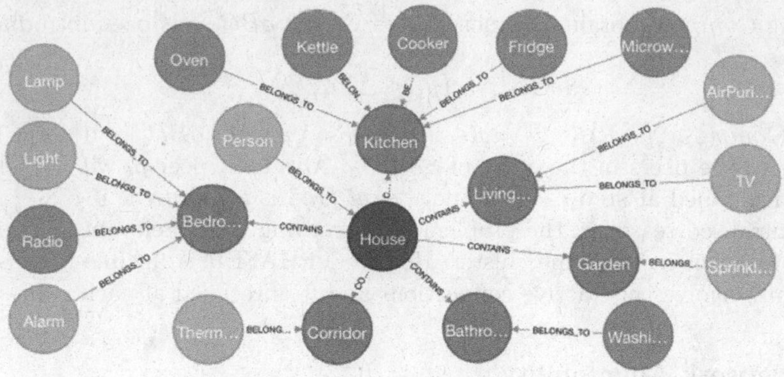

Fig. 4. An example of ontology for smart houses used in PHASER

PHASER should be able to work in different domains just with a limited number of interventions on its configuration, however this paper is focused on the Smart House domain. Each device in the House gathers information about the context from an ontology, structured as in Sect. 3.4 and represented in Fig. 4. Each node interacts with the others as seen in Sect. 3. The final goal of our approach is that each device propagates messages in the network as explained in Sect. 4. Users' perceives themselves as being able to control everything from everywhere, but each device is just expert of the actions it can process. Given this scenario the next challenge is making the interaction as more natural as possible; comments on this issue are reported in the end of Sect. 6. In the next Section, we report some relevant scenarios PHASER can tackle.

5.1 Scenarios

Scenario 1. *John is in the living room, watching TV is on and he is reading a book. Meanwhile, his wife is finishing the housekeeping, interacting with the washing machine and using the radio and their son is in the bedroom playing the guitar. The oven is working to prepare the dinner and John needs to check it, so he asks the TV if the oven is still cooking. The TV checks and answers "no, it has finished". Then the family can have dinner. Later on, it's time to go to bed, so John sets the alarm and falls asleep; the child does the same. The alarms can look the people in the house and can monitor how people are sleeping and, as it is almost time to wake-up, they switch the heating on in the proper bedrooms. John asks to boil the water in the kettle, then takes the breakfast and goes to work.*

Scenario 2. *It is Sunday and Mark is taking a shower; he will reach some friends later. He wants to mow the lawn, with the just bought automatic lawnmower, but it has not been programmed to start yet and, at least on the first time, he does not want to leave it working alone. So Mark asks some device there to start the lawnmower. The lawnmower starts.*

The first scenario is divided in two phases. Multiple users are interacting with the house; in the former part, they are operating independently, in the latter the devices collaborate to responds to users' needs. The second scenario, instead, presents the inclusion of a new device.

6 Experiment and Results

Single PHASER node interaction has been tested in Wizard-of-Oz modalities, where we tested internal dynamics reproducing recorded dialogues. We also conducted stress tests by simulating from one up to 80 input devices. Details are in [9]. In this Section we propose tests focused on network communication with the aim of proving that the algorithm proposed in Sect. 4 reaches the target node in a reasonable time and steps number. Another test, in simulation, uses a realistic network for a smart house. In all the presented results, the target is the node able to provide the desired output. This section ends presenting experiment and results with real users, meeting the scenarios presented in Sect. 5.1.

Simulation. In the considered case of study number of required nodes rarely goes beyond tens, and searching algorithms do not work in very challenging situations, where undetermined solutions are possible. Nevertheless, in order to test convergence features, quality and processing times of our algorithm, we generated networks with 10^3 devices. The network was divided in sub-networks with random arcs: connections within the same area are more probable than connections between different sub-networks. We generated networks with $2^{0..10}$ sub-networks with a number of nodes from 22 to 4134. By defining both the request and the target, we simulated an interaction, starting from a random node, using the algorithm of Sect. 4 as a measure of quality; μ, τ_{max}, τ_i and ϕ have been set to 0.1, 0.5, 0.3 and 0.05 respectively. Figure 5 shows the collected lengths of paths. The first and second columns contain the observed lengths at the first iteration and after 30 adaptation steps, also adding new relevant links; starting from a reference set of N nodes in a graph with $N^2 * 30\%$ connections in total, in repeated simulation, we added up to 7% of the connections. The third column shows the shortest path length on the same initial topology. In the last column we report a stability test; it is calculated by removing both important nodes in the network - after the adaptation - and the new introduced arcs.

Realistic Case Scenario. With the same approach, we generated a realistic network with more realistic connections distributions responding to a possible scenario in the House. We considered 3 bedrooms, 1 bathroom, 1 living room and 1 kitchen with 28 nodes in total. The nodes were pseudo-randomly connected, as connections within the same area and limiting inter-rooms connections were preferred; as far as connections between rooms concerns, once again randomisation was chosen. The more connections the nodes share, the faster could be the response, because each node is more probably connected to the target. However,

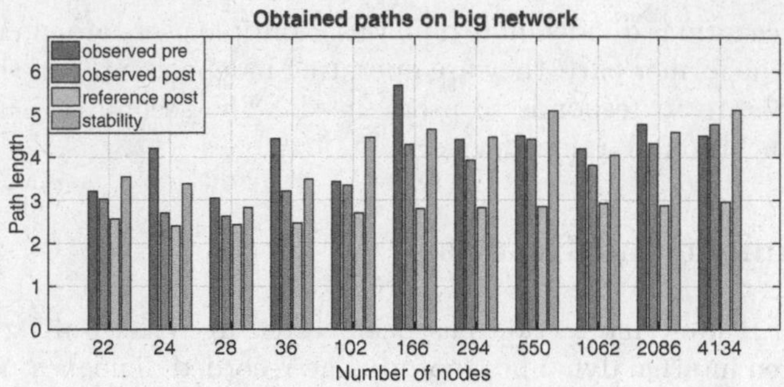

Fig. 5. Observed paths pre and post the adapting phase, comparing post with the shortest path and including stability check

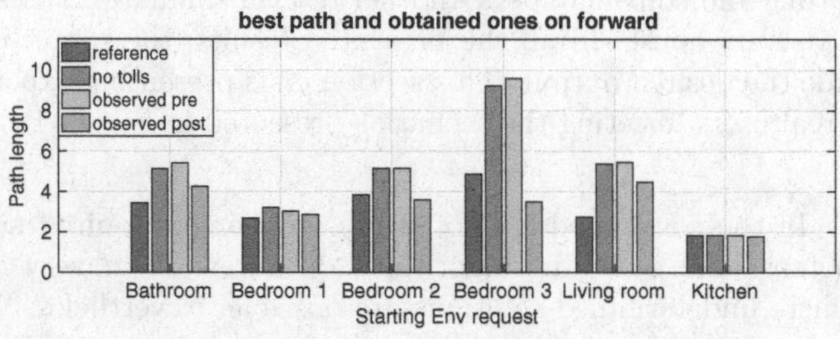

Fig. 6. A comparison in realistic situation with 28 devices and reasonable connections

a full-connected graph is not always feasible because of infrastructure limits, especially with large networks; for this reason it is reasonable that nodes in the same sub-network, that could be *"semantically linked"* are highly connected because it is probable that they will interact. In this case, μ, τ_{max}, τ_i and ϕ have been set to 0.1, 0.5, 0.3 and 0.05 respectively.

The system was tested as follows: similarly as in previous tests, we choose the target node T. A random node R_1 from each room was picked and we calculated the shortest path between R_1 and T; used as reference in comparison with the forwarding algorithm without tolls, with $toll = 0.1$, and the adaptation process as explained in Sect. 4. In the second step, the resulting network is tested picking another node R_2 in the same area. The network was trained in seven iterations. Resulting data are showed in Fig. 6. In order to be statistically relevant, each single experiment has been repeated 50 times; the whole process has been performed on 10 generated topologies having the same structure, but connections among nodes are potentially different.

Smart House. We conducted these experiments at the "Smart Space Lab" at Middlesex University, London. We proposed the scenarios seen in Sect. 5.1 for a network of 8 devices. Each user interacted with the devices through a web-page, where an image represents the associated intelligent device; an avatar has been used as a "personal assistant" for web-pages accessed through a smart-phone. All the nodes run on the same machine, but they can be remotely accessed. The tests have been performed by 10 people. They all perceived the system as a compact block, similarly to a centralised system, but volunteers, asked to express their preference for distributed vs. centralised systems, preferred a distributed system in 8 cases on 10.

Discussions. In the first experiment, we noted that, after the learning phase, the system reached the request in fewer steps than *"observed pre"*, also in big networks. The *t-test* confirmed the hypothesis that "*post* data are lower than *pre* ones", also in the biggest topology, where the *post* average distance is slightly higher than *pre*. Moreover, the removed nodes affected the stability of the result, but the system was able to reach the target anyway. We measured that the reaches the target in 25 ms, even on the biggest network. We just considered time required for the navigation of the request on the same machine; at run-time, average transmission delays and the Dialogue Manager of each node may take additional time.

It appears that our model works better when connections reflect a "semantic links" between two devices, because increases the possibility to use that connection. Two nodes will collaborate if they are semantically connected and if they offer "shared services", so these kind of connections should be fostered. Adopting random connections, preferring intra-area links, proved that our approach can work, improving the results after few steps. However, since an automatic optimised connection highly depends on the context and the offered services, the initial topology should be designed from an expert of the considered domain.

Interesting results came from the last experiments with real users. Although they perceived that they could control the whole house from each device, accomplishing our goal, they found unnatural talking with a specific device to manage everything - e.g. the fridge to switch the light on, etc. This aspect arose questions about which strategies are better to make the users feel the interaction as "natural". A possible strategy they advised is to elect a unit as manager for all the devices in each room. Alternatively, one can coordinate all the devices with the same interface, hiding a shared intelligence. Some studies [19] followed this way: this issue will be argument of future investigations for PHASER as well.

7 Conclusions

In this work we presented PHASER, a framework that manages HCI and Machine Machine interaction in Intelligent Environments. Against other approaches in this area, PHASER is based on a strongly distributed model, where each device carries on a dialogue with the user and the global intelligence is built upon the collection of those capacities. Particular attention has been posed on the presented *Navigation Problem*, seen in Sect. 4; each node of the network forwards the received request to its connected entities if the local Dialogue Manager is not able to produce the expected output. The navigation of the request relies on a *toll*, a context-aware solution adopted to improve the path finding.

The actual use of the network trains the values of each toll: the system learns from real data to foster paths that gave good results in previous interactions. Moreover, the system adds unforeseen connections; they create bridges among different nodes in the network but they are activated just if their use is confirmed during the time. The system has been tested in three cases: we provided a simulated environment in order to test the model in extreme situations; a more realistic scenario has been considered: a case study in a smart house has been proposed with a reasonable number of devices and connections. In each cases, paths found by PHASER were close to the shortest path, without pre-processing the network.

PHASER relies on an external configuration that declares which inputs each node supports, the provided output, the dialogue manager and internal parameters that regulates the behaviour of each node. Currently a configuration is in XML format but a graphical tool is in work in progress to easily design the interaction in an comfortable way.

References

1. Abowd, G.D., Dey, A.K., Brown, P.J., Davies, N., Smith, M., Steggles, P.: Towards a better understanding of context and context-awareness. In: Gellersen, H.-W. (ed.) HUC 1999. LNCS, vol. 1707, pp. 304–307. Springer, Heidelberg (1999). doi:10.1007/3-540-48157-5_29
2. Alegre, U., Augusto, J.C., Clark, T.: Engineering context-aware systems and applications: a survey. J. Syst. Softw. **117**, 55–83 (2016)
3. Augusto, J.C., Callaghan, V., Cook, D., Kameas, A., Satoh, I.: Intelligent environments: a manifesto. Hum.-Centric Comput. Inf. Sci. **3**(1), 1–18 (2013)
4. Bello, O., Zeadally, S.: Intelligent device-to-device communication in the Internet of Things. IEEE Syst. J. **10**(3), 1172–1182 (2016)
5. Bratman, M.: Intention, Plans, and Practical Reason. Center for the Study of Language and Information, Stanford (1987)
6. Busse, B., Fuchs, M.: Prevalence of cell phone sharing. Surv. Method. Insights Field (SMIF) (2013)
7. Chen, H., Finin, T., Joshi, A.: The SOUPA ontology for pervasive computing. In: Tamma, V., Cranefield, S., Finin, T.W., Willmott, S. (eds.) Ontologies for Agents: Theory and Experiences, pp. 233–258. Springer, Heidelberg (2005)
8. Cook, D., Das, S.: Smart Environments: Technology, Protocols and Applications, vol. 43. Wiley, Hoboken (2004)
9. Di Mauro, D., Cutugno, F.: A framework for interaction design in intelligent environments. In: 2016 12th International Conference on Intelligent Environments (IE), pp. 246–249. IEEE (2016)
10. Dooley, J., Henson, M., Callaghan, V., Hagras, H., Al-Ghazzawi, D., Malibari, A., Al-Haddad, M., Al-Ghamdi, A.: A formal model for space based ubiquitous computing. In: 7th International Conference on Intelligent Environments, pp. 74–79 (2011)
11. Dressler, F., Akan, O.B.: A survey on bio-inspired networking. Comput. Netw. **54**(6), 881–900 (2010). New Network Paradigms

12. Ferrando, S.P., Onaindia, E.: Context-aware multi-agent planning in intelligent environments. Inf. Sci. **227**, 22–42 (2013). http://www.sciencedirect.com/science/article/pii/S0020025512007748
13. Karlson, A.K., Brush, A., Schechter, S.: Can I borrow your phone?: understanding concerns when sharing mobile phones. In: Proceedings of the SIGCHI Conference on Human Factors in Computing Systems, pp. 1647–1650. ACM (2009)
14. Li, W., Logenthiran, T., Woo, W.L., Phan, V.T., Srinivasan, D.: Implementation of demand side management of a smart home using multi-agent system. In: 2016 IEEE Congress on Evolutionary Computation (CEC), pp. 2028–2035, July 2016
15. Lison, P.: A hybrid approach to dialogue management based on probabilistic rules. Comput. Speech Lang. **34**(1), 232–255 (2015)
16. Lo, K.W., Tang, W.W., Leong, H.V., Chan, A., Chan, S., Ngai, G.: i*Chameleon: a unified web service framework for integrating multimodal interaction devices. In: Pervasive Computing and Communications Workshops (PERCOM Workshops), pp. 106–111. IEEE (2012)
17. Loseto, G., Scioscia, F., Ruta, M., Di Sciascio, E.: Semantic-based smart homes: a multi-agent approach. In: 13th Workshop on Objects and Agents (WOA 2012), vol. 892, pp. 49–55 (2012)
18. Matthews, T., Liao, K., Turner, A., Berkovich, M., Reeder, R., Consolvo, S.: "She'll just grab any device that's closer": a study of everyday device & account sharing in households. In: Proceedings of the 2016 CHI Conference on Human Factors in Computing Systems, CHI 2016, pp. 5921–5932. ACM (2016). http://doi.acm.org/10.1145/2858036.2858051
19. Mennicken, S., Zihler, O., Juldaschewa, F., Molnar, V., Aggeler, D., Huang, E.M.: "It's like living with a friendly stranger": perceptions of personality traits in a smart home. In: Proceedings of the 2016 ACM International Joint Conference on Pervasive and Ubiquitous Computing, UbiComp 2016, pp. 120–131. ACM (2016). http://doi.acm.org/10.1145/2971648.2971757
20. Musolesi, M., Mascolo, C.: Evaluating context information predictability for autonomic communication. In: Proceedings of the 2006 International Symposium on on World of Wireless, Mobile and Multimedia Networks, pp. 495–499. IEEE Computer Society (2006)
21. O'hara, K., Harper, R., Mentis, H., Sellen, A., Taylor, A.: On the naturalness of touchless: putting the "interaction" back into NUI. ACM Trans. Comput.-Human Interact. (TOCHI) **20**, 5 (2013)
22. Peña-Ríos, A., Callaghan, V., Gardner, M., Alhaddad, M.J.: Using mixed-reality to develop smart environments. In: Intelligent Environments (IE), pp. 182–189. IEEE (2014)
23. Sun, Q., Yu, W., Kochurov, N., Hao, Q., Hu, F.: A multi-agent-based intelligent sensor and actuator network design for smart house and home automation. J. Sens. Actuator Netw. **2**(3), 557–588 (2013)
24. Toch, E., Wang, Y., Cranor, L.F.: Personalization and privacy: a survey of privacy risks and remedies in personalization-based systems. User Model. User-Adap. Interact. **22**(1–2), 203–220 (2012)
25. del Val, E., Rebollo, M., Botti, V.: Combination of self-organization mechanisms to enhance service discovery in open systems. Inf. Sci. **279**, 138–162 (2014)
26. Valero, S., del Val, E., Alemany, J., Botti, V.: Enhancing smart-home environments using Magentix2. J. Appl. Logic (2016)

Which Mobile Health Toolkit Should a Service Provider Choose? A Comparative Evaluation of Apple HealthKit, Google Fit, and Samsung Digital Health Platform

Babak A. Farshchian(✉) and Thomas Vilarinho

Stiftelsen SINTEF, Trondheim, Norway
{babak.farshchian, thomas.vilarinho}@sintef.no

Abstract. Mobile health applications are proliferating. Platform vendors have recently created programming toolkits to support developers. In many healthcare scenarios, mobile health applications are only the end-point of a larger supervised service involving many stakeholders. We want to know how these toolkits support the delivery of such services. Using a case study approach, we study three cases of such platforms and toolkits, i.e. Apple HealthKit, Google Fit and Samsung Digital Health. We collected and analyzed data from blogs, online developer forums, toolkit documentations, and from our own programming of an example health application. We use the boundary resource model to analyze our data. Our findings show that each of the toolkits imposes, through its boundary resources, the business model of its vendor on service providers. This can have important strategic implications for health service providers who want to base their services on each of the three toolkits.

Keywords: Healthcare · Digital health service · Health informatics · Mobile health · Programming toolkit · Health toolkit · Business model · Boundary resource · API

1 Introduction

Health and fitness apps for mobile and wearable devices are proliferating. The majority of users use these apps in stand-alone and unsupervised mode, e.g. for own goal tracking, changing unhealthy habits or gaining awareness of own health and fitness. However, a growing number of Health Service Providers (HSPs) are also examining the potential of smartphones and wearables to deliver supervised health services. Examples include home- and community-based interventions to cope with chronic diseases such as diabetes [1], or assisting community-dwelling elderly in case of e.g. falls [2].

In order to facilitate developers and accelerate this popularity, platform owners – both commercial and research-based –have recently released a range of programming toolkits. A programming toolkit provides a set of programming tools to facilitate the development of a family of software products. Health and fitness toolkits support the development of applications to measure, view and manage health and fitness data.

A. Braun et al. (Eds.): AmI 2017, LNCS 10217, pp. 152–158, 2017.
DOI: 10.1007/978-3-319-56997-0_12

Toolkits create a boundary between what the vendor of the toolkit has already implemented in the platform, and what the application developer can change and build upon. Toolkits are in this sense open innovation tools: "*In this emerging new approach [of using toolkits], manufacturers actually abandon their increasingly frustrating efforts to understand users' needs accurately and in detail. Instead, they outsource key need-related innovation tasks to the users themselves, after equipping them with appropriate 'toolkits for user innovation'*" [3].

At the same time this division brings with it tensions related to e.g. data ownership and vendor lock-in. These tensions become particularly important when we move from the realm of stand-alone health and fitness apps to that of supervised health services provided by e.g. hospitals [4]. Issues such as where data are stored, what investments in hardware and software are needed, how open and interoperable the toolkits are, all become important for HSPs who invest in costly innovation projects.

Although the number of research articles evaluating health and fitness mobile applications is growing, no studies have evaluated mobile health toolkits. Existing evaluations of generic mobile platforms are often at a technical programming level, and focus on mobile devices in isolation from the service context, as in e.g. [5, 6]. In our research we are interested in generating new knowledge about similarities and differences among mobile health toolkits. We believe this type of knowledge is important to inform investments in health platforms, and to inform a dialogue with the vendors of such toolkits. We analyze health toolkit through the *boundary resources* they provide and their impact on service providers. Platform boundary resources are "*software tools and regulations that serve as the interface for the arm's-length relationship between the platform owner and the application developer*" [7]. Examples can be an API (Application programming Interface), or a mandatory server to store health data.

Our research question is "How do existing mobile health toolkits for smartphones support HSPs in providing their services at home and community?" This is a long-term research question for us, whereas the current short paper address a preliminary part. In this paper we explore how three of the most publicized of these toolkits –Apple HealthKit, Google Fit, and Samsung Digital Health Platform (DHP) –support service providers through their deployment architecture, and what requirements they pose on HSPs with respect to deployment and data ownership.

In the following we first present our research method. We then provide a short overview of our preliminary findings, and discuss the implications of these findings.

2 Research Method

We use the case study design with a multiple-case setup [8]. Our cases are the three health toolkits as shown in Fig. 1. The context for the cases is that of *developing supervised health services*. This means services that are provided under supervision of professional HSPs such as hospitals. An example –which we also have used in our case study –is a simple service for home-based monitoring and online reporting of blood sugar levels to a doctor.

We collected and used data from Internet sources –such as blogs, developer forums and vendor's documentation. We collected and analyzed Internet data during a

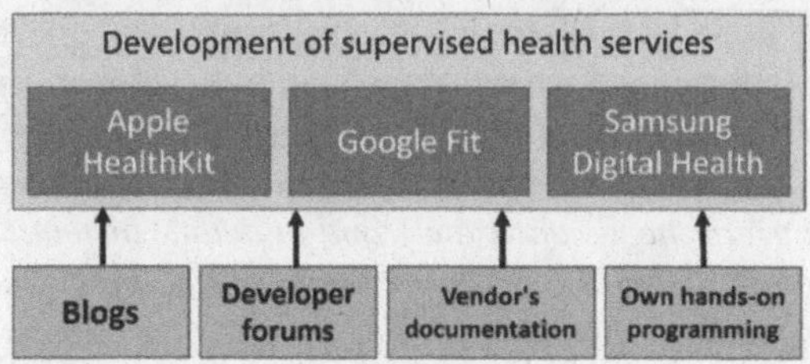

Fig. 1. The case study method used in our research

three-month period in the autumn of 2015. We analyzed the data in several iterations. We used actor network analysis to identify stakeholders and boundary resources for each toolkit. During the same period we developed three versions of a simple blood sugar level reporting service. This exercise was necessary in order to gain detailed knowledge about how each toolkit worked and what technical requirement they posed. For details about the collected data see [9].

3 Findings

In the following we provide an overview of each toolkit, its boundary resources, and its deployment architecture illustrating the role of the boundary resources. The deployment architecture is presented as a three-layer architecture –see e.g. Figure 2 below – showing, from left to right: (1) a health device such as a blood sugar level sensor, (2) a mobile device acting as app container and gateway, and (3) a back-end server containing the service provider's service logic. For each layer and across layers, we show how toolkit vendor's boundary resources (colored in gray in Fig. 2) and third party software and hardware (colored in white) interoperate.

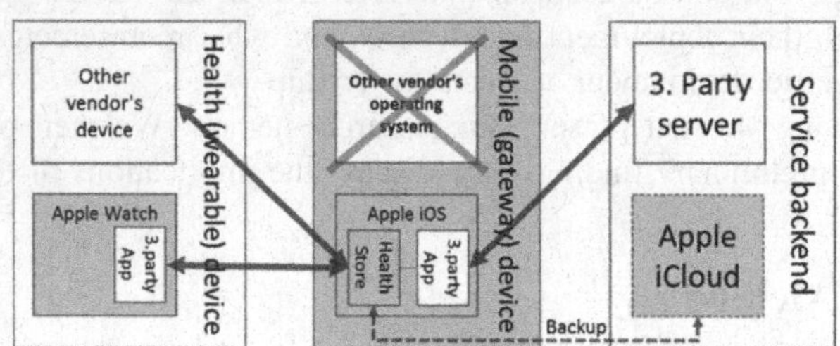

Fig. 2. Service architecture based on HealthKit.

Apple HealthKit. Apple HealthKit's main boundary resources that we have studied are the *Health Store (HS)*, and the *API* to access HS's content (see Fig. 2). HS is the data storage for all health and fitness apps developed for iOS. Apple's own and third party health apps can store data in HS and share it with other apps on the same device. Strict access control mechanisms are in place. The data in HS can only be accessed locally. However, HS's content can optionally be exported to Apple's iCloud servers in form of an encrypted XML file for back-up purposes. Apple has a flexible policy with respect to data types that can be stored in HS. Third party developers can define their own data types and share them through HS. HealthKit, as other Apple products, is restricted to run on iOS devices. A small number of third party Bluetooth devices are certified to work with HealthKit. Moreover, although Apple does not play an active role in the supervised service side, the company has tried to develop partnerships with health service providers in order to promote HealthKit as a healthcare service front-end. Apple has reportedly started a clinical trial in cooperation with Epic Systems and Mayo Clinic.

Google Fit. Figure 3 shows Google Fit's deployment model. All fitness data is stored in Google Fit cloud server and can be accessed in Google Fit web portal and through a REST (REpresentational State Transfer) API. Using a REST API means any mobile device or other web service—e.g. in a hospital—can access the fitness data. Google Fit does not require Android devices. Google provides though an optional Android app, called *Fit App,* to facilitate application development on Android devices. Google has a strict policy regarding what data developers can share via Fit. Google Fit defines a set of fitness data types. If third party developers wish to share other data types using Fit, they need to inform Google and officially register the new data type. Google's policy is that health data cannot be published.

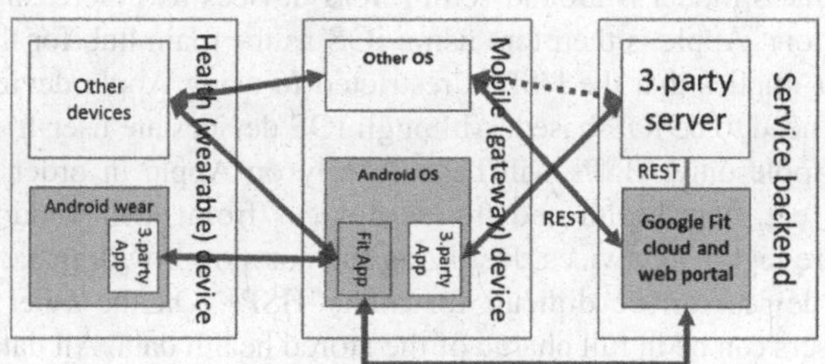

Fig. 3. Service architecture based on Google Fit.

Samsung Digital Health Platform. Figure 4 illustrates Samsung Digital Health (SDH) Platform's deployment model. The main boundary objects are the *Samsung Health* app (*S Health*) and SDH's cloud servers. Similar to Apple's Health Store, app developers can use S Health to store and access all their health data. SDH aims to play an active role also in the service end. Health data stored in S Health are synchronized with SDH's SAMI servers (www.samsungsami.io) and can be accessed directly by other service providers using a secure API. SDH claims to provide an open platform at the device end due to their use of the open source Android OS. Samsung is also involved in developing SIMBAND (www.simband.io), a generic health device. This means both Android Wear-based and SIMBAND-based health and fitness devices can connect to SDH. SDH employs a similar model to Apple regarding its data model. App developers can use an existing set of data types, and can extend this set with own data types.

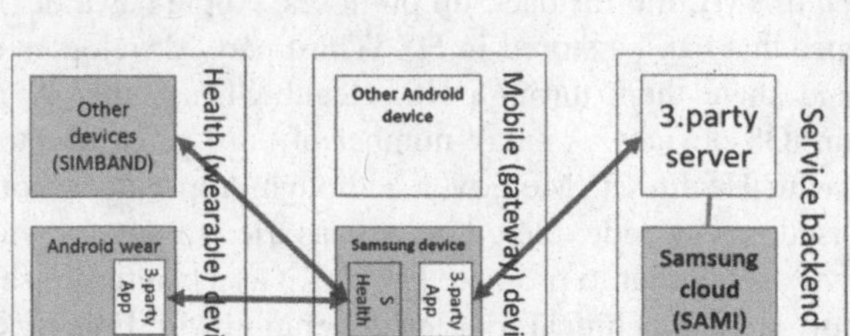

Fig. 4. Service architecture for Samsung Health Platform.

4 Discussion and Implications

Our findings imply that choosing each of the three toolkits can affect a health service provider's (HSP) long-term plans in different ways. Not surprisingly, toolkit vendors have designed their boundary objects in such a way to increase their own revenues. The tensions between the two business models –that of the toolkit vendor and that of the HSP –need to be studied in each case before HSPs invest in a platform.

Apple's business model is around selling iOS devices and increasing app sales in their own AppStore. Apple is therefore using iOS as the main hub for their HealthKit. Using HealthKit implies that the HSP is restricted to using Apple devices. Moreover, third party apps need to be iOS-based. Although iOS devices are user-friendly, they are proprietary to Apple only. HSPs will have to rely on Apple in order to expand the ecosystem with e.g. new health and fitness devices from other vendors. Moreover, Apple devices are high-end devices. Justifying the costs of providing each user with an expensive iOS device can be difficult for many HSPs. On the other hand, service providers and users can be in full charge of the stored health data. All data are stored on the device, the user is in charge of giving access to this data, and SP can access the data via own backend services without any intermediaries.

Google Fit has a cloud-centric model. Google's business model is about selling targeted advertisements. Google Fit is designed to collect and store fitness data from Google's users. Google can then use these data for targeted advertisement. Consequently, Google Fit does not put any restrictions on the type of device used. Even running Android is not a requirement. So HSPs can choose among a wide range of user devices with different form factor and functionality. On the other hand, Google Fit requires integration with Google's own Fit portal. Many countries have strict regulations for HSPs related to storage and access to health-related data, which can make it difficult to use Google servers to store such data. Additionally, Google Fit has a closed data model limited to fitness data, and excluding personal health data such as glucose levels. Healthcare service providers can find this data model limiting, although some service providers currently use fitness data for medical purposes [4].

Samsung's toolkit seems to combine the approaches of HealthKit and Fit. If we consider the recent Samsung initiatives related to SAMI and SIMBAND as part of the company's health platform strategy, we can see that Samsung is looking into the whole value chain. Traditionally Samsung is a device and appliance company, but different from Apple because of Samsung's large variety of devices. This variation seems to have resulted in SIMBAND, an open hardware and device architecture. Samsung also tries to address the needs of service providers, though its SAMI cloud platform can face barriers in different countries due to privacy regulations. Samsung, with its boundary resources on all the three layers of their service architecture, promotes an integrated solution. One disadvantage of this approach is vendor lock-in, which means further technology-driven innovations become difficult due to the vendor-specific interconnections among the different parts of the architecture.

From a research perspective, our preliminary results have implications for the research on boundary resources [7] and platform literature in general. The fact that vendors' products reflect their own business model is not a surprise. Despite this, the relation between business models and platform boundary resources is not studied in depth in the literature. The complexity of the ecosystem of mobile health solutions implies that a thorough understanding of the business models of both technology vendors and HSPs is needed in order to enable sustainable innovation in mobile health.

5 Conclusions

We have in this paper presented some preliminary results from our study of commercial health toolkits and their vendors. Our future work includes expanding the data we have collected, and adding new health toolkits to our analysis.

Acknowledgement. We thank Petter Astrup, Erik G Jansen, and Nemanja Aksic for the collection of data used in our analysis. This paper is partly supported by the Norwegian Research Council project ADAPT (Grant Agreement No. 317631) and the EU Horizon 2020 project MyCyFAPP (Grant Agreement No. 643806).

References

1. Tran, J., Tran, R., White, J.R.: Smartphone-based glucose monitors and applications in the management of diabetes. Clin. Diabetes **30**, 173–178 (2012)
2. Farshchian, B.A., Dahl, Y.: The role of ICT in addressing the challenges of age-related falls: a research agenda based on a systematic mapping of the literature. Pers. Ubiquitous Comput. **19**, 649–666 (2015)
3. von Hippel, E., Katz, R.: Shifting innovation to users via toolkits. Manag. Sci. **48**, 821–833 (2002)
4. Gay, V., Leijdekkers, P.: Bringing health and fitness data together for connected health care: Mobile apps as enablers of interoperability. J. Med. Internet Res. **17**, e260 (2015)
5. Gavalas, D., Economou, D.: Development platforms for mobile applications- status and trends. IEEE Softw. **28**, 77–86 (2011)
6. Anvaari, M., Jansen, S.: Evaluating architectural openness in mobile software platforms. In: 4th European Conference on Software Architecture, pp. 85–92 (2010)

7. Ghazawneh, A., Henfridsson, O.: Balancing platform control and external contribution in third-party development: the boundary resources model. Inf. Syst. J. **23**, 173–192 (2013)
8. Yin, R.K.: Case Study Research: Design and Methods. SAGE Publications, Thousand Oaks (2014)
9. Astrup, P., Jansen, E.G., Aksic, N.: Empirical evaluation of commercial health toolkits. Norwegian University of Science and Technology (NTNU), Trondheim, Norway (2015)

Visual End-User Programming of Personalized AAL in the Internet of Things

Yannis Valsamakis[1(✉)] and Anthony Savidis[1,2]

[1] Institute of Computer Science, FORTH, Heraklion, Crete, Greece
{jvalsam,as}@ics.forth.gr
[2] Department of Computer Science, University of Crete, Heraklion, Greece

Abstract. Ambient Assisted Living (AAL) promotes independent living, while the Internet of Things (IoT) proliferates as the dominant technology for the deployment of pervasive smart objects. In this work, we focus on the delivery of an AAL framework utilizing IoT technologies, while addressing the demand for very customized automations due to the diverse and fluid (can change over time) user requirements. The latter turns the idea of a general-purpose application suite to fit all users mostly unrealistic and suboptimal. Driven by the popularity of visual programming tools, especially for children, we focused in directly enabling end-users, including carers, family or friends, even the elderly/disabled themselves, to easily craft and modify custom automations. In this paper we firstly discuss scenarios of highly personalized AAL automations through smart objects, and then elaborate on the capabilities of the visual tools we are currently developing on a basis of a brief case study.

Keywords: Visual programming · End-user development · Ambient assisted living · Internet of Things

1 Introduction

Ambient Assisted Living (AAL) aims to support the elderly and disabled in their daily routine and health care by extending their independent living as far as possible. Particularly, in the case of elderly people, AAL attempts to encourage and maintain their autonomy by increasing their safety in their home environment, improving their daily life activities and reducing the burden on societal economics from the assisted care of elderly people [1]. Main categories of applications of AAL for the elderly are health (e.g. medications, pill reminder), safety (e.g. emergency button, fall detection), peace of mind, social contact, mobility, security etc. Applications of Ambient Assisted Living can be implemented on top of the Internet of Things [2–4], the emerging paradigm regarding the deployment of network connected smart objects in the environment, including physical things, smart devices, applications, etc.

In our discussion and scenarios throughout the paper we focus mainly on the elderly and on the way their daily life can benefit from the use of smart objects through custom automations supporting everyday activities. The demands for such AAL automations are very personalized, while the requirements may also change on a regular basis due

A. Braun et al. (Eds.): AmI 2017, LNCS 10217, pp. 159–174, 2017.
DOI: 10.1007/978-3-319-56997-0_13

to seasons, social life, health conditions or the progress of ageing. We considered that a good way to enable people fully exploit the capabilities of smart objects and craft whatever custom automations they need is through some sort of end-user programming framework. In fact, it is the wide success of visual programming tools for kids that encouraged as develop the idea of building a framework to allow people around the elderly, even themselves, implement, manage and parameterize applications as personal automations involving smart objects. Also, the results in the domain of end-user programming (EUP) indicate that end-users with virtually no programming background can successfully carry out simple and mode-rate programming tasks.

Contribution

In this paper we propose a full-scale visual end-user programming framework for applications deploying smart objects in the IoT (see Fig. 1[1]), and demonstrate how it can be used to address the highly personalized and fluid requirements of AAL through custom personalized automations. We introduce smart object grouping into tagged environments, supporting environment hierarchies, and provide a real-time smart-object registration process through a discovery cycle, enabling visual programming without requiring direct connection to objects (off-line development). Such a framework, still under development, is running on typical smart phones and tablets and its execution environment is a browser being fully developed in JavaScript. Due to the anticipated fluidity of such automations we also provide ways to easily refine already developed

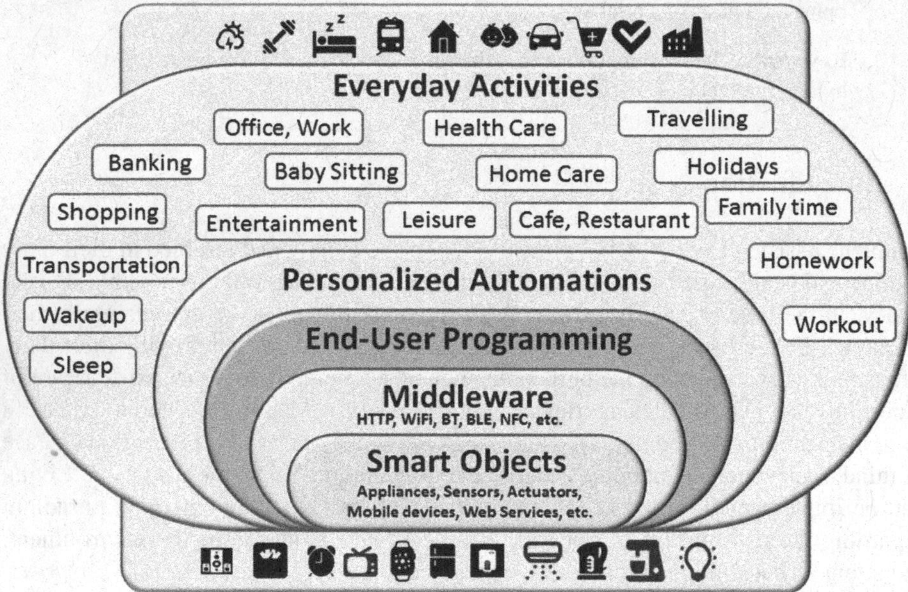

Fig. 1. The notion of personalized custom automations in the Internet of Things through an End-User Programming framework.

[1] Icons are from www.icons8.com.

applications and allow versioning so as to restore previously saved automations or make new ones.

The rest of this chapter is organized as follows. Firstly, we discuss related work in the EUP. Then we outline scenarios of AAL automations for elderly relying on the IoT, followed by a description of the visual tools being developed. Finally, we elaborate on the development case study using the tools.

2 Related Work

Several approaches have been developed to allow End-User Programming. The most popular, and possibly the easiest one, is spreadsheets, widely applied by individuals and businesses. Scripting languages is another popular category, enabling the extension and adaptation of existing applications by end-users. Scripts, while powerful, they have a considerable learning cost and they are prone to errors. A variant of scripting languages is the interpretation of natural languages phrases. While promising, the existing systems are at an early research phase, suffering from various problems and restrictions. Since all previous approaches are text-based they are complicated and less usable for EUP targeted to non-programmers. To address such issues, visual programming languages (VPLs) introduced graphic elements effectively hiding the details of the underlying text program (source code). The most popular visual paradigm for VPLs is *jigsaws* firstly introduced by Scratch [7], then adopted by various other systems such as Blockly [12], MODKit [16], App Inventor [15], etc. Another style is *flow diagrams*, like Microsoft VPL [8] for building robotics applications. Hybrid approaches like EV3 PROGRAMMER AAP [13] existing, blending puzzles and structured flow diagrams.

HomeKit [9] is product from Apple allowing control connected home accessories when compatible with HomeKit, and supports to a certain degree user-defined automations as combinations of accessory control actions. It is not a EUP system as such, and focuses mostly on smart home solutions with emphasis on advanced configurations. Puzzle [17] is a visual development system for custom automations with smart objects in IoT adopting the *jigsaw* metaphor. However, the visual system is primitive and lacks the full-scale capacity of common VPLs like all algorithmic elements, procedures and objects, as well as versioning and application management. Finally, the graphical control logic editor oBeliX [10] is a notable proof of concept for programming on top of IoTSyS [11] without scripts, the latter a common middleware for IoT.

Compared to previous works, we put particular emphasis on: (i) an integrated object-oriented VPL system for EUP, with scalable levels of complexity to match various levels programming concept assimilation and expertise; (ii) first-class support for application management, configuration and versioning; and (iii) hierarchical named environments with smart object registries that can be discovered and used in automations at any time. Finally, since visual language systems seem to be easier to their textual forms, we consider that our target users are the ones supporting and caring the elderly, and for some possible cases the elderly themselves.

3 Scenarios

We firstly discuss the case of Tina, being 72, lives alone, has diabetes and is overweight. Then, we talk about the case of James, being 76, lives alone, has mild cognitive impairments and high blood pressure.

Hypothetical User: Tina

Tina should carry out specific tasks in her daily life due to diabetes, including daily workout, medical therapy and medical examinations (e.g. track insulin glucose), check her weight and have a strict diet. Furthermore, she has to take bath on a regular basis in order to prevent possible infections. Tina's tasks are split in three parts of the day as depicted in Fig. 2 (right), while the people she communicates with are family, nurse which gets blood samples once a week, nutritionist and doctors, as depicted in Fig. 2 (left, top). Tina wakes up every morning at 7 o'clock using an alarm clock in order to get the required pill for her therapy. She has to track her weight, track glucose in her blood, get breakfast with specific ingredients and take her morning bath. However, Tina's morning tasks will be different every Monday for the next two months during which a nurse will be coming to her home once a week. The nurse will take blood samples, which require from Tina not to have received any medication or breakfast on that particular morning. All these changing tasks are difficult to follow for an elderly patient either because they may forget to do some of the tasks (e.g. forget to check weight, remember not to get a pill on the day of blood sampling etc.) or forget to abide by the rules of a strict diet.

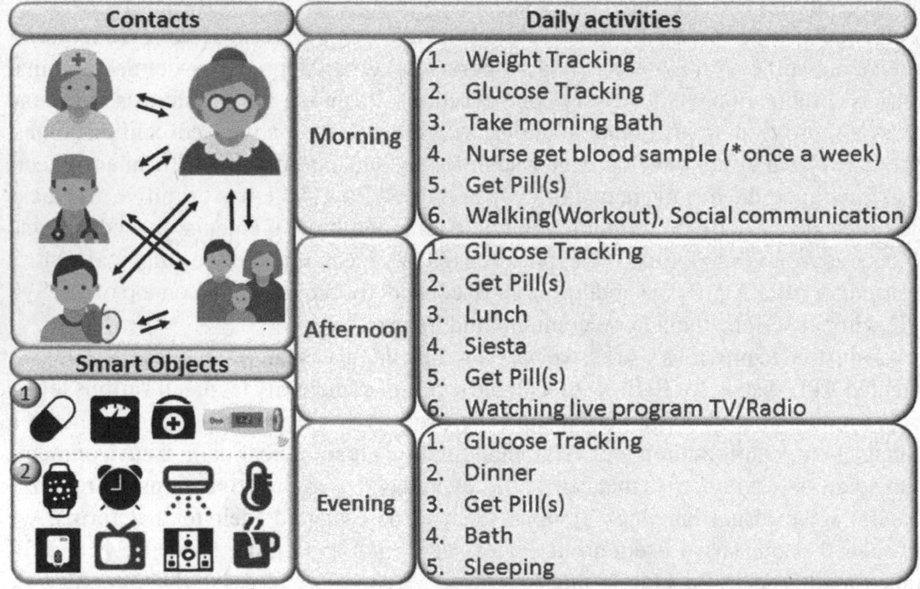

Fig. 2. Tina's daily activities, contacts and smart objects.

Thanks to IoT, Tina is able to use smart objects such as Bee+ [5] tracking glucose, smart scale tracking weight, and smart heater preparing water for bath. In particular, Bee+ is able to track glucose and send data to the doctor directly for further analysis and alert to do this task at a specific time daily. However, Bee+ does not provide functionality to remind her to track glucose after activities such as tracking weight or finishing the bath. Such customized automations require ways to introduce extra algorithmic logic across smart objects.

In Fig. 3, such extra automations are shown to remind and guide Tina for all morning tasks, like track weight and glucose levels, get pills in time, prepare heated water for the morning bath, and regulate home temperature wake up. Furthermore, automations which are depicted in Fig. 3 care to remind Tina not to receive any medication or breakfast every Monday morning before doing her blood tests.

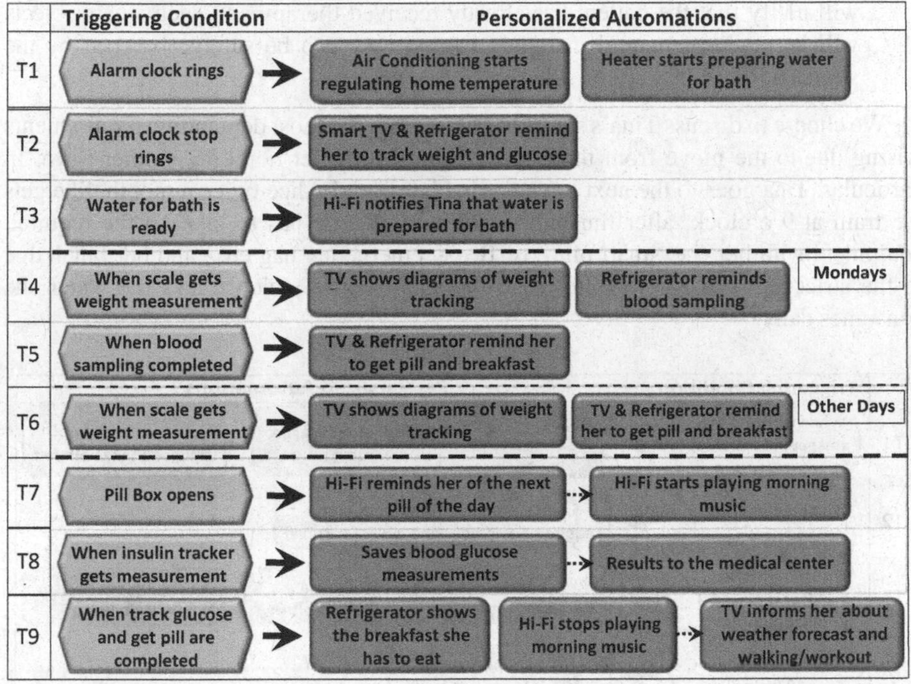

Fig. 3. Tina's morning automations.

Responding to Changing Requirements

All these automations are highly customized on covering Tina's morning requirements. Additionally, such automations are also characterized by a high degree of fluidity due to the frequent changes of Tina's necessities driven by the following factors:

– **Change of seasons**
  - E.g. In summer, people with diabetes need to take more frequent baths to prevent possible infections)

- **Progress of health**
  - E.g. changes in medical therapy, frequency of blood tests, increase of workout/walking sessions, vision issues could arise due to diabetes.
- **Progress of ageing**
  - E.g. Possible hearing issues could arise. As result, this will require a volume up of smart devices.
- **Social life**
  - E.g. Tina visits her friend who lives in another town. She has to get all required things and reminders for therapy will be portable smart devices.
- **Change of technology**
  - This one is an overall evident, but highly decisive factor, requiring ways to accommodate new gadgets or automations for the benefit of the elderly. For instance, consider the era where all pills will be produced as smart objects which will notify that the patient has already received therapy and such smart objects will be made of neutral materials so that they can be safely absorbed by the stomach [6].

We choose to discuss Tina's social life because of the most demanding requirements arising due to the move from the safe environment of her home to another town. In particular, Tina goes to the next town to visit her friend Alice twice a month. She gets the train at 9 o'clock, after finishing her breakfast. She has to take all the required equipment with her (i.e. smart pill box, Bee+, emergency bag etc.) and her lunch due to the strict diet she has to follow and the smart bottle which tracks the water she consumes daily.

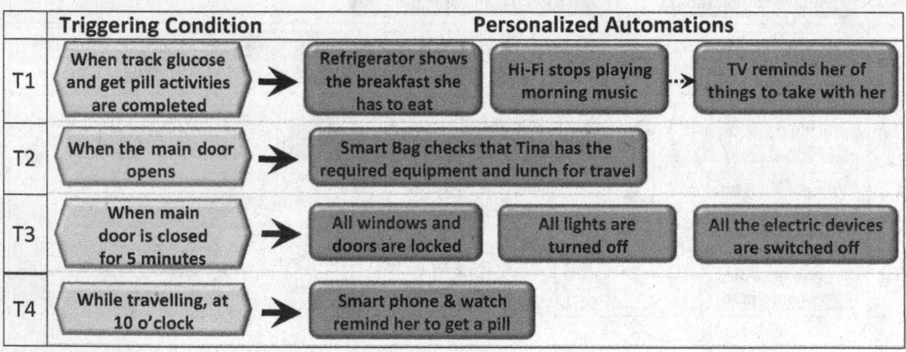

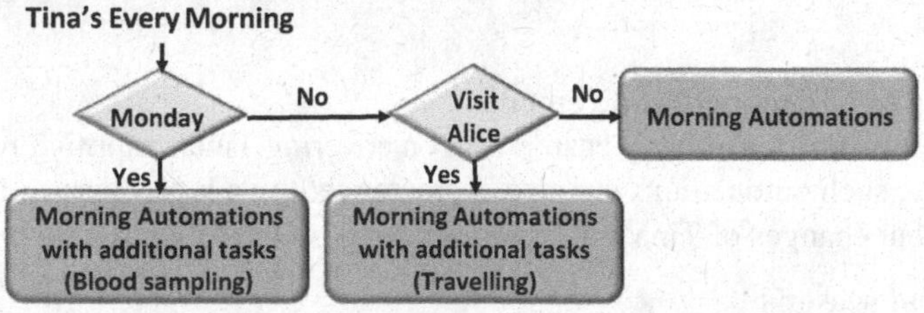

Fig. 4. Additional morning automations when Tina visits Alice (top) and activation of automations based on conditions (bottom).

Leaving her home facilities, total automations could only be executed using portable smart devices such as her smart phone, her smart watch etc. Furthermore, on this day of the week, Tina's workout is postponed for the afternoon when she will be back home. All these changes require respective changes and additions in Tina's automations. Based on the aforementioned requirements Tina's morning automations have to be modified for the day she visits Alice. In particular, the first tasks which are defined are the same with the previous morning automations (see T1–T8, except T4, T5 in Fig. 3) and then tasks concerning travel preparation, leaving home and travelling are depicted in Fig. 4 (top). However, it would be inefficient to change the developed automated tasks for her to travel for one day every two weeks. Nor would it be efficient to change tasks for blood sampling once a week. It would be more efficient to be able to maintain versions of tasks and choose which of them will be active every day as shown in Fig. 4 (bottom).

Hypothetical User: James
James is diagnosed with mild cognitive impairments and he lives alone. He frequently forgets to receive his medical therapy; at other times he forgets to turn off electric devices or lock the door when he leaves home etc. Furthermore, James has a son Nick who worries about his father's daily care. Furthermore, Nick is anxious that his father's condition might deteriorate and he might end up forgetting to drink water, eat, or even worse not find the route to return home after a walk. James's necessities for automations are categorized in five categories as depicted on the right of Fig. 5 and James's contacts are depicted on the left of Fig. 5.

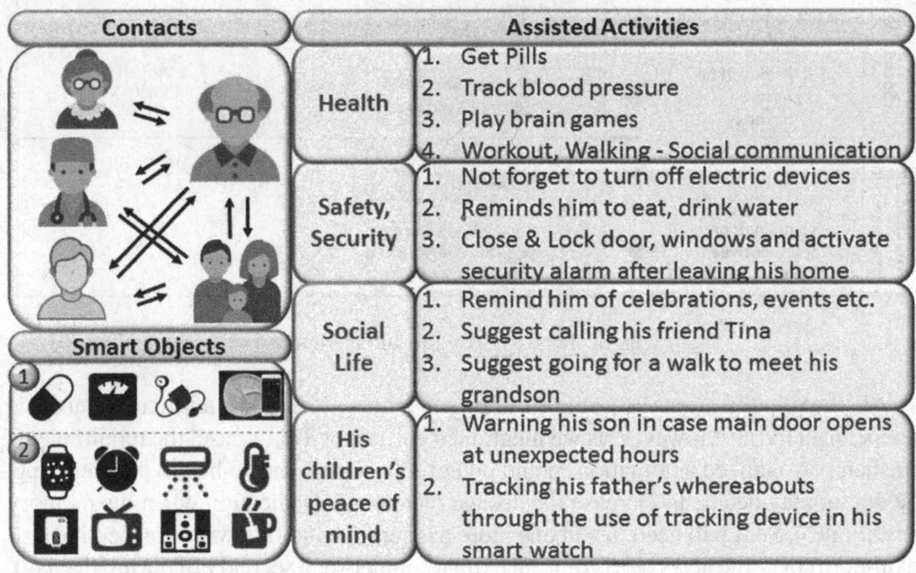

Fig. 5. James's daily activities, contacts and smart objects.

Using smart objects which exist on the market (see in Fig. 5, bottom left), Nick could develop custom automations for his father's necessities. These automations are categorized in respective aforementioned categories as shown in Fig. 6. Firstly, in order to maintain his health, the automation reminds him to receive medical therapy, motivates him to play brain games and have a daily workout. Then, for safety purposes, automated checks are made for possibly forgotten electric devices which have not been turned off (e.g. oven). Furthermore, custom automations care to remind him of celebrations (e.g. the birthday of his grandson) and suggest communicating with his friends etc. In addition, custom automations care to automatically close and lock doors and windows, turn off electric devices and automatically activate security alarm when he leaves home or when he sleeps.

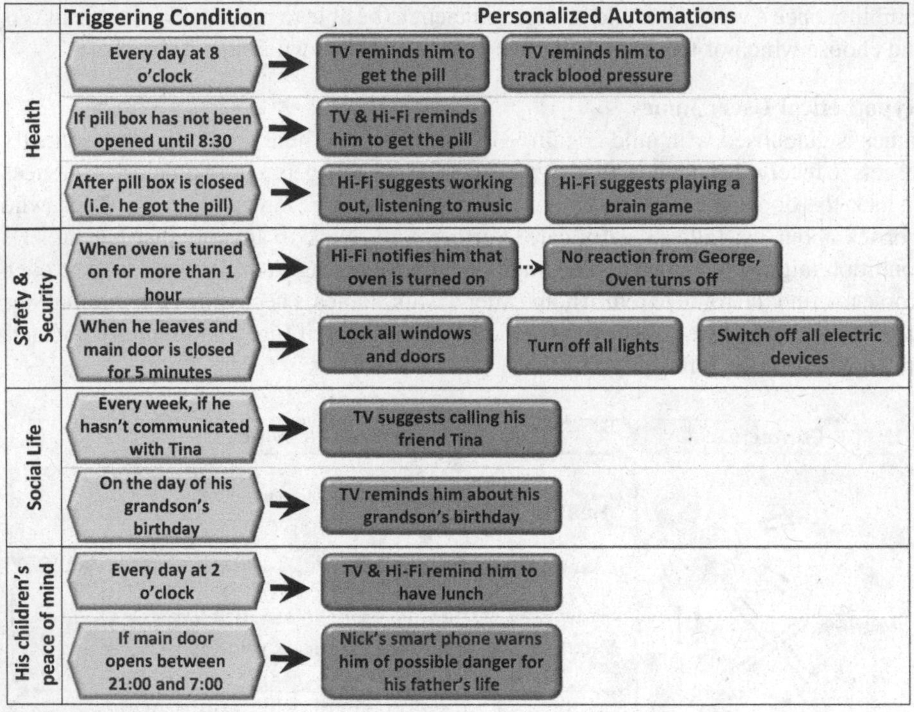

Fig. 6. James's daily life automations.

All these automations are able to improve James's daily life and can extend his independent living. However, as we mentioned earlier for Tina's case, the requirements for such personalized automations could potentially change due to health progress (e.g. the doctor may decide to increase the dosage of James's medication when his memory deteriorates). So it will need to add one more triggering condition with a respective task in order to cover the news needs (e.g. an extra reminder for a second pill during the day). Finally, in order for his son to have peace of his mind, he has additionally programmed personalized automations in order to be notified for unexpected situations i.e. main door opening late at night and GPS data of his father's whereabouts when his father leaves home as depicted in the last two tasks of Fig. 6.

4 Visual Programming Framework

Discovering Proximate Smart Objects

The main building blocks of the IoT are the smart objects. The concept of IoT started in early 2000's with the RFID tags, and network connectivity of physical things. Furthermore, there are numerous smart devices available on the market which are already used in the context of IoT. In particular, devices which are commonly used in daily life (e.g. refrigerator) have been evolved to smart connected devices by offering extra services and automations (e.g. tracking information, remote control, exchanging data with other smart objects etc.). In addition, apart from the physical connected things and the smart devices, there is a huge number of applications online which could be used in the world of IoT and could be considered as smart objects which are connected online and are able to communicate through web-services (e.g. weather forecast, calendar etc.). All the aforementioned categories of smart objects will be available in people's surroundings and require management through the process of developing automations.

The first task end-users have to do in the development process is to discover and register the respective smart objects for their personal automations. The smart objects may be placed in different locations such as the home, workplace, or the gym, and their position may also change (e.g. smart watch). We support the classification of smart objects into named environments, as one or more groups in which a smart object can belong. Nested environments may be defined per environment thus leading to environment hierarchies (e.g. home, home: living room, home: bedroom, home: garden). With the registration of the smart objects, icons can be inserted improving the visualization of smart objects. An example of environments and smart objects is represented on the left part of Fig. 7, showing two environments, home and office, with respective registered smart objects. The registration for a light smart object in the home environment is presented on the right part of Fig. 7. Also, end-users may hide functionalities that they wish to ignore during their development process.

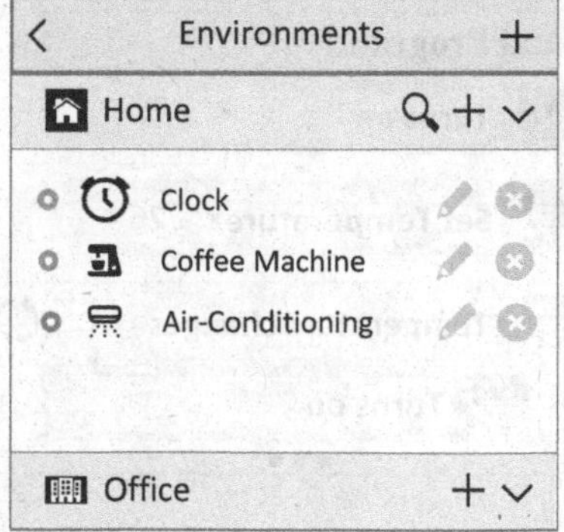

Fig. 7. View of defined environments of smart objects (left). Registration process of a light smart object (right).

Using the environment groups, users may quickly inspect smart objects per environment and continue to develop automations using them. The latter is common practice, and it doesn't restrict the end-users from developing custom automations which include smart objects from more than one environments. Finally, once smart objects are registered, they can be used in the development process without being actively connected at that time. Connection is needed once respective programs are running. For the registration and communication processes of the smart objects, we use the *IoTivity* [18] which is an open source middleware framework for the IoT and the *iotivity-node* [19] which provides the API bindings of *IoTivity* in Javascript.

Programming Custom Automations with Smart Objects

Using the visual end-user programming language of IoT, the end-users main task will be the handling of smart objects that will be involved in their applications. Each of the smart objects provides different functionalities which have to be published via a well-defined API in the context of IoT. Based on this, our system builds the smart object data to a JavaScript object from which the respective visual programming elements are generated and revealed to the visual programming environment.

Using as an example the air-conditioning object, a few control aspects are shown in Fig. 8 providing the mapping of the source code in JavaScript to visual code. There are four main categories identified for the smart object functionalities which are based on their I/O. In particular, there are functionalities without I/O such as the action *"turnOn"* of the *air-condition* which is depicted in the 1st line of the Fig. 8 and functionalities with I/O such as *"setTemperature"* of the *air-condition* which is depicted in the 2nd line of the Fig. 8. The visual element of our VPL is the blue box which consists of the respective smart object icon and the inner white box including the selected functionality. By clicking the white box area, the end-user can view the entire set of control functions and choose one. Then, based on the types of the input arguments, the visual programming editor gives only the valid possible variables, values etc. in order to facilitate the end-users by limiting or eliminating

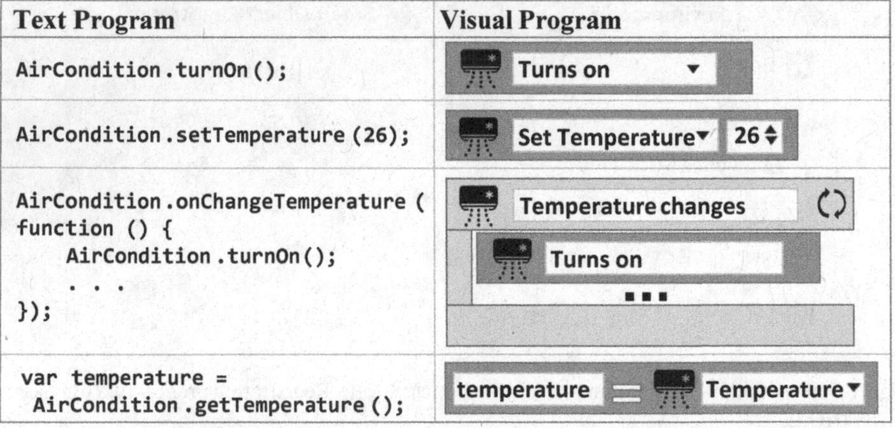

Text Program
Visual Program
AirCondition.turnOn();
Turns on
AirCondition.setTemperature(26);
Set Temperature
26
AirCondition.onChangeTemperature(
function () {
AirCondition.turnOn();
. . .
});
Temperature changes
Turns on
var temperature =
AirCondition.getTemperature();
temperature
=
Temperature

Fig. 8. Air-Conditioning smart object control with source code (*left*); and respective mapping to the visual programming language (*right*). (Color figure online)

their errors. Another category of smart object functionality is based on the responses which are triggered asynchronously and one or more actions could be defined for execution when it responds. The air condition supports an asynchronous response *"onChangeTempetature"* as depicted in Fig. 8. The actions to be executed in response to such an event are provided through an anonymous callback function in JavaScript as shown by the *function() {AirCondition.turnOn();...}* source code.

Furthermore, the main context of the applications in the IoT is focused on the ecosystem of smart objects that exchange data and interact in an automatic or semi-automatic way based on events. This has as a result that the design of events has to be one of the main concepts of the VPL for smart objects. Such events are the aforementioned asynchronous responses; however, these events are not adequate to define total events of applications in the context of IoT efficiently. Firstly, there are smart objects which partially support or not support functionality of asynchronous responses. In this case, the VPL has to support these events by defining such events and core takes on the functionality by using polling which checks the concerned value with appropriate frequency. Moreover, end-user would like to define event actions when combined data of more than one smart objects values change state. In addition, there is the need to define calendar events like the ones presented in Figs. 3 and 6. These events are separated in three different types based on the times to be executed. First category is the non-repeatable events which are executed once (e.g. on Tuesday smart TV will remind James that he has a rendezvous). Second category is the finite number of times that the events will be executed (e.g. On Tuesday, Friday smart TV will remind James that he has a rendezvous). The last category is the periodic execution of events (e.g. Every 14 days the smart TV reminds Tina what to take with her to visit Alice). Also, in case of IoT there are events which could be connected or disconnected to the application system by other events and vice versa. In the next section, we present a case study based on Tina's morning automations using some of the VPL elements see T5, T9 in Fig. 10.

Administering and Versioning Automations

As it is mentioned earlier on, various automations need versioning. Furthermore, each end-user develops several automations for different requirements. For example, Tina's family develops automations for Tina, but also they could design automations for their personal requirements using their smart objects (e.g. for their home requirements, their garden care requirements).

Based on these requirements, our approach provides the end-user with the ability to define groups of automations as depicted on the left of Fig. 9, using the three defined groups of automations that Tina's family has created as an example. In addition, the end-user is able to create new version(s) of the developed automations in order to apply the required changes and at the same time maintain previously developed version(s). As depicted on the right of Fig. 9. using the example of versions of Tina's morning automations. Furthermore, existing versions could be manually activated (i.e. choose to run another version) as shown in Fig. 9, however, versions could be automatically handled through respective visual code, using the aforementioned visual programming language we develop as shown on the right of Fig. 11.

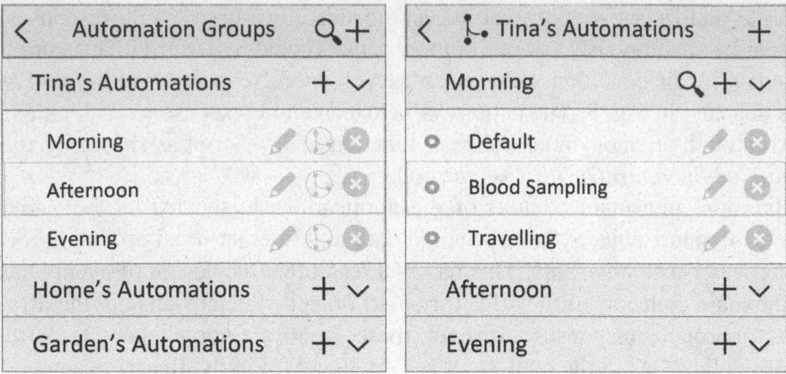

Fig. 9. Automations developed for Tina (left); and tagged versions of the morning automations group (right).

Blending Multiple Visual Paradigms

The plethora of smart objects and the variety of the areas that IoT can be applied such as in the field of AAL, shows that a wide audience would like to be able to use visual programming tools in order to develop automations for their personalized necessities. Furthermore, the audience requirements for such a platform will differ based on their necessities, their available smart objects, their background knowledge and their device sources. This has as a result, that in the case of the visual end-user programming in the context of IoT, only one VPL paradigm is not adequate to cover all requirements which will arise. Moreover, one VPL paradigm may fit a specific purpose of EUP perfectly; however, it can cover efficiently all requirements for the management, development and organization of the personalized smart object applications. For example, on the one hand, the visual programming language we develop is powerful on visualization of programming instruction statements, on the other hand, it lacks on the visualization of dependencies which may arise on the development of defined events. In addition, the most of existing visual EUP approaches are mainly focused on the field of children's learning than in the essential programming of applications (e.g. MODKit [16], Tynker [14] etc.).

We consider that the accomplishment of end-user's total requirements for development of smart object automations will be satisfied by the development of an integrated visual end-user development environment. The latter will able to support multiple visual end-user paradigms. Furthermore, we have identified three visual paradigms; each of them is more appropriate for a specific functionality. In particular, the first is the *hierarchical* which more appropriate for the visualization of program structure. The second is the *grid* which is more suitable to organize workspaces, projects and program units. Third visual paradigm is *graph/network* which is able to properly show and trace dependencies are arising during the development cycle.

5 Implemented Case Study

Using the visual programming tools we develop, we have carried out a case study based on Tina's morning automations earlier defined. All smart objects involved in these automations are shown in Table 1. The control logic for these smart objects is visually defined similarly to the example of Fig. 8 regarding the A/C smart object.

Table 1. Smart objects and their functionality involved in morning automations for Tina.

Smart Object	Functionality	Events
Alarm Clock	Switch On / Off Start / Stop Ringing	When it rings When it stops
Air Condition	Turn On / Off Is Turned On Set / Get Temperature	When temperature changes
Heater	Prepare Water Is water Prepared	When water is prepared
TV	Turn On / Off Message Show	-
Hi-Fi	Message Play / Stop Music	-
Refrigerator	Message Show	When it opens
Door	Open / Close Is Open Lock	When it opens When it closes
Scale	Get Measurement	When it measures
Pill box	Is Open	When it opens When it closes
Bee+	Get Measurement	When it measures

To visually program the morning automations for Tina, actions responding to various events must be defined (i.e. one event for each of T1–T3, T6–T9 of Fig. 3). For most events the logic is simple and directly invokes the necessary functions of the respective smart objects, as shown in Table 1, with the visual code concerning the tasks with tags T1, T2, T3 and T6, T7, T8 of Fig. 10. However, in certain cases the handling is more comprehensive and could require the combination of two events, like the case of T9 of Fig. 10 where actions are defined when pill box closes and Bee+ glucose measurement completes.

Additionally, as previously explained, Tina's morning automations vary for the next two months. In particular, every Monday a nurse visits Tina to collect blood samples, requiring that Tina receives no medication or breakfast before that. Clearly, the latter has to be accommodated in the visual code, requiring to replace the visual code of tag T6 depicted in Fig. 10 with visual code of tags T4, T5 depicted in Fig. 10. Finally, the visual code concerns the tasks of Monday with tags T1, T2, T3, T4, T5 and T7, T8, T9 of Fig. 10.

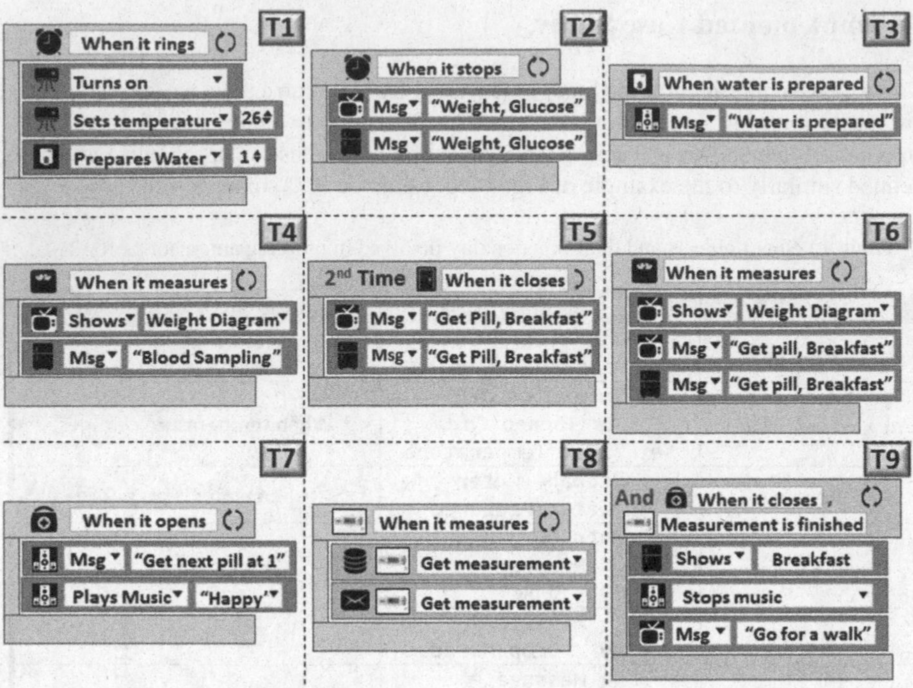

Fig. 10. End-user program regarding the morning automations for Tina (as defined earlier under Fig. 3) using the visual programming tools.

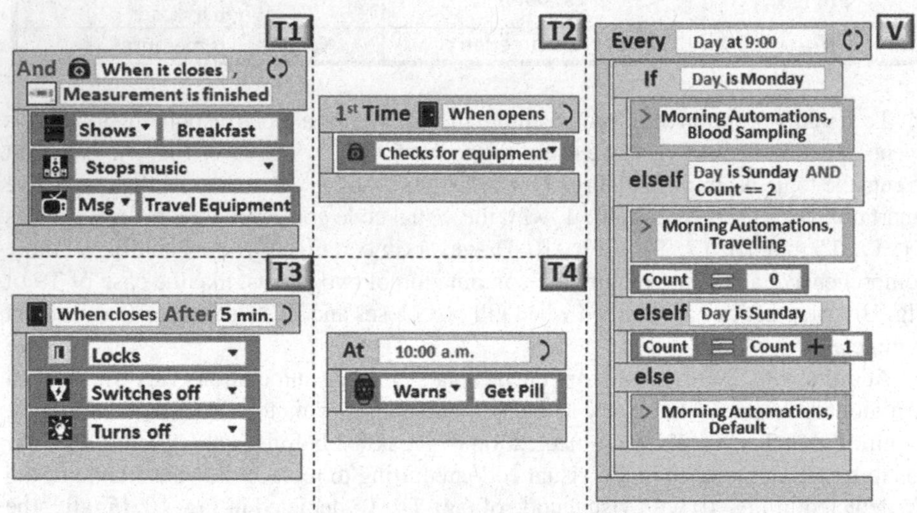

Fig. 11. (T1–T4) Additional EUP for Tina's travelling tasks as defined earlier in the top of Fig. 4; (V) Handling activation of versions through EUP as defined earlier in the bottom of Fig. 4.

Furthermore, Tina travels to the next town to visit her friend twice a month. The latter requires to replace the visual code of tag T9 shown in Fig. 10 with visual code of tags T1, T2, T3, T4 shown in Fig. 11.

Finally, as already mentioned in the previous section, it is not efficient to modify the visual code every time the necessities change with the end-user ending up losing the previously developed features. It is more efficient to maintain versioning that can be handled manually (see Fig. 9) which is an easy task could be applied by end-users even they are beginners. Furthermore, we provide handling of versions in automatic way by using visual code which will refer to these versions (see Fig. 11 in tag V) which can be applied by more advanced end-users.

6 Conclusion and Future Work

An increase in the percentage of elderly people in the general population during the past few decades has made Ambient Assisted Living applications more necessary than ever before. Furthermore, the Internet of Things proliferates as the dominant technological paradigm for the open deployment of networked smart objects in the environment, including physical things with embedded sensors, smart devices and entire applications. Also, applications of Ambient Assisted Living can be developed in the top of the Internet of Things. In this paper, we propose a full-scale visual end-user programming framework for applications deploying smart objects in the IoT, and demonstrate how it can be used to address the highly personalized requirements of AAL through custom personalized automations. We introduce smart object grouping into tagged environments, supporting environment hierarchies, and provide a real-time smart-object registration process through a discovery cycle, enabling visual programming without requiring direct connection to objects. We also provide ways to easily refine already developed applications and allow versioning so as to restore previously saved automations or make new ones.

Furthermore, already existing VPLs are mainly focused on the field of learning than in the essential development of applications. This guide us to focus our future work in the development of an integrated visual end-user development environment in the context of IoT, providing multiple visual programming paradigms which will be able to accomplish total requirements of the end-user development for personalized smart object automations.

References

1. Rashidi, P., Mihailidis, A.: A survey on ambient-assisted living tools for older adults. IEEE J. Biomed. Health Inform. **17**(3), 579–590 (2013)
2. Haller, S., Karnouskos, S., Schroth, C.: The internet of things in an enterprise context. In: Domingue, J., Fensel, D., Traverso, P. (eds.) FIS 2008. LNCS, vol. 5468, pp. 14–28. Springer, Heidelberg (2009). doi:10.1007/978-3-642-00985-3_2
3. Dohr, A., Modre-Opsrian, R., Drobics, M., Hayn, D., Schreier, G.: The internet of things for ambient assisted living. In: Proceedings of the 2010 Seventh International Conference on Information Technology: New Generations (ITNG 2010), pp. 804–809. IEEE Computer Society, Washington, DC (2010)

4. Santos, A., Macedo, J., Costa, A., João Nicolau, M.: Internet of things and smart objects for M-health monitoring and control. Procedia Technol. **16**(2014), 1351–1360 (2014). ISSN 2212-0173
5. Bee+, developed by Vigilant. https://www.arm.com/innovation/products/bee-smart-diabetes-tracker.php. Accessed 12 2016
6. Miller, M.: The Internet of Things: How Smart TVs, Smart Cars, Smart Homes, and Smart Cities Are Changing the World (2015). ISBN-13: 978-0789754004
7. Resnick, M., Maloney, J., Monroy-Hernández, A., Rusk, N., Eastmond, E., Brennan, K., Millner, A., Rosenbaum, E., Silver, J., Silverman, B., Kafai, Y.: Scratch: programming for all. Commun. ACM **52**, 11 (2009)
8. Microsoft VPL. https://msdn.microsoft.com/en-us/library/bb483088.aspx. Accessed 8 2016
9. HomeKit developed by Apple. http://www.apple.com/ios/homekit/. Accessed 8 2016
10. Jung, M., Hajdarevic, E., Kastner, W., Jara, A.: Short paper: a scripting-free control logic editor for the internet of things. In: 2014 IEEE World Forum on Internet of Things (WF-IoT), Seoul, pp. 193–194 (2014)
11. IoTSyS – Internet of Things integration middleware. http://www.iue.tuwien.ac.at/cse/index.php/projects/120-iotsys-internet-of-things-integration-middleware.html. Accessed 8 2016
12. Blocky. https://developers.google.com/blockly/. Accessed 12 2016
13. Lego Mindstorms. http://www.lego.com/en-us/mindstorms. Accessed 12 2016
14. Tynker. https://www.tynker.com/. Accessed 12 2016
15. MIT App Inventor. http://appinventor.mit.edu/. Accessed 12 2016
16. MODKit. http://www.modkit.com/. Accessed 12 2016
17. Danado, J., Paternò, F.: A Mobile End-User Development Environment for IoT Applications Exploiting the Puzzle Metaphor. ERCIM News 101 (2015). http://ercim-news.ercim.eu/en101/special/a-mobile-end-user-development-environment-for-iot-applications-exploiting-the-puzzle-metaphor. Accessed 12 2016
18. IoTivity. https://www.iotivity.org/. Accessed 2 2017
19. iotivity-node. https://www.npmjs.com/package/node-iotivity. Accessed 2 2017

Opportunities for Biometric Technologies in Smart Environments

Olaf Henniger(✉), Naser Damer, and Andreas Braun

Fraunhofer Institute for Computer Graphics Research IGD, Darmstadt, Germany
olaf.henniger@igd.fraunhofer.de

Abstract. Smart environments describe spaces that are equipped with sensors, computing facilities and output systems that aim at providing their inhabitants with targeted services and supporting them in their tasks. Increasingly these are faced with challenges in differentiating multiple users and secure authentication. This paper outlines how biometric technologies can be applied in smart environments to overcome these challenges. We give an introduction to these domains and show various applications that can benefit from the combination of biometrics and smart environments.

Keywords: Smart environment · Biometrics · Multi-biometrics

1 Introduction

Smart environments use a multitude of information-processing methods and technologies to support their inhabitants in daily activities [3]. The basis for most applications are sensors and actuators that are placed in the environment or worn by the user. The purpose of the sensors is to analyse the current situation of the user in the environment – the context [15]. The most common example of a smart environment is the smart home where the system is used to track inhabitants, optimise energy usage, and provide multimedia or comfort functions. However, the concept can be extended to numerous environments, including museums, offices, shopping centers, or cars [3].

Many applications that are built for these context-aware systems are primarily aimed towards single users, with data processing methods that are optimised for this use case and the proliferation of single-user input and output channels. The market for smart homes has been increasing considerably in the past five years, leading to a proliferation of smart environments in multi-user scenarios. Often the systems circumvent the multi-user challenges by simply restricting the automated acquisition of contexts [14].

Within smart environments, the access to certain types of personal data should be restricted to authorised users. This is particularly relevant for health related information, e.g. gathered by devices that remotely measure physiological parameters. In the past few years research into distinguishing multiple users in smart environments and managing their individual contexts in parallel has

A. Braun et al. (Eds.): AmI 2017, LNCS 10217, pp. 175–182, 2017.
DOI: 10.1007/978-3-319-56997-0_14

become more active [4]. The two main approaches are user identification by a specific token or using biometric characteristics.

The strength of biometrics compared to tokens is that biometric characteristics are strongly bound to a person and cannot easily be forgotten or passed on to other people, be it intentionally or unintentionally. Biometrics enables the automated recognition of humans based on their biological or behavioural characteristics. This requires the detection of features that are discriminative for each person and make them recognisable. Some common methods are fingerprint, iris, and face recognition.

A variety of soft biometrics does not attempt to associate the detected biometric features to an individual person, but instead to groups of people, e.g. by detecting age, gender, or group-specific body parameters. This is sufficient for many applications, including several scenarios in smart environments. The multi-user challenge is a typical showcase for the use of soft biometrics, as it provides the opportunity for temporary assignment of user information.

In this paper, we discuss how biometric technologies can be used to provide solutions for the presented challenges that occur in smart environments. In Sect. 2 we give an overview of smart environments. In Sect. 3 we discuss user authentication needs in smart environments. In Sect. 4 we give an overview of biometric technologies that could be applied in smart environments. Section 5 summarises the results and gives an outlook.

2 Overview of Smart Environments

The notion of environments becoming smarter with the aid of information technologies has been a vision for several decades. In a famous article, Mark Weiser established the notion of Ubiquitous Computing where computational resources are invisibly placed in the environment and the computer is reduced to its input and output channel [17]. He envisioned devices similar to today's smartphones and tablets.

Figure 1 shows components hidden in a smart living environment. Early in smart environment research, the notion of platforms has become important. They are software components that manage communication between all devices and enable the creation of domain-specific rules [8]. Due to the heterogeneity of the components involved, they are often service-oriented, semantic platforms that provide a high level of abstraction such as the universAAL platform [7].

All components shown in Fig. 1 benefit from the continuing trend for embedded systems. Computing devices are becoming smaller and more efficient, which enables more advanced computing methods to be used, even on very small devices. Sensing units have become smaller and less energy-consuming over time. They may rely on MEMSs (micro electro-mechanical systems), very small mechanical systems that can be integrated on chips. Thus numerous sensors can be placed on a single chip, reducing cost and making them less obtrusive. Actuators may be all forms of devices that can express an output. They range from the switch that turns on the light, motors that move the blinds, to screens and audio systems, which have also become smaller, using embedded systems.

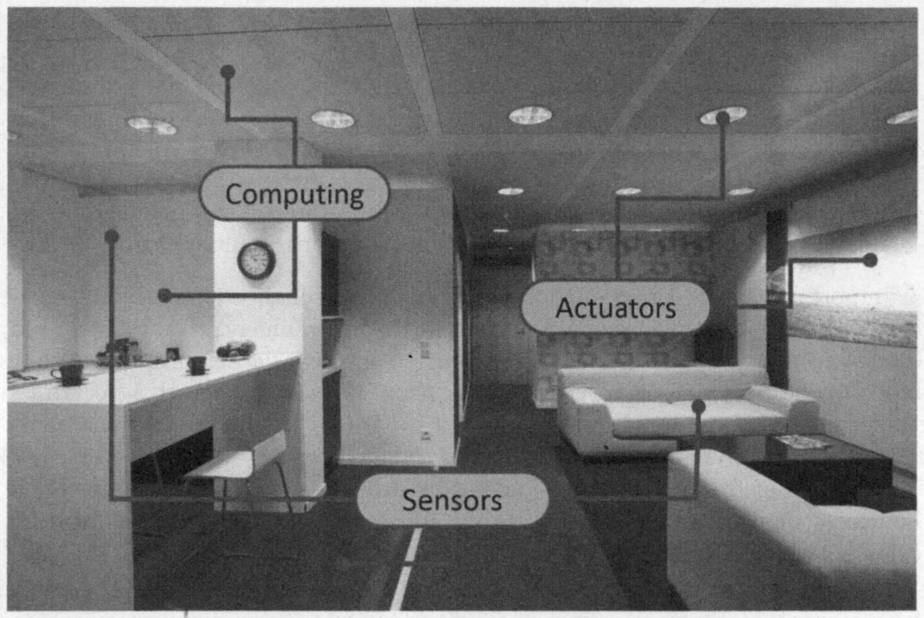

Fig. 1. Example of smart environment and hidden components

So far, most sensing systems do not fulfill the requirement stated by Weiser that they should be unobtrusive and ubiquitous. For example, cameras are powerful and well-suited for public environments, but there is a perceived lack of privacy in the private domain and they are difficult to hide from view. Therefore, recently, entirely invisible sensing systems have become an area of research. Such systems can be put into practice using e.g. capacitive sensing technology, which uses weak electric fields that are disturbed by human bodies moving through. They can be hidden behind any non-conductive material, making them suitable for invisible sensing in smart environments [2].

3 User Authentication Needs in Smart Environments

3.1 Overview

After introducing the technical prerequisites in the previous section, we want to briefly introduce common applications and services that are provided in a smart living environment:

- Information – the inhabitants get targeted and personalised information items, either from general sources, such as news sites on the web, or from personal sources including calendars, emails, and notifications,
- Communication – there are numerous communication services provided, ranging from classic phone systems to video systems in the living room, or telepresence systems, e.g. by special-purpose robots,

- Energy saving – sensor systems detect presence and location and are able to turn off non-essential systems, e.g. lighting and heating,
- Health and care services – health information can be collected by environmental sensors that are connected to the smart environment platform. In addition there can be communication facilities to medical or care personnel, or smart alerts if dangerous situations are recognised,
- Remote configuration, surveillance, and control – smart environments may be configured, monitored, and controlled remotely over the Internet.

Important factors for all of those services are personalisation and data security. As soon as multiple users are present in the environment, the systems need to know from which person they are currently collecting data and to whom they shall provide personalised services. The sensors are able to detect a very fine-grained image of the users' behaviour and eventually medically relevant information. Here it is important to protect the data from any outside access, but in addition also from unauthorised access by other user's in the environment. If the access shall be provided comfortably and seamlessly, smart authentication technologies have to be used.

3.2 Multi-user Challenge

So far, most smart environments have been developed with a focus on a single user. Research into multiple users has been performed for the past few years [14].

The presence of multiple users changes the behaviour of the environment, resulting in the adaptation of scenarios. For example, the smart environment should not turn off the lighting for energy saving as long as there is still another person in the room, and a smart bathroom mirror should only present the news relevant to the user that is currently in front of the mirror. We can distinguish the following classes of scenarios:

- Personalised content presentation,
- Deactivating single-user environment rules,
- Adaptation of sensing and reasoning.

Particularly, the adaptation of sensing and reasoning is an ongoing research topic [13]. Many typical sensing systems cannot inherently distinguish between several people. Therefore, it is necessary to combine multiple sources of information, using multi-sensor fusion.

3.3 Data Security and Continuous Authentication

Data security is an inherent challenge in smart environments [10]. The data that is created has to be protected against unauthorised access from the outside in order to protect behavioural and health-related information from being abused. Speech-recording objects that transmit all recordings by default to the cloud for the purpose of speech recognition[1] are a daunting example. Another example: By remotely accessing the information stored in the smart environment, an attacker could find out times of absence that would be suitable for a break-in or tell the smart environment to unlock doors and open windows for easier access.

Within the smart environment similar issues may occur. Person B may see medical information acquired from Person A or get detailed information about their behaviour or that of potential visitors. Authentication methods can be used to prevent this access, e.g. face recognition methods [11]. The authentication systems should support continuous authentication, for increased user acceptance, while being reliable.

4 Overview of Biometric Technologies

4.1 Biometric Characteristics

Some biometric characteristics are visible or measurable even without the active cooperation of the person. Such characteristics are called static biometric characteristics. Examples of static biometric characteristics include: Fingerprints, face, hand geometry, iris, and vein patterns. In practice, even capturing static biometric characteristics may be an obtrusive process: People have to present their characteristics to a biometric sensor or to remain in a certain pose for a while. The need to simplify and expedite the acquisition of biometric samples has led to the development of innovative biometric sensors (originally targeted at border control applications) including iris-at-a-distance systems and contactless fingerprint systems capturing fingerprints on the fly [16].

In contrast to static biometric characteristics, behavioural characteristics require an action from the person. Examples of behavioural biometric characteristics include: Voice, signature dynamics, keystroke dynamics, and gait.

4.2 Multi-biometrics

The nature of smart environment solutions requires the integration of automatic recognition solutions without jeopardising the overall usability. Ideally, such a biometric system should not require any special actions from the users. However, achieving both, high recognition accuracy and usability have always been a challenge to biometric technologies. An accurate biometric recognition requires limitations such as a specific biometric capture position, strict environment conditions (e.g. illumination), and the collaboration of the users. This trade-off between accuracy and usability/robustness can be eliminated by considering a number of biometric information sources within a smart information fusion approach [5].

[1] http://www.commercialfreechildhood.org/child-advocates-mobilize-stop-mattels-eavesdropping-hello-barbie.

Having more information sources allows each source to be less accurate and thus less sensitive to the environment conditions. Fusing the information provided by these different sources allows to achieve the required high level of accuracy. Most importantly, it allows the biometric system to be operated unobtrusively without requiring special actions from the users. The different biometric sources can be based on different characteristics, captures, algorithms, sensors, or instances.

4.3 Generic Biometric System

Figure 2 illustrates the general model of a biometric system: Biometric samples are acquired from a subject via a biometric capture device (sensor) and sent to a signal processing subsystem in order to extract distinctive, repeatable biometric features. The storage subsystem stores the resulting features or the captured biometric sample in a biometric enrolment database as a biometric reference. The comparison subsystem compares the features extracted from a probe biometric sample with references from the enrolment database to determine whether they match. A distinction is drawn between biometric verification – one-to-one comparison of biometric feature sets to confirm the claimed identity – and biometric identification – one-to-N comparison of biometric feature sets to identify a person among several persons registered in a database. The decision subsystem returns a decision regarding acceptance or rejection of the probe based upon the similarity between the features of probe and reference.

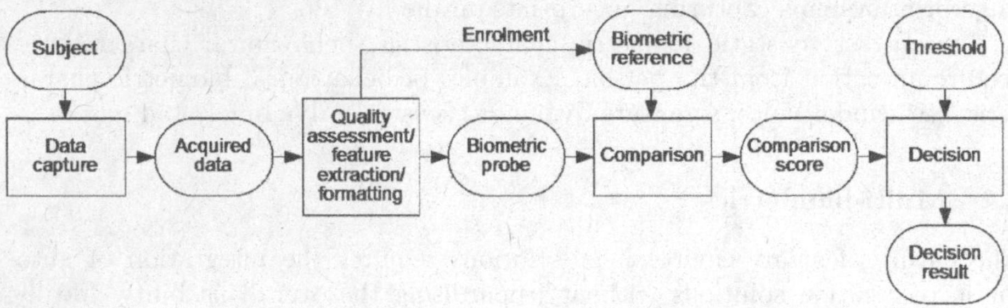

Fig. 2. Generic biometric system

Possible biometric authentication architectures differ in the locations where biometric reference data is stored and where the biometric comparison is carried out: a server, a client, a mobile device, or a security token such as a smart card. Possible architectures for biometric systems include [9]:

- Store on server, compare on server,
- Store on client, compare on client,
- Store on device, compare on device,
- Store on token, compare on server,

- Store on token, compare on device, and
- Store on token, compare on token.

For local authentication in a smart environment, the store-on-server compare-on-server architecture would be appropriate because it allows users to be authenticated anywhere in the environment where biometric sensors are available.

For biometric authentication of a user of a mobile device for remote access to a smart environment, the store-on-device compare-on-device architecture would be appropriate. The FIDO (Fast Identity Online) Alliance has specified a set of mechanisms for using local device authentication, including biometric store-on-device compare-on-device authentication, for secure online authentication [6].

4.4 Security and Usability Requirements and Recommendations

Biometric systems are threatened by attacks on several points: In particular, they may be attacked on the sensors by presenting a biometric look-alike or fake biometric characteristics. An impostor could also try to send recorded or otherwise acquired biometric data to the comparison component, evading the regular data capture device. Another possible point of attack is the data storage containing biometric references and thresholds, which should not be readable or alterable by attackers. Like any information technology system, biometric systems must be sufficiently protected against malicious attacks [12].

More clearly visible biometric characteristics that may be used in a smart living environment such as face, ear, or gait are more prone to presentation attacks (spoofing) as they can be easily captured by attackers. Such attacks can be detected using a presentation attack detection component. Using multi-biometrics makes the biometric system less vulnerable to presentations attacks as it is harder for attackers to collect and mimic a larger number of biometric characteristics simultaneously.

5 Conclusions

We have given an introduction on challenges in smart environments and how biometric technologies can provide solutions. In future applications in this domain the need for supporting multi-user scenarios will become more apparent. The growing number of sensors, particularly in the monitoring of vital signs leads to additional concerns regarding data security and reliable authentication within the smart environments. However, these sensors can be of use for multi-biometric applications, by providing additional features that can be used in the authentication process.

In the future we want to exploit these technologies, e.g. by inclusion of environmental and behavioural information into multi-biometric systems. A candidate are smart floors that provide localisation and potential gait information [1]. The usability of biometric systems in smart environments is to be evaluated. We want to evaluate the user acceptance of various biometric systems in several smart environment pilot sites.

References

1. Braun, A., Heggen, H., Wichert, R.: CapFloor – a flexible capacitive indoor localization system. In: Chessa, S., Knauth, S. (eds.) EvAAL 2011. CCIS, vol. 309, pp. 26–35. Springer, Heidelberg (2012). doi:10.1007/978-3-642-33533-4_3
2. Braun, A., Wichert, R., Kuijper, A., Fellner, D.W.: Capacitive proximity sensing in smart environments. J. Ambient Intell. Smart Environ. **7**(4), 1–28 (2015)
3. Cook, D., Das, S.: Smart Environments: Technology, Protocols and Applications, vol. 43. Wiley, Hoboken (2004)
4. Cook, D.J., Das, S.K.: How smart are our environments? An updated look at the state of the art. Pervasive Mob. Comput. **3**(2), 53–73 (2007)
5. Damer, N., Opel, A., Shahverdyan, A.: An overview on multi-biometric score-level fusion - verification and identification. In: Marsico, M.D., Fred, A.L.N. (eds.) ICPRAM, pp. 647–653. SCITEPRESS, Setúbal (2013)
6. UAF (universal authentication framework) architectural overview. FIDO Alliance Implementation Draft fido-uaf-v1.1-id-20170202 (2017). http://fidoalliance.org
7. Hanke, S., Mayer, C., Hoeftberger, O., Boos, H., Wichert, R., Tazari, M.R., Wolf, P., Furfari, F.: universAAL - an open and consolidated AAL platform. In: Wichert, R., Eberhardt, B. (eds.) Ambient Assisted Living, pp. 127–140. Springer, Heidelberg (2011). http://www.springerlink.com/content/g5k52x925r198q76/
8. Helal, S., Mann, W., El-Zabadani, H., King, J., Kaddoura, Y., Jansen, E.: The Gator Tech smart house: a programmable pervasive space. Computer **38**(3), 50–60 (2005)
9. Study report on biometrics in e-authentication. INCITS M1/07-0185rev, version 1.0 (2007)
10. Nixon, P.A., Wagealla, W., English, C., Terzis, S.: Security, privacy and trust issues in smart environments. In: Smart Environments: Technologies, Protocols, and Applications, pp. 249–270 (2005)
11. Pentland, A., Choudhury, T.: Face recognition for smart environments. Computer **33**(2), 50–55 (2000)
12. Ratha, N., Connell, J., Bolle, R.: Enhancing security and privacy in biometrics-based authentication system. IBM Syst. J. **40**, 614–634 (2001)
13. Roy, N., Misra, A., Cook, D.: Ambient and smartphone sensor assisted ADL recognition in multi-inhabitant smart environments. J. Ambient Intell. Hum. Comput. **7**, 1–19 (2016)
14. Roy, N., Roy, A., Das, S.K.: Context-aware resource management in multi-inhabitant smart homes: a Nash H-learning based approach. In: Proceedings of the Fourth Annual IEEE International Conference on Pervasive Computing and Communications, PERCOM 2006, pp. 148–158 (2006). http://dx.doi.org/10.1109/PERCOM.2006.18
15. Schilit, B., Adams, N., Want, R.: Context-aware computing applications. In: Proceedings Workshop on Mobile Computing Systems and Applications, pp. 85–90. IEEE (1994)
16. Tistarelli, M., Li, S.Z., Chellappa, R. (eds.): Handbook of Remote Biometrics for Surveillance and Security. Springer, Heidelberg (2009)
17. Weiser, M.: The computer for the 21st century. Sci. Am. **265**(3), 94–104 (1991). http://www.ubiq.com/hypertext/weiser/SciAmDraft3.html

New Approach for Optimizing the Usage of Situation Recognition Algorithms Within IoT Domains

Chinara Mammadova[1], Helmi Ben Hmida[1(✉)], Andreas Braun[1], and Arjan Kuijper[2]

[1] Fraunhofer IGD, Fraunhoferstrasse 5, 64283 Darmstadt, Germany
{Chinara.mammadova,helmi.ben.hmida,andreas.braun}@igd.fraunhofer.de
[2] Technische Universität Darmstadt, Karolinenplatz. 5, 64289 Darmstadt, Germany
arjan.kuijper@igd.fraunhofer.de

Abstract. The growth of the Internet of Things (IoT) over the past few years enabled a lot of application domains. Due to the increasing number of IoT connected devices, the amount of generated data is increasing too. Processing huge amounts of data is complex due to the continuously running situation recognition algorithms. To overcome these problems, this paper proposes an approach for optimizing the usage of situation recognition algorithms in Internet of Things domains. The key idea of our approach is to select important data, based on situation recognition purposes, and to execute the situation recognition algorithms after all relevant data have been collected. The main advantage of our approach is that situation recognition algorithms will not be executed each time new data is received, thus allowing the reduction of the situation recognition algorithms execution frequency and saving computational resources.

Keywords: Internet of Things · Smart living · Reasoning usage optimization · Situation recognition · Relevant context information · universAAL IoT platform

1 Introduction

Over the past few years there have been many advancements in technologies that enable the Internet of Things. Sensors, Radio Frequency Identification (RFID), Machine-to-Machine (M2M) communication, etc. are considered as enabling technologies for the Internet of Things. In [9] Friess explains that the goal of the Internet of Things is to enable things to be connected anytime, anywhere, with anything and anyone, ideally using any path, network and any service. The interconnection and communication of things enable numerous applications in many IoT domains. Miorandi et al. identify six application fields for the Internet of Things: environmental monitoring, smart cities, smart business, inventory and product management, smart homes, smart building management, healthcare, security and surveillance.

A. Braun et al. (Eds.): AmI 2017, LNCS 10217, pp. 183–196, 2017.
DOI: 10.1007/978-3-319-56997-0_15

The Internet of Things devices communicate and share data with each other via the Internet. The IoT devices generate vast amounts of data continuously. This data is sent and received through the network to and from the other devices. Usually the data collected from the devices is raw unprocessed data that needs to be interpreted. Context-aware computing plays an important role in understanding such data, and facilitates interpretation and processing of data. Dey provides the following definitions of context:

"Context is any information that can be used to characterize the situation of an entity. An entity is a person, place, or object that is considered relevant to the interaction between a user and an application, including the user and applications themselves [8]*."*

Smart living is one of the major application areas of the Internet of Things where sensors and actuators are deployed inside the smart environment (e.g. homes). Situation awareness is one of the key tasks in a smart living environment [17]. Situation awareness is especially important in AAL environments, where the elderly and people with chronic diseases need to be assisted in their everyday lives.

To recognize situations, data needs to be collected, analyzed, stored and processed. As the number of connected devices in the IoT is growing at a rapid pace, the amount of generated data is increasing too. Processing a huge amount of data is complex for many reasons. Situation recognition algorithms must run incessantly to handle the large amounts of continuously generated data. Continuous execution of recognition algorithms on huge amounts of generated data is inefficient and expensive. The enormous amounts of generated data lead to accumulation of petabytes in a short period of time, increasing the demand for more storage and also slowing down the speed of data processing [14]. High computing power is required to analyze these huge amounts of data. Big data processing is a challenge with regard to computer resources [15]. Continuously running recognition algorithms have a disadvantage in that they are inefficient in using resources. The resource consumption of these algorithms is especially high when they are running on large sets of data. To overcome these problems, there is a need for more intelligent approaches that are able to decide which data should be processed and which data should not be processed. Such approaches have the advantage of not processing all data; instead, they select and process important data, based on target situation recognition purposes.

In Sect. 2 we will review different approaches for starting the situation recognition algorithms. In Sect. 3 we will introduce our approach, which is an intelligent approach that can decide when the situation recognition algorithms must be executed. In Sect. 4 we will describe the architecture of a situation recognition system that we have developed by applying the proposed approach. Implementation of the situation recognition system will be presented in Sect. 5. Section 6 will evaluate the proposed approach. Section 7 will present a conclusion and identify future work.

2 Related Work

In this section we consider two basic approaches for performing reasoning for the recognition of situations in Internet of Things domains. The first approach we consider is the traditional approach, where the reasoning is performed on a prior given dataset [11]. In this approach data is collected for a certain period of time and then given as input into the reasoner. The reasoner executes the reasoning tasks over the collected data and returns the identified situations. The traditional approach does not provide real-time recognition of situations. Therefore this approach is not applicable in ambient assisted living environments. Situation recognition in assistive living is different from situation recognition in traditional data mining, where a prior dataset is available and recognition can be performed offline [11]. Wang et al. apply ontology-based reasoning to identify situations like sleeping, showering, cooking, watching TV, having dinner, etc. [1]. For the evaluation, they create a dataset and pass it as an input to the reasoner. Yau et al. use first order logic-based reasoning to infer situations [2]. They feed the collection of data into the reasoner to detect situations. The paper also acknowledges that first order logic-based reasoning is feasible for non-time critical applications. For time-critical applications, first order logic (FOL) rule-based reasoning is not applicable and for these applications time-efficient processes need to be used. Cheong et al. use an approach that takes a collection of primitive contexts as an input and then applies rules to infer situations [5]. Although this approach can be used to recognize situations, it cannot be applied in the case of real-time recognition. The reasoning engine in this approach is started when some dataset is given. Such reasoning can also be called manual or offline reasoning.

The second approach is a real-time approach, where the reasoning is performed in real-time. Two methods can be used to handle the real-time reasoning [11]. The first method is a listener-based approach, in which a reasoner performs the reasoning each time new data arrives; for example, each time a sensor is activated. Ricquebourg et al. propose an SWRL-based approach for context inferring in a smart home [6]. The presented approach starts the reasoning process each time a new sensor event arrives. Ricquebourg et al. identify the execution time of the inference engine as a problem in their approach. They observe about 5 seconds delay for the reasoning time due to the amount of data contained in the ontology, which is large for real-time recognition. Li et al. present a real-time context reasoner (RTCR) that is designed to satisfy soft real-time requirements on the reasoning process [7]. When an input context changes, every output context may change in response; therefore, RTCR starts the reasoning process to reflect the input changes to the output. Although starting the reasoning process each time new data arrives enables real-time recognition, it can be expensive in IoT domains. In recent years there has been a growth of sensor deployments in the Internet of Things domains. It is predicted that in the future the number of deployed sensors will increase [18]. Therefore, starting the reasoner each time new data is received can cause a lot of computational resources in the IoT environments with millions of deployed sensors.

The second method is a sliding time window-based approach, which uses time windows to collect sensor activations and generate an activity description based on the sensor activations [11]. If some activity description is generated, the reasoner will be started for the activity recognition. If an activity is successfully recognized at a point in time within the time window, the algorithm will clear all sensor activations accumulated so far and restart the time window again from the point in time at which the activity is successfully recognized. This means that the time window is sliding each time an activity is recognized. The sliding time window-based approach can decide which sensors should be discarded and which sensors should be aggregated to form an activity description, which means that the reasoner will not be started each time a sensor is activated. If the algorithm is unable to recognize an activity within the time window and the time window expires, it will discard all existing sensor activations received within the time window and restart the time window again. The disadvantage of this approach is that it clears all sensor activations collected within the time window as soon as an activity is recognized. Therefore, it is not always possible to achieve 100% recognition accuracy with this approach. Chen et al. achieve 94.4% average activity recognition rate [11].

3 Filter Based Approach

This section gives a detailed description of our approach for executing the situation recognition algorithms in Internet of Things domains. The basic idea of this approach is to collect all data that is needed to identify a situation and to start the recognition algorithms after all relevant data has been collected. The difference between our approach and the listener-based approach is that in the listener-based approach the received context information is forwarded directly to the reasoner, and the reasoner outputs the recognized situations. In the suggested filter based approach, the received context information is forwarded to the reasoner if there are some situations which can be recognized by using this information. We assume that the situations that must be recognized are predefined. Furthermore, we assume that for each situation it is known which context information is relevant. This can be low-level context information, which is usually captured through the sensors, and high-level context information, which is inferred from low-level context information through the context reasoner. Sensor information can be low-level context information, and situations, which are generated through the reasoner by aggregating the sensor information, can be high-level context information.

When new context information arrives, the algorithm iterates over the predefined situations and verifies for each situation whether the context information is relevant or not. The context information is relevant if it can be used to recognize the situation. If the context information is not relevant for a situation, the reasoning engine will not be started for this situation, but if the context information is relevant to recognize the situation, it will examine whether all relevant context information has already been received. When the algorithm receives new context data, it saves for each situation, which can be recognized by using this context data, an information about the received context data. In this way the algorithm remembers which relevant context information for each situation has already arrived. This allows selection of all relevant context information, then starting the reasoner when all relevant context information has been collected. If the algorithm has all relevant context information for the situation, it starts the reasoning engine for this situation. One of the expected benefits of the suggested approach is that the frequency of execution of the reasoning engine will be extremely reduced as the recognition operation will not be performed for each received data. Moreover, the number of started threads and the amount of computational resources used by the system, especially the CPU and memory usages, will be reduced (see Fig. 1).

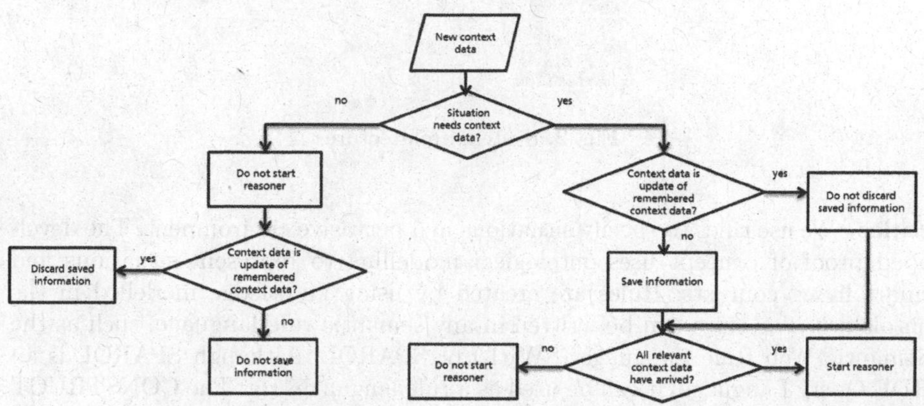

Fig. 1. Filter based approach

4 System Architecture

In this section we introduce the architecture of the situation recognition system, which we have developed by applying the filter based approach from the Sect. 3. The architecture of the system is depicted in Fig. 2. The four components, which are described in the middle box, have been developed within the scope of this paper. The components of the system are described in more detail below.

4.1 IoT Standard Components

Pervasive Environment. A pervasive environment is an environment where sensors and actuators are seamlessly embedded into everyday objects. Sensors have the capability to sense the environment. Actuators can perform actions based on the information gathered from sensors.

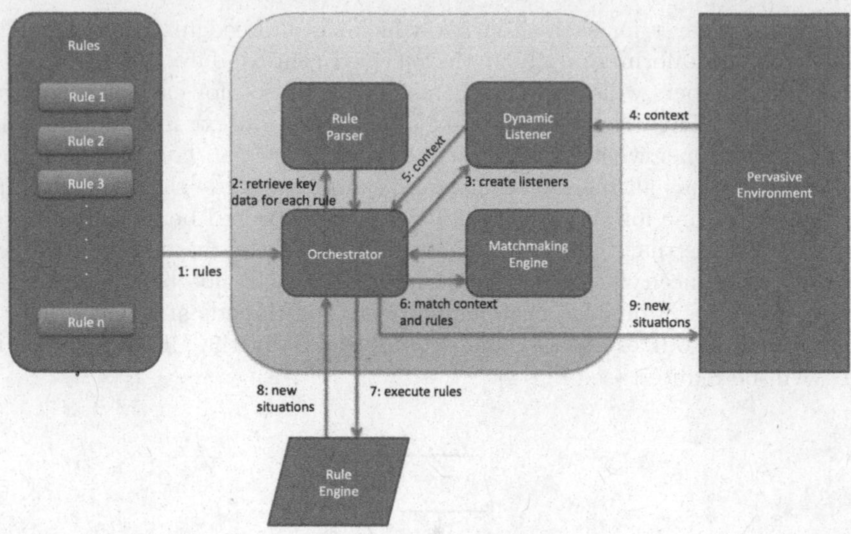

Fig. 2. System architecture

Rules. We use rules to specify situations in a pervasive environment. The developed proof of concept uses ontological modelling to represent situations and smart living contexts. Rules are created by using knowledge modelled in the ontologies. The rules can be written in any semantic rule language, such as the Semantic Web Rule Language (SWRL) or SPARQL. Although SPARQL is an RDF Query Language, it can be used as a rule language [16]. The CONSTRUCT query form in SPARQL can be used to represent the inference rules. As SPARQL CONSTRUCT queries generate new triples, the new triples can be interpreted as inferences, therefore, SPARQL CONSTRUCTs can be interpreted as a rule language.

Rule Engine. The Rule Engine is a reasoning tool that can make inferences over context information. It will be used to derive high-level context information from low-level context information. Our situation recognition system uses an already existing Rule Engine to make inferences. The Orchestrator calls the Rule Engine to execute rules, which the Matchmaking Engine matches to the new context information. After the rule has been executed, the Rule Engine returns the result of the execution (e.g. a new situation) to the Orchestrator.

4.2 Suggested Filter Components

Rule Parser. The task of the Rule Parser is to identify the relevant context information for each rule. Context information is relevant if it can be used to recognize a situation. The rules can have low- and high-level context information. Context information can be built with an ontological model and is usually composed of information including context type and context value. The context types can be sensor or situation types. The context values describe the real values of the context types.

Dynamic Listener. The listener is another important component of the situation recognition system. The task of the listener is to listen to context data arriving from the context providers. Context providers can be sensor nodes, which measure real values. A context provider can also be a reasoner, which infers the high-level context information from the low-level context information. There are some possibilities for creating a listener. One option is to create only one listener that listens to all context information arriving from the context providers. The disadvantage of this possibility is that it can be expensive and inefficient if the listener listens to all context information, but some context information is not used in the recognition process. The other option is to create a listener for each rule, based on the context types that are relevant for this rule. The last possibility is to find unique context types for the set of all rules and to create a listener for each unique context type. Our system uses the third possibility to create a listener; i.e., it creates a listener for each unique context type. The system creates a listener dynamically. The advantage of creating a listener dynamically is that it does not depend on the specific set of context types. A rule can be deleted or a new rule can be added to the set of rules. The definition and requirements of a rule can change. In all these cases the new listeners are automatically created to match the changes.

Matchmaking Engine. The Matchmaking Engine is an essential component of the situation recognition system. The task of the Matchmaking Engine is to find rules that can be executed when new context information arrives. When the Matchmaking Engine receives new context information, it proceeds as follows. It iterates through the rules and checks each rule to identify whether or not the new context information is relevant. If the context information is relevant for a rule, the Matchmaking Engine saves this information. This allows collection of relevant context information for each rule. If the context information is not relevant for the rule, the Matchmaking Engine will not save it. The received context information always reflects the current state of the corresponding context. If the new context information is an update of the previously received and remembered context information and it does not fulfil the requirements of the rule, the Matchmaking Engine will discard the saved information. If the new context information is relevant for the rule, the Matchmaking Engine will not discard the previously saved information. If the Matchmaking Engine receives new context information and it is not relevant for the rule, the rule will not be executed. If the new context information is relevant for the rule, the Matchmaking Engine will check whether the other relevant context information has already been received. For this purpose, the Matchmaking Engine will check the remembered context information for the rule. If all relevant context information has been collected, the Matchmaking Engine will classify the rule as ready for execution and will call the Orchestrator to execute the rule. But if some of the relevant context information is missing, it will classify the rule as not ready for execution and the rule will not be executed.

Orchestrator. The Orchestrator, a central component of the system, is responsible for communication between the components of the system. The Orchestrator retrieves the rules and calls the Rule Parser to find relevant context information for each rule. It creates dynamically a listener for the context information, which is necessary for recognizing the situations. It communicates with the Matchmaking Engine to retrieve the rules that can be executed. Finally, it is responsible for starting the Rule Engine which executes the rules returned from the Matchmaking Engine.

5 Implementation

This section describes the implementation of the developed situation recognition system. The situation recognition system is implemented on top of the universAAL IoT platform. The universAAL IoT platform is an open-source platform that enables the development of IoT solutions. The universAAL IoT development environment is based on Apache Maven and OSGi. The developed system can be used as a modular bundle in the universAAL IoT environment. The universAAL IoT platform defines ontologies that can be used to develop IoT solutions. We use the existing ontologies of the platform to design the rules. The rules are implemented as SPARQL CONSTRUCT queries.

One of the communication arts that the universAAL IoT platform supports is the context communication. The platform provides the Context Bus for this type of communication. Context communication happens between the Context Subscriber, Context Bus and Context Publisher. Context Subscribers are the applications that register themselves at the Context Bus and specify what type of context events they want to receive. A context event is context information built with the ontological model of universAAL IoT platform. The context event is composed of subject, predicate, object and some metadata. Context Publishers are applications that specify the context events they intend to publish. Context Publishers build the context events from the context information with the ontological model and send them to the Context Bus. When the Context Bus receives a context event, it determines which Context Subscribers need this specific context event. If a Context Subscriber needs the context event, the Context Bus sends the copy of the context event to this Context Subscriber. Another copy of the context event will be sent to the central database 'Context History Entrepot' (CHE), which subscribes for all context events that arrive at the Context Bus.

6 Evaluation

For the evaluation we compared our approach with the listener-based approach in which the reasoning engine is executed each time new data is received. For the evaluation, we developed a second situation recognition system by applying the listener-based approach. For the evaluation we specify the following evaluation metrics:

1. Run-time performance
   (a) CPU usage
   (b) Memory usage
   (c) Number of started threads
2. Frequency of execution of the reasoning engine

To evaluate the efficiency of the proposed filter based approach, we measure the amount of computational resources used by the proposed approach. For this purpose, we measure the performance of our approach at run-time. The run-time performance is measured based on the following performance categories: CPU usage, memory consumption and number of started threads. Moreover, the frequency of execution of the reasoning engine is measured. We measure these metrics for both approaches and then compare the results. The purpose of these measurements is to determine whether it is possible to minimize the resource usage and to achieve more efficiency with our approach. The data for the evaluation is generated through a simulator in run-time. For the evaluation, we developed a simulator that triggers a number of sensors automatically. The simulator was developed using the programming language Java and the OSGi framework. We created 14 SPARQL CONSTRUCT rules, which specify situations. Both situation recognition systems run in virtual machines with the following specifications: Ubuntu 16.04.1 LTS, 4x Intel(R) Xeon(R) CPU E5-2680 v2 @ 2.80 GHz, 16432MB RAM. During the run time of both systems we start VisualVM to monitor the applications memory consumption and the runtime behaviour on the same computer on which the situation recognition system will run. To measure the frequency of execution of the reasoner we developed a system logger in the situation recognition systems. The system logger records the frequency of execution of the reasoner into a file. We started both systems with an empty CHE. This guarantees that at the beginning of the execution there are no entries in the database.

The first evaluation was conducted for two days. The simulator generated 77 context events every 10 min. A total of 22176 events were generated within two days. Table 1 shows the results of the evaluation. The filter based system is the situation recognition system which applies our approach. The standard system applies the listener-based approach.

Figures 3 show the measurement results of CPU usage for the filter based and standard systems respectively. The average CPU usage with the filter based system was 2.5% and with the standard on (Without filter) was 10.3%. With our approach, we achieved almost 8% less average CPU usage than the listener-based approach.

Figures 4 show the measurement results of the heap memory usage for the filter based and standard systems respectively. The average heap usage with the filter based system was 1.1 GB and with the standard system was 2.8 GB.

Table 1. Results of the evaluation with 77 context events per 10 min

Metrics	Filter based system	Standard system
Average CPU usage	2.5%	10.3%
Average heap usage	1.1 GB	2.8 GB
Total number of started threads	516227	1566433
Frequency of execution of the reasoner	25197	370420

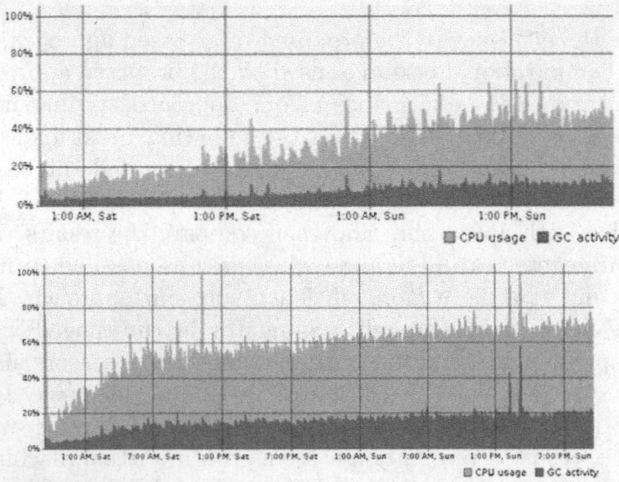

Fig. 3. CPU usage and garbage collector activity of filter based approach (top) and standard system (Below)

Our approach consumed, on average, 1.7 GB less memory than the listener-based approach.

The total number of started threads using the filter based system was 516227, compared with 1566433 using the standard system, which is almost 3 times more. Therefore, using our approach, the number of started threads decreased. The frequency of execution using the filter based system was 25197, and with the standard system, 370420, which is almost 15 times more. So we were able to reduce the frequency of execution of the reasoner with our approach.

The second evaluation was also conducted for two days. The simulator generated 77 context events every 5 min. A total of 44352 events were generated within two days. Table 2 shows the results of the evaluation.

The average CPU usage with the filter based system was 8.7% and with the standard system was 28.6%. With our approach, we achieved almost 20% less average CPU usage than the listener-based approach. The average heap usage with the filter based system was 2.4 GB and with the standard system was 3.1 GB. Our approach consumed, on average, 0.7 GB less memory than the listener-based approach. The total number of started threads using the filter

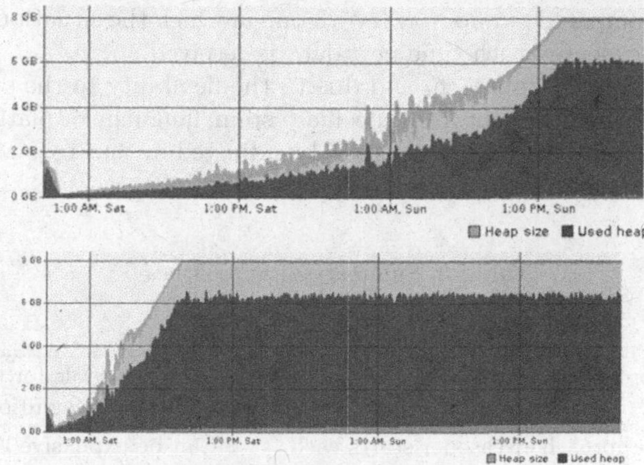

Fig. 4. Heap usage of filter based approach (top) and standard system (Below)

Table 2. Results of the evaluation with 77 context information per 5 min

Metrics	Filter based system	Standard system
Average CPU usage	8.7%	28.6%
Average heap usage	2.4 GB	3.1 GB
Total number of started threads	722384	1981333
Frequency of execution of the reasoner	49522	486292

based system was 722384, compared with 1981333 using the standard system, which is almost 3 times more. The frequency of execution using the filter based system was 49522, and with the standard system, 486292, which is almost 10 times more.

Evaluation of both approaches shows that it is possible to save computational resources with our approach. The filter based approach consumes, on average, less CPU and memory resources. Moreover, the number of total started threads with our approach is much less than with the listener-based approach.

7 Conclusion and Future Work

In this paper, we proposed a new approach for the efficient processing of data in situation recognition systems in Internet of Things domains. The idea of the proposed approach is to select important data based on predefined situation recognition purposes and to execute reasoning algorithms after all relevant data have been collected. We developed a situation recognition system by applying the proposed approach. The situation recognition system was implemented on top of the universAAL IoT platform. Moreover, we developed a simulator for simulating a smart living environment and evaluated the suggested filter based approach. We compared our approach with one in which the situation recognition algorithms are executed each time new data is received.

The new suggested approach, and due to the flexibility to the system architecture, is totally independent from specific system, language or platforms, where the parser is the only module that should be adjusted in that case without influencing the other module of the created engine (Table 3).

Table 3. Summary of approaches

Approaches	Description	Remarks
Traditional approach	Reasoner starts on a prior given dataset	Not applicable for the real-time recognition purposes
Listener-based approach	Reasoner starts each time new data is received	Can be expensive in IoT domains where huge amount of data is continuously generated
Sliding time window-based approach	Reasoner starts if the data collected within a time window is sufficient to generate a situation description. If a situation is recognized, the time window is sliding and collected data is discarded	Not possible to reach 100% recognition accuracy because of the discarding method
Our approach	Reasoner starts only if all necessary facts to recognize a situation are collected	Not based on the sliding time windows. Solves the problem with discarding data

Compared with the sliding time window-based approach, the filter based approach does not discard all existing and collected context information as soon as a situation is successfully recognized. When the sliding time window-based approach recognizes a situation successfully, it discards all existing sensor activations accumulated from the beginning of the time window until the recognition of a situation. The disadvantage of this is that it is not always possible to reach 100 percent recognition accuracy. Our approach does not discard accumulated context information when a situation is successfully recognized. Instead, our approach saves information about each new received context data. New context information describes the update of the value of the old context information. The evaluations showed that it is possible to save computational resources with the presented approach. We achieved, on average, less CPU and memory usages.

Future works can be conducted which will evaluate the proposed approach for a longer period of time, e.g. for months. Furthermore, it can be checked whether it is possible to save network bandwidth with the proposed approach.

References

1. Wang, X.H., Zhang, D.Q., Gu, T., Pung, H.K.: Ontology based context modeling and reasoning using OWL. In: Proceedings of the Second IEEE Annual Conference on Pervasive Computing and Communications Workshops, pp. 18–22 (2004)
2. Yau, S.S., Liu, J.: Hierarchical situation modeling and reasoning for pervasive computing. In: The Fourth IEEE Workshop on Software Technologies for Future Embedded and Ubiquitous Systems, 2006 and the 2006 Second International Workshop on Collaborative Computing, Integration, and Assurance. SEUS 2006/WCCIA 2006, 6 pp. (2006)
3. Bikakis, A., Patkos, T., Antoniou, G., Plexousakis, D.: A survey of semantics-based approaches for context reasoning in ambient intelligence. In: Mühlhäuser, M., Ferscha, A., Aitenbichler, E. (eds.) AmI 2007. CCIS, vol. 11, pp. 14–23. Springer, Heidelberg (2008). doi:10.1007/978-3-540-85379-4_3
4. Miorandi, D., Sicari, S., De Pellegrini, F., Chlamtac, I.: Internet of Things: vision, applications and research challenges. Ad Hoc Netw. **10**(7), 1497–1516 (2012)
5. Cheong, Y.G., Kim, Y.J., Yoo, S.Y., Lee, H., Lee, S., Chae, S.C., Choi, H.J.: An ontology-based reasoning approach towards energy-aware smart homes. In: 2011 IEEE Consumer Communications and Networking Conference (CCNC), pp. 850–854 (2011)
6. Ricquebourg, V., Durand, D., Menga, D., Marhic, B., Delahoche, L., Loge, C., Jolly-Desodt, A.M.: Context inferring in the Smart Home: an SWRL approach. In: 21st International Conference on Advanced Information Networking and Applications Workshops, AINAW 2007, vol. 2, pp. 290–295 (2007)
7. Li, S., Yang, Z., Lin, X.: RTCR: a soft real-time context reasoner. In: Second International Conference on Embedded Software and Systems (ICESS 2005), 6 p. (2005)
8. Dey, A.K.: Understanding and using context. Pers. Ubiquit. Comput. **5**(1), 4–7 (2001)
9. Friess, P.: Internet of Things: Converging Technologies for Smart Environments and Integrated Ecosystems. River Publishers, Gistrup (2013)
10. Vermesan, O., Friess, P., Guillemin, P., Gusmeroli, S., Sundmaeker, H., Bassi, A., Jubert, I.S., Mazura, M., Harrison, M., Eisenhauer, M., Doody, P.: Internet of Things strategic research roadmap. Internet Things: Glob. Technol. Societal Trends **1**, 9–52 (2011)
11. Chen, L., Nugent, C.D., Wang, H.: A knowledge-driven approach to activity recognition in smart homes. IEEE Trans. Knowl. Data Eng. **24**(6), 961–974 (2012)
12. Statista Inc.: Internet of Things (IoT): number of connected devices worldwide from 2012 to 2020 (in billions) (2016). https://www.statista.com/statistics/471264/iot-number-of-connected-devices-worldwide/. Accessed 01 Dec 2016
13. Cisco: The Zettabyte Era: Trends and Analysis (2016). http://www.cisco.com/c/en/us/solutions/collateral/service-provider/visual-networking-index-vni/vni-hyperconnectivity-wp.pdf. Accessed 01 Dec 2016
14. Narendra, N., Ponnalagu, K., Ghose, A., Tamilselvam, S.: Goal-driven context-aware data filtering in IoT-based systems. In: 2015 IEEE 18th International Conference on Intelligent Transportation Systems, pp. 2171–2179 (2015)
15. Kaisler, S., Armour, F., Espinosa, J.A., Money, W.: Big data: issues and challenges moving forward. In: 2013 46th Hawaii International Conference on System Sciences (HICSS), pp. 995–1004 (2013)

16. Meditskos, G., Dasiopoulou, S., Efstathiou, V., Kompatsiaris, I.: SP-ACT: a hybrid framework for complex activity recognition combining OWL and SPARQL rules. In: 2013 IEEE International Conference on Pervasive Computing and Communications Workshops (PERCOM Workshops), pp. 25–30 (2013)
17. Siegel, C., Dorner, T.: Information technologies for active and assisted living- Influences to the quality of life of an ageing society International Journal of Medical Informatics. 2016, Elsevier
18. Kejriwal, S., Mahajan, S.: Smart buildings: how IoT technology aims to add value for real estate companies (2016). https://www2.deloitte.com/content/dam/Deloitte/us/Documents/financial-services/us-dup-smart-buildings-how-iot-technology-aims-to-add-value-for-real-estate-companies.pdf. Accessed 18 Nov 2016
19. Perera, C., Zaslavsky, A., Christen, P., Georgakopoulos, D.: Context aware computing for the internet of things: a survey. IEEE Commun. Surv. Tutorials **16**(1), 414–454 (2014)

HUDConCap - Automotive Head-Up Display Controlled with Capacitive Proximity Sensing

Sebastian Frank[1(✉)] and Arjan Kuijper[1,2]

[1] TU Darmstadt, Darmstadt, Germany
sebastianfrank87@gmx.de

[2] Fraunhofer IGD, Darmstadt, Germany

Abstract. Most of the current Head-Up Display solutions in the automotive domains can not handle user input. Nevertheless, many automotive manufacturers develop and/or implement gesture interaction systems, controlled by the user's hand, into their head-down infotainment displays. The gesture recognition, precisely the hand tracking, is mostly facilitated with camera systems that monitor the driver or with infrared sensors. These systems require a line of sight between the driver's hands and the measurement transducer. Therefore, they require interior design integration and are visible to the user. Moreover, the permanent camera monitoring of the driver, in combination with an internet connected vehicle, can cause privacy issues and increase the driver's feeling of observation.

We therefore present a system that integrates user control into a Head-Up Display, similar to a computer mouse. Moreover, the presented system's capacitive proximity sensors can sense through non-conductive materials. Thus, the system can be invisibly integrated into existing vehicle structures. In our case, it is part of the steering wheel. With our presented system, vehicle manufactures are able to install a Head-Up display control system without any visible design changes. Furthermore, the manufacturer provides more interaction space in driving situations. Additionally, he can rely on the lower level of driver distraction provided by Head-Up displays. Therefore, the presented system can increase driving safety. The systems usability is shown by a small user-study that consists of performance tests on a proof-of-concept prototype and a questionnaire.

1 Introduction

Driver distraction significantly increases the danger of an accident. The National Highway Traffic Safety Administration (NHTSA) names the adjustment of infotainment systems and the looking at navigation commands as one reason for distraction. In 2014, ten percent of all lethal crashes involved driver distraction [15].

To face distraction issues and let the driver keep his eyes on the road, Head-Up Displays (HUD) find their way into the vehicle interior to enrich the driver's line of sight with further information on the windshield. Current HUD not only show static information on the screen, they also adjust the shown items to the

A. Braun et al. (Eds.): AmI 2017, LNCS 10217, pp. 197–213, 2017.
DOI: 10.1007/978-3-319-56997-0_16

Fig. 1. Continental's augmented Head-Up Display prototype with different driving situations [11].

current driving situation. These systems are called augmented Head-Up Displays. Figure 1 shows samples of Continental's augmented HUD [11].

Besides HUD, vehicle development faced driver distraction due to infotainment control with gesture interaction and further control devices, located in the driver's range. It is essential that the driver does not need to take his eyes off the road to initiate a infotainment control command. Due to the introduction of gesture interaction, the vehicle driving safety can be increased [7].

Gesture interaction, supported by infrared sensing is one detection approach. Other systems rely on camera based systems. The driver's upper body is captured by video capturing devices. Afterward, the systems detect hand movements and interpret these as gestures [1].

These systems require a line of sight to the driver or at least to an area in which the driver can interact with. Therefore, the systems must be integrated into the visible interior design of the vehicle. It is a challenge to the manufacturers' designers to integrate these sensors. Moreover, camera based systems can gather more information than only the for the control task required gesture movement. They monitor the whole area of sight and therefore, can capture images of privacy related areas like the driver's head.

Based on these conditions, we developed a Head-Up Display control device based on capacitive proximity sensing (HUDConCap). We provide the following contributions:

- A control device that facilitates interaction between the driver and HUD to give the driver further control about the information displayed.
- A HUD control device that provides a simple direct translation between the driver's hand movement into a computer mouse like cursor.
- A proposal of HUD icons/regions, with which the user can interact on the display.
- Usage of only eight capacitive proximity sensing electrodes that can not capture an image of the driver. Therefore, the system does not show privacy issues.
- Due to the usage of capacitive proximity sensing, we can sense through non-conductive materials. Therefore we can integrate the sensing electrodes invisibly into existing vehicle structures. In our case the structure is the steering wheel.
- Because we can sense through non-conductive materials, the system does not need visible design integration and therefore the interior design is not affected.

- We evaluate the systems usability by comparing user's performance at HUD-ConCap with a popular computer input device, the touch pad, in an user study.

This introduction names information about HUD control and gesture interaction related to driver distraction. Section 2 gives further, detailed information about driving conditions with and without HUD and gesture interaction, in particular, the gesture interaction in vehicles. Beside gesture interaction, we analyze other approaches to capture driver's input intentions and survey the relevant application of capacitive proximity sensors [9,10] in automotive and ambient intelligence [5]. Our HUDConCap starts with the selection of the used sensing system. Together with the sensor selection, we describe our claim for invisible integration in Sect. 3. The sensing system and the selected vehicle structure leads to the design of our position prediction model, also shown in Sect. 3. Because there is no detailed information about interactive HUDs, we furthermore designed an approach to display extendable information to the driver in Sect. 3.

The design of the system covers several claims, but we can not demonstrate and evaluate the systems usability without a real system. Therefore, we present a prototype in Sect. 4. The prototype enables the collection of training data for our model. Furthermore, we let several users test the system. Afterward, we compare their performance on HUDConCap with their performance on the same task with a popular computer input device, the touch pad. This leads to a proof of concept. The model training, the user study and the comparison of the user performance is presented in Sect. 5. Finally, we analyze the captured data. The data gives information about the usability of the system. Furthermore, we can see if the model works stable at a prototype. These findings are presented in Sect. 6. Of course, the project development and the user study lead to further information and ideas how to move on with the development. Moreover, the study shows issues of the system that should be optimized to enhance the systems stability. This is also captured in Sect. 6.

2 Related Work

Braun et al. presented a system that includes capacitive proximity sensors (CAPS) into a vehicle's armrest [4] and seat [2,3]. In [4], they recognized CAPS as design unobtrusive technology to facilitate human machine interaction in cars. The armrest's top cover includes CAPS electrodes. Due to this approach, they enable driver finger gestures, using one or multiple fingers. They enabled single and multiple finger gestures like swiping from left to right and free air gestures like a circular movement. Contrary to our approach, in which we focus on free air gestures, their evaluation shows that the touch based interaction provides a more stable gesture detection. In the paper's outlook, they state that the steering wheel could be a proper vehicle structure for gesture interaction.

Another project utilizes the driver's head rest as CAPS equipped vehicle structure: Ziraknejad et al. provide an accurate measurement method to track the occupants head. Due to their precise investigation of temperature effects on capacitive proximity sensing and an intensive collection of training data, they reached impressive results in all three head position dimensions. They show a mean error of all three dimensions of less than 0.2 cm measured in their evaluation runs [17].

The development of HUD moves forward from static 2-D presentations to 3-D augmented HUD. Broy et al.'s collaborative project, including the BMW Group and the Robert Bosch GmbH, analyzes design and technology affecting parameters of HUD setups [6]. Furthermore, the automotive supplier recognized a lack of HUD control, too. He provides an infrared system based interior installation that can track the driver's hand movements to control a HUD [12,13]. Compared to haptic interaction controlled systems, Geiger shows that gesture interaction outperforms haptic control considering speed and user subjective evaluation of system usability [7].

Not only the control of HUDs is under development. Recent manufacturers present systems that highlight driving lane limits if the vehicle intersects with the lanes limits to support lane keeping assist systems or show different sets of arrows that represent the next navigation command. In dependence on driving situation, Continental's HUD highlights ahead driving vehicles, the current adaptive cruise control safe distance and the current route [11].

3 HUDConCap Concept

The aim of HUDConCap is an automotive human machine interface input device that gives the user the ability to control the HUD. Since HUDs do not provide a pointer yet, we design an interaction concept in Subsect. 3.1. Afterward, we need a significant area to capture the user's input intention. We select the structure in Subsect. 3.2. Moreover, this section describes the sensor selection. Subsequently follows the data processing in Subsect. 3.3, describing the translation of user input into HUD cursor control positions.

3.1 HUD Interaction Concept

The aim of the interaction concept is to provide further interaction space to the user in HUDs. Nevertheless, a HUD should only provide as much information as needed. Therefore, we give the driver the ability to show only his desired information. Figure 2 on the left shows a driving situation. The right image of Fig. 2 shows faded in information that refer to specific situation items. The item samples consist of an icon in the sky that gives information about the weather at the destination at computed time of arrival. There is an item in the right forest area that gives information about the next service station. The forward vehicle run ahead contains an item that shows the current adaptive cruise control distance settings and there is an item about restaurant or gas station signs that shows information about the next food stop.

Fig. 2. Left: Driving situation sample. Right: Same scene with information.

Fig. 3. Left: Driving situation sample segmented. Middle: No information except user points on region of interest. Right: Same scene with semi-transparent rectangles indicating regions of interest

The items' position relies on the progress on driving situation segmentation, provided by augmented HUD systems as shown by Continental [11], or by the segmentation software SegNet (Cambridge University UK [14]). The segmentation process is not part of this project, though we manually segmented the driving scene. The interaction space is now based on two considerations. First: Do not show any information at all and let the driver move the HUDConCap's cursor into an area, where he knows he will get further information, like traffic run ahead. Second: Place semi-transparent rectangles on the screen that indicate regions of information. Figure 3 shows the segmented driving scene on the left. The middle image shows an extended information item where the driver moved his cursor to the run ahead vehicle of the segmentation approach and the right image shows the same scene with semi-transparent rectangles that indicate areas of information.

3.2 Vehicle Structure and Sensor Topology

The driver must be able to control the HUD while driving. Therefore, we need a structure that is close to the driver's region of influence. This lessens the available structures. Furthermore, the driver must use HUDConCap with his hands and it would be of advance if the line of sight between the HUD and the driver's hands is on one area to increase the usability and let the user take a glance at his hands if required to correct his hand position.

We use Capacitive Proximity Sensing (CAPS), which is already applied in automotive applications. An example is CAPS integrated into the steering wheel to detect Hands-On/Hands-Off situation [16]. Because of the constraints to use an existing vehicle structure, the structure should be reachable by the driver

Fig. 4. Left: HUDConCap interaction area. Right: Sensor topology

while driving. Since the steering wheel can already be equipped with CAPS, we selected the vehicle's steering wheel as HUDConCap's vehicle structure.

The steering wheel shows a clearance between the hub and the upper ring area as shown in Fig. 4 on the left. We provide the ability to navigate one hand freely in this area thus allowing a three dimensional hand translation without any contacts. Furthermore, we surround the input area with capacitive proximity sensing electrodes. Labels like "CH0" indicate the sensing electrode's labels in Subsect. 3.3. Electrodes CH0 to CH3 are aligned along the steering wheel ring directed to the input area. Electrodes CH4 to CH7 are aligned in a checkered array at the top area of the steering wheel hub. We define an equal geometric sensor area for electrodes CH0 to CH3. The electrodes CH4 to CH7 have the same size, too.

3.3 Data Processing

Our sensor topology splits the steering wheel into two components: The steering wheel ring and the steering wheel hub. Thus, as shown in Fig. 5, we split the sensing electrodes data into two groups. Group one consists of the data of electrodes CH0 to CH3, the steering wheel ring. Group two consists of the data of electrodes CH4 to CH7, the steering wheel hub.

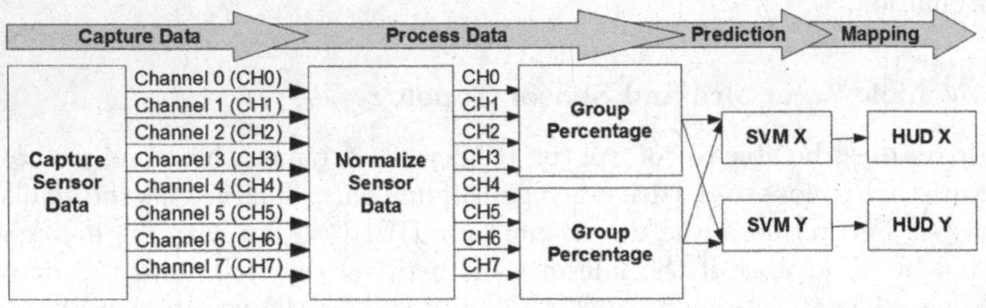

Fig. 5. Data processing flow, from data capture to HUD cursor position

Each electrode's normalized value is divided by the group's sum of normalized values giving it a percentage referred to the electrode containing group.

Equation (1) shows a sample computation for the feature value of electrode CH4 (indicated by the index group). The normalized sensor values are indicated by the index norm.

$$CH4_{group} = \frac{CH4_{norm}}{\sum_{i=4}^{7} CHi_{norm}} \tag{1}$$

The normalization is based on the current minimum value of the whole measurement of the referred electrode and an empirically captured maximum. The maximum is based on data in which a driver touches the electrode cover and the minimum is based on data, captured if there is no person in the range of the sensors at all.

As indicated in Fig. 5, the hands position is predicted by a support vector regression model (**SVM X, SVM Y**). The multivariate regression's independent variables are all channels group values ($CH0_{group}$, $CH1_{group}$, ..., $CH7_{group}$). The dependent variables are the x and the y value of the hand position related to the input area as shown in Fig. 4. Thus, having the hand position, we interpolate the input area dependent x and y values to the HUD area limits to compute the current cursor HUD positions (**HUD X, HUD Y**).

4 Prototype

We selected the steering wheel as used vehicle structure for HUDConCap. Thus, we integrate sensing electrodes into the steering wheel. All sensing electrodes are part of an OpenCapSense toolkit [8] which we use in our system. Due to the designed sensor topology, we integrate four sensing electrodes aligned to the outer steering wheel ring, as shown in Fig. 6. We realized the steering wheel's hub sensing electrode array, too. It consists of four electrodes placed in a two by two checkered array.

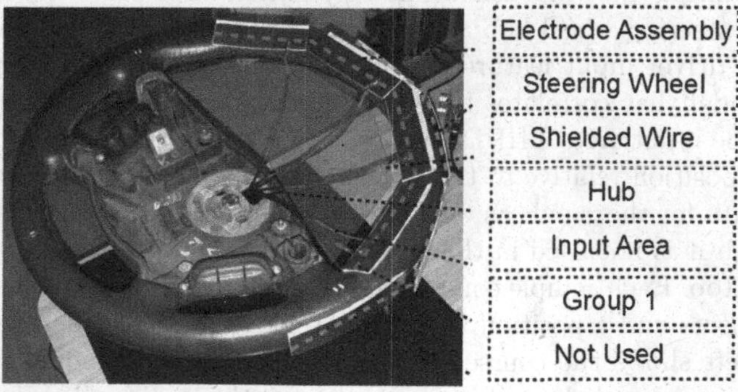

Fig. 6. Sensing electrode topology at the steering wheel

All electrodes are connected to the sensors by shielded wires. The shield is also applied to the sensing electrodes directed to the steering wheels inner material

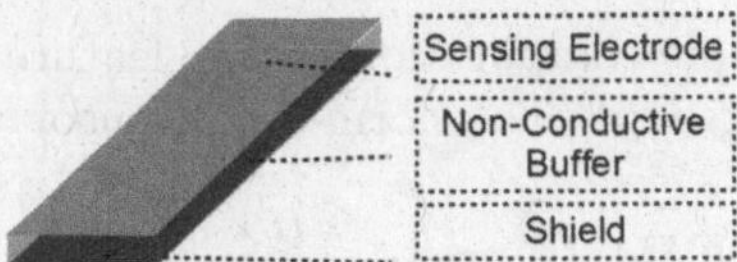

Fig. 7. Single electrode's assembly

to guard any influences of the steering wheel's inner metal structure from the sensing electrodes. Figure 7 shows the assembly of a single electrode. Each sensor is sampled with 25 Hz. Furthermore, we provide an electrode width of 25 mm and a length of 100 mm for the electrodes at the steering wheel ring and a length of 70 mm and a width of 25 mm at the steering wheel hub electrode array. The sensing material is flexible copper foil. Between the sensing electrode and the shield is a clearance of 0.5 mm to increase the measurement range compared to thinner clearances.

5 Evaluation

In Subsect. 5.1 we show the measurement setup. We describe the evaluation procedure in Subsect. 5.2. Six users tested the systems usability. Subsect. 5.3 shows the user's performance on HUDConCap and the touch pad. Furthermore, we asked the users to rate the usability of our system and other human machine interface input devices. In Subsect. 5.4 we discuss the results.

5.1 Evaluation Setup and Model Training

Besides our HUDConCap system, we provide a usual computer monitor that shows a driving situation. The user's input is captured and processed which leads to a pointing two dimensional hand position that refers to the enclosed area between steering wheel hub and the outer ring of the steering wheel.

The basic driver input feature transduction mechanism is a support vector regression model that correlates the CAPS measurement input to planar hand positions in the input area of HUDConCap. Therefore, we measured the absolute (right) hand position relative to the steering wheel. We collected 8,000 samples of training data for the x axis as well as 8,000 samples of training data for the y axis. Although it is not used in this part of the evaluation, we trained a model for the z axis too. Each sample consists of eight sensing outputs of the capacitive proximity sensors and a position value that refers to the considered axis.

Figure 8 left shows the course of the trained regression model (Model output) and the measured data (Data output) for the x axis. The coefficient of determination (R^2) is 0.97. Figure 8 right shows the y axis' course of the trained regression model (Model output) and the measured data (Data output). The coefficient of determination (R^2) is 0.95.

Figure 9 shows the z axis' course of the trained regression model (Model output) and the measured data (Data output). The coefficient of determination

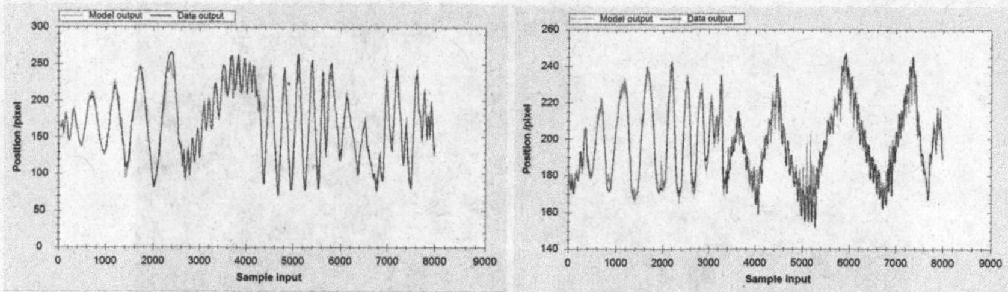

Fig. 8. Comparison of model output and measured data (Left: x axis; Right: y axis).

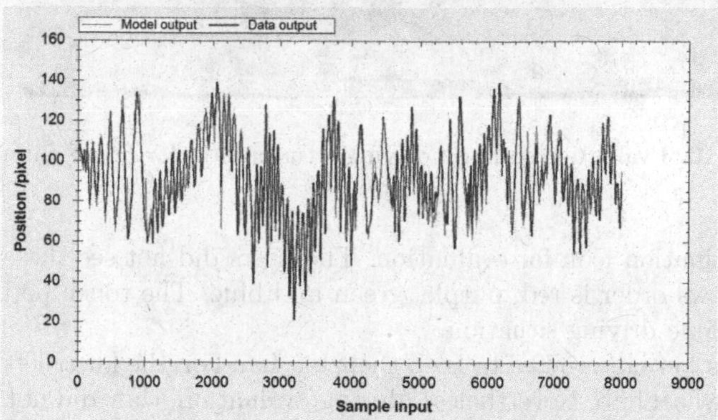

Fig. 9. Comparison model output and measured data of the z axis

(R^2) is 0.88. All samples are captured with the same position of the *left* hand. It grabs the steering wheel at the left lower side of the steering wheel hub. Due to our approach, that specifies an intersection area, the *right* hand is always inside this intersection area for all samples. The grabbing intensity of the left hand is frequently varied during the training data capturing. The evaluation data, gathered in Sect. 5.3, is not used to train the regression models.

5.2 Evaluation Procedure

Each user had to perform several pointing tasks on a static driving situation scene. We gave them two scenarios. In the first scenario they used HUDConCap to reach defined points on the HUD with our new HUD-cursor. In the second one they used a touch pad and repeated the same procedure. We let the user perform on HUDConCap five times and afterward, three times with the touch pad. Figure 10 shows the driving situation in which the user had to act. It shows a ride on the highway at moderate traffic. This situation includes the HUDConCap icons *food*, *next service*, *adaptive cruise control safe distance*, *weather at destination place* and *time till destination reached*. The colored arrows that point from icon to icon show the direct line between the current icon and

Fig. 10. Evaluation scenario driving situation (Color figure online)

the next destination icon for evaluation. The users did not see these lines. Further, the arrows order is red, purple, green and blue. The touch pad evaluation showed the same driving situation.

The user's were instructed to keep their left hand on the lower left position of the steering wheel hub. Nevertheless, during evaluation, they did not always follow that instruction. Furthermore, the user saw the driving situation before they started the evaluation. They knew the HUDConCap icon's positions. Nevertheless, they did not know the icons order. We choose this approach to check the user's acclimatization to HUDConCap. Afterward, with the information about the icons position and the order, they performed on the same task with a touch pad in front of the driving scene without steering wheel. Due to this approach, we expect the touch pad performance to be valid as reference for a comparison between HUDConCap and the touch pad – a popular input device, familiar to the users. In Sect. 5.3, this part of the evaluation is called interactive HUD performance test.

5.3 Evaluation Results

We run the evaluation with six persons. In the following section, each user will have a unique identifier ranging from A to F. After they performed on the interactive HUD in the interactive HUD performance test, we asked them several questions in a questionnaire. Besides the questionnaire about their subjective rating of several human machine interfaces' (HMI) usability, we captured the subject's age, asked them if they own a driving license and a car. All users own a driving license and a car.

Questionnaire Results. The subjects answered the questionnaire after the interactive HUD performance test. The HMI usability scale ranges from 1 to 10, where 1 means not usable and 10 indicates a high usability. The same scale is applied to the question about their experience working with capacitive proximity sensors (CAPS, 1 low to 10 high). Besides subjective ratings on usability and experience, the subjects were asked to answer several questions where they were able to answer with yes, no or no answer.

The first question, about the users experience with CAPS results in four users with an experience assessment less or equal to 2 (Value 1: Users B, E, F; Value 2: User C). Users A and D are experienced in using CAPS giving themselves an experience level of eight (User A) and nine (User D). All of the users state that they use computer mouse, keyboard, and touch screens daily. Important for this evaluation is that all of them, except User A, say that they use touch pads daily.

Since touch pads take place in our interactive HUD performance test, we ask the users about the touch pad usability, too. Table 1 shows the subjects usability rating of both systems. Rating the usability is a subjective estimation. Therefore, we compare the delta usability between HUDConCap and touch pads (Usability(touch pad)-Usability(HUDConCap)). Positive values indicate a better usability of touch pads.

Table 1. Subjects' HUDConCap and touch pad usability rating: 1 (low) to 10 (high)

User	CAPS experience	HUDConCap	Touch pad	Difference
A	8	8	5	3
B	1	3	5	−2
C	2	8	8	0
D	9	8	9	−1
E	1	5	7	−2
F	1	7	8	−1

Users A rates HUDConCap's usability better than the touch pad. User E says that both systems show an equal usability. Users C, D and F rate HUDConCap's usability one point worse than the touch pad and User B rated the usability of HUDConCap two points worse. All of the users say that they think the development of HUDConCap is reasonable. Further they would use a technically mature system daily. Four of the user's think that the system can decrease driving distraction while Users B and E were not sure about that.

Interactive HUD Performance Test Results. Since the users were instructed to reach the HUDConCap icons, as fast as possible, in both tests that include the touch pad and HUDConCap, we compare the required time of the users in both tests. Figure 11 shows the subject's time consumption to complete the whole test. The left side shows their performance with HUDConCap as input device, the right side shows their performance with the touch pad.

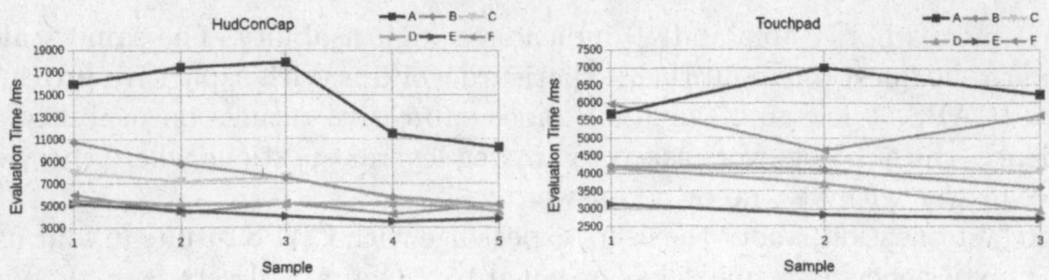

Fig. 11. Interactive HUD performance test task completion time (HUDConCap left, touch pad right)

Between sample one and five, all users reduced their required time to complete the test with HUDConCap. User A shows the greatest progress. He decreased his time consumption by 7.66 s. All other users decreased the time consumption by 5.69 s (User B), 3.1 s (User C), 0.96 s (User D), 1.68 s (User E) and 1.8 s (User F).

The subjects minimum time of all samples are 10.28 s (User A), 5.06 s (User B), 4.9 s (User C), 4.54 s (User D), 3.53 s (User E) and 4.21 s (User F). Table 2 shows the users minimum time consumption in both test cases (HUDConCap and touch pad).

The minimum touch pad time consumption ranges from 2.72 s till 4.11 s. Except User F, all users time consumption with HUDConCap is worse than their performance with the touch pad. User A's performance increases by 4.59 s when he uses a touch pad. The users B and D show a performance difference about 1.5 s and users C and E show a performance about 0.8 s.

Table 2. Interactive HUD performance of the test user's minimum time consumption in seconds

User	HUDConCap	Touch pad	HUDConCap - touch pad
A	10.28	5.69	4.59
B	5.06	3.61	1.45
C	4.9	4.04	0.85
D	4.54	2.95	1.58
E	3.53	2.72	0.8
F	4.21	4.66	−0.45

Since the users performed on the same driving situation in both cases, the increase of performance could be caused by learning the driving situation. Furthermore, the touch pad test followed after using HUDConCap. Therefore, we plotted both tests on one sample axis in Fig. 12. Because we are interested in a correlation between the sample number and the learning rate, we added exponential trend lines to the data points. We could not add a trend line to User F's performance. The coefficient of determination is above 0.9 for users B, C

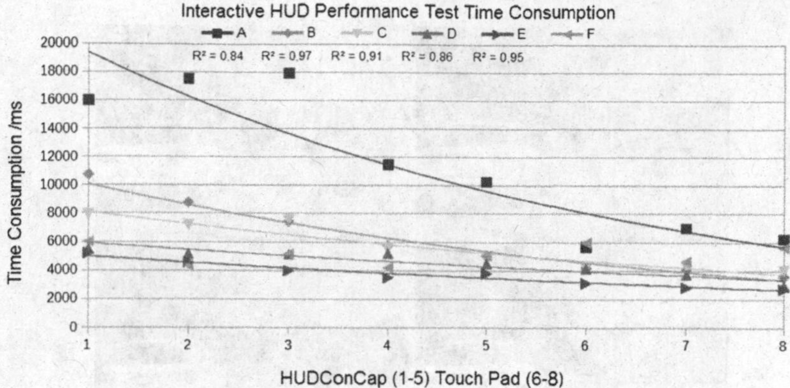

Fig. 12. Interactive HUD performance test task completion time (HUDConCap 1–5, touch pad 6–8)

and E. User A and D's R^2 is at about 0.85. All trend lines show decreasing task completion times with the number of samples.

For further comparison of the touch pad and HUDConCap, we captured the exact course of the users interaction with both devices within the driving situation. We selected the minimum time consumption runs of the users. The direct line between the icons is shown in the same color as the user's curve. The arrows indicate the current direction. The runs of all users are shown in Fig. 13.

5.4 Discussion

The user's usability rating show that HUDConCap's usability is nearly similar to a popular device like the touch pad. Nevertheless, the users rated HUDConCap slightly worse than the touch pad. This is an expected result since HUDConCap was new to the users and they learned the evaluation task from evaluation sample to evaluation sample. The evaluation showed that HUDConCap facilitates a new way of interaction between driver and a HUD, especially the transformation of information on the screen, controlled by the user. This results are remarkable, as a touch pad is a 2D device, whereas we allow the user to point in 3D. Since 3D pointing devices are not commonly used, we chose a vertically placed touch pad.

The core of HUDConCap is its support vector regression model for each axis of the input area. We claimed that our system shows a direct translation between hand position and cursor output like a computer mouse. We thus designed three eight dimensional regression models to predict the absolute hand position and created a device with a direct position translation like a computer mouse. Nevertheless, the evaluation users stated that a lack of a hand shelf makes the feeling of HUDConCap different to a computer mouse. They said that a shelf would increase accuracy. The comparison of both evaluation tasks in Fig. 13 show that the touch pad evaluation curves show a higher accuracy compared to HUDConCap's curves. Clearly, the users had a 2D mouse in mind. A 3D mouse

Fig. 13. Interactive HUD performance test. From top to bottom: user A to F, left: HUDConCap, right: touch pad. (Color figure online)

has the same gravity-enforced accuracy problems as our HUDConCap approach. For fairer comparison we could have glued the touch pad to the steering wheel to capture this gravity effect, but then the touch pad would act as a 2D plane in 3D. This causes additional problems in keeping the finger on the plane while performing the experiment.

Because there was no cursor-like interaction with HUDs yet, we developed two approaches to represent interaction points in the HUD. First, we included squared areas, semi-transparently visible to the user. Second, traffic segmentation algorithms using the front camera show sufficient details about the driving situation. So we proposed that each segment can be an interaction area, activated by the user resting his hand over the interaction area for a short time. However, this requires a stable segmentation during driving, being far beyond the scope of this paper. The evaluation scenario was therefore based on semi-transparent icons. The user succeeded in pointing to these icons. Nevertheless, they asked for a (slightly) bigger icon intersection area.

6 Conclusion and Outlook

In this paper we presented a HUD control device based on capacitive proximity sensing. Due to the sensor topology and the measurement principle, we were able to cover all capacitive proximity sensors. None of them is visible to the user. The used vehicle structure's appearance, the steering wheel, did not need to be redesigned because of the sensors. A small user study showed the intuitiveness of the approach compared to a touch pad. The participants were very well able to select objects in the augmented HUD projection using CPS interaction.

Because of the fast subject acclimatization to the usage of HUDConCap, which nearly reached the task completion time of the touch pad and that the users gave an almost equal usability rating (but less usable as the touch pad), the concept of HUDConCap is proven by this work. Still, predictive models require further training data to increase the general reliability of the output data. Therefore, a further development of HUDConCap requires an extended collection of training data. Similar to the training, the evaluation of the system has to be broadened to capture a more significant group of subjects. Furthermore, the evaluation subjects of this project asked for a hand shelf on the steering wheel hub and further input areas in the region of the steering wheel. In future work, the concept of HUDConCap can be expanded to area independent interaction with hand shelves like on the steering wheel airbag cover. Furthermore, we were not able to test the segmented HUD content with HUDConCap. Therefore, this approach has to be tested, too. This project excludes the left hand. We want the user to keep one hand on the steering wheel. Nevertheless, if required, the system model could be broadened to two handed interaction. Training the system for left-handed persons is of course possible as well. We provide a planar hand detection. Nevertheless, we captured data to train a model for the hands z-axis (pointing from instrument panel to driver). In future optimizations, this degree of freedom could provide further gestures like clicking on our HUD icons.

References

1. Ashley, S.: Touch-less control coming to cars - use of proximity and gesture-recognition systems in auto cockpits could rise fifty-fold within a decade. Automotive Engineering, SAE International, pp. 20–23, March 2014
2. Braun, A., Frank, S., Majewski, M., Wang, X.: CapSeat: capacitive proximity sensing for automotive activity recognition. In: Proceedings of the 7th AutomotiveUI 2015, pp. 225–232 (2015)
3. Braun, A., Frank, S., Wichert, R.: The capacitive chair. In: Streitz, N., Markopoulos, P. (eds.) DAPI 2015. LNCS, vol. 9189, pp. 397–407. Springer, Cham (2015). doi:10.1007/978-3-319-20804-6_36
4. Braun, A., Neumann, S., Schmidt, S., Wichert, R., Kuijper, A.: Towards interactive car interiors: the active armrest. In: Proceedings of the 8th Nordic Conference on Human-Computer Interaction: Fun, Fast, Foundational, Helsinki, Finland, 26–30 October 2014, pp. 911–914 (2014). http://doi.acm.org/10.1145/2639189.2670191
5. Braun, A., Wichert, R., Kuijper, A., Fellner, D.W.: Capacitive proximity sensing in smart environments. J. Ambient Intell. Smart Environ. **7**(4), 483–510 (2015)
6. Broy, N., Höckh, S., Frederiksen, A., Gilowski, M., Eichhorn, J., Naser, F., Jung, H., Niemann, J., Schell, M., Schmidt, A., Alt, F.: Exploring design parameters for a 3D head-up display. In: Proceedings of The International Symposium on Pervasive Displays, PerDis 2014, Copenhagen, Denmark, 3–4 June 2014, pp. 38–43 (2014). http://doi.acm.org/10.1145/2611009.2611011
7. Geiger, M.: Berührungslose Bedienung von Infotainment-Systemen im Fahrzeug. Dissertation, Technische Universität München - Institute for Human-Machine Communication, Munic, Germany, April 2003
8. Grosse-Puppendahl, T., Berghoefer, Y., Braun, A., Wimmer, R., Kuijper, A.: OpenCapSense: a rapid prototyping toolkit for pervasive interaction using capacitive sensing. In: IEEE International Conference on Pervasive Computing and Communications (PerCom), pp. 152–159, March 2013
9. Grosse-Puppendahl, T., Braun, A., Kamieth, F., Kuijper, A.: Swiss-cheese extended: an object recognition method for ubiquitous interfaces based on capacitive proximity sensing. In: Proceedings of the SIGCHI Conference on Human Factors in Computing Systems, pp. 1401–1410. ACM (2013)
10. Grosse-Puppendahl, T., Herber, S., Wimmer, R., Englert, F., Beck, S., von Wilmsdorff, J., Wichert, R., Kuijper, A.: Capacitive near-field communication for ubiquitous interaction and perception. In: Proceedings of the 2014 ACM International Joint Conference on Pervasive and Ubiquitous Computing, pp. 231–242 (2014)
11. Abel, H.: Future HMI trends - concepts and solutions for vehicle instrumentation (2016)
12. Howley, D.P.: Human interactive heads-up display: the future of in-car tech. LAPTOP Magazine, January 2013. http://www.laptopmag.com/articles/harman-interactive-heads-up-display-the-future-of-in-car-tech. Accessed 14 Dec 2016
13. Inovation HUB, Harman International: Looking ahead: solution for connected in-car safety and entertainment, February 2013. http://news.harman.com/blog/looking-ahead:-solution-for-connected-in-car-safety-and-entertainment
14. Kendall, A., Badrinarayanan, V., Cipolla, R.: Bayesian segnet: model uncertainty in deep convolutional encoder-decoder architectures for scene understanding (2015)
15. NHTSA - National Center for Statistics, Analysis: Traffic safety facts - distracted driving 2014, April 2016

16. Rieth, P., Böhm, J., Linkenbach, S., Hoffmann, O., Nell, J., Schirling, A., Netz, A., Stauder, P., Kuhn, M.: Steering handle for motor vehicles and method for recording a physical parameter on a steering handle, US Patent 7,321,311, 22 January 2008
17. Ziraknejad, N., Lawrence, P.D., Romilly, D.P.: Vehicle occupant head position quantification using an array of capacitive proximity sensors. IEEE Trans. Veh. Technol. **64**(6), 2274–2287 (2015). http://dx.doi.org/10.1109/TVT.2014.2344026

E-Textile Couch: Towards Smart Garments Integrated Furniture

Silvia Rus[1(✉)], Andreas Braun[1], and Arjan Kuijper[1,2]

[1] Fraunhofer IGD, Fraunhoferstr. 5, 64283 Darmstadt, Germany
{silvia.rus,andreas.braun,arjan.kuijper}@igd.fraunhofer.de
[2] Technische Universität Darmstadt, Hochschulstr. 10, 64289 Darmstadt, Germany
arjan.kuijper@gris.tu-darmstadt.de

Abstract. Application areas like health-care and smart environments have greatly benefited from embedding sensors into every-day-objects, enabling for example sleep apnea detection. We propose to further integrate parts of sensors into the very own materials of the objects. Thus, in this work we explore integrating smart garments into furniture using a couch as our use-case. Equipped with textile capacitive sensing electrodes, we show that our prototype outperforms existing systems achieving an F-measure of 94.1%. Furthermore, we discuss implications and limitation of the integration process.

Keywords: Capacitive sensing · Conductive materials · E-textiles · Posture detection

1 Introduction

The usage of smart textiles has expanded from an initial state of single prototypes [1] and fashionable technology [2] into a great number of applications, especially in the area of wearables. On-body controls [3,4], easy prototyping of user interfaces for disabled people [5] as well as posture and motion recognition of body parts [6,7] are few of these examples.

The concept of self-aware materials [8] and producing digital textiles at scale [9] enables to view our surrounding materials and surfaces differently, leveraging unexpected invisible ubiquitous interactivity [10,11]. To address these advances, we investigate how smart textiles can be seamlessly integrated within furniture and demonstrate this on the couch as our use-case. The interactions between human and couch, create implications about the surrounding context, creating a self-aware object of every-day use. Measurements conducted by Rus et al. have confirmed the suitability of conductive textile as capacitive sensing electrode [12].

Our contribution with this work, is to extend the usage of smart textiles from the on-body wearables to the seamlessly integrated ambient objects, like furniture. In this paper we cover an ordinary living room couch as our use-case. We extend state of the art by analyzing a set of several fine-grained postures which will contribute to adjusting the environment to the users needs.

A. Braun et al. (Eds.): AmI 2017, LNCS 10217, pp. 214–224, 2017.
DOI: 10.1007/978-3-319-56997-0_17

2 Related Work

Posture recognition has been subject of many works [13,14]. Especially in the area of Ambient Intelligence it is of utmost interest to know as much as possible about the human as interacting counterpart in the surrounding intelligent landscape, to which knowing the posture is an important contribution.

2.1 Posture Recognition Using Smart Textiles

In many works posture recognition has been attempted using different variations of smart textiles [6,7]. Zhou et al. [7] have built a sensing band which monitors gym exercises. They use textile pressure sensors in order to track leg activity during exercising. Focusing on posture monitoring Wang has interconnected smart garments with wearable electronics on a vest for rehabilitation purposes [6]. Few works have already partly integrated smart textiles into furniture. Braun et al. have created a chair to recognize poses and activities creating awareness of correct posture [15]. The chair is endowed with capacitive sensors where one electrode integrated in the backrest woven through the mesh of the chair using conductive thread.

2.2 Posture Recognizing Furniture

Examples of furniture able to recognize the posture of the occupying human are bed, chair and couch. In the bed the sleeping posture is investigated by several works, where different types of unobtrusively placed sensors are used. For example Chang et al., Braun et al. and Rus et al. use capacitive sensors placed underneath the mattress, attached to the frame of the bed, respectively underneath the bed-sheet in order to detect sleeping postures, lying postures and prevent decubitus ulcers as a consequence [16–18]. Liu et al. use capacitive pressure sensors in a high density sensor bed sheet for monitoring the patients rehabilitation exercises [19].

First approaches of detecting seating postures have been made by Tan et al. using a pressure sensor mat [20]. They classify 14 postures achieving more than 90% accuracy per posture. Eight postures were identified by using pressure sensors endowed in an office chair created by Nazari et al. [21]. Braun et al. have created several prototypes of sensing chairs by using capacitive sensing [22,23]. One prototype is meant to support training micro-breaks in the office while another is a sensing system for car seats. The second one is based on 16 electrodes connected to capacitive sensors with the goal of identifying different properties of the driver, like e.g. drivers head posture.

Couches have been endowed with sensors several times, mostly using capacitive sensors. Kivikunnas et al. present a sofa equipped with six metal foil capacitive sensors analyzing basic sensor data [24]. Grosse-Puppendahl et al. evaluate nine different postures with a couch equipped with 8 capacitive proximity sensors achieving 97% precision and recall [25]. By creating a network of furniture composed of bed, couch and chair Heikkil et al. envisage posture and activity tracking throughout the day [26]. Even though, the couch has been also equipped with sensors only long time evaluations with chair and bed have been reported. More recently, the couch has been used as a sensing device by Pohl et al. for context sensing in a livingroom, controlling ambient lightning, music and tv [27]. The couch is equipped with six capacitive proximity sensors, evaluating eight postures with an achieved accuracy of 92.9%.

3 Prototype

The production of conductive textiles at large scale envisages that sensing electrodes will one day be fully integrated into the covering materials and thus into the production process of furniture. Following this chain of thought our interactive couch prototype is enhanced by placing eight textile electrodes on the surface of the couch, see Fig. 1. We created the electrodes by using pieces of 15 x 16 cm^2 conductive fabric, sewing a loop of wire to the fabric using conductive thread and gluing it to pieces of ordinary couch cover, as shown in Fig. 2. This process ensures that the electrodes are isolated and utilize materials used for the production of an actual couch.

The electrodes are connected to sensors which are connected to a capacitive sensing prototyping board, the OpenCapSense board [28]. The raw sensor data is collected and processed in the following steps in order to extract the posture of a person on the couch.

Fig. 1. Couch endowed with eight textile electrodes.

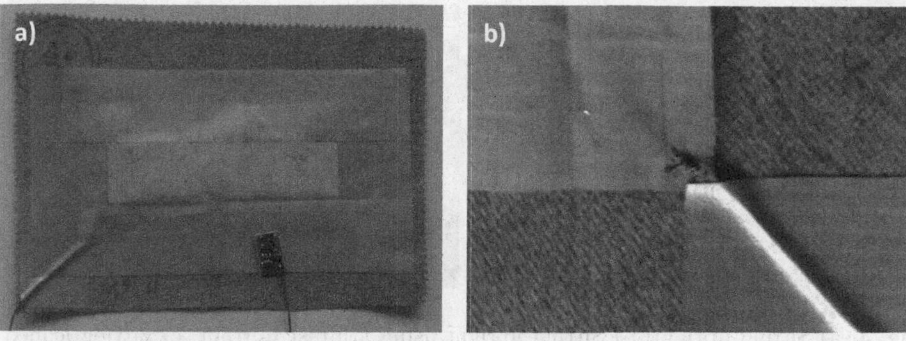

Fig. 2. a) Sensor and connected electrode made of conductive textile taped to regular couch cover sample. b) Sewn connection with conductive thread between textile and wire.

4 Evaluation Setup

We evaluated the couch by asking 15 test persons (2 female) to execute 14 different postures: 12 sitting poses, of which 3 using the armrest of the couch (see Fig. 3), and 2 lying postures. At all times there was only one person on the couch. Including the empty couch we have evaluated 15 distinguished classes:

- **Class 1** Empty couch
- **Class 2** Sitting upright, on right side
- **Class 3** Sitting on edge, on right side
- **Class 4** Sitting leaned back, on right side
- **Class 5** Sitting upright, on right side, using armrest in front
- **Class 6** Sitting leaned back, on right side, using armrest in front
- **Class 7** Sitting leaned back, on right side, using armrest at back
- **Class 8** Sitting upright, in the middle
- **Class 9** Sitting on edge, in the middle
- **Class 10** Sitting leaned back, in the middle
- **Class 11** Sitting upright, on left side
- **Class 12** Sitting on edge, on left side
- **Class 13** Sitting leaned back, on left side
- **Class 14** Lying down, head on right side
- **Class 15** Lying down, head on left side

For each class we collected 30 data samples per sensor, which correspond to spending about 10 s in a given posture. The test persons were verbally instructed on how the posture should be executed. Only the desired position of the arm using the armrest has been marked at the position in front and back due to the more specific and smaller change in posture, harder to convey verbally.

We evaluated the data with leave-one-subject-out cross-validation using four different classifiers form the WEKA [29] framework. All classifiers were applied with their standard settings. The four classifiers are k nearest neighbors (kNN),

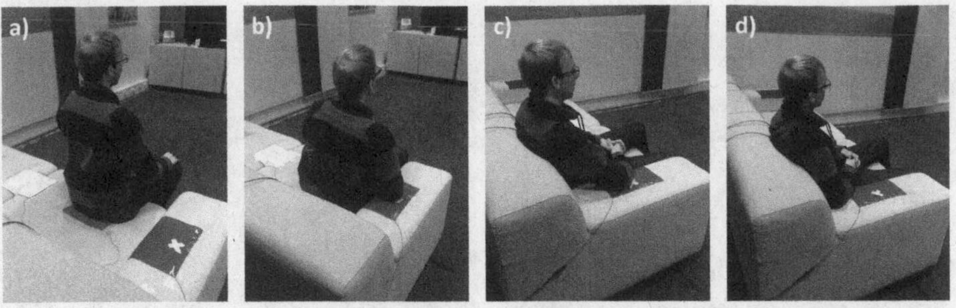

Fig. 3. a) Sitting upright; b) Sitting upright using armrest in front; c) Sitting leaned back using armrest in front; d) Sitting leaned back using armrest at back;

naive Bayes, C4.5 decision tree (Weka J.48) and Support Vector Machine (SVM). At first we applied them on the raw sensor data and subsequently on the normalized sensor data. In order to be able to compare the performance of conductive fabric electrodes with the performance of proximity capacitance measurements we selected the classes equivalent to the ones which were evaluated within the work of Pohl et al. [27]. These correspond to our classes 1–4 and 11–15.

5 Evaluation Results

As described in Sect. 4 we have collected the raw data of 15 subjects and evaluated it with different classifiers. As input we used the raw data, the per sensor normalized data and a subset of classes of the raw respectively the normalized data. The subset was chosen in order to compare the results of the fabric electrodes to the proximity sensing electrodes. The detailed results of the leave-one-subject-out cross-validation F-measure are shown in Fig. 5. For each classifier we have calculated the overall accuracy and F-measure by compiling the mean of all leave-one-subject-out cross-validation results for the particular classifier. Table 1 shows an overview of the results.

Table 1. Overview of classification results for C4.5, kNN, naive Bayes and SVM on different data sets.

	C4.5 decision tree		kNN		Naive Bayes		SVM	
Data	Acc.[%]	F-m.[%]	Acc.[%]	F-m.[%]	Acc.[%]	F-m.[%]	Acc.[%]	F-m.[%]
Raw	82.3	77.0	80.7	75.6	84.0	79.8	85.7	81.9
Normalized	89.1	86.0	88.9	86.2	87.2	84.1	**91.2**	**88.8**
Subset raw	83.3	78.9	87.5	83.9	89.7	87.0	90.45	88.1
Subset normalized	89.9	87.2	91.6	88.9	95.3	94.1	**95.5**	**94.1**

Comparing the overall results of the different classifiers, SVM produces the highest accuracy and F-measure. SVM performs on the normalized data an accuracy of 91.3% and an F-measure of 88.8%. On the subset of classes 1–4 and 11–15 SVM reaches even higher values of 95.5% accuracy and 94.1% F-measure.

These results outperform the results achieved by Pohl et al. [27]. Table 2 compares the accuracy achieved with the two classifiers kNN and naive Bayes which we used in common. For kNN our results were significantly better 91.6% compared to 79.4%. Pohl et al. achieved their best results with the naive Bayes classifier, reaching 92.9% accuracy, whereas our prototype has achieved slightly more 95.3% accuracy, only 0.2% less than our overall best result of 95.5% accuracy using SVM.

Grosse-Puppendahl et al. [25] have evaluated their prototype with a total of 9 classes. Six of these classes correspond to the classes evaluated using the current prototype. These classes are sitting upright on left, middle and right side and lying down with the head on the right and the left side which correspond to classes 1, 2, 8, 11, 14, 15. The F-measure calculated from their precision and recall values of the individual classes is 97.5% achieved using the RBF network. Selecting the same classes, using the current prototype, we achieve an F-measure of 99.8%.

These results indicate, that using conductive textile electrodes reaches equally good results, slightly outperforming a system with electrodes placed under the couch cushions.

Table 2. Performance comparison to related work.

	kNN	Naive Bayes	SVM
Pohl et al. [27]	79.4 %	92.9 %	-
Our work	91.6 %	95.3 %	95.5 %

The difference between the results of SVM on the normalized data and on the subset of normalized data is of 6%. In order to find out, which of the classes cause the miss-classification, we inspected the confusion matrices of particular subjects. We chose to look at the subject with the lowest success rate, subject 4 (see Fig. 4), and a middle success rate, subject 3. The confusion matrices indicate that classes sitting on the right, upright and on the edge were not differentiated at all for both test persons. Looking at the performance over all classes, in the case of subject 4 sitting upright and on edge were correctly identified, however differentiating between leaned back with arm in front and arm at the back were miss-classified as can be observed in Fig. 4.

6 Discussion

Taking only the miss-classification of sitting upright and on the edge on the right side, we could consider improving this by placing two electrodes on the sitting area, as has been done by Pohl et al. However, the fact that the two classes were

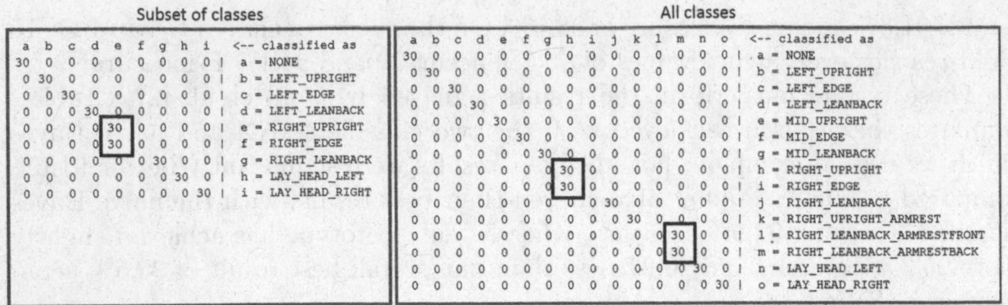

Subset of classes

a	b	c	d	e	f	g	h	i	<-- classified as
30	0	0	0	0	0	0	0	0	a = NONE
0	30	0	0	0	0	0	0	0	b = LEFT_UPRIGHT
0	0	30	0	0	0	0	0	0	c = LEFT_EDGE
0	0	0	30	0	0	0	0	0	d = LEFT_LEANBACK
0	0	0	0	30	0	0	0	0	e = RIGHT_UPRIGHT
0	0	0	0	30	0	0	0	0	f = RIGHT_EDGE
0	0	0	0	0	0	30	0	0	g = RIGHT_LEANBACK
0	0	0	0	0	0	0	30	0	h = LAY_HEAD_LEFT
0	0	0	0	0	0	0	0	30	i = LAY_HEAD_RIGHT

All classes

a	b	c	d	e	f	g	h	i	j	k	l	m	n	o	<-- classified as
30	0	0	0	0	0	0	0	0	0	0	0	0	0	0	a = NONE
0	30	0	0	0	0	0	0	0	0	0	0	0	0	0	b = LEFT_UPRIGHT
0	0	30	0	0	0	0	0	0	0	0	0	0	0	0	c = LEFT_EDGE
0	0	0	30	0	0	0	0	0	0	0	0	0	0	0	d = LEFT_LEANBACK
0	0	0	0	30	0	0	0	0	0	0	0	0	0	0	e = MID_UPRIGHT
0	0	0	0	0	30	0	0	0	0	0	0	0	0	0	f = MID_EDGE
0	0	0	0	0	0	30	0	0	0	0	0	0	0	0	g = MID_LEANBACK
0	0	0	0	0	0	0	30	0	0	0	0	0	0	0	h = RIGHT_UPRIGHT
0	0	0	0	0	0	0	30	0	0	0	0	0	0	0	i = RIGHT_EDGE
0	0	0	0	0	0	0	0	0	30	0	0	0	0	0	j = RIGHT_LEANBACK
0	0	0	0	0	0	0	0	0	0	30	0	0	0	0	k = RIGHT_UPRIGHT_ARMREST
0	0	0	0	0	0	0	0	0	0	0	0	30	0	0	l = RIGHT_LEANBACK_ARMRESTFRONT
0	0	0	0	0	0	0	0	0	0	0	0	30	0	0	m = RIGHT_LEANBACK_ARMRESTBACK
0	0	0	0	0	0	0	0	0	0	0	0	0	30	0	n = LAY_HEAD_LEFT
0	0	0	0	0	0	0	0	0	0	0	0	0	0	30	o = LAY_HEAD_RIGHT

Fig. 4. Confusion matrices of subject 4 for the subset and for all classes.

correctly identified in the case of sitting on the left side and in the middle shows that it is possible to differentiate these poses in most of the cases. This means that one needs to consider a trade-off between the cost of using one ore more additional sensors and accuracy.

Regarding the placement of the arm, one single electrode does not seem to be enough to detect the position of the arm in a robust way. We are considering to improve recognition rates with placing two electrodes on the armrest, one towards the front and one towards the back.

The evaluation results show, that using conductive textile electrodes is equally suitable in order to detect postures. However, while attaching the textile electrodes to the couch cover, it became clear that integrating the electrodes with the couch cover has to be done by taking the design and shape of the couch into account. On a couch where three persons can sit down, but the sitting surface is made up of only two couch cushions one needs to consider the placement of the electrodes. Placing the electrodes underneath the couch cushion needs only one electrode to sense the user. Integrating the electrode into the cushion cover material would mean in the case of our couch creating two different electrodes, which could be connected to two sensors or connecting the two electrodes to one single sensor. Connecting multiple electrodes to one sensor could be used in order to increase the sensing area, and would still send their signal to one single sensing unit. This approach could reduce conductive fabric material costs.

Combining proximity sensing electrodes and multiple smaller cover electrodes all connected to one sensing unit could be used to create sensing electrode pairs which act as stand-alone sensor and are connected to a single sensing unit. This approach has been recently proposed by Tsuruta et al. [30].

7 Conclusion and Outlook

In this paper we have contributed to extending the usage of smart textiles from the on-body wearables to seamless integration within ambient objects, like a couch. We have shown that conductive textile used as capacitive electrode yields as good results as capacitive proximity electrodes, slightly outperforming previous works. Next steps to be considered are: exploring conductive thread as

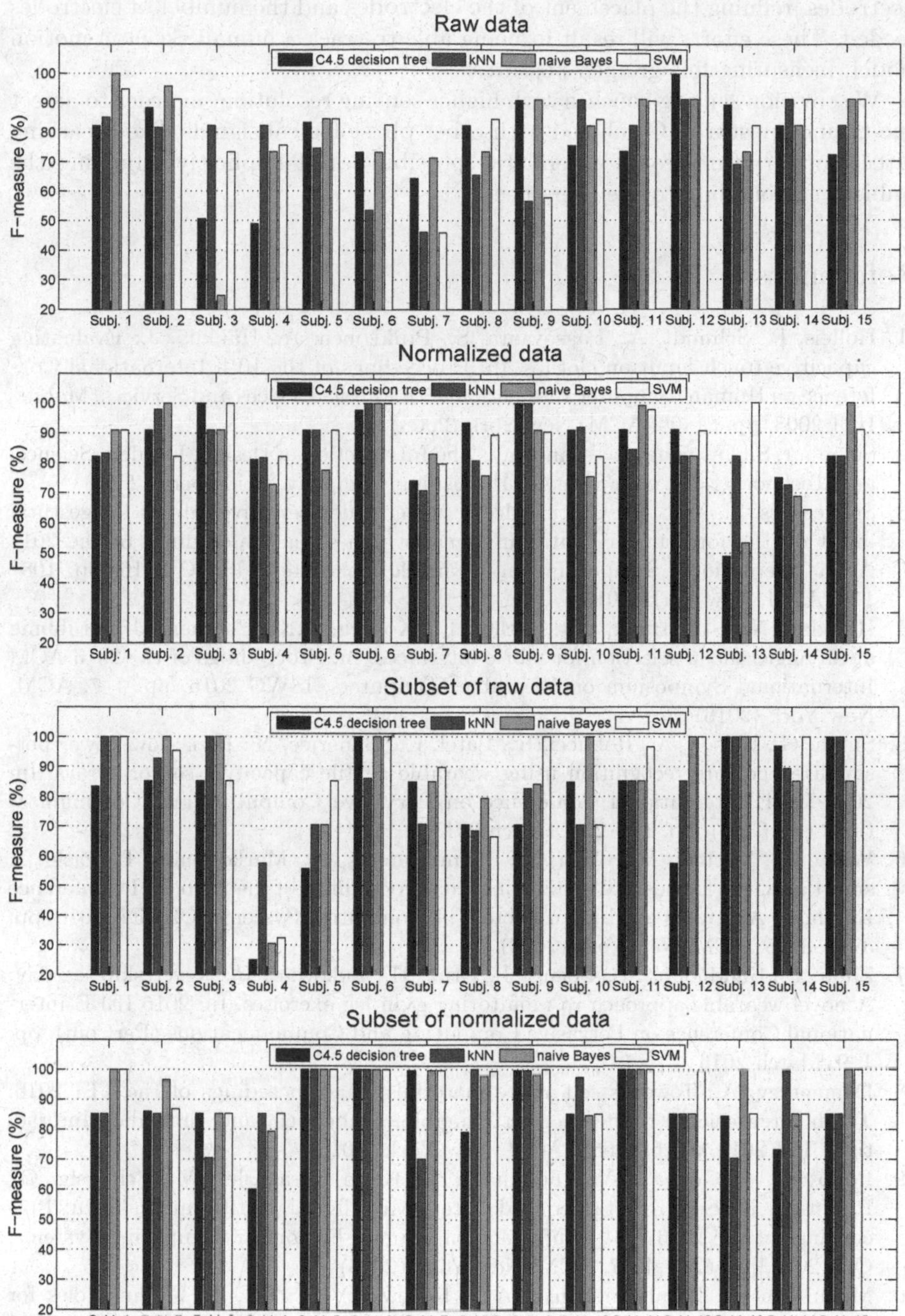

Fig. 5. F-measure of leave one subject out cross-valuation using different classifiers and on different data sets.

electrodes, refining the placement of the electrodes and the number of electrodes needed. These efforts will result in being able to track a human skeleton motion model, measuring fine-grained postures.

We envision sensing couches with higher sensing resolution, in order to detect fine-grained postures. Combined with other physiological signals, like breathing detection, furniture would extend the possibilities of implicitly adjusting the ambient surrounding to the users needs.

References

1. Holleis, P., Schmidt, A., Paasovaara, S., Puikkonen, A., Häkkilä, J.: Evaluating capacitive touch input on clothes. In: Proceedings of the 10th International Conference on Human Computer Interaction with Mobile Devices and Services, MobileHCI 2008, pp. 81–90. ACM, New York (2008)
2. Seymour, S.: Fashionable Technology: The Intersection of Design, Fashion, Science, and Technology, 1st edn. Springer Publishing Company, Heidelberg (2008)
3. Schneegass, S., Voit, A,: GestureSleeve: using touch sensitive fabrics for gestural input on the forearm for controlling smartwatches. In: Proceedings of the 2016 ACM International Symposium on Wearable Computers, ISWC 2016, pp. 108–115. ACM, New York (2016)
4. Hamdan, N.A.-H., Blum, J.R., Heller, F., Kosuru, R.K., Borchers, J.: Grabbing at an angle: menu selection for fabric interfaces. In: Proceedings of the 2016 ACM International Symposium on Wearable Computers, ISWC 2016, pp. 1–7. ACM, New York (2016)
5. Singh, G., Nelson, A., Robucci, R., Patel, C., Banerjee, N.: Inviz: low-power personalized gesture recognition using wearable textile capacitive sensor arrays. In: 2015 IEEE International Conference on Pervasive Computing and Communications (PerCom), pp. 198–206, March 2015
6. Wang, Q., Toeters, M., Chen, W., Timmermans, A., Markopoulos, P.: Zishi: A smart garment for posture monitoring. In: Proceedings of the 2016 CHI Conference Extended Abstracts on Human Factors in Computing Systems, CHI EA 2016, pp. 3792–3795. ACM, New York (2016)
7. Zhou, B., Sundholm, M., Cheng, J., Cruz, H., Lukowicz, P.: Never skip leg day: A novel wearable approach to monitoring gym leg exercises. In: 2016 IEEE International Conference on Pervasive Computing and Communications (PerCom), pp. 1–9, March 2016
8. Dementyev, A.: Towards self-aware materials. In: Proceedings of the TEI 2016: Tenth International Conference on Tangible, Embedded, and Embodied Interaction, TEI 2016, pp. 685–688. ACM, New York (2016)
9. Poupyrev, I., Gong, N.-W., Fukuhara, S., Emre Karagozler, M., Schwesig, C., Robinson, K. E.: Project Jacquard: interactive digital textiles at scale. In: Proceedings of the 2016 CHI Conference on Human Factors in Computing Systems, CHI 2016, pp. 4216–4227. ACM, New York (2016)
10. Mennicken, S., Bernheim Brush, A.J., Roseway, A., Scott, J.: Finding roles for interactive furniture in homes with Emotocouch. In: Proceedings of the 2014 ACM International Joint Conference on Pervasive and Ubiquitous Computing: Adjunct Publication, UbiComp 2014 Adjunct, pp. 923–930. ACM, New York (2014)

11. Mennicken, S., Bernheim Brush, A.J., Roseway, A., Scott, J.: Exploring interactive furniture with EmotoCouch. In: Proceedings of the 2014 ACM International Joint Conference on Pervasive and Ubiquitous Computing: Adjunct Publication, UbiComp 2014 Adjunct, pp. 307–310. ACM, New York (2014)
12. Rus, S., Sahbaz, M., Braun, A., Kuijper, A.: Design factors for flexible capacitive sensors in ambient intelligence. In: Ruyter, B., Kameas, A., Chatzimisios, P., Mavrommati, I. (eds.) AmI 2015. LNCS, vol. 9425, pp. 77–92. Springer, Heidelberg (2015). doi:10.1007/978-3-319-26005-1_6
13. Xu, X., Lin, F., Wang, A., Hu, Y., Huang, M.C., Xu, W.: Body-earth mover's distance: a matching-based approach for sleep posture recognition. IEEE Trans. Biomed. Circ. Syst. **10**(5), 1023–1035 (2016)
14. Enokibori, Y., Ito, Y., Suzuki, A., Mizuno, H., Shimakami, Y., Kawabe, T., Mase,K.: Spirovest: An E-textile-based wearable spirometer with posture change adaptability. In: Proceedings of the 2013 ACM Conference on Pervasive and Ubiquitous Computing Adjunct Publication, UbiComp 2013 Adjunct, pp. 203–206. ACM, New York (2013)
15. Braun, A., Frank, S., Wichert, R.: The capacitive chair. In: Streitz, N., Markopoulos, P. (eds.) DAPI 2015. LNCS, vol. 9189, pp. 397–407. Springer, Cham (2015). doi:10.1007/978-3-319-20804-6_36
16. Chang, W.-Y., Chen, C.-C., Chang, C.-C., Yang, C.-L.: An enhanced sensing application based on a flexible projected capacitive-sensing mattress. Sensors **14**(4), 6922–6937 (2014)
17. Djakow, M., Braun, A., Marinc, A.: MoviBed - sleep analysis using capacitive sensors. In: Stephanidis, C., Antona, M. (eds.) UAHCI 2014. LNCS, vol. 8516, pp. 171–181. Springer, Heidelberg (2014). doi:10.1007/978-3-319-07509-9_17
18. Rus, S., Grosse-Puppendahl, T., Kuijper, A.: Recognition of bed postures using mutual capacitance sensing. In: Aarts, E., et al. (eds.) AmI 2014. LNCS, vol. 8850, pp. 51–66. Springer, Cham (2014)
19. Liu, J.J., Xu, W., Huang, M.-C., Alshurafa, N., Sarrafzadeh, M., Raut, N., Yadegar, B.: A dense pressure sensitive bedsheet design for unobtrusive sleep posture monitoring. In: IEEE International Conference on Pervasive Computing and Communications (PerCom), p. 22 (2013)
20. Tan, H.Z., Slivovsky, L.A., Pentland, A.: A sensing chair using pressure distribution sensors. IEEE/ASME Trans. Mechatron. **6**(3), 261–268 (2001)
21. Shirehjini, A.A.N., Yassine, A., Shirmohammadi, S.: Design and implementation of a system for body posture recognition. Multimedia Tools Appl. **70**(3), 1637–1650 (2014)
22. Braun, A., Schembri, I., Frank, S.: ExerSeat - sensor-supported exercise system for Ergonomic microbreaks. In: Ruyter, B., Kameas, A., Chatzimisios, P., Mavrommati, I. (eds.) AmI 2015. LNCS, vol. 9425, pp. 236–251. Springer, Heidelberg (2015). doi:10.1007/978-3-319-26005-1_16
23. Braun, A., Frank, S., Majewski, M., Wang, X.: Capseat: capacitive proximity sensing for automotive activity recognition. In: Proceedings of the 7th International Conference on Automotive User Interfaces and Interactive Vehicular Applications, AutomotiveUI 2015, pp. 225–232. ACM, New York (2015)
24. Kivikunnas, S., Strmmer, E., Korkalainen, M., Heikkil, T., Haverinen, M.: Sensing sofa and its ubiquitous use. In: 2010 International Conference on Information and Communication Technology Convergence (ICTC), pp. 559–562, November 2010

25. Große-Puppendahl, T.A., Marinc, A., Braun, A.: Classification of user postures with capacitive proximity sensors in AAL-environments. In: Keyson, D.V., Maher, M.L., Streitz, N., Cheok, A., Augusto, J.C., Wichert, R., Englebienne, G., Aghajan, H., Kröse, B.J.A. (eds.) AmI 2011. LNCS, vol. 7040, pp. 314–323. Springer, Heidelberg (2011). doi:10.1007/978-3-642-25167-2_43
26. Heikkil, T., Strmmer, E., Kivikunnas, S., Jrviluoma, M., Korkalainen, M., Kyllnen, V., Sarjanoja, E.M., Peltomaa, I.: Low intrusive Ehealth monitoring: human posture and activity level detection with an intelligent furniture network. IEEE Wirel. Commun. **20**(4), 57–63 (2013)
27. Pohl, H., Hettig, M., Karras, O., Ötztürk, H., Rohs, M.: CapCouch: home control with a posture-sensing couch. In: Adjunct Proceedings of the 2015 ACM International Joint Conference on Pervasive and Ubiquitous Computing and Proceedings of the 2015 ACM International Symposium on Wearable Computers, UbiComp/ISWC2015 Adjunct, pp. 229–232. ACM, New York (2015)
28. Grosse-Puppendahl, T., Berghoefer, Y., Braun, A., Wimmer, R., Kuijper, A.: OpenCapSense: a rapid prototyping toolkit for pervasive interaction using capacitive sensing. In: IEEE International Conference on Pervasive Computing and Communications (PerCom), pp. 152–159, March 2013
29. Hall, M., Frank, E., Holmes, G., Pfahringer, B., Reutemann, P., Witten, I.H.: The WEKA data mining software: an update. SIGKDD Explor. Newsl. **11**(1), 10–18 (2009)
30. Tsuruta, M., Nakamae, S., Shizuki, B.: RootCap: touch detection on multi-electrodes using single-line connected capacitive sensing. In: Proceedings of the 2016 ACM on Interactive Surfaces and Spaces, ISS 2016, pp. 23–32. ACM, New York (2016)

Context-Aware Monitoring Agents for Ambient Assisted Living Applications

Sofiane Bouznad[1(✉)], Abdelghani Chibani[1], Yacine Amirat[1], Sabri Lyazid[1], Edson Prestes[2], Faouzi Sebbak[1], and Sandro Fiorini[1]

[1] Laboratory of Images, Signals and Intelligent Systems, University of Paris-Est, 122 Rue Paul Armangot, Vitry sur Seine, France
sofiane.bouznad@univ-paris-est.fr

[2] Institute of Informatics, Federal University of Rio Grande do Sul, Bento Gonçalves, Porto Alegre 9500, Brazil

Abstract. This paper presents a knowledge-based engineering framework for the design, deployment and running of context-aware monitoring agents that are dedicated to ambient assisted living applications. A new modeling approach of agent knowledge, that combines the advantages of both ontologies and object oriented modeling and programming, is proposed. In this approach, the agents' logic is implemented using a micro-ontology and production rules based on the closed world assumption, called smart rules. These rules are managed using a standard reasoning system embedded in the agent core. Unlike semantic web approaches, the proposed approach rely on the closed world and unique name assumptions. These features are required for monitoring purposes in ambient intelligence and robotics domains. We present a practical work, where monitoring agents are instantiated in the user environment and their reasoning rules operate to handle the detection and confirmation of abnormal and emergency situations with respect to user's context. These rules allow the agents to trigger appropriate actions with help of companion robot.

Keywords: Ambient assisted living · Monitoring agent · Ontologies · Smart rules · Context-awareness

1 Introduction

Independent living and active ageing are two complementary concepts in the Ambient Assisted Living (AAL) research area, which target the building of intelligent and responsive services that allow elderly people to live and do daily tasks on their own, participate of social activities and, when possible, work [1]. AAL services can be supplied through smart spaces, which contain personal mobile assistants such as smartphones, tablet or ubiquitous robots. In this topic, ambient monitoring for the elderly safety is an AAL service of a major importance. The intelligence of such a service is based on the ability of the robots and the other entities of the environment to capture the context of the elderly person

A. Braun et al. (Eds.): AmI 2017, LNCS 10217, pp. 225–240, 2017.
DOI: 10.1007/978-3-319-56997-0_18

situation and react accordingly. This can be achieved by adopting a knowledge-driven distributed approach, in which the monitoring system abstracts the heterogeneity of the environment and infers high-level contextual information about the user situation to take appropriate decisions. The abstraction and inference processes are very challenging requirements that are currently being addressed by the international community, which needs to deal with information coming/going from/to a wide set of objects (e.g. devices, sensors and actuators) implemented using the different IoT middleware technologies and standards present in smart spaces.

Regarding the knowledge driven approaches for AmI, they are usually based on reasoning system that operates using rules and ontologies according to the Open World Assumption (OWA). OWA states that if a certain information is not present in the knowledge base, it is not necessarily false. For example, if we have no axiom stating that John is a student, this does not mean that John is *not* a student [9]. In contrast, the closed world assumption (CWA) is based on negation-as-failure (NAF) principle [3] witch assumes as false any formula that the system fails to prove using the currently available information. NAF can be useful for making decisions when complete information about the world is missing. For example, if an accident happens for an elderly person and it is not known if a caregiver was successfully contacted at that time, the safe measure is to assume the procedure failed and fire a safety rule accordingly. Using rules with NAF can lead to a non-monotonic reasoning system [7] where new facts can change old information.

In general, monitoring systems are also non-monotonic systems, since they often need to make fast decisions on incomplete knowledge. The knowledge can lead to later retraction of the assumed values of the properties they measure insofar as new information is gathered or old information is reinterpreted. Therefore, non-monotonic reasoning techniques are powerful tool for monitoring systems.

In this paper, we present a knowledge-driven approach for designing context-aware agents that can monitor elderly safety during their daily activities in indoor spaces. Our contributions are

- a context-aware monitoring of abnormal and emergency situations that has as a core an ontology, which describes essential concepts to real world AAL scenarios, and a set of inference rules defined according to CWA. These rules called *smart rules* are expressed using production rules to deal with dynamic scenarios in standalone and independent contexts. A rule-based procedure is proposed to handle the confirmation of abnormal situations in the different contexts, using the interaction with human, and thus avoids false alarms.
- a loosely coupled middleware platform made of virtual objects and monitoring agents. Virtual objects are used to abstract the sensors observations and actuations in the real world hiding for the designers sensors and actuators implementations. Monitoring agents are software agents composed of communication and reasoning layers. They are endowed with cognitive procedures for confirming that an abnormal situation lead to an emergency or not, removing false-positive events. These agents include reasoning core that

run a production rule engine and store commonsense knowledge composed of RDF triples stored in the agent run-time memory. The implementation of new monitoring scenarios do not require any specific programming of the reasoning core. These new scenarios need only the update of smart rules and the conceptual description of the context, as well as the instantiation of virtual objects if new wireless sensors, actuators and robots are introduced in the real-world.
- an implementation of an AAL application in a real environment. A fall monitoring scenario is fully implemented within the premises of the Ubistruct Living Lab[1].

This paper is organized as follows. Section 2 gives an overview of main works related to the subject of this paper. Section 3 describes in detail the main components of our proposal i.e. both virtual objects and monitoring agents. Section 4 describes the modeling of our system using production rules to deal with one shot abnormal situations as *falls*, and finally, Sect. 5 presents some conclusions and discusses future works.

2 Related Works

Several approaches have been proposed during last decade for developing AmI systems that supply Ambient Assisted Living Services. These approaches span a wide range of aspects, such as how to recognize activities, anticipate users' needs and intensions, react to actions in a timely manner, exhibit autonomous commonsense behaviour, communicate through multi-modal, non-intrusive ways and many others. The most interesting approaches are those proposing context-awareness models and reasoning systems that endow AmI agents with capabilities to be able, from one hand, to recognize users' activities and situations, and on the other hand, decide in autonomous manner to supply the suitable services to users or react in a real-time fashion to a given situation [2]. These approaches can be categorized into two classes: data driven and knowledge-driven approaches.

On the one hand, data driven approaches are valuable for recognizing specific patterns from a limited and predefined set of physical activities of daily living using machine-learning techniques on raw, noisy and uncertain sensory data without considering their contexts or semantics. Usually these approaches require retraining the reasoning system again every time a change occurs in the configuration of the environment. Moreover, it is in general complex to take into account complex structures of a priori expert knowledge that are needed for the decision-making. On the other hand, knowledge-driven approaches facilitate the elicitation and communication of the high-level contextual information relevant to the task. Moreover, they are independent from the data characteristics and support a large variety of data-sources such as IoT devices, databases and web services. Ontological models are the most frequent approaches used in AmI and Robotics Research. Ontologies provide a formal, explicit specification of a shared

[1] http://ubistruct.ubiquitous-intelligence.eu/lissi_living_lab.

conceptualization [11]. In our scenario, they allow heterogenious agents to share a common formal description of context concepts and their relationships providing them a support for reasoning to obtain a meaningful interpretation of situations and human activities. SOUPA Ontology, CONON, PalSPOT, Dog, mIO! Ontology, PiVOn, ORO, Knowrob Ontology [8,12], are representative examples of ontology models that have been used to develop ambient assisted living applications. These ontologies are mostly structured in two main parts. The core part is used to describe the generic concepts, whereas the second part is composed of several sub-ontologies dedicated to describe specific aspects of the context and the application domain. While the aforementioned ontologies lack general design patterns for context modeling and sensors, the SSN ontology has been developed from Stimulus-Sensor-Observation ontology design pattern [6]. The SSN ontology was proposed by W3C Semantic Sensor Networks Incubator Group (SSN-XG) which is responsible to build a semantic model for describing the capabilities, deployment process and discovery of sensors. SSN uses a lightweight version of the upper ontology called Dolce Ontology (DUL). This alignment with a upper ontology is fundamental, since it makes explicit the ontological commitment which facilitates system interoperability [10]. These ontologies are used in combination with production rules to implement specific reasoning on the context information and endow agents with the ability to act adequately to their current contextual situation.

Rule-based languages have been used as an extension to OWL language to increase its expressiveness in order to model complex context relationships and ensure the consistency of ontology knowledge bases [5,8]. The two representative rule-based languages supported by OWL are SWRL and SPIN. SWRL is a standard rule language based on the combination of OWL sublanguages (OWL-DL and OWL Lite) with RuleML (Rule Markup Language) while SPIN is an extension of SPARQL that allows for querying and inferring on both RDF and OWL ontologies.

3 Monitoring Platform Architecture

The architecture of the monitoring platform proposed in this paper consists of the following three main software components (see Fig. 1):

1. **Virtual Objects** are software components that handle the observations and the actuations. They are connected to the sensors, actuators and/or robots present in the real world;
2. **Monitoring Agents** manage, on the one hand, the insertion of new instances of sensors observations, the updates of the existing instances properties and the deletion of the instances that are no longer valid in the knowledge base; and from the other hand, the triggering of actions on real world actuators. The observations and actions are messages exchanged between monitoring agents and (virtual or physical) objects connected to the web.
3. **Messaging Bus**, also called the faade, which is used for registering IoT devices as Virtual Objects, routing their observation messages to the monitoring agents and routing the actuation decisions from monitoring agents

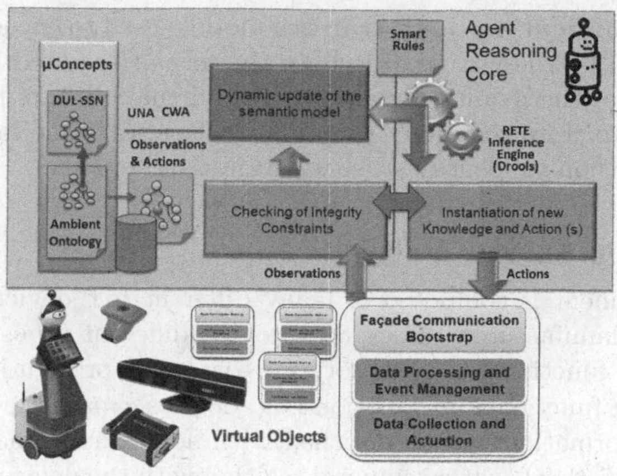

Fig. 1. Monitoring agent and virtual objects architecture

to virtual objects. The faade bus includes a mechanism of generic encoders that allows for translating IoT devices outputs into ontology instances and actuation decision, from ontology instances, into specific input requested by the IoT devices.

3.1 Virtual Objects Architecture

Virtual objects are used as elements that abstract the complexity and heterogeneity of the sensing and actuation infrastructure of the ambient environment. They are software components dedicated to a specific sensor or actuator whose main characteristic is autonomy since they are able to self register and self monitor their execution in a safe manner. For instance, when a virtual object is deployed, it sends a XML message for registering its description in the working memory of the monitoring agents. Once registered, it starts transmitting raw sensor data or ontology instances in XML format.

Thus, the designer of monitoring agents will focus only on their logic implementation disregarding the details related to the kind of IoT devices protocols in use. Therefore, the interaction between the monitoring agents and virtual objects is totally abstracted from the real-world and is made through a unique messaging bus.

The architecture of a virtual object is composed of three modules:

- **data collection and actuation** contains the effective implementation of the communication drivers of the IoT device, which can be based on serial port, wireless communication API (e.g. Bluetooth, ZigBee, Z-Wave) or through an IoT protocol (e.g. CoAP, XMPP and DPWS).
- **data processing and events management** is a module dedicated to make post-processing sensory data to extract interesting clues or trigger events of interest.

- **facade communication bootstrap** is a module used to encode the information exchanged by the virtual objects in the format required by the communication layer of the monitoring agents. The virtual objects initiates a registration phase to store communication informations into the faade repository, to be used later on to identify sensors and initiate actions.

3.2 Monitoring Agents Modeling

A smart environment is composed of many different IoT devices produced by a multitude of manufacturers. They can provide different types of information that ranges from functional (e.g. sensory raw-data and/or high level data interpretation) to non functional information (e.g. devices capabilities and execution status). This information can be enriched with additional semantics, like user capabilities and his(her) spatio-temporal relation with the devices present in the environment, to infer high level and rich description of the user context.

For this purpose, Ontologies offer an expressive language to represent formally, normally in some logic language, the relevant abstractions used by people to solve problems in some domain [8]. Ontologies may rely on Description Logics reasoning, which is used mainly for checking the consistency of contextual knowledge or for context matching queries. In addition, ontologies can be combined within inference rules and logic programs to deduce high-level and implicit context information from multiple context sources; expressing more complex and real world settings; modeling the cognition process needed for recognizing situations, activities and their context; and also implementing reactive responses, which are closed to the notion of actions and events.

Knowledge Representation. The abstraction model used to describe the monitoring agents knowledge is a micro ontology, which is a low scale domain ontology often used as semantic model for the working memory of reasoning engines of a cognitive agent. A micro-ontology contains only the concepts and relations needed for the problem handled by the cognitive agent. In AAL scenarios, this ontology describes the contextual sensors which are present in the ambient environment and also all concepts related to observations, situations and activities of daily living that can influence the elderly safety. For instance, this ontology contains the relevant concepts that characterize typical contexts, such as *sleeping* and *preparing a breakfast*. The concept *sleeping* is defined with properties that describe that the user may be located in the bedroom or in the living room and that (s)he is in a lying posture close to objects such as sofa or bed. The concept *preparing a breakfast* is defined with properties that indicate the user should be located in the kitchen and (s)he is interacting with fridge, micro-wave, dishes, etc. The list of objects necessary for the context is defined according to the user activity profile (i.e. the list of objects frequently used for a given activity).

The core concepts defined in this ontology are:

- **sensor output** is used to transform the raw sensor data into sensor observation instances;

- **space region** corresponds to a specific environment region from witch two specialized concepts *indoor space region* and *outdoor space region* are derived. The indoor space region is specialized into subconcepts that describe all the spaces of a house that need to be monitored, like kitchen, bedroom, living room, toilets and corridor. Each monitored space can includes a small space regions called zones and used to fine-grade the user, object, sensors, actuator and robot location.
- **object** is associated to physical and software objects that are used for performing system monitoring and acting. It is specialized into subconcepts like sensors, actuators, device, appliances, dishes and furniture; and also like multimedia documents, applications and web services objects.
- **robot** is used to describe the features and the services provided by a robot. It is specialized into several sub concepts, according to the services supplied by the robot, like mobile companion robot, mobility assistance robot (e.g., exoskeleton robot, walker robot or wheelchair robot), tele-presence robot, etc.

Our micro-ontology is defined in the μConcept/RDF [9] representation to allow the definition of inference rules according to the CWA. This representation is a variant of OWL2/RDF that makes a micro ontology close to an UML metamodel. It can be easily mapped to class diagrams that are needed in object oriented production rule systems such as Drools[2].

In general, μConcept ontologies can be even defined from scratch using the μConcept language or elaborated from existing OWL2/RDF ontology. The additional features that are not supported in OWL2, such as the unique name assumption, qualified restrictions and default values, are handled directly in the reasoning software that supports the μConcept language.

As introduced before, SSN is good domain ontology to describe background knowledge about sensors and their readings. The concepts included in this ontology makes it easy to define reasoning rules that involve sensors observations and reactive actions. For this reason, all domain specific concepts of the proposed micro-ontology and that are used to model the ambient context, are mapped respectively with DUL and SSN concepts.

In order to represent the SSN conceptualization in the μConcept language, an ontology editor designed during the SEMbySEM project was used to translate the OWL2 concepts description of SSN to their corresponding ones in the μConcept language. The axioms that cannot be translated into μConcept concept primitives, such as, restrictions on concepts, when necessary, were encoded using smart rules language. The μConcept version of the ontology was further enriched by adding the domain concepts, including actions, which are needed for the scenario. Moreover, only a subset of all the axioms available in the OWL2 version of the SSN ontology are useful for specifying the different reactive reasoning cases of the scenario. Therefore, for practical reasons, we have made fusion on the name spaces of the SSN/DUL concepts and properties with micro-ontology and

[2] http://www.drools.org.

kept only concepts and properties related to the sensors description and observations, which are needed for designing the reasoning rules. Description Logics restrictions have been removed as they are not needed for reactive reasoning requirements.

Reasoning System. The core of the reasoning system is a set of rules which are executed by the monitoring agents. Rules are defined by the experts and are used together with up-to-date observations from sensors outputs for inferring human situations and activities; and also for triggering agent reactive actions.

The underlying logic of the smart rules language is a choice that depends on the expressivity needed to represent a scenario and the complexity of the required reasoning. Smart rules allow the monitoring agents designers to design rules in different logics languages without caring about how they will be executed by the different reasoners.

For this reason, in our architecture, rules are classified according to four reasoning categories:

- **recognition rules:** classify situations based on the observations made by the available sensors. For example, the observations made by the lock door sensor (ZLock) are translated into a fluent that represents the current status of the door. This contextual information is aggregated by other rules to form situations. For example, if the door is said to be both opened and locked at the same time, it is possible that an intruder has forced it and entered the house.
- **confirmation rules:** confirm the situations recognized from recognition rules. For example, the fire situation inferred from the observations provided by the fire detector sensor can be confirmed by the temperature information gathered by the temperature sensor (TelosB);
- **diagnosis rules:** evaluate qualitatively the global system status. Once the fire is confirmed, the agent diagnoses the context and determine if it was accidental or criminal. In case of criminal fire, the agent will try to track the intruder by analyzing the events that are triggered by different virtual objects associated to the cameras.
- **reaction rules:** respond to the inferred context using the available actuators and agents. Once any abnormal situation is detected, the informed virtual object reacts by trying to contact the person in charge of dealing with this situation. For example, in case of a supposed fire, the virtual object tries to contact the resident for confirmation.

To handle these reasoning categories, the current implementation of smart rules in our proposal is based on production rules to model one shot abnormal situations, such as *a fall* which can happens in different contexts, see Sect. 4. The RETE based inference engine [4] is used to fire the defined rules. The implementation of this reasoning system have been conducted in the context of the EU SEMbySEM project[3] and the Web of Object project[4].

[3] https://itea3.org/project/sembysem.html.
[4] https://itea3.org/project/web-of-objects.html.

The reasoning core has also a module for checking the constraints related to the observation messages coming from the sensors before inserting them into the working memory. This avoids to insert instances that either do not have corresponding concepts or have properties values that exceed the maximum allowed value.

4 Fall Monitoring for Elderly Safety

This section details the implementation of the monitoring agent and its validation in abnormal situations after a fall. Let us consider the case of an elderly person living alone and suffering from mild cognitive impairment. The family doctor noticed that the elderly had a worsening of his mobility and falls several times a week. Then, the elderly agreed with his doctor and family members to use a bracelet, install an RGB-D camera and have a companion robot at home.

In this scenario, the monitoring agent can recognize abnormal situation, by aggregating observations obtained from sensors in different contexts; and, then, infer if the situation is an emergency by using a verification process through a stimulus to the user. For the latter situation, if the user does not react to the stimulus, the agent considers that the situation is an emergency and triggers a reactive action such as sending an alarm to elderly caregivers.

4.1 Virtual Objects

Virtual objects used for abstracting the sensing and actuation infrastructure are listed below:

- **Health Virtual Object (H-VO)** is associated to ZCare CLEODE^{TM} bracelet and it is responsible to detect falls and monitor the elderly cardiac activity.
- **Activity Recognition Virtual Object (AR-VO)** encapsulates the SUP (*Scene Understanding Platform*) platform[5] which allows to recognize events from RGB-D video streams. SUP virtual object is setup to detect human postures, posture change, human proximity to objects, and so on. Its architecture is composed of three modules: (i) a *vision module* which allows to identify and track moving objects in a scene; (ii) an *event recognition module* which allows to recognize scenarios according to the activities of mobile objects moving in a scene; (iii) a *knowledge base module* which stores 3D information about a scene and the description of events of interest made by experts.
- **Robot Virtual Object (R-VO)** allows to control the Kompai companion robot which is used to perform the assistive services. These services are implemented mostly using sensory and actuation of the robuBOX middleware functionalities that include robot mapping, path planning and navigation in indoor environments; user localization relative to the robot position; voice recognition and translation which are used for capturing the user verbal instructions into text; voice messages synthesis to supply users with advices, recommendations and alerts, etc.

[5] https://pal.inria.fr/ressources/scene-understanding-platform-sup.

- **Objects Detection and Identification Virtual Object (ODI-VO)** used to identify close objects and humans that are present in the proximity.

4.2 Fall Situation

Normal contexts of lying down are associated to those related to sleeping and/or relaxing activities. They can be inferred from the user location and his(her) proximity/position with regards to furnitures such as sofa or bed. Abnormal contexts are identified when the user is localized in non-suitable places such as corridor, toilet, bathroom or kitchen. In these cases, probably, a falling situation happened.

Context Analysis. Falling situations are detected from the aggregation of the following context attributes: user lying posture; user position; absence of an object (bed or chair) near the user location.

The first two attributes are directly observable by the AR-VO while the third one is inferred by the denial of the presence of objects in the area (Negation by Failure). AR-VO has several SUP event configurations that allow to determine specific events in the AmI scenario. For instance, the event *a person is lying down* is a compound state, as shown in SUP Configuration 1, that connects a physical object (person) to a simple event (lying) adding a constraint. In this event, if the person *p* stays more than 5 s lying down, the AR-VO sends a message with this information to the monitoring agent. When this message is received, the monitoring agent processes it and executes the smart rule, defined in SmartRule 2. This smart rule updates the current user posture according to the concept *posture observation* (Posture Observation).

SUP Event Configuration 1: Posture Observation

```
CompoundState(Person_LyingDown,
    PhysicalObjects (p : Person)
    Components (c : PrimitiveState Lying(p))
    Constraints (c duration > 5))
```

Determining the user location and his(her) proximity to the furnitures involves to identify the user presence in a specific area of the environment. Hence, the user is near a sofa or bed if his(her) location is the same location of the sofa or bed, respectively. In this study, the location of any physical object (person or objects) is defined by a cuboid that contains that object. These areas are static and defined *a priori*. As result, the user location corresponds to one of these areas that contains his(her) 3D position.

The SUP configuration to inform that a user is in a zone A is given in SUP Configuration 3. The execution of this event is followed by the execution of the Smart Rule 4. Every time, the user is in the zone A, the AR-VO broadcasts an

Smart Rule 2: Posture Observation

```
Conditions
    PostureObservation(?posture:=hasQualityValue);
    ?inhabitant:=Person();
Actions
    ?inhabitant.hasPosture:=?posture;
    update(?inhabitant);
End
```

Fig. 2. Detection of the users' posture by the Activity Recognition Virtual Object

observation message informing the user location. This zone A can be associated to a sofa, bed, kitchen region, etc. (Fig. 2).

Using this observation, the system can infer abnormal context (see Smart Rule 5). After identifying that the user is in a lying posture, the system searches for the presence of bed or sofa near the user location. If these objects are not present then, an instance of a fall situation concept is created and inserted in the knowledge base making reference to the user location, thanks to the CWA feature of the micro-ontology that allows to handle negations of facts.

Fall Near the Personal Computer. In this context a fall alarm is raised by the virtual object ZCare Cleode^{TM} bracelet (Fig. 3); a typical device for human fall detection and triggering SOS alerts. The Smart Rule 6 allows to update the semantic model.

Confirming an Emergency Situation. Confirming that an abnormal situation is an emergency one requires a cognitive procedure to remove false-positive events. To handle this situation, we propose a reactive reasoning procedure based

SUP Event Configuration 3: Location Observation

```
PrimitiveState(Person_Inside_ZoneA,
    PhysicalObjects ((p : Person) (z: Zone))
    Constraints ((p.Position in z.Vertices)
                 (z.Name=ZoneA))
    Alarm(Level : URGENT)
```

Smart Rule 4: Location Observation

```
Conditions
    LocationObservation(?location:=hasQualityValue);
    ?inhabitant:=Person();
Actions
    ?inhabitant.hasLocation:=?location;
    update(?Inhabitant);
End
```

Smart Rule 5: Fall Situation in Context 1

```
Conditions
    Person(?location:=hasLocation,
    hasPosture=='LyingDown');
    ?location(?object:=one(contains));
    (not?object(isInstanceOf(Sofa)) and
    (not?object(isInstanceOf(Bed))
Actions
    FallSituation ?fall:=createInstance(FallSituation);
    ?fall.locatedAt:= ?location;
    insert(?fall)
End
```

on the user response to a specific stimulus. This procedure contains two generic inference rules that are complementary. The first rule is conditioned on the existence of an interaction device type near the user (see Smart Rule 7). The second

Fig. 3. Fall event detected by ZCare Cleode™ bracelet

Smart Rule 6: Fall Situation in Context 2

```
Conditions
    ?output:=FallSensorOutput(?virtual_object:=isProducedby);
    Person(?location:=hasLocation);
Actions
    FallSituation ?fall:=createInstance(FallSituation);
    ?fall.observedBy:= ?virtual_object;
    ?fall.observationResult:=?output;
    ?fall.locatedAt:= ?location;
    insert(?fall)
End
```

rule is fired if the first one is not fired i.e., there is no interaction device near the user. In this situation, a robot is instructed to move to the current user position to apply a stimulus (see Smart Rule 8). Moving the robot is also conditioned by the accessibility of the space where the falling situation was observed. Once the robot arrives at its destination, the first rule fired and the interaction device is the robot itself, see Fig. 4.

The user response to the stimulus allows to confirm or not that the abnormal situation is a real emergency situation. In our scenario, the user responds to false alarms by pressing on the robot screen. This action triggers an event that broadcasts a *button observation* containing the information "false alarm". If no action is triggered, an alert is emitted (to the first response center and/or relatives). However, to avoid false positive situations due to the system delay, a waiting time is used between the inference of the fall situation and the decision to trigger the alert.

This waiting time is defined by the presence of an instance of the concept *deadline expiry observation* in the rule condition, as shown in SmartRule 9.

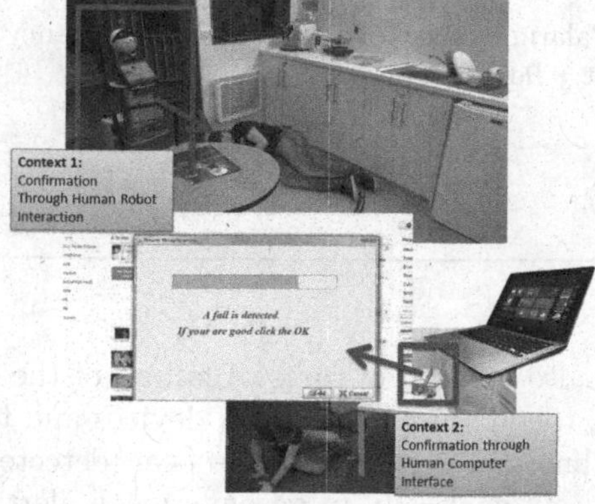

Fig. 4. A reasoning and interaction procedure for the confirmation of abnormal situations depending on the current context

Smart Rule 7: Apply Stimulus in Fall Situations

```
Conditions
    FallSituation();
    Person(?deviceId :=nearTo);
    ?deviceId(isInstanceOf(MultimediaDevice));
Actions
    VisualMessage ?message:=createAction(?deviceId, VisualMessage);
    ?message.content:='If you feel good, please ok';
    execute(?message)
End
```

Smart Rule 8: Moving the Robot

```
Conditions
    FallObservation(?location:=locateAt);
    ?location(isAccessibleSpace=='true');
    Person(not(nearTo isInstanceOf(MultimediaDevice)));
    ?robot:=CompanionRobot();
Actions
    MoveRobot ?action:=createAction(?robot,MoveRobot);
    ?action.moveTo:=?location;
    execute(?action);
End
```

Smart Rule 9: Confirmation 1

```
Conditions
    ?fall:=FallSituation(?location:=locateAt);
    not exists(ButtonObservation(
hasQualityValue=='False Alarm'));
    ?timer:=DeadlineExpiryObservation(
hasQualityValue=='Fall deadline');
Actions
    FallEmergency ?alarm :=createInstance(FallEmergency);
    ?alarm.locatedAt:=?location;
    insert(?alarm);
    retract(?fall);
    retract(?timer);
End
```

The emergency is also inferred in cases of failure of the confirmation procedure. In our scenario, the absence of stimulus devices and the inaccessibility of the area where the abnormal observation has been detected are considered as failure and translated automatically in an emergency alert to be checked by a human (see Smart Rule 10).

Smart Rule 10: Confirmation 2

```
Conditions
    ?fall:=FallObservation(?location:=locateAt);
    ?location(isAccessibleSpace=='False');
    Person(not(nearTo isInstanceOf(MultimediaDevice)));
Actions
    FallEmergency ?alarm :=createInstance(FallEmergency);
    ?alarm.locatedAt:=?location;
    insert(?alarm);
    retract(?fall);
End
```

5 Conclusion

Developing monitoring agents that react to heterogeneous situations by considering their context requires a suitable engineering approach that must have the advantages of ontologies as well as object oriented data modeling and programming. The approach presented in this paper allows developing easily context-aware monitoring agents for ambient assisted living application that can support users in any predefined situation without specific programming of the agent's reasoning core. Agents' knowledge base contains a semantic model describing the real world and rules to infer from the one hand non-observable contexts and situations and to trigger the corresponding reactive actions on the other hand. The semantic model is defined by using micro concepts and smart rules languages, which support respectively the unique name assumption, closed world assumption and negation as failure features. Therefore, the agent knowledge base is implicitly viewed as being complete and any missing information are considered by default as false. In addition, the knowledge base will never include redundant facts. These important features are unfortunately not supported in OWL, which means that OWL-based knowledge bases are potentially representing partial contextual knowledge and cannot be used in monitoring applications. In contrary of state of the art approach where the detection of situation is completed automated, in the propose approach a general procedure for confirming possible abnormal situations is implemented. The abnormal situations that can be detected by monitoring agents are confirmed through a reliable stimulus-response interaction. The latter is triggered by the monitoring agent and may involve different modes that are related to the context of the user. Moreover, our engineering approach allows designers to enhance agents to support new context types only through the extension of the micro-ontology with few concepts and smart rules without any additional programming. The semantic description of sensors and their output types, including the transformation of output data into knowledge are handled by a middleware of virtual objects, which assure an abstraction with regards to the heterogeneity of sensing technologies and their architecture remains independent from the architecture of the monitoring agents.

The ongoing works are focusing to solve two main issues. The first issue concern the possible conflicts (inconsistencies) that may arise when context information about the same situation are provided by different virtual objects that transmit to the monitoring agent at the same time. The second issue concerns the exploitation of the temporal relations between observations in order to better recognize non-trivial situations and take into account the effects of these changes before triggering reactive actions.

References

1. Aaliance2 Consortium: Aaliance2 aal roadmap (2014). http://www.aaliance2.eu
2. Chibani, A., Amirat, Y., Mohammed, S., Matson, E., Hagita, N., Barreto, M.: Ubiquitous robotics: recent challenges and future trends. Robot. Auton. Syst. **61**, 1162–1172 (2013)
3. Clark, K.L.: Negation as failure. In: Fagerberg, J., Mowery, D., Nelson, R. (eds.) Readings in Nonmonotonic Reasoning, pp. 311–325. Morgan Kaufmann Publishers, San Francisco (1987)
4. Forgy, C.L.: RETE: a fast algorithm for the many pattern/many object pattern match problem. Artif. Intell. **19**(1), 17–37 (1982)
5. Hervás, R., Bravo, J., Fontecha, J.: A context model based on ontological languages: a proposal for information visualization. J. UCS **16**(12), 1539–1555 (2010)
6. Janowicz, K., Compton, M.: The stimulus-sensor-observation ontology design pattern and its integration into the semantic sensor network ontology. In: Proceedings of the 3rd International Conference on Semantic Sensor Networks, pp. 64–78 (2010)
7. Poole, D.L., Mackworth, A.K.: Artificial Intelligence: Foundations of Computational Agents. Cambridge University Press, Cambridge (2010)
8. Rodríguez, N.D., Cuéllar, M.P., Lilius, J., Calvo-Flores, M.D.: A survey on ontologies for human behavior recognition. ACM Comput. Surv. (CSUR) **46**(4), 43 (2014)
9. Sabri, L., Chibani, A., Amirat, Y., Zarri, G.P.: Semantic reasoning framework to supervise and manage contexts and objects in pervasive computing environments. In: Advanced Information Networking and Applications (WAINA), pp. 47–52, March 2011
10. Schneider, T., Hashemi, A., Bennett, M., Brady, M., Casanave, C., Graves, H., Gruninger, M., Guarino, N., Levenchuk, A., Lucier, E., et al.: Ontology for big systems: the ontology summit 2012 communique. Appl. Ontol. **7**(3), 357–371 (2012)
11. Studer, R., Benjamins, V., Fensel, D.: Knowledge engineering: principles and methods. Data Knowl. Eng. **25**(1–2), 161–197 (1998)
12. Tenorth, M., Beetz, M.: KnowRob - knowledge processing for autonomous personal robots. In: IEEE/RSJ International Conference on Intelligent Robots and Systems (IROS) (2009)

Mobility Competencies of People with Down Syndrome Supported by Technical Assistance

Results of the Requirement Analysis in POSEIDON Project

Anne Engler(✉), Anna Zirk, Monique Siebrandt, Eva Schulze, and Detlef Oesterreich

Berlin Institute for Social Research, Brandenburgische Straße 16, 10707 Berlin, Germany
a.engler@bis-berlin.de

Abstract. The POSEIDON project aims to increase the independence and autonomy of people with Down syndrome (DS) with the help of technical assistants. To find out which daily activities people with DS can manage on their own and where help can lead to a greater independence, a survey was conducted as a first step of the project. All in all, 583 questionnaires were filled in by carers of people with DS. Data indicate that help increases the number of people with DS being able to manage certain activities with the help of technical assistants.

Keywords: Down syndrome · Smart environment · Technical assistance · Integration into society · Autonomy · Mobility

1 Introduction

The POSEIDON project (PersOnalized Smart Environments to increase Inclusion of people with DOwn's syndrome) focuses on the task of bringing some of the latest technological advances to people with Down Syndrome (DS). The aim was to develop technological infrastructure to help people with DS to achieve greater independence and inclusion in their everyday lives. It is a three-year project (2013–2016) which has been founded by the European Commission. Nine partners[1] from the United Kingdom, Norway and Germany are involved. The idea generation and the developmental process of POSEIDON´s technical assistants based on a user centred approach. This means that all stakeholders as there are people with DS, parents, carers and teachers were included in all stages of the developmental process. The first step in the project was to find out were support is needed in order to provide technical assistance for those situations. So, an extensive scientific online survey was conducted; selected results are presented in this paper. Based on these results different technical applications were developed and tested in two usability tests.

[1] Karde AS, Middlesex University, Fraunhofer IGD, Berlin Institute for Social Research, Funka Nu, Tellu AS, Norwegian Network for Down Syndrome, Down's Syndrome Association – UK, Association Down-Syndrome – Germany.

A. Braun et al. (Eds.): AmI 2017, LNCS 10217, pp. 241–246, 2017.
DOI: 10.1007/978-3-319-56997-0_19

2 Theory

Down syndrome, also known as trisomy 21, is caused by extra genetic material in chromosome 21. According to the WHO, 1 in 1000 to 1 in 1100 live births worldwide is affected by DS. People with DS have many different symptoms as there are physical limitations [1], but it also affects mental areas being responsible for cognitive, linguistic and sensomotoric skills [2]. Even though the capabilities and disabilities often vary to a high extent, there is a general perception that people with DS can achieve little within the society they live in. One reason might be that they have problems in expressing themselves [3]. Problems in expressive language can cause an underestimation of intelligence and other competencies [4]. But in some cases, they successfully complete university [5] and become as independent as possible. This leads to the assumption that people with DS can achieve much more than they are expected to, especially when help is provided. Research has shown that people with DS have a high affinity for technology and that it seems to be of great importance for them [6]. Due to that fact, we assume that technology can be an opportunity to increase their independence and to strengthen their self-confidence.

3 Method

The aim of this requirement survey was to find out which activities of daily life people with DS can do on their own, where help is needed to fulfil certain tasks and where they, even with help, cannot manage to do things. Our main interest was to get an idea about what they can accomplish when help is offered in order to provide support for these certain activities. To examine a large sample as possible a quantitative research design was planned and a questionnaire created[2] which focused on IADL (Instrumental Activities of Daily Living) - skills and on the use of modern information technology in daily life. It was important to find out how people with DS cope with different situations in daily life, including time management, handling money, travelling, health, communication and school/work/learning. It was asked if the person with DS is able to do a certain activity on his/her own, with very little help, with some degree of help, with a lot of help or if he/she is not able to do this activity. We also focused on the estimated impact assistive technology might have to improve the living situation of people with DS. The questionnaire addressed everybody caring for people with DS because people with DS are often not able to fill in a questionnaire. An online version of the questionnaire was published on various platforms of the national Down Syndrome Organisations in UK, Norway, Germany, Italy, Slovenia and Portugal. The survey was conducted from December 2013 until the end of 2016. All in all, 583 questionnaires had been filled in.

---

[2] Available under www.bis-berlin.de/POSEIDON/Quest/RequirementAnalysis.pdf.

4 Results

It became clear that people with DS mainly need support in the areas of mobility, money handling and time management. For this paper, we decided to focus on mobility where most help is required and most assistive technologies in the POSEIDON project were developed. Data are analysed for three age groups[3]: 10–19 years, 20–29 years and 30 years and older. The distribution for the age groups (N = 372) is presented in Table 1.

Table 1. Age and gender distribution

	Male	Female	All
10–19 years	125	84	209
20–29 years	63	51	114
30 years and older	26	23	49
Sum	214	158	372

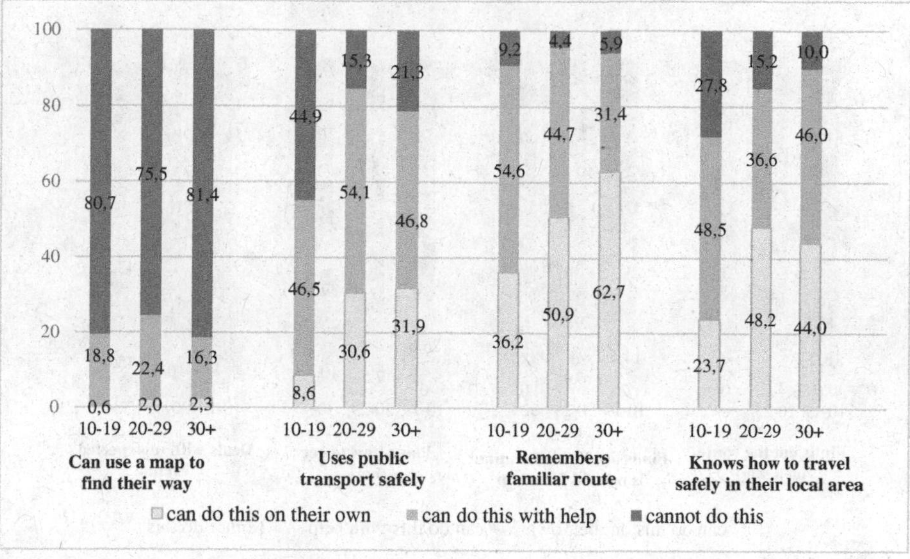

Fig. 1. Mobility -part 1 - in percent

Results indicate that competencies regarding mobility vary highly between age groups and items. As shown in Fig. 1, competencies increase with increasing age. Whereas remembering a familiar route seems to cause less problems and most of the people with DS are able to do this, at least with help[4], almost none of the people with DS is able to use a map to find his or her way alone. Help seems to be very promising, especially for using

[3] Children under 10 years and people who have not reported their age are excluded.

[4] All people who need very little, some degree or a lot of help are summarized in one group who "can do this with help".

public transport, remembering a familiar route and knowing how to travel safely in local areas. This is true for all age groups. Without help, almost none of the people with DS can use a map to find his or her way. But help can increase the number of those managing this activity up to 22.4%, at least if they are between 20 and 29 years old.

Figure 2 indicates that especially planning activities seems to cause problems for people with DS. This is true for finding routes on maps, finding out how much time is needed for a trip and planning how to get somewhere. Data indicate that among of those aged between 10 and 19 almost no one is able to do these activities alone. No matter how old people with DS are, even with help these activities seem to be challenging. However, data show that the older people are the more likely they are able to deal with these activities when help is provided. Providing help leads to a huge increase of the number of people being able to do things. This is especially true for those aged 30 years and older and finding out how much time is needed for a trip and dealing with unexpected events. When help is provided, 39.6% and 42.2% are able to do this among those older than 30 years.

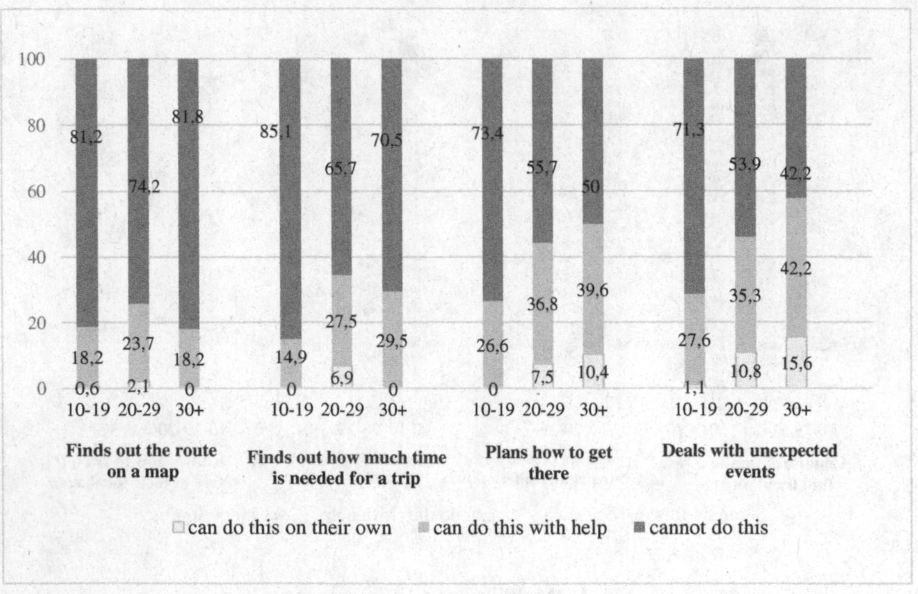

Fig. 2. Mobility – part 2 - in percent

Carers were also ask if they think assistive technology, like an app on a smartphone or tablet, might help to overcome daily challenges. Most of them (54.5%) think that technical assistants can help manage daily activities. 12.1% do not see a benefit in using such a technology. One-third (33.5%) indicates that this question is difficult to answer.

5 Discussion

The survey provides a broad overview on the competencies and problems people with DS have in their daily life. The major result of the survey is they have highly divergent competencies - some of them can do a lot of things on their own, some cannot do things at all, and a larger group is able to do things with help. These are promising results considering assistive technologies as being helpful to support the challenges in daily life. The large number of carers demonstrate the immense interest parents and relatives have to improve the everyday life of those they are caring for. The results of the survey clearly indicate that people with DS can do many things when help is provided. The questionnaire allows only limited explanations. We especially do not know why people with DS are doing things not on their own. We cannot say to what extent they are not able to do them and to what extent they are not doing them because of an overprotective system they live in. However, the results can be seen as a good basis for developing assistive technologies for people with DS.

6 Conclusion and Prospects

POSEIDON contributes to the field of smart environments where there is little done before for people with DS. Not much is really known about their interaction with technology. User-centerdness was paramount for the success on adoption of Intelligent Environments. The first step was the online-survey. The results lead to the assumption that people with DS can achieve a lot when help is provided. The results also indicate that assistive technologies should be quite flexible since their capabilities vary to a high extent. Based on the results, different technical assistants were developed in the POSEIDON project to support these activities. To help people with DS in terms of mobility, a navigation app and a Home Navigation System (HNS) was developed and for carers a Route Creator app to create routes. These routes can be rehearsed with the HNS on the PC and they can be used on smartphones to navigate outside. Carers can adapt the routes to the needs of their protégées with pictures, text and speech. All applications were evaluated regarding their usability and usefulness in field studies with people with DS and their families. Results indicate that POSEIDON has a great potential to increase their independence.

References

1. Hickey, F., Hickey, E., Summar, K.L.: Medical update for children with Down syndrome for the pediatrician and family practitioner. Adv. Pediatr. **59**(1), 137–157 (2012)
2. Abbeduto, L., Pavetto, M., Kesin, E., Weissman, M.D., Karadottir, S., O'Brien, A., Cawthon, S.: The linguistic and cognitive profile of Down syndrome: evidence from a comparison with fragile X syndrome. Down Syndr. Res. Pract. **7**(1), 9–15 (2001)
3. Buckley, S., Bird, G.: Speech and language development in individuals with Down syndrome (5–11 years): an overview. Technical report. Down Syndrome Educational Trust, Portsmouth, UK (2001)

4. Kumin, L.: Early Communication Skills in Children with Down Syndrome: A Guide for Parents and Professionals. Woodbine House, Bethesda (2003)
5. Down Syndrom Regensburg: What about the intelligence of children with Down syndrome? (Was ist mit der Intelligenz bei Kindern mit Down-Syndrom?) (2016). http://www.down-syndrom-regensburg.org/das-down-syndrom/was-ist-mit-der-intelligenz-bei-kindern-mit-down-syndrom/
6. Feng, J., Lazar, J., Kumin, L., Ozok, A.: Computer usage by young individuals with Down syndrome: an exploratory study. In: Proceedings of the 10th International ACM SIGACCESS Conference on Computers and Accessibility, pp. 35–42. ACM (2008)

An Exploratory Study on Electric Field Sensing

Julian von Wilmsdorff[1(✉)], Florian Kirchbuchner[1], Biying Fu[1], Andreas Braun[1,2], and Arjan Kuijper[1,2]

[1] Fraunhofer IGD, Fraunhoferstr. 5, 64283 Darmstadt, Germany
{julian.von.wilmsdorff,florian.kirchbuchner,biying.fu,andreas.braun, arjan.kuijper}@igd.fraunhofer.de

[2] Technische Universität Darmstadt, Karolinenplatz 5, 64289 Darmstadt, Germany
arjan.kuijper@mavc.tu-darmstadt.de

Abstract. Electric fields are influenced by the human body and other conducting materials. Capacitive measurement techniques are used in touch-screens, in the automobile industry, and for presence and activity recognition in Ubiquitous Computing. However, a drawback of the capacitive technology is the energy consumption, which is an important aspect for mobile devices. In this paper we explore possible applications of electric field sensing, a purely passive capacitive measurement technique, which can be implemented with an extremely low power consumption. To cover a wide range of applications, we examine five possible use cases in more detail. The results show that the application is feasible both in interior spaces and outdoors. Moreover, due to the low energy consumption, mobile usage is also possible.

Keywords: Electric field sensing · Capacitive sensing · Motion detection · Sensors · Gesture recognition

1 Introduction

The advent of touch-screen technologies in smartphones, tablets, and automotive human-machine-interfaces has sparked an increasing trend towards natural interaction paradigms that enable a user to interact with a machine using the same means as with interaction between persons - speech, gestures, and mimics. In recent years capacitive sensing systems have become a major input modality for small computing devices but have also found their way into the domain of ubiquitous interaction. Regarding the detection range, modern capacitive sensing systems can detect the proximity to objects at distances up to 50 cm. However, these systems use actively generated electric fields to sense their environment. In contrast to active capacitive sensing, our proposed electric field sensing is completely passive and picks up changes in ambient electric potential, generated by human movements. It can detect the presence of a human body in distances up to 2 m [6]. Working through any non-conductive material, they are especially suited for integration into the typical home environment as they can be placed into furniture. An array of electric field sensors can be used to detect passive

A. Braun et al. (Eds.): AmI 2017, LNCS 10217, pp. 247–262, 2017.
DOI: 10.1007/978-3-319-56997-0_20

interaction patterns, e.g. the presence of a person, but also active interaction, e.g. gestures performed by a user over an equipped surface. The low power consumption is also a major benefit for mobile usage.

In the following sections we will first introduce the technology of electric potential sensing, and then we will examine some potential applications.

2 Related Work

It's easily possible to turn most of the everyday objects into smart objects by simply applying the active capacitive sensing technique. Sato et al. [14] published in their work Touch? different everyday objects equipped with interactive capabilities, like e.g. a smart doorknob to sense different grasp gestures and a smart desk to sense body gestures. Besides, Kaila et al. [9] embedded capacitive sensing techniques into furniture to make it smart enough to interact with users unobtrusively for smart home applications. It automatically fades into the background, if it is not used and offers visual input help as the user interacts with it. Braun et al. [1] worked on a smart wooden table called CapTap, which combines capacitive hand tracking and acoustic touch sensing. Ivan Poupyrev et al. even go a step further and turned flowers into electrodes to interact with the surroundings as introduced by the project called Botanicus Interacticus [11]. However, these active capacitive techniques possess the same disadvantage in the sense of power consumption.

The concept of passive electric field sensing has been explored more and more in recent years by various researchers. Cohn et al. [4] use the human body as receiving antenna and turn the electromagnetic noise which already exists in our environment into useful signals for home automation applications. His group further developed an ultra-low power wearable device to detect human body motion using static electric field sensing [3]. Another example for wearables based on electric field sensing that can detect movements of legs and even the touch of human hair is shown by Pouryazdan et al. [12]. Prance et al. [13] use electric field sensing to detect remotely heart rate signals (ECG). They are able to detect the electric field change almost 40 cm apart from the surface of the body. Grosse-Puppendahl et al. [6] deployed a prototype called Platypus using the passive electric field sensing to perform indoor localization and person identification. The most important advantage of these type of technologies lies is its low power consumption. Therefore, our research also relates to the field of passive electric field sensing. In this paper, we will present further explorative studies we performed to show the wide range of application possibilities using this technology.

3 Electrical Field Sensing

Electric field sensing is a measuring technique that relies on the same physical principles as capacitive sensing. Capacitive sensing uses a constant current to charge and discharge an electrode. If an object comes near this electrode, the time needed to charge and discharge the electrode is altered because of the change in electrical capacity, which determines the amount of charge that the electrode is able to store. In this approach, the charging time is measured and correlates linearly to the electrical capacity. Capacitive sensing is, therefore, an active measurement, as the electrode emits an electrical field.

Since electric field sensing is similar to capacitive sensing, electric field sensing also reacts on the change of electrical capacity. But the main influence on the measurement is the charge carried by the object in nature itself. In contrast to capacitive sensing, voltage is measured. The voltage U of an electrode to ground correlates as follows to the charge Q and the electrical capacity C:

$$U = \frac{Q}{C}$$

Due to the triboelectric effect and other sources of static electricity, nearly every object carries a charge Q. The capacity C of the electrode, which can be interpreted as a virtual capacitor to ground, can be derived as:

$$C = \epsilon_0 \epsilon_r \frac{A}{d}$$

where ϵ_0 is the vacuum permittivity, ϵ_r is the relative permittivity, A is the Area of the electrode and d the distance to the ground. If a charged object moves near the electrode, it causes the charge in the electrode to move accordingly, resulting in a current that can be measured. That is why electric field sensing is a purely passive measurement; no electrical fields are emitted. Because of Ohm's law and because the induced current is very small, the resistance on the electrode has to be high to measure the change in voltage. To achieve a high resistance in a giga-ohm range, an operation amplifier is used in a unity gain buffer configuration, as shown in Fig. 1.

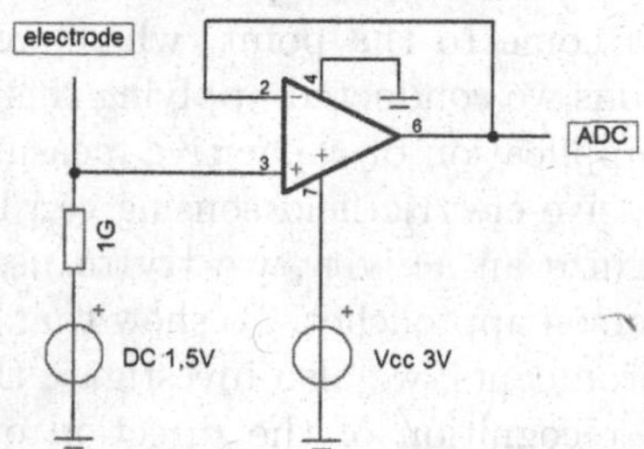

Fig. 1. The basic measurement circuit.

An advantage over classical capacitive sensing is the increased range. Electric field sensing can be used to measure objects several meters away from the sensing electrode, as shown for example in Mirage by Mujibiya et al. [10]. Active capacitive sensing is well suited in close range proximity sensing [7]. Another advantage over capacitive sensing is the reduced energy consumption since no electrical field is formed. The measurement itself as shown in Fig. 1 only consumes several nano-amps. A similar efficient system is shown by Cohn et al. [3]. The operation amplifier used in our electric field sensor implementation, the MCP604x from Texas Instruments, only uses 600 nA as quiescent current. All other components drain even less power so that the sensor consumes overall less than 800 nA.

A disadvantage with the purely passive electric field sensing is that only moving objects can be detected since a current has to be induced in the electrode, which is only possible by moving electrical charge. This can be done mainly in two different ways:

1. A charged object moves by, similar to a charged balloon moving close to some hair, moving it in the process.
2. A constantly changing electrical field is emitted, as, for example, every cable in households does that transmits an alternating current.

Classical capacitive sensing, on the other hand, can measure the distance of objects despite the fact that they are moving or not. The sole presence of a conducting object changes the capacitance and hence can be detected.

Electric field sensing also cannot measure the distance to the approaching object. That is because the measured voltage is a function of charge and capacitance. The electrical charge of the same object can vary over time and even change its sign. Trivial everyday activities, such as walking over a carpet or washing hands are affecting the amount of charge carried by a person. For this reason, the amplitude and the sign of such a voltage measurement give only limited information.

4 Exploratory Studies

After introducing the basic working principle of passive electric field sensing in the last Section, we now come to the point, where we would like to present several possible applications we conducted applying this sensing technology. We first imitate a standard application of capacitive measurement: the recognition of presence. However, passive electric field sensing can be used for much more. Since we primarily recognize an activity, we try to use this fact to recognize from which direction a person approaches. To show that this is not only possible in controlled indoor environments, we also investigate the application outdoors in our third study. The recognition of the direction of motion thus leads us to a refined application for gesture recognition. This is shown in our fourth study. Finally, we demonstrate a further advantage over the plain old capacitive technology by the mobile application of passive eclectic field sensing.

4.1 Whiteboard Sensor

A limitation of passive electric field sensing is, as discussed in Sect. 3, that it is hard to detect non-moving entities. With classical capacitive sensing, this is not an issue. To show how it is possible with passive electric field sensing to detect static situations without any movements, we face a standard application for capacitive sensing - Touch detection.

In this first experiment, we turned an unmodified whiteboard into an interactive touch sensor. Until now, the sensors used in other proposed experiments always filter out all frequencies above 50 Hz including the 50 Hz itself. In this experiment, an electric field sensor was modified such, that it filters out frequencies below 50 Hz. This is useful to overcome the constraint of the sensors that only movements can be detected. We especially deploy the 50 Hz component to detect the presence of a user. This experiment features a common whiteboard, which consists of at least one conductive layer. The surface of the whiteboard itself is non-conductive. For measuring the electric potential of the conductive layer, an electrode was attached on top of the non-conductive layer of the whiteboard. This means that the electrode has no direct contact with the conductive layer, but the electrode and the conductive layer are coupled in a capacitive way since they both resemble a small capacitor. Figure 2 shows the sensor as well as the attachment of the electrode.

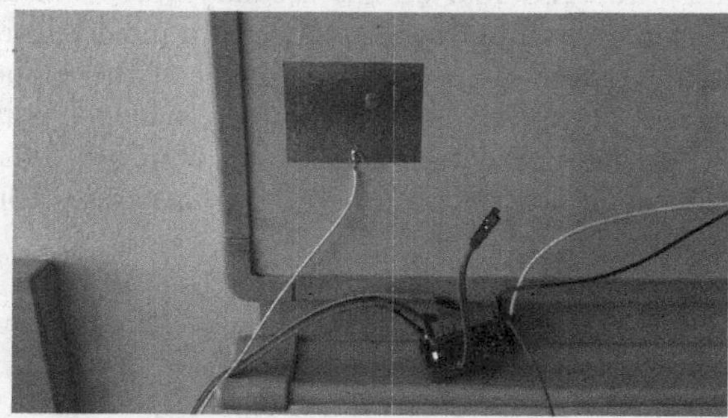

Fig. 2. Modified EF-sensor attached to a whiteboard.

As can be seen in Fig. 3, a touch on the whiteboard caused by a user will result in an increase in the amplitude. This increased amplitude remains as long as the user touches the whiteboard. By constructing the envelope curve of the measurement, a simple touch sensor can be created. The sensor is able to deliver the information whether the whiteboard is touched.

This approach shows that electric field sensing is capable of substituting classical capacitive sensing. It also shows that electric field sensors can easily turn everyday objects into interactive entities. As long as the object features some conductive behavior, attaching sensors like the above can turn our surroundings into components of the Internet of Things. Especially in this context, low power consumption plays an important role.

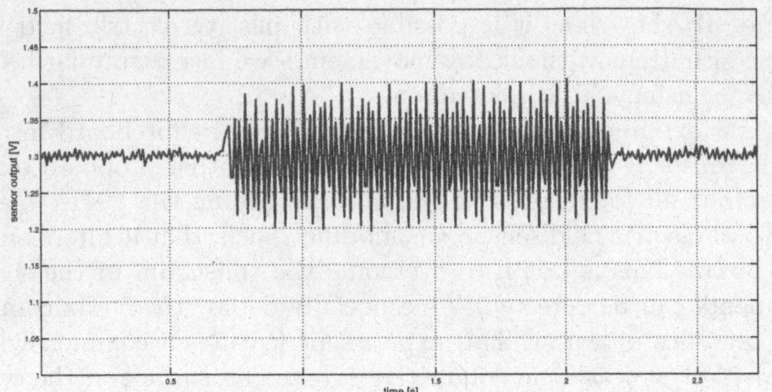

Fig. 3. Touch event on a whiteboard.

4.2 Door Sensor

The electrode of the electric field sensor was placed all around the door, in the form of a thin wire. The goal of this second experiment is not only the detection of persons in a room but also to detect if a moving person is entering or exiting the room. Because of the small diameter of the copper cable of the electrode that was used, the electrode was completely hidden within the rubber on the doorframe. The doorframe itself is made out of metal. This property is no requirement for the experiment but can be used to generate more information, as shown later on.

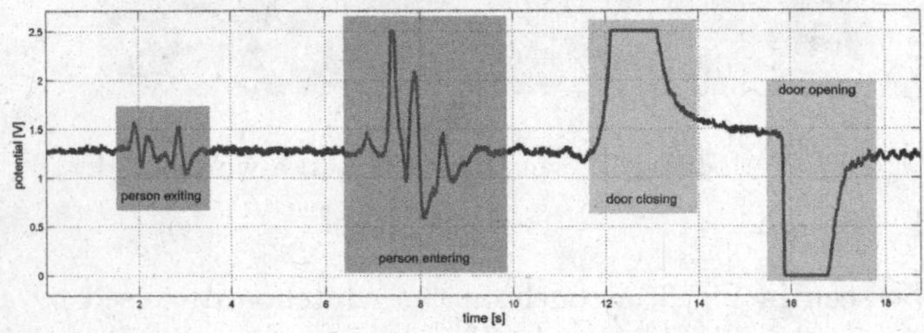

Fig. 4. Four different electrical footprints: a person exiting the room, a person entering, closing the door, and opening the door

Figure 4 illustrates four simple classes that can be easily distinguished. As shown, the entry event of a person and the corresponding exit-event of the same person differ in magnitude. The reason for this is the location of the electrode. The electrode was placed on the outside of the doorframe, which consists of metal. The electrode was facing the inside of the room. The metal shielding of the doorframe reduces the amplitude of the measurement in the direction of the hallway.

Likewise, the amplitude of any activity inside the room can be detected better. That is the reason that the exit event of a person will always have a larger amplitude than entering the room. This holds only for the same person within a small time-frame, since the charge of any entity, can vary over time. The closing and opening of a door can, in contrast to many other activities, be classified by the sign and form of the event recorded. Normally, the sign of the voltage amplitude of moving entities can change over time, as described in Sect. 3. However, in the case of a installed door, the door is permanently connected to the ground potential and hence cannot build up much static charge, except for small charges on the surface of the door. By closing the door, the ϵ (the electrical permittivity) of the virtual capacitor created by the electrode and the ground, will change. That influences its capacitance which results in a change of the measured voltage.

This experiment showed that it is possible to detect the direction of moving entities with a single electrode, even if only in a small timing window. To have a more reliable way to determine the direction, multiple electrodes should be used, as shown in a later experiment. In order to achieve the same functionality, the classical capacitive system needs larger transmitter electrodes and thus consumes way more power.

4.3 Traffic Observation

In the third application, the electric field sensor was deployed on the street, to test the sensor in a more open environment. This experimental setup should answer the question, if it is possible to distinguish between different participants of the traffic, like e.g. trucks, cars, bicycles or longboards. Since cars should influence the electric field significantly, electric field sensing could be an excellent technology for vehicle classification.

Figure 5 depicts the deployment of an electric field sensor on the street. Note that the deployment of the sensor did not take longer than a minute, this system is in particular suitable for fast and uncomplicated acquisition of traffic data. Vehicles and passengers are crossing the sensor deployed on the ground, and their electric footprint will be collected. Since only one electrode was used, it does not matter in which direction the vehicles are moving.

Figures 6, 7, and 8 illustrate three different vehicles (a car, a truck and a bicycle) crossing the sensor electrode. The curves depict the electric footprint of the respective vehicles. The peaks are due to the wheels crossing the sensing electrode. Based on the spacing in time and the known distance of the wheels, we can further deduce the speed of the driving vehicles. The difference of the signal form and duration can be seen clearly. The peaks in signal were caused by the wheels crossing the sensing electrode. Therefore, by counting the time of two successive wheels generated a signal and the distance between the wheels, it is further possible to detect the velocity of the driving vehicle. A similar approach using the classical capacitive sensor should be investigated in the future.

Fig. 5. Deployment of one electric field sensor on the street

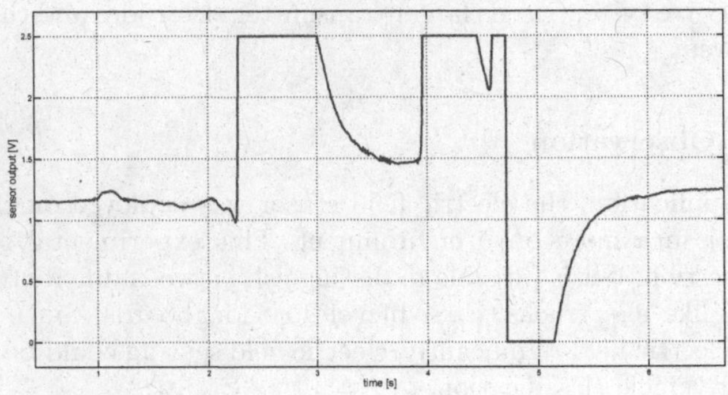

Fig. 6. Electric footprint of a truck

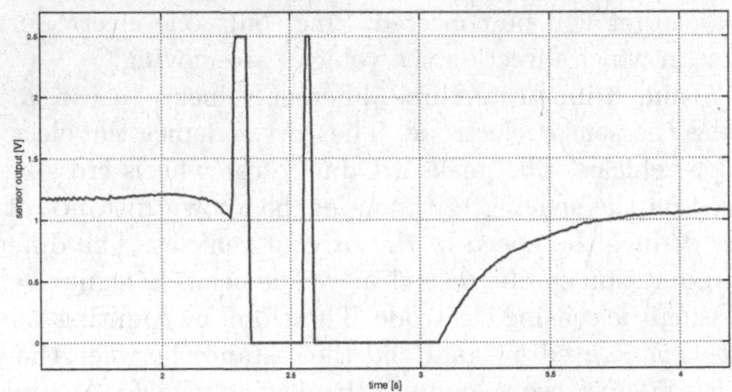

Fig. 7. Electric footprint of a car

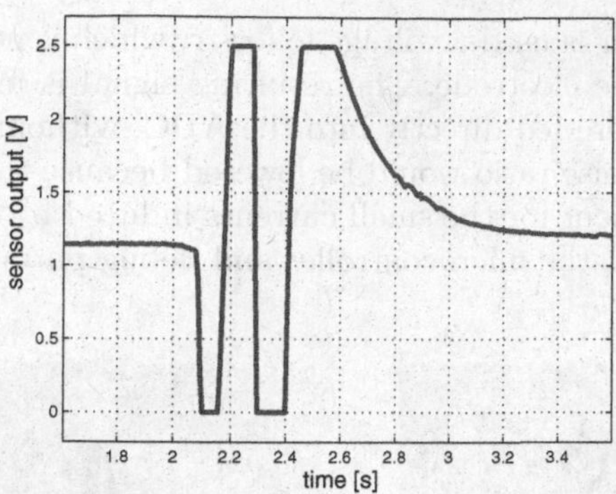

Fig. 8. Electric footprint of a bicycle

4.4 Gesture Recognition

As a fourth use case, we show an example of refined classification of movement directions with multiple electrodes, as suggested in the second experiment. To demonstrate this, we propose a system for gesture recognition based on electric field sensing. We developed a prototype in the style of a smartwatch, called GeFish (Fig. 9). The aim was to recognize gestures in a two-dimensional space. In order to measure the direction of a gesture, the electrodes are arranged symmetrically on four opposing edges of our "clock face". The direction of the movement can be calculated by considering the order in which the electrodes were activated.

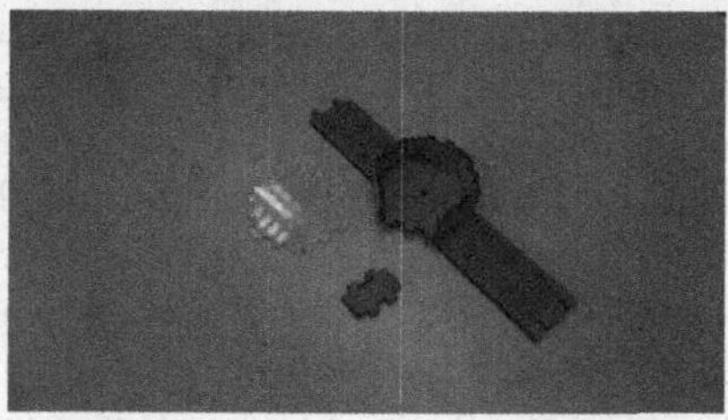

Fig. 9. The housing of GeFish.

For reasons of space and cost optimization, electrodes are built-in and are part of the PCB which is illustrated in Fig. 10. Distinctive components are the operational amplifiers at the center, the big 1G Ω resistors, and four electrodes. Every electrode is connected to two measurement groups. In comparison to the classical capacitive sensors, such small electrodes design would not be possible. The measuring distance would be too low for remote sensing. The signal without filters could be used to analyze the ambient 50 Hz field so that not only movements can be registered, but even the sheer presence of body parts. The second measurement group only consists of a 1G Ω resistor and an operation amplifier.

An operation amplifier is used a voltage follower, which is needed to increase the input resistance of the electrode. The resulting signal is fed into an additional ADC. If the signal were fed directly into the ADC, without using a voltage follower, the signal to noise ratio would be lowered because the input resistance of the ADC is not sufficient for the small currents induced by the user. At the bottom side of the board, the microcontroller and debug ports are placed (Fig. 11).

Fig. 10. GeFish top view.

Fig. 11. GeFish bottom view.

The time difference between the signals of the four electrodes is used for determining the direction of movement. As depicted in Fig. 12 a difference can be seen in the course of the four measurement curves. A simple state-machine is used to analytically find the typical pattern for a movement over a single electrode. This pattern is a sequence of a local extremum, followed by a zero-crossing, followed by another local extremum. After recognizing this pattern, the position of the zero-crossing is calculated. This procedure is done for every set of measurements of every electrode. A valid gesture in this context is if all four electrodes report an extremum-zero-extremum pattern within a certain amount of time. Another indicator is the relative time difference between those events. Absolute timing values will not do any good because every user executes gestures with different speeds. For this reason, a system was implemented which calculates the confidence of every direction and a confidence value for the situation that a gesture was done at all. So if the software is certain that the user has interacted with the system, it will output the direction, but only if a certain level of confidence is reached. That minimizes false positives since a user who walks past the sensor generates a similar pattern than a user making a gesture.

The functionality was shown in a small evaluation with 13 users. This experiment confirmed our thesis formulated in the second experiment, that it is possible to use electric field sensing for a robust detection of moving directions.

4.5 Wearables

In the previous experiments, the electrode of the sensors was always placed on a solid structure. That means that the potential to the ground of the electrode itself remained the same every time. The question arises what happens if the electrode

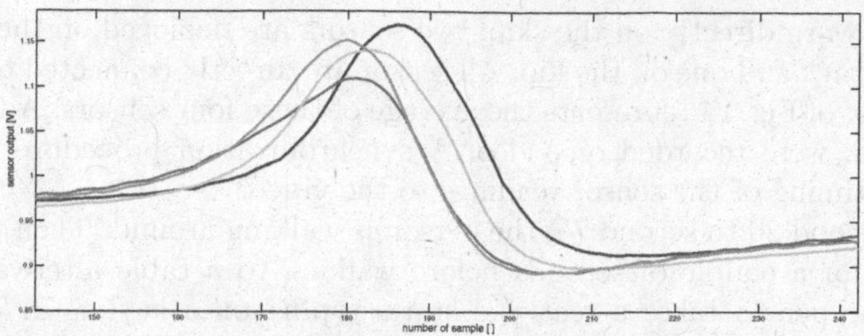

Fig. 12. A recording of all four electrodes of GeFish.

is worn on the body so that the potential to the ground changes over time. The following experiment was conducted in cooperation with the University of Sussex. The electric potential sensor used in this experiment was designed by the University of Sussex [2,5,8] and further embedded into our custom-designed circuits. The used external sensor device is also known under the name electric potential integrated circuit (EPIC) and can be commercially purchased from the Plessey Semiconductors[1].

Fig. 13. A person wearing multiple electric field sensors.

Figure 14 illustrates the sensor recording of approximately three minutes of activities. In this experiment, the person moving around is equipped with a variety of different sensors (see Fig. 13). Accelerometers and gyroscopes are embedded in each shoe to serve as a reference to our electric field measurement. This reference sensor system embedded in the shoes was also in courtesy from the Sensor Technology Research Centre of the University of Sussex. Four electric field

[1] http://www.plesseysemiconductors.com/

sensors are worn directly on the skin; two sensors are deployed on the shoulder, one on the back and one on the hip. All sensor are directly connected to the skin. The last row of Fig. 14 represents the average of these four sensors. Additionally, all activities were recorded on video. A synchronization procedure is used to match the timing of the sensor readings to the video.

From second 20 to second 75, the person is walking around. Then the person stood still for a couple of seconds before walking to a table afterward. At 90 seconds, the person takes a seat and starts typing on a keyboard. The signal at each time, when the person is in motion can clearly be seen in the recording from Fig. 14.

Figure 15 illustrates the sensor readings while walking over a pad of rubber. As seen in the recording, a natural step results in a pattern with two bulges. The pattern arises from the typical movement of a foot while rolling off the floor. When walking over a different type of floor, like a pad of rubber, a change of amplitude in the recording can be noticed. Exactly three steps were made on the rubber pad as marked in yellow in the measurement, where three step-pattern have got a smaller amplitude. This implies that electric field sensors, when worn on the body, can provide information not only for the activities of a person but for the environment itself.

Another example for monitoring external influences can be seen around second 150 in Fig. 14. At this point, the person wearing electric field sensors was touched by another person, resulting in a big change of amplitude. Again, the problem of ambiguity occurs. By looking at all available contextual information, it is easy to come to the conclusion that an external influence caused the distortion since all other accelerations and gyroscopic sensors have no deflections. However, to spot the reasons of the distortion at second 150, there is not enough data just by looking at all sensor graphs without further knowledge. To identify the source of such external influences, a bigger sensor array of electric field sensors is needed than in this recording.

Surprisingly, even without a big array of sensors, very small movements and activities like typing on a keyboard can easily be spotted. Figure 14 focuses on the activities at second 120. The person wearing the sensors is sitting still, which can be deduced from the acceleration sensors. With acceleration and gyroscopic sensors only, it is impossible to spot such small movements if the sensors are not worn directly on the fingers or near the fingers. However, even without wearing an electric field sensor on the arms, typing on a keyboard produces a unique pattern in the recording.

The experiment showed that electric field sensing in mobile applications can generate a lot more information than currently used technologies such as accelerometers while being more energy efficient. We have shown how sensitive this measurement method can be. This application opens up a wide range of possible applications in the areas of sports and fitness, as well as in health care.

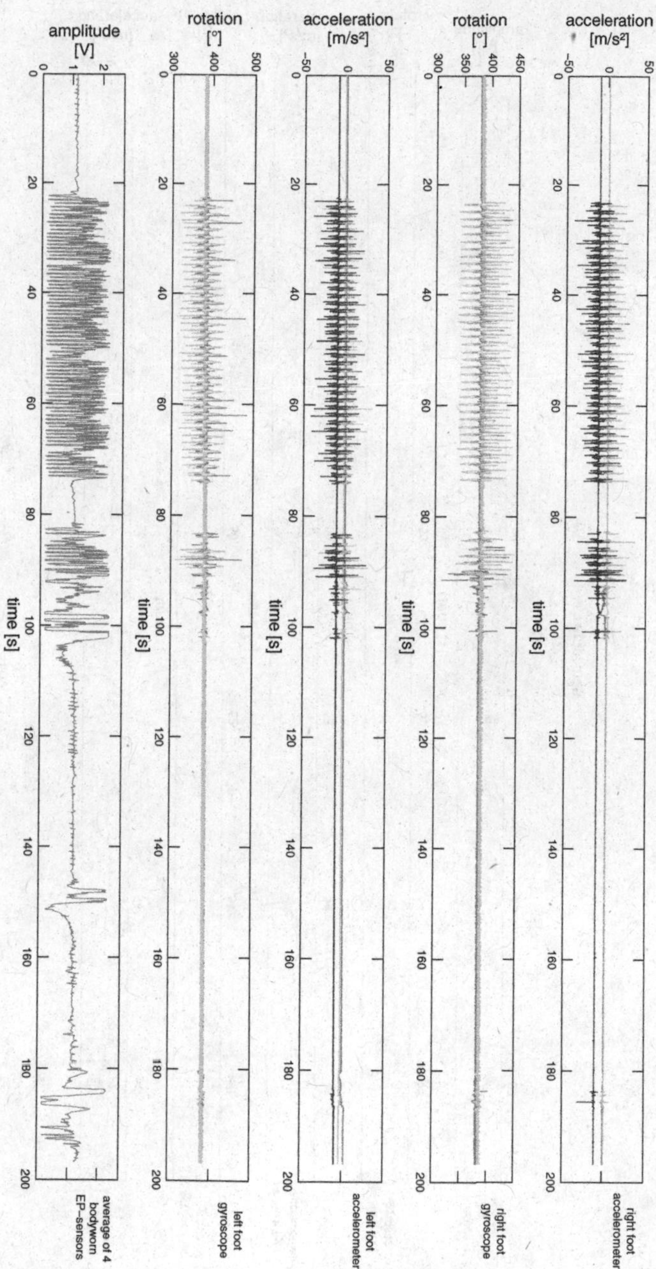

Fig. 14. 3 min walking and typing.

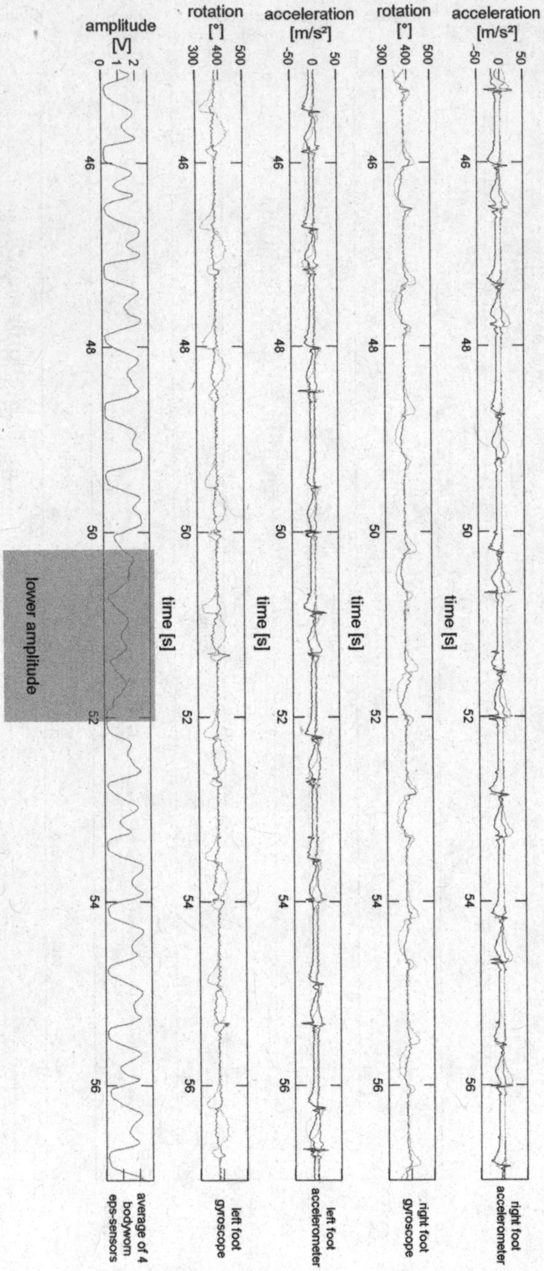

Fig. 15. Walking over a pad of rubber.

5 Conclusion and Outlook

In this paper, we compared capacitive sensing to passive electric field sensing and discussed various use-cases for this technology. Not only did we describe theoretically possible fields of application, with our data we are able to prove that this technology is really potent and that in some scenarios it would be beneficial to use electric field sensing instead of currently established technologies. That is because in the cases presented in this paper we can generate much information with electric field sensing without the need of fusing several sensor technologies. In the five use cases, we have shown that the presence and activity of persons and machines are recognized. The direction of activity can also be determined by a simple construction. Thus, gesture detection is also easy to implement even with a small electrode surface. We also showed the advantage of the mobile application.

Since we only presented a small compilation of conceivable use-cases, there is a lot of other applications that should be explored with this sensing technology. Future work with electric field sensing could involve a variety of new uses. For example, the detection of water damage in large structures, since it is a cheap technology with the possibility of large and flexible layouts for electrodes, or new devices for x-ray like machine-vision in non-harmful ways by creating large electric field sensor arrays. Alternatively, high-resolution localization of charged entities with only very few sensors based on the "time of flight" of charge redistribution. There are still a lot of scenarios worthwhile exploring.

References

1. Braun, A., Dutz, T., Kamieth, F.: Capacitive sensor-based hand gesture recognition in ambient intelligence scenarios. In: Proceedings of the 6th International Conference on Pervasive Technologies Related to Assistive Environments, PETRA 2013, pp. 5:1–5:4. ACM, New York (2013). http://dx.doi.org/10.1145/2504335.2504340
2. Clippingdale, A.J.: The sensing of spatial electrical potential. Ph.D. thesis, University of Sussex (1993)
3. Cohn, G., Gupta, S., Lee, T.J., Morris, D., Smith, J.R., Reynolds, M.S., Tan, D.S., Patel, S.N.: An ultra-low-power human body motion sensor using static electric field sensing. In: Proceedings of the 2012 ACM Conference on Ubiquitous Computing, UbiComp 2012, pp. 99–102. ACM, New York (2012). http://dx.doi.org/10.1145/2370216.2370233
4. Cohn, G., Morris, D., Patel, S.N., Tan, D.S.: Your noise is my command: sensing gestures using the body as an antenna. In: Proceedings of the SIGCHI Conference on Human Factors in Computing Systems, pp. 791–800. ACM, New York (2011). http://dx.doi.org/10.1145/1978942.1979058
5. Gebrial, W., Prance, R., Harland, C., Clark, T.: Noninvasive imaging using an array of electric potential sensors. Rev. Sci. Instrum. **77**(6), 063708 (2006). http://dx.doi.org/10.1063/1.2213219
6. Grosse-Puppendahl, T., Dellangnol, X., Hatzfeld, C., Fu, B., Kupnik, M., Kuijper, A., Hastall, M., Scott, J., Gruteser, M.: Platypus - indoor localization and identification through sensing electric potential changes in human bodies. In: 14th ACM International Conference on Mobile Systems, Applications and Services (MobiSys). ACM (2016). http://dx.doi.org/10.1145/2906388.2906402

7. Grosse-Puppendahl, T., Berghoefer, Y., Braun, A., Wimmer, R., Kuijper, A.: Opencapsense: a rapid prototyping toolkit for pervasive interaction using capacitive sensing. In: 2013 IEEE International Conference on Pervasive Computing and Communications (PerCom), pp. 152–159. IEEE (2013). http://dx.doi.org/10.1109/PerCom.2013.6526726
8. Harland, C., Clark, T., Prance, R.: Electric potential probes-new directions in the remote sensing of the human body. Measur. Sci. Technol. **13**(2), 163 (2001)
9. Kaila, L., Raula, H., Valtonen, M., Palovuori, K.: Living wood: a self-hiding calm user interface. In: Proceeding of the 16th International Academic MindTrek Conference, MindTrek 2012, pp. 267–274. ACM, New York (2012). http://dx.doi.org/10.1145/2393132.2393191
10. Mujibiya, A., Rekimoto, J.: Mirage: exploring interaction modalities using off-body static electric field sensing. In: Proceedings of the 26th Annual ACM Symposium on User Interface Software and Technology, UIST 2013, pp. 211–220. ACM, New York (2013). http://dx.doi.org/10.1145/2501988.2502031
11. Poupyrev, I., Schoessler, P., Loh, J., Sato, M.: Botanicus interacticus: interactive plants technology. In: ACM SIGGRAPH 2012 Emerging Technologies, p. 4. ACM (2012). http://dx.doi.org/10.1145/2343456.2343460
12. Pouryazdan, A., Prance, R., Prance, H., Roggen, D.: Wearable electric potential sensing: a new modality sensing hair touch and restless leg movement. In: Proceedings of the 2016 ACM International Joint Conference on Pervasive and Ubiquitous Computing: Adjunct, pp. 846–850. ACM (2016). dx.doi.org/10.1145/2968219.2968286
13. Prance, R., Beardsmore-Rust, S., Watson, P., Harland, C., Prance, H.: Remote detection of human electrophysiological signals using electric potential sensors. Appl. Phys. Lett. **93**(3), 033906 (2008). http://dx.doi.org/10.1063/1.2964185
14. Sato, M., Poupyrev, I., Harrison, C.: Touché: enhancing touch interaction on humans, screens, liquids, and everyday objects. In: Proceedings of the SIGCHI Conference on Human Factors in Computing Systems, pp. 483–492. ACM (2012). http://dx.doi.org/10.1145/2207676.2207743

A Framework for Responsive Environments

Ben Salem[1,2(✉)], Jorge Alves Lino[1,3], and Jan Simons[1]

[1] Department of Media Studies, University of Amsterdam, Amsterdam, The Netherlands
mail@bsalem.info

[2] School of Engineering, University of Liverpool, Liverpool, UK

[3] Department of Industrial Design, Eindhoven University of Technology, Eindhoven, The Netherlands

Abstract. In this paper, we define Responsive Environments as adaptive venues that possess context awareness, deliver ubiquitous computing and natural interaction. They also yield a pre-determined User Experience. We propose a framework for the development and assessment of such environments and we discuss applying the framework to some examples. Highlighting benefits and usefulness of the framework.

Keywords: Ubiquitous computing · Pervasive computing · Ambient intelligence · Responsive environments · User experience · Design and evaluation framework

1 Introduction

Responsive Environments (ResEnv) are venues augmented with interactive technologies and enriched with digital content. They were defined as spaces enhanced with media and technology to provide a user experience (UX) that is interactive, rich, and changing; being engaging with their visitors and adaptive to them [1]. Our main motivation in developing ResEnv is to crate a comprehensive experience, which combines ubiquity, ambience and pervasiveness. We believe that ResEnv combine the functionalities a space should provide, with the desired user experience, relying on interactions that are meaningful for the users, yet simple, without the urge for "more" – and unnecessary – complexity [2–4].

To clarify the concept of Responsive Environments within a contemporary context, we list comparable research areas in Table 1. These areas of research are about distributed information and communication technologies (ICT) as well as interaction channels, creating a digital ecosystem that surround the user. All of Ubiquitous Computing (UbiComp), Pervasive Computing, Ambient Intelligence (AmI) and ResEnv rely on a combination of media, modalities, interactions and technologies. However, only ResEnv includes a spatial and architectural embodiment as an essential component. Another key difference is that the constituent elements of each of these approaches have different prominence, priority, and level of engagement with the user. UbiComp prioritises the availability of information, Pervasive Computing prioritises the optimal use of technology in integration within objects and devices; as for AmI, it makes use of

A. Braun et al. (Eds.): AmI 2017, LNCS 10217, pp. 263–277, 2017.
DOI: 10.1007/978-3-319-56997-0_21

Table 1. Research areas related to responsive environments

Research areas	Main focus
Ubiquitous computing	Information technology – information is accessible, present and surrounding the user, relying on a collection of devices
Pervasive computing	Technology everywhere – computing is embedded into everyday objects and devices
Ambient intelligences	Content everywhere – the whole surrounding (i.e. all the physical objects used) is enhanced with digital content
Smart environments	More comfortable life – an environment of connected and interacting devices in an ordinary setting for everyday tasks
Responsive environments	User experience everywhere – the user experience the venue in a designed way

technology and information availability to provide content that has an effect on the entire environment. UbiComp relies on a push of information through the use of technology implemented on platforms of different sizes [5, 6]. Pervasive Computing prioritises the minimizing and hiding of technology to provide content and functionalities [7]. It is a disappearing technology that supports mobility and is in part worn/held by the user and in part embedded in buildings. To do so, Pervasive Computing relies on smart spaces, and a stable and scalable interaction [8]. AmI on the other hand relies on distributed integrated technology into everyday objects and deliver "social interaction" [2]. While information, content and technology are building components of ResEnv, in similar fashion to AmI. However, in the case of a ResEnv, it is the user experience that guides the design process and is the major focus of attention.

1.1 A Short Historical Perspective on Responsive Environments

American artist and researcher Myron Krueger is one of the early pioneers in the field. He took the implementation of media within spaces to a next level in the late 1960's: at the heart of Krueger's contribution was the notion of the artist as a "composer" of intelligent, real-time computer-mediated spaces, or "responsive environments", as he defined them [9]. Krueger "composed" environments, such as Videoplace, a computer-projection of graphic content designed in 1969. The projection was reactive to the gestures of the audience, and even anticipating some of their actions, thanks to sensors on the floor, graphic tables, and video cameras [10, 11]. Hand movements and manipulations were the modalities available. With such installations, Krueger pioneered the development of unencumbered, full-body participation in computer-created telecommunication experiences and coined the term "artificial reality" to describe it. Much later, by the 1990's, the relationship between media and architecture grew in strength as ideas became technologically and practically feasible. The application of kinetics in architecture, as the application of motion in the design of spaces, was by then re-examined under the premise that buildings' performance could be optimised if they delivered physical adaptation of forms and spaces [12]. The evolution of the field of human-computer interaction and ubiquitous computing became the driving force behind the interest in adaptive spaces and architecture [13].

More recent developments have focused on a combination of sounds and lights, such as "Audio Grove" [14]. A light and sound installation that consists of a circular wooden platform, on which vertical steel posts extend toward the ceiling. These vertical steel posts are an interface through which light and sound can be physically experienced and controlled. Visitors touching the posts evoke a soundscape, which always results in a harmonic melody whatever the combination of interactions. This is similar to the "Dune" interactive landscape, combining nature and technology [15]. Another development has seen the emergence of building as interactive systems. The Prada Transformer pavilion in Seoul is a good example. It is a pioneering structure, flipped using cranes; each side plan is designed to host a different event, hereby creating a building with four cultural identities. Whenever one shape becomes the floor surface, the other three shapes become the walls and the ceiling defining the space, as well as referencing past – or anticipating future – event [16]. The "Illumina" building in Singapore is another approach; it features an interactive facade, where visitors use mobile phone to send messages, images and graphics to be projected onto the building [13].

One last installation is worth mentioning: The "Ada Experience", it merges effectively the design of the space with interactive flooring and rich audio-visual content. The installation interacts with visitors and communicates through sound, lights and visuals [17]. Ada relies on visitors' actions such as walking, standing and jumping around to immerse them in an environment where their sensory stimulation comes from the installation and, to a lesser degree, from other visitors. Like an organism, Ada's output is designed to have a certain level of coherence, and to convey an impression of behaviour towards visitors [17].

1.2 Similar Work

In this section we review some projects that closely relate to Responsive Environments, and in doing so highlight some of their key features.

Smart Homes
Smart homes were defined as incorporating a network that links the key appliances and services and allow for their remote control, monitoring and access; as such these homes are equipped with a network to connect all appliances and systems, a control and management system to set preferences and an automation system that connects with services and contents [18].

Interactive Architecture
It about architectural projects that address changeability, adaptability and interaction issues [19]. To design such architecture, four "informative steps" are suggested: (1) Analysis (what aspects of the architecture should be interactive, and to which extent), (2) Concept generation (finding a comprehensive solution to the design problem), (3) Simulation (to check if the proposed design meets the requirements and needs of the users), and (4) Assessment (to find out the degree of compliance of the design with the requirement and needs of the user).

Interactive Public Spaces
They are about the distribution of technology into public spaces and context dependent social applications; resulting in crowd behaviour and social interaction [20]. They can be classified as performative (each user interact independently and in isolation of the others), allotted (each user share the venue of interaction with others), or responsive ambient (where all the users share the interaction and content).

Smart Environments
These are venues that rely on the acquisition of information, about the environments and their users and the processing and merging of information to improve users' experience [21]. They also are environments that adapt to their users and in doing so improve their users' experience [22]. Smart Environments were made possible via the miniaturisation of ITC and the increased functionality of everyday objects and their transformation into "smart artefacts" [23].

Intelligent Environments
Intelligent Environments were defined as comprising Sensors and Actuators (e.g. position, pressure, biometric data), Network and Middleware (e.g. wired and wireless network, sensor data processing software), Pervasive and Ubiquitous Computing (e.g. various distributed devices with small computing capabilities), Artificial Intelligence (e.g. Activity recognition, cognitive inference for decision making, Autonomy), and Human-Computer Interaction (e.g. no need for user training or specialisation) [24]. In a further development, Intelligent Environments have been defined as having reached a certain level of maturity and being ready to be implemented within real applications. Intelligent Environments are also defined as enriching the environment with technology, and relying on real-time and stored data for adaptation and interaction with the user [25]. Furthermore, intelligent Environments have the potential to proactively support their users in their daily lives [26].

2 Responsive Environment Framework

While the concept have been defined, there is a lack of a design and evaluation tool that could help design, develop, assess and classify ResEnv. A tool for a multidisciplinary design team to adopt and use in the design process leading to the successful implementation of a ResEnv. We believe this is essential, because to be responsive, a variety of channels of interaction between the users and the ResEnv need to be relied on. To be at the same time an environment, implies the emergence of a media and digital eco-system that surrounds and immerses the users. These are endeavours that clearly cannot easily be achieved without the help of a methodical approach. In this perspective, some attempts at establish a framework leading to ResEnv can be found in the literature [16, 27, 28]. Unfortunately, the proposed methods do not consider a comprehensive set of design elements and a combination of disciplines that such environments' development necessitates. ResEnv require different creative, development and implementation skills. Content, delivery platforms, modalities of interaction, methods of adaptation and finally the technology relied upon are all challenges to be addressed. Designing a ResEnv is, in this perspective, an iterative process that requires informed design decisions from various disciplines and stakeholders' perspectives. We therefore propose a framework that offers guidelines for the design and assessment of ResEnv (see Fig. 1). This framework includes a combination of quantitative and qualitative design dimensions, each with several elements that may or may not be applicable and relevant, depending on the environment's specifications and requirements. These design dimensions relate to the architecture, technology, media, modalities, interaction, adaptation and, user experience.

One of the particularities of the proposed framework is that it includes an architecture dimension, and here architecture refers to the design of the built environment. Indeed, ResEnv are an extension of the work of Krueger [9], and Bentley et al. The latter defined such concept as a manual for designers of the built environment [29].

The framework should be used as a reference tool by designers and operators of ResEnv, helping them address each of the key elements that contribute to the environment responsiveness and deciding what level of sophistication to reach and to maintain. The framework can be used in a bottom-up fashion, starting at the architecture dimension and adding features at each of the successive dimensions, up to the user experience. In this case the design follows a system-centric approach – first defining the built environment, the technology and the content before addressing the interaction and moving on to more user related issues. Symmetrically, the framework can be used in a top-down approach, in a user-centric approach, focusing first on the user experience and the adaptation of the installation.

Another noticeable feature of the proposed framework is that its seven dimensions are correlated and interdependent. Media and modalities are an obvious case, but even architecture and experience are related (the first defines the second, and experience influences the perception of the architecture).

Looking at the framework and starting at the architecture dimension (e.g. the build environment) the properties of the environment relate to access, it is where the users can go in the environment and what are the alternative paths they can follow. It also relates to visibility and legibility, which is the awareness and the understanding users have of what is available. The environment has to possess variety: a range of possible actions and experiences for the user, as well as richness, which is the choice and the complexity of sensory experience rendered. Finally the space has to possess some personalisation, allowing users to adjust and personalise the space surrounding them. (Table 2 summarises the dimension and its specifications, inspired by [29]).

Table 2. Architecture dimension of the framework

Specifications	Measurements
Accessibility	How is the access to the different spaces granted to the users?
Availability	Is the architecture of the venue prominent within its context?
Legibility	Are the architectural spaces recognisable, from a functional and aesthetic perspective?
Variety	Is there a diversity of spaces, of layouts and styles provided?
Richness	How much architectural features and content are there in the venue?
Personalisation	Is the architecture customisable or changeable by the visitors?

After considering the different architectural features of an installation, the next dimension is technology. It is about what devices are used in the environment, how they are available to the users. Connectivity via networking between the devices, the environment and beyond needs also to be considered. Reliability (robustness, security) is also important alongside scalability (see Table 3).

Table 3. Technology dimension of the framework

Specifications	Measurements
Devices	What are devices that can be used? Are they everyday objects or specialised devices? Small (handheld), medium sized (tablet) or large (display)?
Availability	Is the technology available anytime, anywhere in the environment?
Connectivity	What connectivity is provided within the environment? Between users? Beyond the environment?
Reliability	How redundant, fail-safe and fault-tolerant is the technology? How secure and private is the environment?
Scalability	Is the technology capable of handling increased number of users, higher bandwidth, richer content and more intense usage?

The next dimension of the framework relates to the media that is delivered in the environment (see Table 4). The intrusiveness is about how significant in the user landscape is the media in question – the degree of prominence in the user's perception. The disruptiveness of the media is another feature, relating to the level of interruption it produces and how important the resulting attention it receives from the user is. Flow disruption is also to be taken into account. Other properties relate to how information and entertainment are provided. How the media is delivered and whether it is independent or embedded in an interaction context. Finally, the way media are combined in multimedia content and whether or not they are narrating a story throughout the users' visit, are also to be evaluated.

Table 4. Media dimension of the framework

Specifications	Measurements
Intrusiveness	To what degree is the delivery of content with (our without) the need for user actions?
Disruptiveness	How significantly does the media delivered changes the user's behaviour, focus of attention or experience?
Informative	What amount of knowledge is communicated? What is the information entropy of content?
Entertaining	Is the media delivered for entertainment or serious effect?
Interactive	To what degree is the media interactive?
Combinative	Is the multitude of media combined to deliver a single message?
Narrative	Is there an underlying narrative or story?

Continuing through the framework, the next dimension is modalities, the means by which the users perceive the installation and act within it (see Table 5). The modalities include our senses as well as all the actions that we can perform in particular body movements (e.g. displacements, orientations, postures), Manipulations (e.g. pushing, grabbing) or, gestures (e.g. signs, pointing). Body movements are better for navigation interaction (by just waling across the installation), Manipulations are suited for handling devices and controllers; while gestures can be relied upon for specific interactions (such as menu option selection).

Table 5. Modalities dimension of the framework

Specifications	Measurements
Address	Does the users address the installation explicitly and directly?
Readiness	How much of indication does the installation gives to the users that it is ready for interaction?
Feedback	How much are the users allowed to know about current state of the installation and what is going on?
Attention	Are the users' focuses of attention influencing the installation?
Action	Frequency and number of actions required from the user?

Closely related to the modalities, the next step is to evaluate the interaction and ensure that it facilitates and contributes to the responsiveness of the environment (see Table 6).

Table 6. Interaction dimension of the framework

Specifications	Measurements
Effectiveness	Can users comprehensively achieve intended tasks with?
Efficiency	Are resources provided allow for the completeness of a task with minimum efforts?
Affect	What subjective effect(s) does the installation has on the users?
Learnability	Can the interaction with the installation be learned and memorised? How easily can it be so?
Intuitiveness	How much of prior knowledge and experience are necessary or sufficient to use the installation?
Discoverability	How little perceptive and cognitive efforts are necessary to find out the interactive features of the installation?
Context	Does the installation render an alternate reality/context?
Usability	Is the installation free from errors, delays, failures and confusing features?
Usefulness	How purposeful is the installation? Does it address the users intents and motivations?
Comfort	Is the user comfortable and satisfied while in the installation?

ResEnv rely heavily on adaptation and personalisation (see Table 7). The next dimension of the framework adaptation is related to adjustments and changes in the service delivery to match user profile to the service provided. It is a change to fit the user (e.g. language selection). It is about adapting the service being provided to the current surrounding context (e.g. currency used in prices to match user location).

Table 7. Adaptation dimension of the framework

Specifications	Measurements
Individuals vs. group	Does the installation adapt to single users or to users as groups?
Adaptation level	What is the adaptation level of the installation: reactive, interactive, perceptive, receptive or proactive?
Personalisation	Are the installation and the content rendered anonymous, or do they rely on user identities, preferences, profiles or models?
Resources allocation	How does the installation operate when there are limited resources available? How does it resolve conflicting demands and needs

By personalisation we refer to the different levels of user information that is being addressed by the system (anonymous: or no user recognition, to model: full user recognition including preferences and interests). It is about giving experience of a service that matches details and characteristics, that are not necessarily relevant to the service provided, or do not make any difference to it (e.g. background music matching personal preferences). Finally, it is about ascribing qualities to the service such as private, individual or discretionary.

There is an overlap between levels of personalisation of an environment, and the adaptation of an environment, in the sense that both imply changes in some of its features. The contrast lies in the fact that while adaptability is a dynamic feature: the ability of an environment to change according to certain rules; personalisation is related with how much information about the user is being recognised and processed to trigger these changes, and how much these changes yield content that is specific to the user.

The final dimension of the framework is the User Experience. Interacting with an environment involves the whole body and has the potential to yield a strong experience if the environment triggers a variety of perceptions, actions and emotions with a narrative to link the variety of media and modalities, and make sense of it [7, 12]. User experience encompasses the experiential, affective, meaningful and valuable aspects of the interaction with ResEnv, but it also includes a person's perceptions of the practical aspects such as utility, ease of use and efficiency of the environment [30]. It is subjective in nature, because it is about an individual's feelings and thoughts towards the environment being considered [31, 32]. Furthermore, the involvement of the whole body makes difficult the avoidance of emotion and mood influences on the behaviour and experience: The immersive experience of a ResEnv cannot be without emotional influence(s). Experiencing emotion is dependent on the media used as well as the modalities chosen and is also influenced by the changing context and situation [33].

To support the designers of a ResEnv installation in rendering a desired user experience, inspiration can be sought from interactive art installations, where artists and designers explore further than elsewhere the rendering of feelings and meanings [15]. The desired user experience is selected for relevance and meaning in the context of the ResEnv and its prevailing theme [34]. Accomplishment, Beauty, and Wonder are good examples of experiences that might be considered (see Table 8).

Table 8. Experience dimension of the framework

Specifications	Measurements
Competence	Do the users experience dexterity and fluency?
Influence	Can the users create or modify events in the installation?
Self development	Does the installation contribute to the users skills improvements and to their better awareness of the content presented?
Enjoyment	Does the installation trigger a feeling of fulfilling entertainment?
Control	Are the users in charge of what is happening?
Autonomy	How much independence do the users have in their choice of actions?
Self esteem	Does the installation positively influence how users feel about themselves?
Engagement	How rich and intense is the installation's immersion?
Attention	Does the installation capture the users focus of attention?

The experience of the ResEnv depends on the interaction with the installation that is performed thanks to one's body, as such; our learned and cultural behaviours are essential. It makes sense to rely on social and cultural values to design the embodied interactions. The richness and complexity of the interaction in a responsive environment can be such that users need familiar guidance to help them choose what behaviour and course of action to take. A ResEnv is, after all, a space (public or private) where social and cultural values are embedded.

For each of the seven dimensions of the framework (architecture, technology, media, modalities, interaction, adaptation and experience), we have defined specifications and measurements (e.g. for architecture: accessibility, visibility, legibility, variety, richness and personalisation) that we include in our framework (see Fig. 1). This set of dimensions can be used to determine the performance and completeness of an installation in terms of responsiveness. Some of the measurements are nominal, others are ordinal and finally some are scales. Using our framework, we are able to evaluate an installation according to each of the seven elements that we have defined as contributors to its responsiveness. It is important to take in account that for each installation, some of these elements and dimensions are more relevant than others (e.g. in the case of the Prada Transformer [16], the relevance is clearly the architecture, whereas in Water Zone [35] the relevance is in the media and interaction).

While it is important to have clear measurements, we have to understand that responsiveness depends to a significant extent on the perception and experience of the user, which varies, is subjective and not always clearly defined. In this evaluation, it is therefore important to be reminded that the whole issue is about responsiveness that is

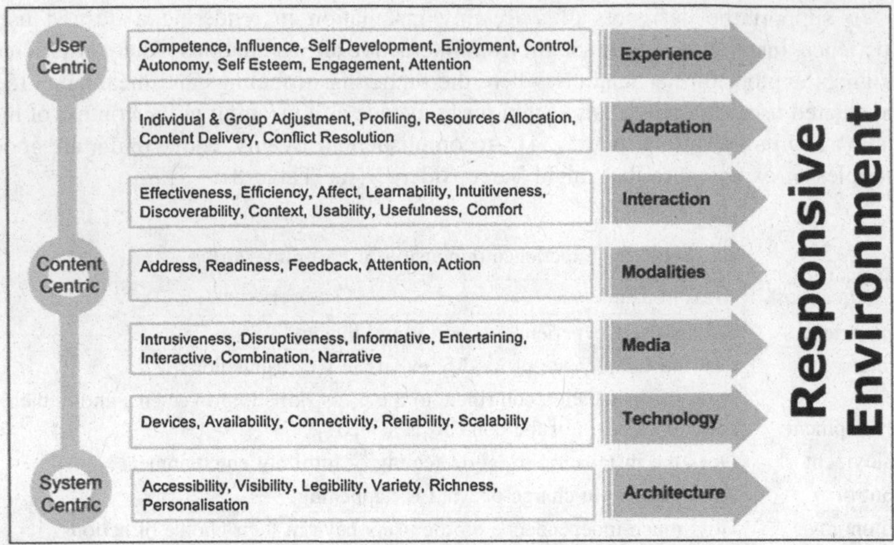

Fig. 1. Proposed responsive environments framework

perceived by the user. While our framework is useful from an analytical perspective, the evaluation process needs to be conducted with an acute awareness of the primacy of the user's perception of the installation and it's content. Furthermore, assessing ResEnv implies the consideration of addressability (when a user addresses a system, how does the system know the user is addressing it), attendance (when a user asks a system to do something, how does the user know it is attending), intention (when the user issues a command, how does the system know what it relates to), interaction (how does the user know the system understands the command) and recovery of content (how does the user recover from mistakes) [27].

2.1 Three Possible Approaches When Using the Framework

We posit that three possible approaches can be undertaken when using the proposed framework (see Table 9):

A System-Centric Approach
The use of this framework in a bottom-up prioritisation of the different dimensions would mean that the design of an installation would have a system-centric approach. In this case, the design process would begin by specifying the architecture of the environment. An example of this approach is the Prada Transformer building [16]. The design objective focuses on the architecture to deliver changing venue and context for a variety of events.

A Content-Centric Approach
In the context of responsive environments, the media are the components of the installation that are used as channels for the delivery of content, and are integrated

within the fabric of the environment. A good example of an installation focusing on media is the "Water Zone", an immersive environment that triggers feelings about, reflections on, and experimentations with sensations [35]. The visitors' displacements within the installation trigger the interaction with a projected content on the floor. Visitors are involved with the space in a playful and immersive manner; they can collectively take action in order to achieve changes in the content rendered.

A User-Centric Approach

In a third approach, this framework can be used top-down, where user experience takes priority: it is a user-centric approach. The enhancements of the environment thanks to

Table 9. Review of ResEnv with different approaches

Dimension	System centric *Prada Transformer*	Content centric *SmartEx*	User centric *Ada Experience*
Overview	A structure that can be flipped over as a mean to transform it into a different venue	An adaptive exhibition booth relying on prioritisation of visitor profiles to deliver exhibit content	Immersive experience that actively attracts user attention and give them the opportunity to make compositions of sound and light
Experience	A changing venue for a variety of events	According to their profile ranking, users can modify content	Dexterity and fluency thanks to changes in sound and colour
Adaptation	It is the physical space that change to host different events	Content displayed on screens is matching the interests of the user with higher priority	Users behaviour (individually and as a group) trigger changes in audio-visual content
Interaction	Limited to visiting the installation as a venue for events	Navigation through the exhibition booth, attention toward displays	The whole floor of the installation is interactive via pressure sensitive tiles
Modalities	Limited to attention being paid to the event happing in the venue	Users address the installation by focusing on the displays, their attention trigger a change of content	Users address the installation explicitly and directly by standing on pressure pads. Feedback is delivered in proportion to the number of different floor pads pressed
Media	Fashion events	Audio-visual Presentation on large displays	A combination of different coloured light combinations and sound. This combination does not address any narrative or story
Technology	Transformable architecture, cranes pick up the installation and rotate it	Displays, Tracking of users location and orientation	Displays, floor tiles, tracking of user location
Architecture	Highly original as it is designed to flip over and each side of the space is a floor for different events	Designed to render a corporate identity and help visitors discover exhibitor and products	Poorly explored as the installation is within an interior space with no particular architectural features. Accessibility somewhat easy, by limiting the number of access points to one
Responsive environments	Focus on a new experience of spaces and venues for fashion events	Smart exhibition booth, with a focus on delivering tailored and relevant information	Engaging, entertaining and immersive experience. Media, modalities, interaction and adaptation are used in strong clustering and combinations

media and technology are there to facilitate the desired experience, and not solely to be experienced per se. The installation becomes a result and consequence of the designed user experience, and its materialisation exists to give form to and to deliver this experience. Here a good example to illustrate this approach is the "Ada Experience", which encourages users to develop interaction skills, by allowing them to make compositions of sound and light [17]. This is made possible because the behaviour of the users controls what is happening in the installation.

3 Conclusion – A Direction for Responsive Environments

Our agenda for future research is to apply this framework in the design, development, assessment and classification of installations that focus on personalisation and adaptation. We see the design of a responsive environment and of its components, as a combination of installation, media, modalities and content that can provide users with experiences that are rendered in a new fashion, opening up opportunities for interaction and adaptation. We have already had a glimpse of such an environment thanks to our SmartEx installation [36]. Through our experiments we have demonstrated that profiled non-adaptive presentations are better suited, compared to a generic presentation for an effective and efficient information display strategy. We have also demonstrated that the improvement is significant and measurable. We have also indicated that the use of profiled and adaptive presentations is promising as a whole and across profiles.

In the perspective of architecture and space, it is also clear that content cannot be a mere conversion of traditional formats towards digital and space-integrated formats. One of the key features of ResEnv is that architectural elements are turned into media. Designers creating ResEnv need to take into account the purposes addressed, and choose what media or technologies can deliver these efficiently, effectively and in a user-friendly manner.

When adaptive components, services and content are focused on the user experience, the environment becomes responsive. The responsiveness can be in the form of the physical structure of the space (e.g. movable panels and partition walls). The changes can also be related to the ambient features of the space such as lighting, acoustics and temperature. Finally, the changes can relate to the content presented in the space, such as media, information, and interactivity available. Clearly there are many avenues to adaptation and ultimately responsiveness. We believe in the need to build system demonstrators to investigate various content, design, technology and interaction solutions. As seen in the reviewed examples (and beyond), ResEnv are emerging from architecture, which is moving from static to dynamic forms, through the use of technology. In some cases, the technologies are an obvious choice and are clearly visible to the visitors (e.g. involving tangible interfaces), while in others it is rather innovative and invisible (e.g. involving sensors). It is interesting to compare, in terms of meaningful experience, how these technologies are applied. While in first case, users tend to feel the installation is mechanically responding to their actions, in the second case users feel the installation is naturally responding to their behaviour.

Most developers of ResEnv have been focusing on creating spaces, environments, objects, application that prioritised usability, functionality, or positive user experience.

The design process was always associated with the installation, technology and content involved, while the human contribution to the installation, shall it be from the end user or from the installation staff was mainly ignored. We advocate that the user and the staff of the installation can, and should, have a significant contribution to it. If, on the one hand, the design of spaces can strongly influence the user experience, on the other hand it is undeniable that the behaviour and "choreography" followed by the environment "staff" and user can be a significant contributing element to the environment. A user experience, in this context, is not only facilitated by the space, the installation and its content, but also by the staff and their behaviour and "rule of engagement". The design of staff services and behaviour can be seen as the design of choreography: a performance. This choreography or performance becomes the "human contribution" that triggers the user experience, which long before being triggered by technology or design, were triggered by human contact, within social behaviour, as design history has shown us with the pioneering work of Charles Mackintosh: his architecture proposals included the design of the house, the furniture, the cutlery, the dishes, the costumes and even how staff should behave. It seems to be an interesting future direction: to integrate into the spaces the design of such "performed actions".

We are proposing a framework to provide guidance for the design, development, assessment and classification of ResEnv, hopefully allowing for a critical, informed and objective analysis.

References

1. Alves Lino, J., Salem, B., Rauterberg, M.: Responsive environments: user experience for ambient intelligence. J. Ambient Intell. Smart Environ. **2**(4), 347–367 (2010)
2. Aarts, E., de Ruyter, B.: New research perspectives on ambient intelligence. J. Ambient Intell. Smart Environ. **1**, 5–14 (2009)
3. Fox, M., Kemp, M.: Interactive Architecture. Princeton Architectural Press, New York (2009)
4. Maeda, J.: The Laws of Simplicity. MIT Press, Cambridge (2006)
5. Mahajan, S., Mishra, A., Singh, L.: Systematic review of ubiquitous computing system models. Int. J. Comput. Eng. Technol. **5**, 46–55 (2014)
6. Weiser, M.: The computer of the 21st century. Sci. Am. **265**(3), 94–104 (1991)
7. Bargas-Avila, J., Hornbæk, K.: Old wine in new bottles or novel challenges? A critical analysis of empirical studies of user experience. In: Proceedings of CHI 2011. ACM, Vancouver (2011)
8. Satyanaryanan, R.: Pervasive computing: vision and challenges. IEEE Pers. Commun. **8**(4), 10–17 (2001)
9. Krueger, M.: Responsive environments. In: Proceedings of 1977 National Computer Conference, New York, USA, pp. 423–433 (1977)
10. Krueger, M.: Documentary video of Myron Krueger's videoplace. http://www.youtube.com/watch?v=dqZyZrN3Pl0. Accessed Jan 2017
11. Krueger, M., Gionfriddo, T., Hinrichsen, K.: Videoplace - an artificial reality. In: Proceedings of 1985 CHI Conference, San Francisco, USA, pp. 35–40 (1985)

12. Forlizzi, J., Battarbee, K.: Understanding experience in interactive systems. In: Proceedings of 5th Conference on Designing Interactive Systems: Processes, Practices, Methods, and Techniques, Cambridge, USA, pp. 261–268 (2004)
13. WOHA Architects Online documentary video of Iluma. http://www.youtube.com/watch?v=r5CQWv3HfSY. Accessed Jan 2017
14. Moeller, C.: Online project description and documentary video of audio grove. http://www.christian-moeller.com/display.php?project_id=6&play=true. Accessed Jan 2017
15. Chong, A., de Rijk, T.: Daan Roosegaarde: interactive landscapes. NAi Publishers, Rotterdam (2010)
16. Koolhaas, R.: Online documentary video of Prada Transformer. http://www.youtube.com/watch?v=23kCsdQiPxU. Accessed Jan 2017
17. Eng, K., Balber, A., Bernadet, U., et al.: Ada: constructing a synthetic organism. In: Proceedings of Intelligent Robots and Systems, vol. 2, pp. 1808–1813 (2002)
18. Jiang, L., Liu, D.-Y., Yang, B.: Smart home research. In: Proceedings of 3rd International Conference on Machine Learning and Cybernetics, Shanghai, pp. 659–663 (2004)
19. Achten, H., Kopriva, M.: A design methodological framework for interactive architecture. In: Proceedings of 28th eCAADe Conference ETH Zurich (Switzerland), 15–18 September 2010, pp. 169–177 (2010)
20. Hespanhol, L., Tomitch, M.: Strategies for intuitive interaction in public urban spaces. Interact. Comput. **27**(3), 311–326 (2015)
21. Youngblood, G.M., Heierman, E.O., Holder, L.B., Cook, D.J.: Automation intelligence for the smart environment. In: International Joint Conference on Artificial Intelligence, vol. 19, p. 1513 (2005)
22. Cook, D.J., Das, S.K.: Overview. In: Cook, D.J., Das, S.K. (eds.) Smart Environments: Technologies, Protocols and Applications, pp. 3–10. Wiley, Hoboken (2005)
23. Streitz, N.A., Rocker, C., Prante, T., van Alphen, D., Stenzel, R., Magerkurth, C.: Designing smart artifacts for smart environments. Computer **38**(3), 41–49 (2005)
24. Augusto, J.C., Callaghan, V., Cook, D., et al.: Intelligent environments: a manifesto. Hum.-Centric Comput. Inf. Sci. **3**(12), 1–18 (2013)
25. Augusto, J.C., Coronato, A.: Introduction to the inaugural issue of the journal of reliable intelligent environments. J Reliab. Intell. Environ. **1**, 1–10 (2015)
26. Aztiria, A., Augusto, J.C., Basagoiti, R., Izaguirre, A., Cook, D.J.: Discovering frequent user-environment interactions in intelligent environments. Pers. Ubiquitous Comput. **16**(1), 91–103 (2012)
27. Bellotti, V., Back, M., Keith Edwards, W., Grinter, R.E., Henderson, A., Lopes, C.: Making sense of sensing systems: five questions for designers and researchers. In: CHI 2002, Minneapolis, Minnesota, USA (2002)
28. Loke, L., Larssen, A., Robertson, T., Edwards, J.: Understanding movement for interaction design: frameworks and approaches. J. Pers. Ubiquitous Comput. **11**(8), 691–701 (2007)
29. Bentley, I., Alcock, A., Murrain, P., McGlynn, S., Smith, G.: Responsive Environments: A Manual for Designers. Architectural Press, Oxford (1985)
30. Law, E., Roto, V., Vermeeren, A., Kort, J., Hassenzahl, M.: Towards a shared definition of user experience. In: CHI 2008 Proceedings, pp. 2395–2398 (2008)
31. Hassenzahl, M., Tractinsky, N.: User experience - a research agenda. J. Behav. Technol. Inf. **25**(2), 91–97 (2006)
32. Hassenzahl, M.: Experience design: technology for all the right reasons. Synth. Lect. Hum.-Cent. Inform. **3**, 1–95 (2010)
33. Stahl, A., Sundstrom, P., Hook, K.: A foundation for emotional expressivity. In: Proceedings of DUX 2005, no. 33 (2005)

34. Diller, S., Shedroff, N., Rhea, D.: Making Meaning: How Successful Business Deliver Meaningful Customer Experiences (2005)
35. Ming Mekka Documentary video of Water Zone. http://www.mingmekka.com/projects/waterzone.html. Accessed Feb 2012
36. Salem, B., Alves Lino, J., Rauterberg, M.: SmartEx: a case study on user profiling and adaptation in exhibition booths. J. Ambient Intell. Human. Comput. **1**(3), 185–198 (2010)

Author Index

Alekseew, Michael 80
Alves Lino, Jorge 263
Amirat, Yacine 225

Ben Allouch, Somaya 110
Ben Hmida, Helmi 183
Bouznad, Sofiane 225
Braun, Andreas 64, 80, 175, 183, 214, 247
Büttner, Sebastian 33

C. Augusto, Juan 136
Chibani, Abdelghani 225
Cutugno, Francesco 136

Dalpiaz, Fabiano 94
Damer, Naser 175
Di Mauro, Dario 136
Dragoni, Aldo Franco 94

Engler, Anne 241

Farshchian, Babak A. 152
Fiorini, Sandro 225
Frank, Sebastian 46, 197
Fu, Biying 64, 247

Gries, Stefan 17
Grosse-Puppendahl, Tobias 64
Gruhn, Volker 17

Henniger, Olaf 175
Hesenius, Marc 17
Hosio, Simo 130

Jaschinski, Christina 110

Kirchbuchner, Florian 64, 247
Konomi, Shin'ichi 130
Kuijper, Arjan 46, 64, 183, 197, 214, 247

Lyazid, Sabri 225

Maekawa, Takuya 124
Mammadova, Chinara 183
Mettel, Matthias Ruben 80

Oesterreich, Detlef 241
Ollesch, Julius 17
Origlia, Antonio 136

Prestes, Edson 225

Röcker, Carsten 33
Rus, Silvia 214

Sakumichi, Yuki 124
Salem, Ben 263
Sand, Oliver 33
Sasao, Tomoyo 130
Savidis, Anthony 159
Schulze, Eva 241
Sebbak, Faouzi 225
Sernani, Paolo 94
Serral, Estefanía 94
Sezaki, Kaoru 130
Siebrandt, Monique 241
Simons, Jan 263
Stocklöw, Carsten 80
Streitz, Norbert 1

Valsamakis, Yannis 159
Vilarinho, Thomas 152
von Wilmsdorff, Julian 64, 247

Wessling, Florian 17

Zirk, Anna 241

Printed in the United States
By Bookmasters